The
Art
of the
Essay

The
Best
of

1999

The
Best
of

1999

Selected and Introduced by
Phillip Lopate

The
Art
of the
Essay

Anchor Books
A Division of Random House, Inc., New York

First Anchor Books Edition, October 1999

Library of Congress Cataloging-in-Publication Data

The art of the essay 1999 / selected and introduced by Phillip Lopate.
—1st ed.
  p. cm.
1. English essays—20th century. 2. American essays—
20th century. I. Lopate, Phillip, 1943– .
PR1367.A78   1999
824′.91408—dc21   99-28844
CIP

ISBN: 0-385-48415-1

www.anchorbooks.com

Printed in the United States of America
10 9 8 7 6 5 4 3 2 1

Contents

SEEING

COLLECTIONS

THE LENS OF ART

AGING AND FATE

Phillip Lopate

Introduction

The essay lives a double life in our culture: a dreaded competence test (ink-stained bluebooks), a dessert of the mind. Meant to support a nonfiction prose text, it can be as clumsy and utilitarian as a schooldesk, or as elegant as an escritoire designed by Josef Hofmann. We rarely consider the relationship between these two essay species—unless we are forced to.

Recently, the Educational Testing Service devised a way for college essays to be graded by a robot, who (which?) would give higher marks for transition words such as "since," "while," and "therefore," or for semicolons and parentheses, which seemed to point toward a student's possessing more sophisticated syntax and argumentation. To most professional essayists, myself included, the idea of ignoring an essay's content and judging it merely by its syntactical sign posts seemed initially laughable. After all, did not the greatest essayist of all, Montaigne, frequently jump from topic to topic without so much as a single transitional warning? The more densely packed the mind, the more abrupt the leap from insight to insight. A great stylist like Stendhal, in his heady essay "On Love," assumed that readers would follow his epigrammatic constructions, without having to help them along with all the lumbering scaffolding of a lesser thinker.

Okay, okay, the ETS replied; but we're not judging geniuses here, we're trying to evaluate millions of incoming college students, for the most part uninspired and ill-prepared for higher education, who could no sooner write a sentence worthy of Stendhal than the proverbial pool of typing monkeys could achieve a line of Shakespeare. Frankly, as someone who has taught freshman composition, as well as prepared dropouts to take their high school equivalency exam, I can sympathize with the desire for some mechanical apparatus to help lighten the essay-grading grind. And perhaps there is an underlying structure to the superior essay, which in time will be discovered, allowing each potential essay to be X-rayed, thereby ascertaining how good its bones are. Though I have never been able to find— or put into words—what the underlying structure of a superior essay might be, I sometimes have the dim intuition that it exists. When I am grappling with one of my own essays, I seem to write toward that Holy Grail, that elusive, phantom structure which keeps teasing me with its promises of intellectual plot, emotional tension, and final resolution. When I am reading an essayist I admire, I am sure that he or she possesses the demon matrix, the blueprint, and no longer has to grapple at all. In my capacity as editor of this Anchor essay annual series, having read thousands of essays these past three years (I confess to taking my own equivalent of DNA scrapings from the first paragraphs), in order to pick the most exciting twenty-five or so for each volume, I can only hope that the scientists will hurry up and make my job easier. In any case, we can safely predict that the next generation of high school students will be taught to use lots of "sinces" and "therefores" and "howevers" in their compositions. The problem with "since" and "therefore" as predictors of excellence, however, is that not all good essays need to be arguments. Some do argue, of course (see, for instance, the closely reasoned polemics by Marilynn Robinson and Margaret Talbot in this volume), but others meander and experiment, eschewing the noose of closure (check out Wayne Koestenbaum's essay, collaged out of fragments which undercut each other), or recollect, interrogating the guilt or innocence of one's younger self (witness Siri Hustvedt's piece on eros), or appreciate (Susan Sontag's sensitive reading of a Debussy opera), or elegize (Floyd Skloot's very moving portrait of his brother), or take inventory (as in Anne Fadiman's or Alexander Theroux's collections). All essays, in a sense, are both arguments and collections, which exhibit conflicting impulses: on the one hand, to plead the case, like a good lawyer; on the other hand, to keep expanding and digressing, like a Whitmanesque poet, so as to take in more of the amusing, infuriating world.

The best essays display a sparkling literary style that is pure pleasure to follow, make us recognize painful home truths and experience pangs of honesty, awaken our capacity for mental adventure, and put us in touch with a human voice that we want to follow for as long as he/she will talk to us. If the robot at the other end can be taught to appreciate the timbre and texture of that vulnerable humanity, so much the better. I have my doubts—but then, essayists are notoriously willing to wallow in doubt. I am sure the robot is doing the best job it can, and I take my hat off to a fellow essay eater.

A common dilemma faced by editors and anthologists is how to handle a situation when two good pieces on the same topic show up. Such was the case when I came upon a marvelously robust essay by Edward Hoagland on the subject of going blind. Now, to include Hoagland in an essay annual is something of a no-brainer: he's rightfully considered one of the best in the field. But then I stumbled upon a beautiful essay by Erin McGraw, "Bad Eyes," which treated the same situation though from a very different angle. What to do? Most of the time, the weaker of the two essays (or the one by a lesser name—it may, in fact, be stronger) gets cut. This time, I thought, maybe I can include them both. . . . Then I noticed that I also had two strong contenders on politics of the left (Richard Rorty, George Packer), on religion (Jonathan Rosen, Kathleen Norris), on sports (Gerald Early, Vijay Seshadri), on fathers, and on and on.

How bizarre. What to do indeed? I had been planning to

swallow hard and ruthlessly eliminate one of each at the end of the decision process, when it occurred to me: Why not make a virtue of duplication—or theme and variation—and try an experiment in intentional "pairing"? After all, the essay is an inherently conversational medium, both in its tonal contract with the reader and in its tendency to respond to talking points from earlier essayists. Friendship, antipathy, manners, city versus country, infirmity, spectatorship, skepticism and belief: historically, these and a half-dozen other subjects have been the bread and butter of the essay form. By placing two essayists under one umbrella, it seems to me, we might become more attuned to intriguing conversations between them, while at the same time picking up on their exchanges with other contributors in the annual. So the pairings issue came about: not an earth-shaking arrangement, but a companionable one. I hope you like it.

It only remains for me to thank the friends and associates who helped me these past three years by reading some of the essays I was struggling to evaluate and giving me their honest opinions: Jeff Bockman, Brigitte Frase, Vivian Gornick, Tom Beller, Paul McRandle, Jack Schwartz, and my three hardworking Anchor editors, Charlie Conrad, Rob McQuilkin, and Gerry Howard.

The
Art
of the
Essay

The
Best
of
1999

Family

Marilynn Robinson

Family

We are all aware that "family" is a word which eludes definition, as do other important things, like nation, race, culture, gender, species; like art, science, virtue, vice, beauty, truth, justice, happiness, religion; like success; like intelligence. The attempt to impose definition on indeterminacy and degree and exception is about the straightest road to mischief I know of, very deeply worn, very well traveled to this day. But just for the purposes of this discussion, let us say: one's family are those toward whom one feels loyalty and obligation, and/or from whom one derives identity, and/or to whom one gives identity, and/or with whom one shares habits, tastes, stories, customs, memories. This definition allows for families of circumstance and affinity as well as kinship, and it allows also for the existence of people who are incapable of family, though they may have parents and siblings and spouses and children.

I think the biological family is especially compelling to us because it is, in fact, very arbitrary in its composition. I would never suggest so rude an experiment as calculating the percentage of one's relatives one would actually choose as friends, the percentage of one's relatives who would choose one as *their* friend. And that is the charm and the genius of the institution. It implies that help and kindness and loyalty are owed where they are perhaps by no means merited. Owed, that is, even to ourselves. It implies that we are in some few circumstances excused from the degrading need to judge others' claims on us, excused from the struggle to keep our thumb off the scales of reciprocity.

Of course families do not act this way, always or even typically, certainly not here, certainly not now. But we recognize such duty and loyalty as quintessentially familial where we see it. And if the institution is culturally created, what we expect of it has a great deal to do with determining what it will be in fact.

Obviously if we are to employ the idea that behaviors are largely culturally created, we must humble that word "fact." It seems very plausible to me that our ceasing to romanticize the family has precipitated, as much as it has reflected, the weakening of the family. I am sure it is no accident that the qualities of patience and respect and loyalty and generosity which would make family sustainable are held in very low regard among us, some of them even doubling as neuroses such as dependency and lack of assertiveness. I think we have not solved the problem of living well, and that we are not on the way to solving it, and that our tendency to insist on noisier and more extreme statements of the new wisdom that has already failed gives us really very little ground for optimism.

Imagine this: some morning we awake to the cultural consensus that a family, however else defined, is a sort of compact of mutual loyalty, organized around the hope of giving rich, human meaning to the lives of its members. Toward this end they do what people do—play with their babies, comfort their sick, keep their holidays, commemorate their occasions, sing songs, tell jokes, fight and reconcile, teach and learn what they know about what is right and wrong, about what is beautiful and what is to be valued. They enjoy each other and make themselves enjoyable. They are kind and receive kindness, they are generous and are sustained and enriched by others' generosity. The antidote to fear, distrust, self-interest is always loyalty. The balm for failure or weakness, or even for disloyalty, is always loyalty.

This is utopian. And yet. Certainly it describes something of which many of us feel deprived. We have reasoned our way to uniformly conditional relationships. This is at the very center of the crisis of the family, since the word means, if it means anything, that certain people exist on special terms with each other, which terms are more or less unconditional. We have instead decided to respect our parents, maybe, if they meet our stringent standards of deserving. Just so do our children respect us, maybe.

Siblings founder, spouses age. We founder. We age. That is when loyalty should matter. But invoking it now is about as potent a gesture as flashing a fat roll of rubles. I think this may contribute enormously to the sadness so many of us feel at the heart of contemporary society. "Love is not love / Which alters when it alteration finds," in the words of the sonnet, which I can only interpret to mean, love is loyalty. I would suggest that in its absence, all attempts to prop the family economically or morally or through education or otherwise will fail. The real issue is, will people shelter and nourish and humanize one another? This is creative work, requiring discipline and imagination. No one can be scolded or fined into doing it, nor does it occur spontaneously in the demographically traditional family.

Nor does it occur predictably even where it is earnestly sought and desired. Life is in every way full of difficulty, and that is the great variable that confounds all generalization, as I am eager to concede, even while discussions of this kind oblige one to generalize.

But we have forgotten many things. We have forgotten solace. Maybe the saddest family, properly understood, is a miracle of solace. It seems to me that our multitude of professional healers and comforters are really meant to function like the doctor in a boxer's corner, there to slow bleeding and minimize swelling so that we will be able to last another round. Neither they nor we want to think about the larger meaning of the situation. This is the opposite of solace.

Imagine that someone failed and disgraced came back to his family, and they grieved with him, and took his sadness upon themselves, and sat down together to ponder the deep mysteries of human life. This is more human and beautiful, I propose, even if it yields no dulling of pain, no patching of injuries. Perhaps it is the calling of some families to console, because intractable grief is visited upon them. And perhaps measures of the success of families that exclude this work from consideration, or even see it as failure, are very foolish and misleading.

We tend to think, now, of the ideal family as a little hatchery for future contributors to the Social Security system, non-criminals who will enhance national productivity while lowering the cost per capita of preventable illness. We have forgotten that old American nonsense about alabaster cities, about building the stately mansions of the soul. We have lowered our hopes abysmally, for no reason obvious to me, without a murmur I have ever heard. To fulfill or to fall short of such minor aspirations as we encourage now is the selfsame misery.

For some time we seem to have been launched on a great campaign to deromanticize everything, even while we are eager to insist that more or less everything that matters is a romance, a tale we tell one another. Family is a narrative of love and comfort which corresponds to nothing in the world but which has formed behavior and expectation—fraudulently, many now argue. It is as if we no longer sat in chairs after we learned that furniture was only space and atoms. I suppose it is a new upsurge of that famous Western rationalism, old enemy of reasonableness, always so right at the time, always so shocking in retrospect.

Well, we have exorcised the ghost and kept the machine, and the machine is economics. The family as we have known it in the West in the last few generations was snatched out of the fires of economics, and we, for no reason I can see, have decided to throw it back in again. It all has to do with the relationship of time and money. When we take the most conscientious welfare mothers out of their homes and neighborhoods with our work programs, we put them in jobs that do not pay well enough to let them provide good care for their children. This seems to me neither wise nor economical. We do it out of no special malice but because we have lately reorganized society so that even the children of prosperous families often receive doubtful care and meager attention. The middle class are enforcing values they themselves now live by, as if these values would reduce the social pathologies of the poor, as if they were not in fact a great cause of the social pathologies of the middle class.

An employed American today works substantially longer hours than he or she did twenty-five years ago, when only one adult in an average household was employed and many more households had two adults. The recent absence of parents from the home has first of all to do with how much time people spend at work. Some of them are ambitious businesspeople or professionals, but many more patch together a living out of two or three part-time jobs, or work overtime as an employer's hedge against new hiring. Statistically the long hours simply indicate an unfavorable change in the circumstances of those who work. If an average household today produces more than twice as much labor in hours as an average household did twenty-five years ago, and receives only a fraction more in real income, then obviously the value of labor has fallen—even while the productivity of labor in the same period has risen sharply. So, male and female, we sell ourselves cheap, with the result that work can demand always more of our time, and our families can claim always less of it.

This is clearly a radical transformation of the culture, which has come about without anyone's advocating it, without consensus, without any identifiable constituency. It would be usual to imagine a conspiracy of some sort. That is a good enough reason to do otherwise. Our usual approaches have by now an impressive history of fruitlessness, as we would notice if we were at all a reflective people.

Conspiracy theories are childish and comforting, assuming as they do that there are smart people somewhere who are highly efficient at putting their intentions into effect, when history and experience combine to assure us that nothing could be more unlikely. We long imagined that the great corporations contrived against our good, but if any institution has been as staggered as the family in the last twenty-five years, it is surely the great corporation. Workers who are well paid and secure are good consumers, and in the new economy there are always fewer people who suit that description. The faltering of the economy has always been interpreted as a problem of "competitiveness" with other countries, and this notion has accelerated the cheapening of labor and the reduction of the labor force in traditional industries. That is, it has accelerated the increase of insecurity among those who work. Surely it is a tribute to the vast power of the economy that it has weathered this nonsense as well as it has.

This whole notion of competitiveness was pitched by many of its exponents as a "war" we must "win," which could surely mean nothing else than the crippling of those same foreign markets upon which our future prosperity supposedly depends. If we force wages down in competitor countries, or if we weaken their industries and lower the value of their currencies, they will simply be less able to buy from us no matter how lean we are, or how mean we are. One could say public opinion has been cynically manipulated with this talk of "challenge" and "war," but I think we should face the harder fact that a public silly enough to be persuaded by such arguments would very likely produce a class of experts silly enough to propose them in good faith.

The family as we know it in the modern West has been largely willed and reformed into existence. European culture was long distinguished by the thoroughness with which it coerced labor out of its population—slavery and industrialization, contemporary phenomena equally indifferent to such inconveniences as considerations of family, were natural extensions of feudalism, only more ambitious and ingenious in their exactions. The case has been made that childhood was invented, which it was, at least in the sense that certain societies began to feel that young children should be excluded from the workforce, and women with them, to some extent at least.

Working conditions in trades and factories were brutal into the present century. We tend to forget that women of working age were often pregnant or nursing and often obliged to leave infants and small children untended. Sometimes they gave birth on the factory floor.

Children of working age, that is, as young as five, were spared no hardship. The British documented these horrors quite meticulously for generations, and one may read all anyone could care to read about the coffles of children driven weeping through morning darkness to the factories; children lying down to sleep in the roads because they were too exhausted to walk home at night; children dismembered by machines they were obliged to repair while the machines ran; children in factory dormitories sleeping by hundreds, turn and turn about, in beds that were never empty until some epidemic swept through and emptied them, and brought hundreds of new children, orphans or so-called child paupers, to work away their brief lives. There is nothing to wonder at, that the ideal of mother and children at home, and father adequately paid to keep them from need, was a thing warmly desired, and that for generations social reform was intended to secure this object.

By comparison with Britain, America was late in industrializing, and its agricultural economy was based on widely distributed ownership of land. Nevertheless the societies were similar enough to be attentive to each other's reform movements. The decisive innovation was the idea that one wage earner should be able to support a wife and a few children, rather than that every employable person in a household should support himself or herself and some fraction of a baby or two. The idea of the "living wage" became much more important in America, where labor was usually in demand and therefore able to command a higher price and to set other limits and conditions governing employers' access to it. Where labor is cheap, the market is flooded with it, assuring that it will remain cheap. Other goods will, over time, be withheld if they do not command a reasonable price, but the cheaper labor is, the less it will be withheld, because people have to live, and to hedge against the falling wages and unemployment which are always characteristic of a glutted labor market. These phenomena have been observed and analyzed since the seventeenth century. Now they are recrudescent like other old maladies we thought we had eliminated.

This glut of cheap labor was the characteristic state of

things in England and Europe until the postwar period—and it is increasingly important among Americans now. That is why we sometimes see such anomalies as employment and unemployment rising at the same time. The two-tier economy we are developing, with accelerating inequality between those who are trained or educated and those who are not, reflects the scarcity relative to demand of skilled labor. If schemes to educate more of our workforce are carried out successfully, the increased availability of skilled labor will lower its value, and the erosion of the prosperity of those who work will simply become more widespread.

It is because the family as we have known it in this country over the last three-quarters of a century was the goal and product of reform that a radiance of idealization hung over it, and that it was so long and so confidently invoked as a common value, as a thing deserving and also requiring political and economic protection. This has had many important consequences for policy and law. Yet for some reason we are convinced at the moment that the ways of our economy should be identical with the laws of the market, and therefore we depart resolutely from norms and customs that controlled economic behavior among us through our long history of increasing prosperity. No one is more persuaded of the rightness of this course than those who claim to especially cherish the family.

Take for example the weekend, or that more venerable institution, the Sabbath. Moses forbade that servants, even foreigners, should work on the seventh day. If their wage was subsistence, as it is usually fair to assume in premodern societies, then his prohibition had the immediate practical effect of securing for them seven days' pay for six days' work. He raised the value of their labor by limiting access to it. In all its latter-day forms the Sabbath has had this effect.

Now those among us whose prosperity is eroding fastest are very likely to be at work on Sunday, because they cannot afford not to work when they have the chance, and because they cannot risk losing a job so many others would be happy to take. Absent legal or contractual or religious or customary constraints, work-

ers without benefits or job security or income that is at least
stable relative to the economy have no way of withholding their
labor. Now all those constraints are gone, in the name of liberal-
ization, I suppose. I do not recall hearing a single murmur about
the effect of such changes on the family, though it is always easy
to find journalistic wisdom to the effect that parents should
spend more time with their children. The last great Sabbatarian
institution is the school system—even the Postal Service makes
deliveries on Sunday—so the quondam day of rest is now a special burden for families with young children or children who
need supervision.

Of course the shops must be open on Sundays and at night
because the rate of adult employment is so high and the working
day is so long that people need to be able to buy things whenever
they can find the time. I would suggest that such voracious demands on people's lives, felt most mercilessly by the hardest
pressed, for example the employed single parent, are inimical to
the family, and to many other things of value, for example the
physical and mental health of such parents, though these are
utterly crucial to the well-being of millions of children, and
therefore of extraordinary importance to the society as a whole.

Clearly a calculation could be made in economic terms of
the cost to the society of this cheapening of labor. It is no great
mystery that statistics associate social problems with single-
parent families. And social problems, crime for example, are an
enormous expense, an enormous drag on the economy. We are
conditioned to think that the issue for single mothers, say, is
work or welfare. In fact the issue is decent working hours and
reasonable pay. These are important people, holding the world
together for children who in many instances have been half
abandoned. It is grotesque that their lives should be made impossible because of some unexamined fealty to economic principles that are, if we would pause to consider, impoverishing to us
all in many ways, some of them extremely straightforward.

To consider again the weekend. It is often remarked, in an
odd spirit of censoriousness, that American culture was never a
melting pot. We are given to know that it was wrong to have

aspired to such an ideal, and wrong to have fallen short of it. There seems to me to be little evidence that the ideal ever was aspired to, at least in the sense in which critics understand the phrase. Since religion is central to most special identities within the larger national culture, religious tolerance has been the great guarantor of the survival of the variety of cultures. It was characteristic of European countries for centuries to try to enforce religious uniformity on just these grounds. If earlier generations in America chose not to follow this example, presumably they knew and accepted the consequence of departing from it, that assimilation would have important limits. This strikes me as a happy arrangement, all in all.

Now there is great anxiety about the survival and recognition of these cultures of origin. I suggest that this sense of loss, which reflects, it seems, novel and unwelcome assimilation is another consequence of the disruption of the family I have been describing. Civic life is expected to be ethnically neutral, and at the same time to acknowledge our multitude of ethnicities and identities in such a way as to affirm them, to make their inheritors all equally glad to embrace and sustain them. These are not realistic expectations. One acquires a culture from within the culture—for all purposes, from the family.

And acculturation takes time. I suggest that those groups who feel unvalued are the very groups who are most vulnerable to the effects of the cheapening of labor, least able to control the use of their time. They look for, or are promised, amendment in the correction of images and phrases, in high school multicultural days and inclusive postage stamp issues. Such things can never supply the positive content of any identity.

The crudeness of public institutions in their attempts to respond to these demands is clearly in large part due to the fact that they are wholly unsuited to the work that is asked of them. Obviously they cannot supply the place of church or synagogue. The setting apart of the weekend once sheltered the traditions and institutions that preserved the variety of cultures. French Catholics and Russian Jews and Dutch Protestants could teach morals and values wholly unembarrassed by the fact that the general public might not agree with every emphasis and particular, and therefore they were able to form coherent moral personalities in a way that a diverse and open civic culture cannot and should not even attempt. It seems to me likely that the openness of the civic culture has depended on the fact that these groups and traditions have functioned as teachers of virtue and morality, sustaining by their various lights a general predisposition toward acting well. When the state attempts to instill morality, the attempt seems intrusive and even threatening precisely because that work has traditionally been reserved to family, community, and religion, to the institutions of our diversity, a thing we have cherished historically much better than we do now, for all our talk. Or rather, our talk arises from a nervous awareness that our traditional diversity is eroding away, and we are increasingly left with simple difference, in its most negative and abrasive forms.

I do not think it is nostalgia to suggest that it would be well to reestablish the setting apart of time traditionally devoted to religious observance. If there is any truth in polls, the American public remains overwhelmingly religious, and religion is characteristically expressed in communities of worship. To take part in them requires time. It may be argued that there are higher values, for example the right to buy what one pleases when one pleases, which involves another's right to spend Saturday or Sunday standing at a cash register or to compel someone else to stand there. If these are the things we truly prefer, there is no more to be said. But the choice is unpoetical and, in its effects, intolerant. When we were primitive capitalists we did much better. Now people in good circumstances have their Saturdays and Sundays if they want them. So observance is an aspect of privilege, though the privileged among us tend to be the least religious. No wonder the churches are dying out.

Those among us who call themselves traditionalists, and who invoke things like "religion" and "family" in a spirit that makes these honest words feel mean and tainted, are usually loyal first of all to a tooth-and-nail competitiveness our history does not in fact enshrine. Religion and family must shift as they will when there is a dollar at stake. But the exponents of these notions are no better economists than they are historians. Reforms meant to raise the price of labor! they will say. Think of the cost to the employer! But what is the cost to the employer of this steady impoverishment of the consumer—who is, after all, simply someone else's employee, spending what he dares of what he earns? This wisdom has prevailed for twenty years and more. Its methods are not in fact traditional, and their results are not good.

Well-compensated labor tends to be marketed selectively, and this protects its market value. Badly compensated labor tends to overwhelm demand, and this erodes its market value. Or, one might say, cost rations access, thereby enhancing the price for which work can be sold. This was the effect of the minimum wage law, while it was meaningful. But high levels of employment at low wages create more low-wage employment, for example in services like fast food and child care, services which reflect the fact that people have sold a great deal of their time for relatively little money. Since these services fill needs created by low-wage employment, they must keep their own costs low, and this is an inevitable downward pressure on the pay of their own employees. The accelerating disparity of wealth among us is no great mystery. But it is even now inspiring recondite speculations, electrifying learned brains to the point of re-animating ideas anyone might have thought long and utterly dead, of sclerosis or spleen or intractable primitivity.

I think the history of ideas is easily as peculiar as anything that exists on our planet, that its causalities are whimsical altogether. We know that Communism was a theology, a church militant, with sacred texts and with saints and martyrs and prophets, with doctrines about the nature of the world and of humankind, with immutable laws and millennial visions and life-pervading judgments about the nature of good and evil. No doubt it failed finally for the same reason it lasted as long as it did, because it *was* a theology, gigantic and rigid and intricate, taking authority from its disciplines and its hierarchies even while they rendered it fantastically ill suited to the practical business of understanding and managing an economy. It seems to me that, obedient to the great law which sooner or later makes one the image of one's enemy, we have theologized our own economic system, transforming it into something likewise rigid and tendentious and therefore always less useful to *us*. It is an American-style, stripped-down, low-church theology, its clergy largely self-ordained, golf-shirted, the sort one would be not at all surprised and only a little alarmed to find on one's doorstep. Its teachings are very, very simple: There really are free and natural markets where the optimum value of things is assigned to them; everyone must compete with everyone; the worthy will prosper and the unworthy fail; those who succeed while others fail will be made deeply and justly happy by this experience, having had no other object in life; each of us is poorer for every cent that is used toward the wealth of all of us; governments are instituted among men chiefly to interfere with the working out of these splendid principles.

This is such a radical obliteration of culture and tradition, let us say of Jesus and Jefferson, as to awe any Bolshevik, of course. But then contemporary discourse is innocent as a babe unborn of any awareness of culture and tradition, so the achievement is never remarked. It is nearly sublime, a sort of cerebral whiteout. But my point here is that unsatisfactory economic ideas and practices which have an impressive history of failure, which caused to founder that great nation California, which lie at the root of much of the shame and dread and division and hostility and cynicism with which our society is presently afflicted, are treated as immutable truths, not to be questioned, not to be interfered with, lest they unleash their terrible retribution, recoiling against whomever would lay a hand on the Ark of Market Economics, if that is the name under which this mighty power is currently invoked.

There is a great love of certitude implicit in all this, and those impressed by it often merge religious and social and economic notions, discovering likeness in this supposed absolute clarity, which is really only selectivity and simplification. Listening to these self-declared moralists and traditionalists, it seems to me I hear from time to time a little satisfaction in the sober fact that God, as our cultures have variously received him through the Hebrew Scriptures, seems to loathe, actually abominate, certain kinds of transgression. Granting this fact, let us look at the transgressions thus singled out. My own sense of the text, based on more than cursory reading, is that the sin most insistently called abhorrent to God is the failure of generosity, the neglect of widow and orphan, the oppression of strangers and the poor, the defrauding of the laborer. Since many of the enthusiasts of this new theology are eager to call themselves Christians, I would draw their attention to the New Testament, *passim.*

I have heard pious people say, Well, you can't live by Jesus' teachings in this complex modern world. Fine, but then they might as well call themselves the Manichean Right or the Zoroastrian Right and not live by *those* teachings. If an economic imperative trumps a commandment of Jesus, they should just say so and drop these pretensions toward particular holiness— which, while we are on the subject of divine abhorrence, God, as I recall, does not view much more kindly than he does neglect of the poor. In fact, the two are often condemned together.

I know those who have taken a course in American history will think this merger of Christian pretensions and bullyboy economics has its origins in Calvinism and in Puritanism. Well, Calvin and the Puritans both left huge literatures. Go find a place where they are guilty of this vulgarization. Or, a much easier task, find a hundred or a thousand places where they denounce it, taking inspiration, always, from the Bible, which it was their quaint custom to read with a certain seriousness and attention. We have developed a historical version of the victim defense, visiting our sins upon our fathers. But I will say a thing almost never said among us: we have ourselves to blame.

Communism demonstrated the great compatibility of secularism with economic theology, and we may see the same thing now in the thinking of many of our contemporaries. On the assumption that American society is destined to extreme economic polarization, certain brave souls have written brave books arguing that those who thrive are genetically superior to those who struggle. They have higher IQs.

So we are dealing with a Darwinian paradigm, again, as people have done in one form or another since long before Darwin. The tale is always told this way—the good, the fit, the bright, the diligent prosper. These correspond to the creatures who, in the state of nature, would survive and reproduce. But—here our eyes widen—civilization lumbers us with substandard types who reproduce boundlessly and must finally swallow us up in their genetic mediocrity, utterly confounding and defeating the harsh kindness of evolution. This peril once posed itself in the form of the feckless Irish. But they became prosperous, enjoying, one must suppose, a great enhancement of their genetic endowment in the process, since I have never heard that the arts and professions have had to stoop to accommodate their deficiencies. This theory is so resilient because it can always turn a gaze unclouded by memory or imagination on the least favored group in any moment or circumstance, like the Darwinian predator fixing its eye on the gazelle with the sprained leg, perfectly indifferent to the fact that another gazelle was lame two days ago, yet another will be lame tomorrow.

The Social Darwinist argument always arises to answer, or to preclude, or in fact to beg, questions about social justice—during trade wars or in the midst of potato famines. We are not quite at ease with the chasm that may be opening in our society, and some of us seek out the comforts of resignation. And these comforts are considerable. Viewed in the light of science, or at least of something every bit as cold and solemn as science, we see manifest in this painful experience the invisible hand of spontaneous melioration, the tectonic convulsions meant to form the best of all possible worlds.

But, at the risk of a little discomfort, let us try another hypothesis, just to see if it has descriptive power as great or even greater than the one favored by sociobiology. Let us just test the idea that our problems reflect an inability to discover or prepare an adequate elite. Obviously the thought of deficiency at the top of society is more alarming than deficiency at the bottom, but that is all the more reason to pause and consider.

When we speak of an elite, do we mean people of high

accomplishment, people who do valuable work with great skill, people who create standards and articulate values? Are we speaking of our brilliant journalists, our noble statesmen, the selfless heroes of our legal profession? To be brief, what part of the work of the culture that is properly the responsibility of an elite actually functions at the level even of our sadly chastened hopes? Are our colleges producing great humanists and linguists? Is spiritual grandeur incubating in our seminaries? How often do we wonder if the medical care we receive is really appropriate?

For the purposes of these sociobiologists, membership in the elite seems to be a matter of income. But doctors and professors and journalists are so much a part of the morphology of our civilization that they will be with us until goats are put to graze in our monuments, and will probably be pulling down a decent salary, too, by whatever standards apply. Their presence in roles that are ideally filled by competent people does not make them competent. "But IQ!" they will answer. Yes, and since our society is, statistically speaking, in the hands of people with high IQs, we have no trouble at all finding a good news magazine, and we can always go to a good movie, and we are never oppressed by a sense of vulgarity or stupidity hardening around us. "But that is condescension to the masses," they will say. "You have to do things that are very stupid to make enough income to qualify for a place in this elite of the bright and worthy." Yes. That accounts, I suppose, for the rosy contentment of the man in the street.

Or perhaps they would offer no such tortuous defense. Perhaps they would say that if an elite is defined as a group of highly competent, responsible people with a special gift for holding themselves to exacting standards, we have at present rather little in the way of an elite. Then perhaps a high IQ correlates strongly with sharpness of the elbows, and simply obtains for people advantages to which they have no true right. Qualities consistent with the flourishing of the individual can be highly inconsistent with the flourishing of the group. History makes this point relentlessly. We have forgotten that democracy was intended as a corrective to the disasters visited upon humanity by elites of one kind and another. Maybe the great drag on us all is not the welfare mother but the incompetent engineer, not the fatherless child but the writer of mean or slovenly books. When our great auto industry nearly collapsed, an elite of designers and marketing experts were surely to blame. But the thousands thrown out of work by their errors were seen as the real problem. No doubt many of these workers figure among the new lumpenproletariat, as the Marxists used to call them, people who just are not bright enough.

These grand theories are themselves no proof of great intelligence in the people who formulate them. Obviously I am shaken by the reemergence of something so crude as Social Darwinism. But my point here is that regrettable changes in our economy may not simply express the will of the market gods, but may instead mean something so straightforward as that those whose decisions influence the economy might not be good at their work. If they were brighter, perhaps no pretext would ever have arisen for these ungracious speculations about the gifts of the powerless and the poor.

It seems to me that something has passed out of the culture, changing it invisibly and absolutely. Suddenly it seems there are too few uses for words like humor, pleasure, and charm; courage, dignity, and graciousness; learnedness, fairmindedness, openhandedness; loyalty, respect, and good faith. What bargain did we make? What could have appeared for a moment able to compensate us for the loss of these things? Perhaps I presume in saying they are lost. But if they were not, surely they would demand time and occasion—time because every one is an art or a discipline, and occasion because not one of them exists except as behavior. They are the graces of personal and private life, and they live in the cells of the great cultural reef, which takes its form and integrity from them, and will not survive them, if there is aptness in my metaphor.

Why does society exist, if not to accommodate our lives? Jefferson was a civilized man—clearly it was not his intention to send us on a fool's errand. Why do we never imagine that the happiness he mentioned might include a long supper with our children, a long talk with a friend, a long evening with a book? Given time, and certain fading habits and expectations, we could have comforts and luxuries for which no one need be deprived. We could nurture our families, sustain our heritages, and, in the pregnant old phrase, enjoy our*selves*. The self, that dear and brief acquaintance, we could entertain with a little of the ceremony it deserves.

It will be objected that we are constrained by the stern economics of widget manufacture. Perhaps. If that argument is otherwise persuasive, there is no real evidence that it is true. In either case, we should at least decide when such considerations should be determining. There is a terse, impatient remark in Paul's letter to the Galatians: "For freedom Christ has set us free." And why are *we*, by world and historical standards, and to the limit of our willingness to give meaning to the word—why are *we* free? To make hard laws out of doubtful theories, and impose them and obey them at any cost? Nothing good can come of this. Great harm has come of it already.

Margaret Talbot

The Perfectionist

This is an auspicious time for shallowness. Seriousness—and moral seriousness especially—is so rare these days that we are inclined to cut all sorts of slack for those who seem to possess it. The appearance of hard thinking is increasingly mistaken for the thing itself. Attitudes more and more do the work of arguments. Sincerity, solemnity, sanctimony: these are now the marks of moral and intellectual elevation; and the feeling of elevation is what matters. After all, logical and empirical rigor are so unedifying. And there is already so much cynicism loose in the land.

This is an auspicious time, therefore, for a moralist such as Bill McKibben. He seems like such fine and edifying company. He cares so much. Never mind that he may strike us as a bit precious, a bit self-regarding in his various renunciations and refusals. We all know people a little like him, and we are timid about criticizing them, too. We all have friends or relatives who periodically declare that Christmas or Hanukah have become too commercialized (who, in the materialist madness of boom-time America, would deny it?), and therefore they will be boycotting the holidays, which is to say, not giving us any presents. (The adherents of Voluntary Simplicity, a diffuse movement of affluent Americans who have decided that they can live better by buying less and band together on the Internet for self-congratulatory chats about the frisson of frugality, like to call this "non-gifting.") And we have all met the sort of people who will announce that the world is already overloaded with the human pollutants otherwise known as children, and so they have made the decision not to reproduce.

Privately, we may wonder whether these are the right sacrifices, or even whether, for these particular people, they are sacrifices at all. We may wonder whether a 3,000-page Web site devoted to Voluntary Simplicity, or a series of best-selling books on the same topic (all duly promoted by multicity author tours, point-of-purchase displays, and the like) quite embody the Shaker-like humility to which their votaries lay claim. We may ask whether the very notion of voluntary simplicity is itself an expression of overrefinement, as inseparable from advanced consumerist civilization as, say, the ideal of a pristine wilderness is from the culture that dreamed *it* up. We may even wonder— privately, again, when the effect of all that earnestness has worn off—whether some of the non-gifters or the non-breeders might be thought of as, well, cheap or selfish. ("I got caught up in the 'remember when' of being disappointed by others and I decided to be very limited as to giving," confided one non-gifting Internet chatterer. "I splurged on a gift for my granddaughter, asked my parents to share the cost, which they did, and observed that when opened, there was a temper-tantrum from my three-year-old granddaughter.")

But since this skepticism may strike us as we wander the aisles of Toys R Us, feeling free-handed and maybe a little guilty, we probably won't admit to it out loud. I mean, we're the problem, aren't we? And so a set of ideas about what constitutes the virtuous life will escape the scrutiny that it deserves. It's not as if panting consumerism or the environmental implications of population growth are trivial topics. Quite the contrary. So we may be inclined to say of anyone who speaks dourly enough of these topics, bless their delicate, prickly, abstemious souls, and their gifts in our name to charities of their choice, and their deeply committed childlessness. Let them do as they please. All that we ask is that they don't start holding themselves up as models for the rest of us.

Except that so often that's just what they do. Consider Bill McKibben. He began his writing career a decade ago as a nature-loving journalist who chronicled environmental depredation, and that is what he still does. With each of his books—he has written four and a fifth is on the way—McKibben's tone has become less reportorial and more personal, less analytical and more homiletical. It's as though John Muir had clambered down Half Dome to sit at the feet of Robert Fulghum.

McKibben's first book, *The End of Nature* (1989), was the first general interest work to explain the threat of global climate change, and it did so with clarity and conviction. Still, it had its McKibbenish flaws. One could argue, along with some other students of the subject, that *The End of Nature* was marred by its embrace of the sort of eco-dualism in which the human and the natural are seen as utterly separate and inevitably at odds. Nature is dead and man is the perp, for any and all manipulation of the natural world is a violation of its essence. (Never mind that conservation itself is a manipulation of nature.) Thus, in a trenchant essay called "The Trouble with Wilderness," the historian William Cronon has written rather witheringly that the McKibbenish perspective is possible

> only if we accept the wilderness premise that nature, to be natural, must also be pristine—remote from humanity and untouched by our common past. In fact, everything we know about environmental history suggests that people have been manipulating the natural world on various scales for as long as we have a record of their passing. Moreover, we also have unassailable evidence that many of the environmental changes we now face also occurred quite apart from human intervention at one time or another in the earth's past. The point is not that our current problems are trivial, or that our devastating

effects on the earth's ecosystems should be accepted as inevitable or "natural." It is rather that we seem unlikely to make progress in solving these problems if we hold up to ourselves as the mirror of nature a wilderness we ourselves cannot inhabit. To do so is merely to take to a logical extreme the paradox that was built into wilderness from the beginning: if nature dies because we enter it, then the only way to save nature is to kill ourselves.

These are serious objections. The point is not only that an overly pious view of nature can actually inspire a debilitating fatalism about the prospects for preserving it. Cronon's criticism suggests a more far-reaching problem: the sort of thinking in which a theological awe of nature is supposed to furnish a basis for human ethics. Such thinking is now widespread; but humanist philosophers have been warning against this fallacy at least since Mill, and with good reason. For there is nothing moral in nature—nothing, that is, that we have not ascribed to it.

There is beauty in nature, beauty unbounded, but there is no justice and there is no mercy. "Either it is right that we should kill because nature kills," Mill wrote in his great essay on nature, "torture because nature tortures; ruin and devastate because nature does the like; or we ought not to consider at all what nature does, but what it is good to do." The urge to restore nature, to undo the damage that humans have done to the environment, is itself an impulse of culture. It is a supremely civilized—which is to say, a supremely unnatural—urge.

Its philosophical fallacy notwithstanding, *The End of Nature* was full of useful information. It was also pretty free of the exemplary presence of its author. The same, alas, cannot be said of McKibben's more recent writings. Increasingly the subject of Bill McKibben's books has been the rightness of the choices made by Bill McKibben. In *The Age of Missing Information,* he found that he had been right to abstain from television. Up in the Adirondacks, in that patch of primeval neo-wilderness to which McKibben and his wife had retreated, the reception was lousy; but after watching thousands of hours of randomly taped TV broadcasts mailed to him by more corruptible friends with cable, McKibben was able to reassure himself that he wasn't missing a thing.

It was an ordeal, of course; not even the moldiest couch potato takes in eighteen hours a day of television. Yet the experiment paid off, insofar as it allowed McKibben the satisfaction of confirming what he knew all along. "What keeps me more truly in touch with the world," he asked rhetorically, "watching all this TV, or taking a simple walk in the woods?" To which his reader might reply with a question of her own: By what artificial dichotomy must television and nature, information and contemplation, technology and spirituality, cancel one another out? It was only McKibben who was asking us to choose.

In *Hundred Dollar Holiday,* another manual of moral improvement that Simon and Schuster has announced for next winter, McKibben appears to discover that he is also right to spend less money at Christmas, and that the rest of us ought to follow his antimaterialist example. As the publisher's catalog explains, "a more satisfying and meaningful Yule could be had by making it, financially, at least, a far more modest affair." Now there's a revelation suitable for needle-pointing. If there is anyone out there to whom this hoary platitude has not yet occurred, there is surely no book in the world that will enlighten him.

I would like to know, though, what McKibben has to say about the jobs that would be lost—starting with minimum-wage retail positions—if all of the privileged Americans at whom his exhortations are directed quit throwing their money around at Christmas. There is something so privileged about such renunciations of privilege. And the same question may be posed more generally to McKibben's kindred spirits in the Voluntary Simplicity movement. Disdain the market all you like, but we cannot all live by bartering our lightly used Armani and growing our own arugula.

The most egregious of McKibben's sermons, though, is certainly his current one. In *Maybe One,* McKibben concludes that he and his wife were right to stop with just one child, and that the rest of us ought to do the same. The next fifty years "will be crucial to our planet's future," he writes. "[T]hey are the years that could so devastate the earth's biology that it will never again be able to support life as abundantly as it does at present." The best way McKibben now sees for us to limit the damage that humans wreak on the planet is to make the only child a "cultural norm."

In its broad outlines, McKibben's neo-Malthusianism is nothing new. What distinguishes him from other population doomsayers is his yuppieish determination to see moral virtue and the opportunity for self-betterment where they see only stark, terrible necessity. Saving the earth isn't enough? Apparently not. McKibben wants to convince us not only that one-child families are environmentally sound, but also that they are psychologically enriching—superior, in certain important ways, to the messier constellations of bigger families.

The "real reason" he did the research for this book, McKibben explains, bore no relation to the planet. "I did it because of Sophie, my four-year-old daughter. I wanted to make sure that growing up without brothers or sisters would not damage her spirit or her mind. That's why the first chapters of this book have nothing to do with the environment and everything to do with kids." As a preamble to a manifesto of sorts, this is rather bizarre. For if the population crisis is as grave as McKibben portrays it, then the psychological niceties of the singleton status are irrelevant. And if it is not as grave as he portrays it, then why get into the business of defining a politically correct family size at all? Why try to dictate for others what is, or ought to be, a fiercely intimate choice?

To his credit, McKibben asks himself these questions, too. He agonizes that he and his wife did not make the deep ecological decision to forgo children altogether. "What eventually made up our minds was largely simple desire; like most, though certainly not all, people we felt some need deeper than deep to raise and nurture a child. Anything else may simply be justification." He offers the acknowledgement (it is a little stiff, but at least it is there) that "this book may not persuade most readers to limit themselves to one child—there are many deep factors involved in that decision." And he returns again and again to the idea that we are living in a "special moment," a fifty-year moment of truth during which we can open up more of a margin for environmental error and experimentation if we in affluent America have fewer children.

Of course, the attentive reader will recall that in affluent America we already have fewer children, fewer than we used to have and fewer than our counterparts have in the developing world. The fertility rate in the United States first sank below what demographers call the replacement level—roughly 2.1 children per woman—in 1973. Since then, the American birth rate has risen slowly back to replacement levels, but this is a minor increase in comparison to the soaring fertility rates of the late nineteenth century and the more recent baby-boom period. "Few demographers would forecast either a resurgence of fertility equivalent to the baby boom of 1940–1957," the demographers Douglas Anderton, Richard Barrett, and Donald Bogue write in *The Population of the United States*, "or a dramatic fall in fertility to below the replacement level in the near future. Instead, the likely prospect seems to be small ripples in a plateau hovering either just below or at the replacement level."

The reasons for this are fairly clear, and they hinge on the changing role of women. Generally speaking, the more women work outside the home, and the higher the professional status they achieve, the more likely they are to postpone childbearing and the fewer children they are likely to have. (High divorce rates in the United States probably also contribute to lower birth rates.) The reality, then, is that most of us already live in smaller families. As Anderton, Barrett, and Bogue put it, "Only 10 percent of married-couple families contained 3 or more children in 1992. . . . The trend since 1980 is towards an increase in childless families and a reduction in large numbers of children present in families."

Today, roughly one in four American families has just one

child, compared to one in ten in the 1950s. And if you want to measure this new fertility regime in terms of attitudes rather than numbers, you can do that, too. Twenty-three times in the last 60 years, the Gallup Poll has asked Americans for their opinion about the ideal size of a family. In 1938, 66 percent of those polled said three or more children in a family was ideal. In 1962—the last hiccup of the baby boom—an astonishing 80 percent did. In 1997, just 36 percent of those polled thought three or more kids would be swell.

There is a population problem of sorts in the United States, but it is not one that can be conceived of in McKibben's terms, as a problem of human bulk. The answer to this population problem, moreover, is not a general thinning of the herd. Our problem is that half of all the pregnancies in the United States are unintended; and so the children who result from these pregnancies (about half of them come to term) are probably less likely to get the love and the care they need than children who are planned. "When people are born whose parents don't want them," as the demographer Joel Cohen succinctly observes, "there is definitely a population problem."

These unintended pregnancies are more common than average among the young and among the poor. Yet impoverished teenagers are not the group most likely to read McKibben's book, or to make decisions about their lives on the basis of abstract arguments about global climate change. And among his likely readers—the college-educated, the eco-savvy—what McKibben calls the "taboo" on one-child families has long since broken down. Only children are more common than they used to be, especially in the higher income brackets; and the advice-giving apparatus that attends modern parenthood has caught up with this reality.

It is not at all unusual to flip through magazines aimed at striving parents and find an article such as "Only Kids Aren't Lonely . . . and other Reassuring Research for Parents of One Child" (*Parents* magazine). Popular how-to books such as *What to Expect in the Toddler Years* tell parents that "children aren't like potato chips; you can stop at just one, if you want to." (The authors go on to tout research showing that "only children performed better academically than children with siblings, and were strongly represented among the population of highly successful people.") So McKibben is really preaching to the converted.

But he is ready with an answer. It is true that affluent First Worlders do not drop big litters, but it is also true that affluent First Worlders suck up more resources. One kid in Larchmont is more of a drag on Mother Nature than six kids in Lahore. We tromp on the earth, while others are obliged (by grinding poverty, it must be said, rather than by Earth Firstism) to tiptoe. They are woodland sprites; we are teletubbies. As McKibben unflatteringly puts it, "The richest tenth of Americans—the people most likely to be reading this book—each emit eleven tons of carbon annually. . . . My daughter, age four at the time of this writing, has already used more stuff, added more waste to the environment than most of the world's residents in a lifetime."

What a costly little girl! But if this is the problem, then surely the solution lies in renewed attempts at conservation—recycling, fuel efficiency, solar energy and other corrections yet to come. On this point, however, it turns out that McKibben has become something of a fatalist. All those changes in lifestyle and technology happen too slowly to make a difference, he believes. Worse, they may not happen at all. We are naïve to keep putting our faith in them: "You'd think offhand that compared to changing fertility—the number of kids we bear—changing consumption patterns would be a breeze," he writes. "Fertility, after all, seems *biological*—hard-wired into us in deep Darwinian ways. But in fact, I would guess that it's easier to change fertility than lifestyle. For better or for worse, we live in a culture that can say 'that's enough' in regard to children at least as easily as it can regarding cars."

"It's easier to change fertility than lifestyle": a purer expression of the yuppie view of the world was never uttered. And if this is so, if it is really true that we would sooner interfere with our commitment to children than with our taste in cars, then surely this is for the worse—so much for the worse, in fact, that we ought not to resign ourselves to it. There is something deeply dispiriting about McKibben's straitened sense of what is possible. For the yearning to have children, and the having of children and the caring for them, are part of what makes us believe in the continuity of life, and gives us hope in a future; part of what frees us from the bonds of self; part of what ties us to this earth and to everyone else on it. More than work, more than nature, more even than God, children are what confer meaning on the lives of most people around the world. Before we surrender all this—and restricting yourself to one child when you long for more children and you firmly believe that a family is properly comprised of sisters and brothers *is* a surrender—why not try to make the kind of changes that do not violate something so fundamental?

McKibben's homey moralism disguises the fact that he has surprisingly little confidence in moral agency. If moral agency were enough, then he would not have had a vasectomy, which is, after all, an anatomical fix intended to vanquish forever the temptation, if it is one, to procreate. Yet McKibben describes his vasectomy proudly, and alas, in some detail: "So I sat on the table, and pulled my pants down my ankles, and he swabbed my scrotum with iodine ('the iodine needs to be a little warm—the last thing we want is shrinkage before we start') and then he injected a slug of anesthetic into each side of my testicles. Yes, it was a needle down there, but no, it didn't hurt much; by chance I'd spent the previous afternoon in the dentist's chair and this was much less painful. (And no flossing!)" I suppose it was noble of McKibben to go for the operation himself; vasectomies are less invasive than tubal ligations, the procedure that his wife would have had to endure to achieve the same end. (Women generally do most of the worrying about birth control.) Noble, and no flossing!

McKibben wants to persuade his readers that there would be no real loss entailed in making one-child families the norm. For him, this means first and foremost overcoming what he calls, a bit melodramatically, the "prejudice" against only children. And this in turn means assembling recent psychological research showing that singletons grow up to be no more spoiled or selfish or lonely or misanthropic than children with siblings.

To do so, McKibben relies on the work of a psychologist named Toni Falbo who, along with her colleague Denise Polit, reviewed 141 studies on the personalities, the peer relations, the intelligence, and the achievement of only children. They concluded that only children scored slightly higher than other groups on some measures, especially those having to do with achievement and motivation in school. In almost all other areas, they were virtually indistinguishable from children with siblings.

In a way, this conclusion is not surprising; or what is surprising is how easy it is to assimilate. For if there is a prejudice against only children, it is not the sort of prejudice that slams doors in their faces or girds anyone's heart against them. It is more like the notion that redheads have tempers: you may vaguely believe it, but you are happy enough to have it overturned. I am certainly content to accept Falbo's findings, and to credit the obvious explanations that only children might do better in school on average because they get more of their parents' attention and because they live in households in which adults set the tone. It is clear, too, that if only children risk growing up with an exaggerated sense of their own importance, they risk it less now than ever, since so many more kids of all kinds are in day care at early ages.

Alas, McKibben does not stop with such sensible reassurances about onlies. He crows over their achievements—"disproportionate numbers of only borns have had their faces on the cover of *Time*"—even when he slyly admits that such evidence is anecdotal. (The cover of *Time* is not supposed to matter in the woods.) Worse, McKibben's spirited defense of singletons leads him to pathologize the sibling relationship, which he portrays as a teeming petri dish of resentments. "[A]s more children enter the family, there's a dilution of resources," he writes. "Everyone tries to give their second, third, and fourth child as much of their attention as their first, but there are only so many hours in the day, only so much stress a father can tolerate, only so many Frisbees a mother can throw."

This sounds true, and it probably feels true, to many parents; but it cannot actually be true that younger siblings get consistently less attention from their parents. If it were, then psychological woes of all kinds would be more liberally distributed among younger siblings than among older ones. Anyway, the particular size of the family matters. In a family of eight children, somebody probably will be overlooked, but there is no reason why this should necessarily be the case in a family of two or three children.

Of sibling rivalry, McKibben notes bathetically that "sometimes the hurts go on forever: Bank and Kahn [the authors of a book called *The Sibling Bond*] tell the story of a chronically unhappy older sister who feels perpetually anxious and driven and cannot understand why she and her sister still don't get along." And when sibs form especially strong ties, he says, it is usually only to compensate for a lousy relationship with their parents. "Your sister can be, in other words, a kind of fallback mechanism, a relationship of last resort." This seems to me a rather bleak and attenuated way to describe what for many people is a vital and joyous and irreplaceable bond. It is always hard to generalize about such things, and it is certainly true that siblings can form powerful trauma bonds if they come from families where their parents abused or neglected them; but my own experience has taught me that remarkably close relationships between brothers and sisters can and do flourish under happier circumstances. (Even if you like and love your parents, they are still a source of bafflement, and who besides your sister or your brother will try, with a curiosity like your own, to figure them out with you?)

The pitfalls of sibling relationships—jealousy, competition, the anxiety that one loves more than one is loved, the eventuality that your cute new cardigan will be pilfered from your closet— are to some extent the pitfalls of attachment to others. They are nothing worse than the cost of loving. And when McKibben goes on to cite the incidence of sibling incest ("[S]ometimes the hurts are very deep. Sibling incest has been estimated to be at least five times as frequent as parent-child incest, and many researchers think that's an underestimate"), presumably as a way of saying that sibling relationships are more trouble than they're worth, he loses me entirely.

Anyway, answering for the psychological health of only children does not exhaust the argument about the morality of a one-child norm. This is grimly clear in McKibben's chapter on China, "the nation with the world's largest population of only children, as well as the source of some of the most potent images of their wickedness." If all those number-one sons are not "spoiled," whatever that means, then we can charge ahead with a commitment to having tiny litters, free of the worry that a preponderance of onlies might change our culture for the worse. And what do you know, the useful Toni Falbo has done a study in China, too; and she has found, again, that onlies are pretty much like everybody else. The Chinese are not producing a generation of "little emperors," after all!

In fact, it is hard to consider Falbo's study definitive proof of anything, given what one imagines the cultural barriers might be between an American social scientist brandishing questionnaires about self-esteem and a population of provincial Chinese children for whom onlyness is already the norm. More importantly, a study such as this one misses what would seem to be the more urgent point about China's population regime. The real trouble with China's one-child policy is not that it may result in the cossetting of some boys, but that it has apparently resulted in the abandonment or the infanticide of many girls. The distortion of morality that results when a heavy-handed state intrudes on the private sphere is what matters here. McKibben's Chinese example is grotesque.

Not that McKibben wants a state policy mandating one child per family. He takes some pains to make this clear. No, he wants only to appeal to our higher selves, to the saint in us that will forsake our deepest and in some ways our most generous longings in order to do the right thing—or what McKibben thinks is the right thing—for the planet. Yet there is something anti-humanistic in such a message, something morally troubling about demanding such extraordinary commitments of ordinary people as a matter of course. For it really is extraordinary to give up one's idea of a family on the chance that we may emit a little less carbon dioxide, to deny parents the hope that their children will enrich one another's lives long after they themselves are dead, and to turn a primary human bond into a relic. Surely this is too much to ask—unless, of course, there is an emergency, and it may be claimed with some certainty that we are facing an extraordinary population crisis.

Are we? Maybe. The pace of world population growth has certainly accelerated dramatically in the last century, so dramatically that we cannot know what impact it will have on the earth or the quality of human life. It took until 1830 for the earth's population to get to 1 billion, but it took only one hundred years for it to reach 2 billion and only 45 years for it to reach 4 billion. On the other hand, the rate of global population growth hit a peak in 1965 and has now fallen to 1.5 percent a year. The total fertility rate worldwide dropped by nearly two-fifths between 1955 and 1995; from about 5 children per woman to about 3.1 children per woman. In one scenario, advanced by a respected Austrian demographer named Wolfgang Lutz and endorsed by others, the world's population will peak at 10.6 billion in the later half of the next century and then begin to shrink. A number of leading demographers now dispute the global doomsday scenario, and some of them are worrying about a population implosion.

The paradox for environmentalists such as McKibben is that these numbers are falling largely as the result of social and economic development in the Third World—that is, as a result of the sort of development that means more cars, more factories, more pollution, more living heavily on the land. McKibben himself is a bit coy about this: "It's relatively easy to explain why populations grew so fast after World War II, it's much harder to explain why that growth is now slowing." But that isn't exactly true. A strong scholarly consensus supports the observation that economic and social development—in Europe and America as they industrialized, and more recently in Asia—have tended to bring reductions in family size.

Development and an improvement in the status of women, has been generally more successful than coercion or exhortation in reducing fertility. In a way, this is not a mystery. People have fewer children, Amartya Sen writes, "when they have some basic education, know about family planning methods and have access to them, do not readily accept a life of persistent drudgery, and are not deeply anxious about their economic security." They also have fewer children when health care and sanitary conditions improve to the point that babies no longer die quite so regularly: if parents can count on more of their children surviving, they need not have "extras" as an insurance policy against infant mortality. "In country after country," Sen observes, "the birth rate has come down with more female education, the reduction of mortality rates, the expansion of economic means and security, and greater public discussion of ways of living." Sen points out that we cannot even say with certainty that China's one-child policy lowered the birth rate any further than it would have been lowered by development alone.

McKibben is right when he says that population prediction is a notoriously unreliable business. Yet the ambiguity can cut both ways—and in the past it has cut most often against pessimists such as himself. From Malthus onward, the field is littered with failed forecasts of demographic armageddon, most of them based on the idea that population will inevitably outstrip food supply. In 1968, in his bestselling book *The Population Bomb,* Paul Ehrlich thundered that "the battle to feed humanity is already lost, in the sense that we will not be able to prevent large-scale famines in the next century." In that same year, an equally popular and even scarier book called *Famine-1975!* predicted mass hunger worldwide in less than a decade. Doom galore; but the fact is that food production has consistently outpaced population since Malthus's time, and in recent decades food prices worldwide have been falling.

Of course, even if the demographic Cassandras have been wrong in the past, they may be right now. And even if they were wrong about food supply, they may be right about the threat to the environment. The trouble is that we really don't know how many people is too many people. Estimates of the earth's "carrying capacity," or the number of humans it can sustain, have ranged in recent decades from fewer than a billion to more than a trillion. Such elasticity is probably unavoidable, since both "carrying capacity" and "overpopulation" are essentially subjective terms.

It makes sense to talk about carrying capacity when you are assessing a habitat for boll weevils or wolves; but it makes no sense at all in relation to humans, who are capable of adapting and altering both their culture and their physical environment, and so of defying almost any formula that might settle the matter. (Also they vary from nation to nation and culture to culture in their use of resources.) The number of people that the earth can support depends on how we on the earth want to live, on what we want to consume and on what we regard as a crowd. Population density is not an adequate measure, since we can easily point to densely packed cities (Amsterdam, Tokyo) that are considered among the most functional and livable cities in the world.

For some environmentalists, it seems to come down to an aesthetic judgment. They like the idea of what Dave Foreman, the founder of Earth First!, calls the "Big Outside." They are suckers for grandeur, snobs for solitude. McKibben typically complains that there are crowds at every national park and state campground. (Every one? Two summers ago, on a road trip from San Francisco to Bend, Oregon, I stopped in several national forests and campgrounds where I scarcely saw another soul.) And he regards this overcrowding as a spiritual danger. "We can live without big wilderness," he frets, "but it's not clear we can live as Americans, not in the way we have in the past." We must be singletons in the face of the sublime, too.

But do we really wish to continue to "live as Americans" in this regard? Surely it would be best for the environment if Americans stopped thinking of nature in a certain American way, that is, if we ceased to regard nature as the antidote to culture, as a people-free zone where some of us go to flex our muscles and save our souls. Maybe it would be better if we gave up our Ansel Adams fantasy of unsullied nature, so that if it isn't sublime, well, we might as well turn it into a strip mall. The choice between arcadia and Monsanto is a spurious choice. For it is a primary fact of our history that the wild and the cultivated have blended together more or less successfully, if not altogether seamlessly. The human mastery of nature is hardly an occasion for shame; and it is hardly incompatible with a sense of awe.

Indeed, it is McKibben's proposal that marks a collapse of awe. This critic of the liberties taken with nature takes liberties with nature. He is licensed by perfectionism. Like all perfectionists about human life, however, McKibben seems unattractively detached from it. His consecration to the ideal has caused him to demean the real—the real existence of ordinary people, who love their children and do not hate the rain forest, who strive to live morally on this side of sainthood. McKibben puts me in mind of Orwell's strictures against Gandhi: "The essence of being human is that one does not seek perfection, that one *is* sometimes willing to commit sins for the sake of loyalty, that one does not push asceticism to the point where it makes friendly intercourse impossible, and that one is prepared in the end to be defeated and broken up by life, which is the inevitable price of fastening one's love upon other human individuals. . . . In this yogi-ridden age, it is too readily assumed that 'non-attachment' is not only better than a full acceptance of earthly life, but that the ordinary man only rejects it because it is too difficult: in other words, that the average human being is a failed saint. It is doubtful whether this is true. Many people genuinely do not wish to be saints, and it is probable that some who achieve or aspire to sainthood have never felt much temptation to be human beings."

McKibben is the yuppie yogi. He is irritating not only because he is so wrong, but also because he is so sanctimonious. And his sanctimony has nothing to do with the truth or the falsity of his beliefs. After all, one may hold a true belief and not be sanctimonious. Sanctimony is something more. It is the promotion of a belief into a judgment of those who hold or do not hold that belief. In this way, the distinction between rightness and righteousness disappears. Yet the distinction should be reasserted against McKibben. He is righteous, but not right. It is delightful to be a worse person than he is.

Politics

Richard Rorty

The Eclipse of the Reformist Left

It is impossible to discuss leftist politics in the twentieth century, in any country, without saying something about Marxism. For Marxism was not only a catastrophe for all the countries in which Marxists took power, but a disaster for the reformist Left in all the countries in which they did not.

At the end of the twentieth century, Marxism is in the position of Roman Catholicism at the end of the seventeenth. By then the full horror of the Renaissance papacies and of the Inquisition had been made known. Many Christians thought that it would be best for the bishops of Rome to close up shop. Christianity, they pointed out, had long antedated the papacy, and would be much better off for its demise.

Many present-day eastern and central Europeans hold an analogous view about Marxism, and I think they are right. The ideals of social democracy and economic justice, these people say, long antedated Marxism, and would have made much more headway had "Marxism-Leninism" never been invented. Now that the last general secretary of the Communist Party of the USSR has pointed out how much better off Russia would have been if Lenin had failed, people on the Left should stop being sentimental about the Bolshevik Revolution. Leftists should repudiate links with Lenin as firmly as the early Protestants repudiated the doctrine of the Primacy of Peter.

For us Americans, it is important not to let Marxism influence the story we tell about our own Left. We should repudiate the Marxists' insinuation that only those who are convinced capitalism must be overthrown can count as leftists, and that everybody else is a wimpy liberal, a self-deceiving bourgeois reformer. Many recent histories of the Sixties have, unfortunately, been influenced by Marxism. These histories distinguish the emergent student Left and the so-called Old Left from the "liberals"—a term used to cover both the people who administered the New Deal and those whom Kennedy brought from Harvard to the White House in 1961.

In such histories, you are counted as a member of the Old Left only if you had proclaimed yourself a socialist early on, and if you continued to express grave doubts about the viability of capitalism. So, in the historiography which has unfortunately become standard, Irving Howe and Michael Harrington count as leftists, but John Kenneth Galbraith and Arthur Schlesinger do not, even though these four men promoted mostly the same causes and thought about our country's problems in pretty much the same terms.

I think we should abandon the leftist-versus-liberal distinction, along with the other residues of Marxism that clutter up our vocabulary—overworked words like "commodification" and "ideology," for example. Had Kerensky managed to ship Lenin back to Zurich, Marx would still have been honored as a brilliant political economist who foresaw how the rich would use industrialization to immiserate the poor. But his philosophy of history would have seemed, like Herbert Spencer's, a nineteenth-century curiosity. People on the Left would not have wasted their time on Marxist scholasticism, nor would they have been so ready to assume that the nationalization of the means of production was the only way to achieve social justice. They would have evaluated suggestions for preventing the immiseration of the proletariat country by country, in the pragmatic, experimental spirit which

Dewey recommended. The contrast between genuine revolutionary leftists and wishy-washy liberal reformers would never have taken hold.

I think we should drop the term "Old Left" as a name for the Americans who called themselves "socialists" between 1945 and 1964. I propose to use the term "reformist Left" to cover all those Americans who, between 1900 and 1964, struggled within the framework of constitutional democracy to protect the weak from the strong. This includes lots of people who called themselves "communists" and "socialists," and lots of people who never dreamed of calling themselves either. I shall use "New Left" to mean the people—mostly students—who decided, around 1964, that it was no longer possible to work for social justice within the system.

In my sense of the term, Woodrow Wilson—the president who kept Eugene Debs in jail but appointed Louis Brandeis to the Supreme Court—counts as a part-time leftist. So does FDR—the president who created the rudiments of a welfare state and urged workers to join labor unions, while obdurately turning his back on African-Americans. So does Lyndon Johnson, who permitted the slaughter of hundreds of thousands of Vietnamese children, but also did more for poor children in the United States than any previous president. I cannot offer, and we do not need, a criterion specifying how much time a politician must spend on leftist reforms to be counted as a man or woman of the Left. My term "reformist Left" is intended to cover most of the people who were feared and hated by the Right, and thereby to smudge the line which the Marxists tried to draw between leftists and liberals.

Erasing that line is easier if we reflect that the Communist Party of the United States was of very little importance to the political life of our country. It marshaled some good picket lines, and it recruited a few good agents for Soviet intelligence. But the most enduring effects of its activities were the careers of men like Martin Dies, Richard Nixon, and Joseph McCarthy. On the other hand, we should remember that individual members of that party worked heroically, and made very painful sacrifices, in the hope of helping our country to achieve its promise. Many Marxists, even those who spent decades apologizing for Stalin, helped change our country for the better by helping to change its laws. So did many managerial technocrats in the Kennedy White House, even those who later helped Johnson wage the Vietnam War.

It would be a good idea to stop asking when it was unforgivably late, or unforgivably early, to have left the Communist Party. We should also stop asking when it was too late, or too early, to have come out against the Vietnam War. A hundred years from now, Howe and Galbraith, Harrington and Schlesinger, Wilson and Debs, Jane Addams and Angela Davis, Felix Frankfurter and John L. Lewis, W. E. B. Du Bois and Eleanor Roosevelt, Robert Reich and Jesse Jackson, will all be remembered for having advanced the cause of social justice. They will all be seen as having been "on the Left." The difference between these people and men like Calvin Coolidge, Irving Babbitt, T. S. Eliot, Robert Taft, and William Buckley will be far clearer than any of the quarrels which once divided them among themselves. Whatever mistakes they made, these people will deserve, as Coolidge and Buckley never will, the praise with which Jonathan Swift ended his own epitaph: "Imitate him if you can; he served human liberty."

If we look for people who made no mistakes, who were always on the right side, who never apologized for tyrants or unjust wars, we shall have few heroes and heroines. Marxism encouraged us to look for such purity. Marxists suggested that only the revolutionary proletariat could embody virtue, that bourgeois reformers were "objectively reactionary," and that failure to take Marx's scenario seriously was proof of complicity with the forces of darkness. Marxism was, as Paul Tillich and others rightly noted, more of a religion than a secularist program for social change. Like all fundamentalist sects, it emphasized purity. Lenin, like Savonarola, demanded complete freedom from sin and undeviating obedience.

Some socially useful thinkers—for example, Cornel West, Fredric Jameson, and Terry Eagleton—still speak of themselves, for what seem to me purely sentimental reasons, as "Marxists." Such sentimentality appalls Poles and Hungarians who never want to hear Marx's name again. I suspect it would baffle the Chinese dissidents starving in the laogai. Nevertheless, there is little harm in such nostalgic piety. For in the mouths of these people the word "Marxism" signals hardly more than an awareness that the rich are still ripping off the poor, bribing the politicians, and having almost everything their own way.

One way to convince oneself that the American Left could have gotten along perfectly well without Marxism is to look back to the best-known manifesto of the Progressive Era, Herbert Croly's *The Promise of American Life.* This book is filled with the same national pride that filled *Democratic Vistas,* but Croly makes a distinction Whitman rarely made: that between America before and America after the coming of industrial capitalism. Whitman was the first Romantic poet to celebrate an industrial and technological civilization, but he did not worry about the phenomenon that Marx and Croly recognized: the immiseration that would occur whenever the capitalists became able to maintain a reserve army of unemployed, and thus to pay starvation wages to those they hire. In late nineteenth- and early twentieth-century America, this reserve army was drawn from the endless supply of European immigrants—the people whose working and living conditions Upton Sinclair described in *The Jungle,* published three years before Croly's book.

Croly begins his book by saying that Americans are entitled to their "almost religious faith" in their country. But then he gets down to the problem which the Progressives wanted to solve, the problem created by the fact that "the traditional American confidence in individual freedom has resulted in a morally and socially undesirable distribution of wealth." This new distribution of wealth, Croly realized, threatened to make nonsense of Hegel's suggestion that America might become something gloriously different from Europe, and of Whitman's hope that Lincoln's heirs would see an unending series of new births of human freedom. "So long as the great majority of the poor in any country are inert and are laboring without any hope in this world," Croly wrote, "the whole associated life of that community rests on an equivocal foundation. Its moral and social order is tied to an economic system which starves and mutilates the great majority of the population, and under such conditions its religion necessarily becomes a spiritual drug, administered for the purpose of subduing the popular discontent and relieving the popular misery."

Croly, like Dewey, urged people to set aside the individualist rhetoric of nineteenth-century America. That rhetoric has been the mainstay of the American Right throughout our century, and is now, bafflingly, being treated as characteristic of liberalism by the so-called communitarians. But neither Croly nor Dewey, nor the leaders of the trade union movement, had any use for what the communitarians call "liberal individualism." Croly wrote that "a more highly socialized democracy is the only practicable substitute on the part of convinced democrats for an excessively individualized democracy." It is time, he believed, to set about developing what he called "a dominant and constructive national purpose." In becoming "responsible for the subordination of the individual to that purpose," he said, "the American state will in effect be making itself responsible for a morally and socially desirable distribution of wealth." From 1909 until the present, the thesis that the state must make itself responsible for such redistribution has marked the dividing line between the American Left and the American Right. We Americans did not need Marx to show us the need for redistribution, or to tell us that the state was often little more than the executive committee of the rich and powerful.

To the many readers who found Croly convincing, American nationalism became indistinguishable from what they sometimes called "Christian socialism" and sometimes simply "socialism"—their name for the attempt to create a cooperative commonwealth, a classless society in which nobody should be deprived of his or her dignity as an American citizen by "laboring without any hope of reward in this world." As Croly put it, "In this country, the solution of the social problem demands the substitution of a conscious social ideal for the earlier instinctive homogeneity of the American nation."

Many Progressives who never dreamed of fomenting a revolution or urging the nationalization of the means of production were happy to call themselves "socialists." Twenty years before Croly, the great Wisconsin economist Richard Ely had identified the "New Nationalism" with "the American type of socialism," and had asked his audience to realize that "from every land the wage-earning classes are looking to America for inspiration and direction." Ely's book *Social Aspects of Christianity* argued that industrial capitalism had produced "the farthest and deepest reaching crisis known to human history." He hoped that American intellectuals would throw themselves into the struggle to give the masses what they wanted and deserved.

Eldon Eisenach has argued persuasively that Croly's manifesto of 1909 summarizes two decades' worth of what we should nowadays call "communitarian" criticisms of American individualism—criticisms made by social scientists like Ely and social workers like Jane Addams. These criticisms produced what Eisenach calls a redefinition of American identity "in nationalist and historicist terms," thereby devaluing "prevailing constitutionalist, legalistic and party-electoral expressions of citizenship." These criticisms helped substitute a rhetoric of fraternity and national solidarity for a rhetoric of individual rights, and this new rhetoric was ubiquitous on the Left until the 1960s.

Eisenach has also shown how Progressive intellectuals turned American universities into what he calls "something like a national 'church'—the main repository and protector of common American values, common American meanings, and common American identities." This new church preached that America could be true to itself only if it turned left—that socialism, in some form or another, was necessary if our country, its government, and its press were not to be bought up by the rich and greedy. The ministers of this national church told America that it would lose its soul if it did not devote itself to "a conscious social ideal."

The period in which the state universities of the Midwest emerged as power bases for redistributivist social initiatives was also the era of the first great strikes. These strikes were examples of the kind of solidarity, and of comradeship in suffering, which Americans had previously witnessed only in wartime. Now Americans were making sacrifices, and sometimes dying, not to preserve the republic from political division, but to preserve it from dividing into a nation of rich and a nation of poor.

I can sum up by saying that it would be a good thing if the next generation of American leftists found as little resonance in the names of Karl Marx and Vladimir Ilyich Lenin as in those of Herbert Spencer and Benito Mussolini. It would be an even better thing if the names of Ely and Croly, Dreiser and Debs, A. Philip Randolph and John L. Lewis were more familiar to these leftists than they were to the students of the Sixties. For it would be a big help to American efforts for social justice if each new generation were able to think of itself as participating in a movement which has lasted for more than a century, and has served human liberty well. It would help if students became as familiar with the Pullman Strike, the Great Coalfield War, and the passage of the Wagner Act as with the march from Selma, the Berkeley free-speech demonstrations, and Stonewall. Each new generation of students ought to think of American leftism as having a long and glorious history. They should be able to see, as Whitman and Dewey did, the struggle for social justice as central to their country's moral identity.

To bring this about, it would help if American leftists stopped asking whether or not Walter Reuther's attempt to bourgeoisify the auto workers was objectively reactionary. It would also help if they emphasized the similarities rather than the differences between Malcolm X and Bayard Rustin, between Susan B. Anthony and Emma Goldman, between Catharine MacKinnon and Judith Butler. The sectarian divisions which plagued Marxism are manifestations of an urge for purity which the Left would be better off without.

America is not a morally pure country. No country ever has been or ever will be. Nor will any country ever have a morally pure, homogeneous Left. In democratic countries you get things done by compromising your principles in order to form alliances with groups about whom you have grave doubts. The Left in America has made a lot of progress by doing just that. The closest the Left ever came to taking over the government was in 1912, when a Whitman enthusiast, Eugene Debs, ran for president and got almost a million votes. These votes were cast by, as Daniel Bell puts it, "as unstable a compound as was ever mixed in the modern history of political chemistry." This compound mingled rage at low wages and miserable working conditions with, as Bell says, "the puritan conscience of millionaire socialists, the boyish romanticism of a Jack London, the pale Christian piety of a George Herron, . . . the reckless braggadocio of a 'Wild Bill' Haywood, . . . the tepid social-work impulse of do-gooders, . . . the flaming discontent of the dispossessed farmers, the inarticulate and amorphous desire to 'belong' of the immigrant workers, the iconoclastic idol-breaking of the literary radicals, . . . and more."

Those dispossessed farmers were often racist, nativist, and sadistic. The millionaire socialists, ruthless robber barons though they were, nevertheless set up the foundations which sponsored the research which helped get leftist legislation passed. We need to get rid of the Marxist idea that only bottom-up initiatives, conducted by workers and peasants who have somehow been so freed from resentment as to show no trace of prejudice, can achieve our country. The history of leftist politics in America is a story of how top-down initiatives and bottom-up initiatives have interlocked.

Top-down leftist initiatives come from people who have enough security, money, and power themselves, but nevertheless worry about the fate of people who have less. Examples of such initiatives are muckraking exposés by journalists, novelists, and scholars—for example, Ida Tarbell on Standard Oil, Upton Sinclair on immigrant workers in the Chicago slaughterhouses, Noam Chomsky on the State Department's lies and the *New York Times*'s omissions. Other examples are the Wagner and Norris-Laguardia Acts, novels of social protest like *People of the*

Abyss and *Studs Lonigan,* the closing of university campuses after the American invasion of Cambodia, and the Supreme Court's decisions in *Brown v. Board of Education* and *Romer v. Evans.*

Bottom-up leftist initiatives come from people who have little security, money, or power and who rebel against the unfair treatment which they, or others like them, are receiving. Examples are the Pullman Strike, Marcus Garvey's black nationalist movement, the General Motors sit-down strike of 1936, the Montgomery bus boycott, the creation of the Mississippi Freedom Democratic Party, the creation of Cesar Chavez's United Farm Workers, and the Stonewall "riot" (the beginning of the gay rights movement).

Although these two kinds of initiatives reinforced each other, the people at the bottom took the risks, suffered the beatings, made all the big sacrifices, and were sometimes murdered. But their heroism might have been fruitless if leisured, educated, relatively risk-free people had not joined the struggle. Those beaten to death by the goon squads and the lynch mobs might have died in vain if the safe and secure had not lent a hand.

These loans were unheroic but indispensable. The Luce journalists of 1937 who filled the pages of *Life* magazine with pictures of the National Guard beating up striking United Automobile Workers were not taking many risks. Nor were the TV reporters who kept the cameras focused on Bull Connor's dogs and cattle prods in 1961. But if they had not been there, and if a lot of secure and well-off Americans had not reacted to those images as they did, the UAW strike against Ford and the Freedom Ride through Alabama would both have been ineffectual. Somebody has to convince the voters that what the authorities are calling senseless violence is actually heroic civil disobedience.

The conviction that the vast inequalities within American society could be corrected by using the institutions of a constitutional democracy—that a cooperative commonwealth could be created by electing the right politicians and passing the right laws—held the non-Marxist American Left together from Croly's time until the early 1960s. But the Vietnam War splintered that

Left. Todd Gitlin believes August 1964 marks the break in the leftist students' sense of what their country was like. That was the month in which the Mississippi Freedom Democratic Party was denied seats at the Democratic Convention in Atlantic City, and in which Congress passed the Tonkin Gulf Resolution.

Gitlin argues plausibly that these two events "fatefully turned the movement" and "drew a sharp line through the New Left's Sixties." Before them, most of the New Left's rhetoric was consensual and reformist. After them, it began to build up to the full-throated calls for revolution with which the decade ended. Whether or not one agrees with Gitlin about the exact date, it is certainly the case that the mid-Sixties saw the beginning of the end of a tradition of leftist reformism which dated back to the Progressive Era. For reasons I shall be saying more about in my final lecture, this tradition was never fully reconstituted after the Sixties came to a close.

Those who admire the revolutionary turn which the New Left took in the late Sixties have offered us their own accounts of the history of the American Left. Much of the tone and emphasis of these accounts comes from the writings of C. Wright Mills and Christopher Lasch. I think the description of mid-century America which these two men helped put in circulation needs to be replaced. It should be replaced with a story which gives the reformers their due, and thereby leaves more room for national pride and national hope. Emphasizing the continuity between Herbert Croly and Lyndon Johnson, between John Dewey and Martin Luther King, between Eugene Debs and Walter Reuther, would help us to recall a reformist Left which deserves not only respect but imitation—the best model available for the American Left in the coming century. If the intellectuals and the unions could ever get back together again, and could reconstitute the kind of Left which existed in the Forties and Fifties, the first decade of the twenty-first century might conceivably be a Second Progressive Era.

Here is a rough sketch of the argument which convinced Mills, Lasch, and many young leftists of the Sixties to break with the old, reformist Left: The Vietnam War, they rightly said, is an atrocity of which Americans should be deeply ashamed. But, they continued, the Vietnam War is just the latest phase of the anticommunist Cold War. Most of the people in the universities, the unions, and the Democratic Party who call themselves either "liberals" or "leftists" are anticommunists; so we who oppose the war must form a Left which is not anticommunist.

Any attempt to replace the Mills-Lasch account of the history of the post–World War II Left must begin by asking: Granted that the Vietnam War was an atrocity of which America must always be ashamed, does this mean that the Cold War should not have been fought? This question will be debated as long as members of my generation of leftists survive. Those of us who were, like myself, militantly anticommunist believe that the war against Stalin was as legitimate, and as needed, as the war against Hitler. Some of my contemporaries, like Fredric Jameson, still agree with Jean-Paul Sartre. Sartre said that he had always believed, and would always believe, that anticommunists are scum. Such people see the Cold War as nothing more than an American drive for world domination. They mock the idea that America could have prosecuted that war without propping up right-wing dictators. My anticommunist side of the argument gets a lot of support from leftists in central and eastern Europe. Jameson's side of the argument gets a lot of support among leftists in Latin America and Asia—people who have first-hand knowledge of what the CIA can do to a poor nation's hopes for social justice.

People on my side of the argument never took seriously C. Wright Mills's suggestion that American intellectuals should have refused to fight the Cold War, and should have "attempted to get in touch with [their] opposite numbers in all countries, above all in the Sino-Soviet zone . . . [and] make our own separate peace." Our Russian and Polish opposite numbers did not want a separate peace. They wanted liberation from a thuggish, cruel, and seemingly invincible tyranny. Unless America had fought the Cold War, they now believe, they would never have been freed. People on my side of the argument think these Russians and

Poles are right. Despite the suggestions of revisionist historians of the Cold War, we do not believe the liberation of 1989 would ever have occurred if the United States had come to terms with Stalin in the late 1940s in the way these historians have suggested was possible. We think that history will see the Cold War as having been fought, like most wars, from thoroughly mixed motives, but as having saved the world from a great danger.

My leftmost students, who are also my favorite students, find it difficult to take my anticommunism seriously. When I tell them that I was a teenage Cold War liberal, they react as they would to the title of a particularly tasteless horror film. So I try to explain to them what it was like to be what Gitlin calls a "red-diaper anticommunist baby." There were lots of babies like me in the Thirties and Forties, but Gitlin's term puzzles his younger readers. I shall spend a few minutes on autobiography in the hope of giving you a sense both of what it was like to grow up on the anticommunist reformist Left in mid-century, and of the continuity between that Left and the Left of 1910, the time of Debs and Croly.

My parents were loyal fellow-travelers of the Communist Party up through 1932, the year after I was born. In that year my father ran a front organization called the League of Professional Groups for Foster and Ford (the Communist Party's candidates for president and vice-president). My parents broke with the party after realizing the extent to which it was run from Moscow, and so I did not get to read the *Daily Worker* when I was a boy. By 1935 the *Worker* was printing cartoons of my father as a trained seal, catching fish thrown by William Randolph Hearst. But my parents did subscribe to the organ of Norman Thomas' Socialist Party, *The Call,* as well as to those of the DeLeonite Socialist Labor Party and the Shachtmanite Socialist Workers' Party. I plowed through these papers, convinced that doing so would teach me how to think about my country and its politics.

Few of the people who wrote for leftist periodicals, either those aimed at workers or those aimed at bourgeois intellectuals like my parents, had any doubt that America was a great, noble, progressive country in which justice would eventually triumph. By "justice" they all meant pretty much the same thing—decent wages and working conditions, and the end of racial prejudice.

They sometimes quoted my maternal grandfather, the Social Gospel theologian Walter Rauschenbusch. An ally of Ely and Croly, Rauschenbusch preached against those he described as "servants of Mammon . . . who drain their fellow men for gain, . . . who have made us ashamed of our dear country by their defilements, . . . [and] who have cloaked their extortion with the gospel of Christ."

Because Rauschenbusch had remained a pacifist even after America's entry into World War I, because my father had been an unarmed stretcher-bearer in that war, and because one of my uncles had been staff director of the Nye Committee's investigation of the "merchants of death" in the mid-Thirties, I associated leftism with antimilitarism. But even though my father had, like John Dewey and Norman Thomas, opposed America's entry into World War II, I rejoiced that we had fought and won the war against Hitler. Because my father had once been thrown in jail for reporting on a strike, I associated the police with the goon squads who, in those days, were still being regularly hired to beat up strikers. I thought of the strikers in the coal fields and the steel mills as the great heroes of my time. When the Taft-Hartley Labor Act was passed in 1947 I could not understand how my country could have forgotten what it owed the unions, how it could fail to see that the unions had prevented America from becoming the property of the rich and greedy.

Because a lot of my relatives helped write and administer New Deal legislation, I associated leftism with a constant need for new laws and new bureaucratic initiatives which would redistribute the wealth produced by the capitalist system. I spent occasional vacations in Madison with Paul Raushenbush, who ran Wisconsin's unemployment compensation system, and his wife, Elizabeth Brandeis (a professor of labor history, and the author of the first exposé of the misery of migrant workers on Wisconsin farms). Both were students of John R. Commons, who had passed on the heritage of his own teacher, Richard Ely. Their friends included Max Otto, a disciple of Dewey. Otto was the in-house philosopher for a group of Madison bureaucrats and academics clustered around the La Follette family. In that circle, American patriotism, redistributionist economics, anticommunism, and Deweyan pragmatism went together easily and naturally. I think of that circle as typical of the reformist American Left of the first half of the century.

Another such circle was made up of the so-called New York Intellectuals. As a teenager, I believed every anti-Stalinist word that Sidney Hook and Lionel Trilling published in *Partisan Review*—partly, perhaps, because I had been bounced on their knees as a baby. My mother used to tell me, with great pride, that when I was seven I had had the honor of serving little sandwiches to the guests at a Halloween party attended both by John Dewey and by Carlo Tresca, the Italian anarchist leader who was assassinated a few years later. That same party, I have since discovered, was attended not only by the Hooks and the Trillings, but by Whittaker Chambers. Chambers had just broken with the Communist Party and was desperately afraid of being liquidated by Stalin's hit men. Another guest was Suzanne La Follette, to whom Dewey had entrusted the files of the Commission of Inquiry into the Moscow Trials. These files disappeared when her apartment was burgled, presumably by the Soviet agents.

The warnings against Stalin in Hook's and Trilling's articles were buttressed by remarks I overheard in conversations between my parents and their friends, in particular one of their neighbors: J. B. S. Hardman, an official of the Amalgamated Clothing Workers of America. Hardman had been revolutionary governor of Odessa in the 1905 Revolution, and had come to America to escape the Cheka and to organize the workers. It was in Hardman's house that I first heard of the Katyn Forest massacre, and of Stalin's murder of the Polish trade union leaders Ehrlich and Alter.

Growing up with the image of Stalin that such conversations produced, I did not find it surprising when my father, toward the end of World War II, helped Norman Thomas organize the Post-War World Council. The aim of this organization was to publicize what Stalin was preparing to do to central Europe, and to warn Americans that the wartime alliance with the USSR should not be allowed to carry over into the postwar period. The council did its best both to incite the Cold War and to prevent the American Right from monopolizing anticommunism. The latter aim was shared by a subsequent organization, the Americans for Democratic Action—an outfit slapped together in 1948 by Eleanor Roosevelt, Arthur Schlesinger, Walter Reuther, and others to counter the Communist-backed candidacy of Henry Wallace.

Inciting the Cold War struck me as continuous with the rest of the good work being done by my family and their friends, and it still does. I am still unable to see much difference between fighting Hitler and fighting Stalin. I still find nothing absurd in the idea that, if the reformist Left had been stronger than it was, post–World War II America could have had it both ways. Our country could have become both the leader of an international movement to replace oligarchy with social democracy around the world, and the nuclear superpower which halted the spread of an evil empire ruled by a mad tyrant.

When it was revealed, in 1967, that one of the organizations with which Thomas, Hook, Trilling, and my father were associated—the Congress for Cultural Freedom—had received CIA money, I was neither surprised nor appalled. It seemed to me perfectly predictable that the CIA should contain both rightist hirelings of the United Fruit Company (the people who had gotten Eisenhower to order the overthrow of Colonel Arbenz—the leftist leader of Guatemala—in 1952) and leftist good guys who used the taxpayers' money to finance what Christopher Lasch was to describe disdainfully as the "Cultural Cold War." The cohabitation of bad guys with good guys in the CIA seemed to me no more surprising than that the Labor and Commerce Departments contained some bureaucrats who conspired with the capitalists against labor, and other bureaucrats who conspired with the unions against the bosses. When in 1967 Lasch triumphantly proclaimed that the CIA's connection with the pre-Sixties Left showed how bankrupt the reformist Left had proved to be, I could not see what he was making such a fuss about.

So much for autobiography. I hope that I have given you some sense of what it was like to take for granted that one could be both a fervent anticommunist and a good leftist, and of the distrust with which I read books like Lasch's *The Agony of the American Left*. This was and is a very influential book, written by a distinguished scholar who was also a very useful social critic. Despite its author's intellectual and moral virtues, however, his book helped propagate the false idea that when the student Left burst into the headlines in the early Sixties, it replaced a discredited older Left.

Lasch began his book with the following quotation from Paul Goodman: "We now have the abnormal situation that there is no persuasive program for social reconstruction, thought up by many minds, corrected by endless criticism, made practical by much political activity . . . The young are honorable, and see the problems, but they don't know anything because we have not taught them anything." Lasch noted that Goodman attributed the absence of a persuasive program to "the failure of the intellectuals during the late forties and fifties." Lasch went on to say: "It is true that the defection of intellectuals in the period just past is the immediate cause of our troubles . . . My experience and the experience of many of my friends and contemporaries fully bears out the contention that the intellectuals' acquiescence in the premises of the cold war made it unusually difficult to get a political education in the fifties." However, he continued, "The deeper explanation of the present crisis of radicalism . . . lies in events that happened in the early part of the century. It lies in the collapse of mass-based radical movements which grew up for a time, and then aborted: populism, socialism, and black nationalism." Lasch proceeded to dismiss the period between 1910 and 1964, the period which I think of as American leftism at its best. "Even when they originated in humanitarian impulses," Lasch wrote, "progressive ideas led not to a philosophy of liberation but to a blueprint for control . . . Manipulative and managerial, twentieth-century liberalism has adapted itself without difficulty to the corporation's need to soften conflicts."

Lasch was no Marxist, but his ideas about the elites and masses paralleled those of the Marxists. Lasch thought that a movement which is not mass-based must somehow be a fraud, and that top-down initiatives are automatically suspect. This belief echoes the Marxist cult of the proletariat, the belief that there is virtue only among the oppressed. Lasch brushed aside fifty years' worth of off-and-on cooperation between the elites and the oppressed. He thereby encouraged the New Leftists' delusion that they were the first real leftists America had seen in a long time, or at least the only ones who had not sold out.

The New Leftists gradually became convinced that the Vietnam War, and the endless humiliation inflicted on African-Americans, were clues to something deeply wrong with their country, and not just mistakes correctable by reforms. They wanted to hear that America was a very different sort of place, a much worse place, than their parents and teachers had told them it was. So they responded enthusiastically to Lasch's claim that "the structure of American society makes it almost impossible for criticism of existing policies to become part of political discourse. The language of American politics increasingly resembles an Orwellian monologue."

When they read in Lasch's book that "the United States of the mid-twentieth century might better be described as an empire than as a community," the students felt justified in giving up their parents' hope that reformist politics could cope with the injustice they saw around them. Lasch's book made it easy to stop thinking of oneself as a member of a community, as a citizen with civic responsibilities. For if you turn out to be living in an evil empire (rather than, as you had been told, a democracy fighting an evil empire), then you have no responsibility to your country; you are accountable only to humanity. If what your government and your teachers are saying is all part of the same Orwellian monologue—if the differences between the Harvard faculty and the military-industrial complex, or between Lyndon

Johnson and Barry Goldwater, are negligible—then you have a responsibility to make a revolution.

In saying things which the young leftists of the late Sixties wanted to hear, Lasch was not playing to the crowd. He was as harsh on the New Left as he was on every other aspect of contemporary America. But his writing, along with that of Goodman, Mills, and others, reconfirmed the leftist students' impression that there was nothing in America on which they could rely, except perhaps the most militant of the African-American protest movements. So they started to look for moral and intellectual support in the wrong places—the China of Mao-Tse Tung, for example. They reasoned that, since anti-Communism was the dominant theme of the Orwellian monologue Lasch described, the only way to escape from this monologue was to appreciate the achievements of the Communists. Michael Harrington's argument—that there was no reason the student Left should not also be an anticommunist Left—went unheard.

The heirs of that student Left and the heirs of the older, reformist Left are still unreconciled with one another. I want to suggest that such a reconciliation could be started by agreeing that the New Left accomplished something enormously important, something of which the reformist Left would probably have been incapable. It ended the Vietnam War. It may have saved our country from becoming a garrison state. Without the widespread and continued civil disobedience conducted by the New Left, we might still be sending our young people off to kill Vietnamese, rather than expanding our overseas markets by bribing kleptocratic Communists in Ho Chi Minh City. Without the storm that broke on the campuses after the invasion of Cambodia, we might now be fighting in the farther reaches of Asia. For suppose that no young Americans had protested—that all the young men had dutifully trotted off, year after year after year, to be killed in the name of anti-Communism. Can we be so sure that the war's mere unwinnability would have been enough to persuade our government to make peace?

America will always owe an enormous amount to the rage which rumbled through the country between 1964 and 1972. We do not know what our country would be like today, had that rage not been felt. But we can be pretty certain that it would be a much worse place than it is. The CIA would undoubtedly be even more of a loose cannon than it is now. It is even possible that the Defense Department might lie to the public more frequently and fluently than at present, though I admit that this is hard to imagine. The anti-anti-Communism of the New Left, and its counterproductive habit of spelling "America" with a "k," are not important in comparison to what it achieved. By saving us from the Vietnam War, the New Left may have saved us from losing our moral identity.

It would be pointless to debate whether the New Leftists were justified in breaking with the reformist Left, and with the hope of participating in ordinary old-fashioned reformist politics, by the events of 1964–1966. There is no way to decide whether their patience should have run out in those years, rather than earlier or later. But if their patience had not run out at *some* point, if they had *never* taken to the streets, if civil disobedience had *never* replaced an insistence on working within the system, America might no longer be a constitutional democracy. Their loss of patience was the result of perfectly justified, wholly sincere moral indignation—moral indignation which, the New Left rightly sensed, we reformists were too tired and too battered to feel.

For reformers like Walter Reuther, seating the white delegates from Mississippi in the 1964 Democratic Convention was, despite the outrageous insult to the incredibly brave African-Americans who had contested those seats, justified by the need to keep the South voting Democratic. The reformers were divided as to whether the Tonkin Gulf Resolution was just one more example of the spinelessness of Congress or rather a prudent attempt to give President Johnson room to maneuver. But Gitlin may be right that for the New Left these two events were the last straws. There had to be a last straw sooner or later if American leftism was ever to be revitalized. The New Left was right to say that America was in danger of selling its soul in order to defeat Communism. Even if one agrees with me in thinking that the Cold War was a necessary war, that does nothing to diminish the service which the New Left did for our country.

American leftism was revived in the 1960s by calls for revolution which, fortunately, were not successful. They did, however, lead to reform—to the passage of the legislation which Johnson rammed through Congress after being elected in 1964, and, eventually, to the withdrawal of our troops. These successes are a sufficient excuse for the Left's many and varied stupidities—even for what Paul Berman has called its "slightly crazy attempt to raise insubordination into a culture." Analogously, the labor movement did succeed in getting American workers a forty-hour week and some collective-bargaining rights. This is quite enough to excuse the many instances of venal corruption in the unions and of insouciant featherbedding, which rightists prefer to dwell on. When compared with the ruthless greed, systematic corruption, and cynical deceit of the military-industrial establishment, both the New Left and the American labor movement look very good indeed.

But the old-timey Trotskyites and the people whom Lasch called "managerial liberals"—the Howes and the Schlesingers, the Hooks and the Galbraiths—do not look so bad either. A battered and exhausted Left, a Left too tired to experience rage when only rage will work, and too chastened by knowledge of the results of revolutions elsewhere to urge a revolution in America, is not the same as a Left that has sold out or become discredited.

Lasch was simply wrong when he said that it was hard to get a political education in the Fifties because of "intellectuals' acquiescence in the premises of the cold war." My friends and I got an admirable leftist education in that decade from such books as Schlesinger's *The Vital Center* and Galbraith's *The Affluent Society*. Paul Goodman was simply wrong when he said that there was no "persuasive program for social reconstruction, thought up by many minds," available for the inspection of the young in the Forties and Fifties. He can be thought right only if one takes the phrase "program for social reconstruction" to mean a proposal for revolution, rather than a list of reforms.

As I see it, the honors should be evenly divided between

the older, reformist Left and the New Left of the Sixties. The heirs of that older Left should stop reminding themselves of the stupid and self-destructive things the New Left did and said toward the end of that decade. Those who are nostalgic for the Sixties should stop reminding themselves that Schlesinger lied about the Bay of Pigs and that Hook voted for Nixon. All of us should take pride in a country whose historians will someday honor the achievements of both of these Lefts.

George Packer

Sisyphus in the Basement

Nine years ago, I chose of my own accord to become a late-twentieth-century object of political ridicule: a card-carrying socialist, a comrade. The comic potential of this decision was not lost on me at the time. Joining the socialist movement in 1989 was like converting to Catholicism at the height of the Reformation, or coming out as a flat-earther during the Enlightenment. The whole world, from Poland to Ghana, was moving in the other direction, ridding themselves of outdated political fantasies and waking up to the wonders of market capitalism. Here at home, the century's winning ideology was summed up best by Senator Phil Gramm. "If America is going to be saved," Gramm has said, "it's going to be saved at a profit."

Why, then, did I make my quixotic decision? No one sat me down and convinced me of a theoretical truth. I didn't come across some lines in *Das Kapital* and, like the young Augustine opening the Bible at random, see my destiny there upon the page. When I joined I couldn't even have said exactly what socialism was, and I still can't. In fact, I found that even for party veterans, who spoke of worker self-management and "market socialism," the contours of the future were extremely vague.

But socialism has always had less significance as a program than as an ideal. Earlier this century, when the Socialist Party drew almost a million votes in the 1912 presidential election, and eleven socialist weekly papers were published in Oklahoma alone, and large numbers of working people across the country believed that socialism was America's future, most of its adherents were driven by motives no different than mine. That is to say, they became socialists out of a keen sense of objection and hope.

What I objected to in 1989 was the idea that plant closings and bought political representation and the Disney Channel exemplified the best of all possible social arrangements. What I hoped for was a potentially different arrangement, one in which America would become something like the classless society that it has always pretended to be, or at least one in which the management consultant and the line worker felt as though they inhabited the same land and lived by more or less the same rules.

It was a leap of faith. Three hundred years ago I might have immigrated to the colonies and joined a congregation in New Hampshire. A hundred and fifty years ago I might have bought a cooperative share of stock in Brook Farm. Eighty-five years ago I might have manned a strikers' barricade with the Wobblies. In every age there are those who attempt to find their own utopia. I went looking for a just society in a shrinking organization of fewer than ten thousand people that called itself "the left wing of the possible." I was improvising. At the end of the American century there was a shortage of available utopias.

For seven years I labored in the ruins of an idea that had once been associated with giants—Eugene Debs and Big Bill Haywood and Mother Jones—an idea that had once had the power to attract millions of people. And what strikes me now is the significance of that futility. No idea has risen to take socialism's place, and yet it's clear how badly Americans could now use one. Every year wealth and power grow more concentrated and the blessings of the unregulated market grow less equal. But we've had to accept it as inevitable, like continental drift or tooth decay. The irony is that just when we need a serious challenge to global corporate capitalism, the old beliefs are discredited and the energy for new ones is spent. These circumstances make objection and hope difficult for anyone to sustain. In this sense, the minor history I'm about to relate might have something to do with you.

Half of this country has no adult memory of a left that wasn't in decline—a remarkable fact for which the left itself bears a good deal of blame. Anyone who grew up, as I did, with progressive political sentiments in the Nixon-Reagan era has endured a chronic sense of siege and isolation, of being a loser. Earlier generations that experienced the destructive temptation of Communism in the Thirties, or the apocalyptic thrill of campus revolution in the Sixties, enjoyed for at least a short while the notion that they were on the winning side of history. It was the small-town Babbitt, the fascist priest, the corporate executive, the sellout college administrator, who were consigned to the dustbin of history or ordered up against the wall. In dialectical pseudoscience or romantic hallucination, members of both the Old and the New Left believed that they represented the future, and this belief infused them with energy and no small amount of arrogance.

Their betrayals, excesses, and failures helped make it impossible for my generation to share their beliefs with any certainty; the glamour of their communal passions afflicted my generation with a feeling of having come too late. As far back as I can remember, defeat hung in the political air. For the better part of my adult life it was difficult to imagine that there would ever be another Democratic president, let alone a cooperative commonwealth. It's been the right that seemed to own the future: Microsoft, biotechnology, the stock market, these things all seem to belong to conservative ideology. Ronald Reagan is the only president in the last thirty years to articulate a utopian vision. Appropriating John Winthrop's speech to the Massachusetts Bay Company en route to the New World, he called

America "the shining city on the hill," in which unleashed individual self-interests would combine to create the beautiful and
good community.

By contrast, in the past quarter century a leftist has been a
sour, defensive creature, mumbling stale slogans and clinging to
unexamined dogmas that crumble at the first contact with reality.
Style plays a crucial role in political movements. The songs,
clothing, language, tone of voice, even the physical appearance
of adherents will attract or repel potential recruits regardless of
the legitimacy of a cause. Left-wing style in the Popular Front
Thirties, following orders from Moscow, went grittily native.
"Communism Is Twentieth-Century Americanism" was their slo-
gan, and this belief was both embodied in and emboldened by
their overalls and their Jeffersonian rhetoric, by Woody Guthrie
songs and Paul Robeson. In the Sixties, the New Left came to
cultivate a style that was defiant of mainstream values and yet, in
the manipulation of publicity and calculation of the power of
images—especially violent images—typically American.

Since then, however, left-wing style has been rigid, insular,
and self-consciously symbolic. The high drama of Sixties' protests
gave way to ritual theater, most notable in the protests of intervention in Latin America, where even English words were suddenly spoken with Latino accents, and public die-ins amused
passersby without persuading them of anything. Politics reduced
to a series of dramatic gestures is a sign of powerlessness and
probably of weakening conviction. It wins few converts, and it
ends by focusing on the self-expressive and soul-saving satisfac-
tions of its participants.

The reigning leftist ideology of the past two decades has
been the identity movements—black, Hispanic, female, gay,
deaf, and others—that fall under the term "multiculturalism."
But beyond wishing them success in their struggles to find a
place in the sun, there's not much an outsider can do to belong
meaningfully. The point of identity politics is that some people
don't belong. "Diversity" as a hardened system of thought
(rather than as a justified struggle for equality) has given us the
spectacle of full-scale war over English department hirings,

sensitivity-training consultants, and a fragmented and unstable Democratic Party: on the whole, not a very promising direction for a political movement to take. Meanwhile, the left has abandoned its historic claim to speak for a universal humanity against the privileged few. This claim has now fallen into the hands of conservatives. On the left, people speak of "group interest" and "decentered knowledge"; on the right, they speak of reason, virtue, freedom, and responsibilities, when what they really mean is "tough luck."

Insularity, eccentricity, rigidity: these are the symptoms of political atrophy and decay. By the end of the Reagan years the left was thoroughly demoralized and beaten. It was at this point that I joined the Boston chapter of the Democratic Socialists of America.

"I didn't know there were any more democratic socialists," a friend said at the time, as if he were talking about California condors. But I knew they weren't extinct. I had seen them at rallies, with their sign bearing the old fist and rose of the Socialist International: strength and beauty. A number of things made the socialists attractive. They didn't cultivate weirdness or theatrics. They were genuinely open to discussion. They had a long tradition—mostly of failure, but not completely (the New Deal was, in part, a response to the demands of early socialism). They had an international network, with parties in power in several European and Caribbean countries. They claimed intellectually serious members as diverse as Meyer Schapiro and Cornel West. And the issues that concerned me preoccupied them: economic inequality, between the West and the rest of the world, between the privileged few in America and the rest of the country. Their short-term goals were practical, focusing on unions and electoral work. The basis for their larger critique was humanistic. "I am now inclined to think the case for socialism must be made increasingly on moral grounds," one of our national leaders wrote. That was enough for me. Mercifully, this wasn't a sect or a cult.

In fact, the reigning mood on "the left wing of the possible" was irony. The style was understatement, deflation, self-mockery: a low-key Götterdämmerung. We held forums on the topic of "How Dead Is Socialism?" Our T-shirt proclaimed, "Socialism in my lifetime"—wistfully and half-jokingly, like the bumper sticker that says, "My other car is a Mercedes." When the word "comrade" turned up, it always wore an affectionate smirk. One member, Comrade Mike, knew the entire history of left-wing sectarianism in the twentieth century, and he would tease the rest of us with hyperbolic analogies. "You know, Comrade George, as newsletter editor you hold what Lenin said is the key to party power." Or: "Comrade Guy is moving toward right deviationism. The politburo should consider a purge." No one was ever "purged." We had anti-abortion Catholics, orthodox Marxists, and Clinton Democrats. As editor of our newsletter, the *Yankee Radical,* I published anything that came in—terrible poetry, pseudonymous rants, arguments for abandoning the "S word." "Comrade George!" Comrade Mike would mock-exhort me, "more Leninist discipline!"

The organization acquainted me with the pathos of left-wing activism in twilight. It was marginal, pedestrian work, based on the eternal postponement of gratification: three-hour board meetings in a narrow room in a church basement; a two-year fund drive to buy a used computer; a snowbound forum on the Canadian left, whose announcement reached most of the membership too late because the nonprofit mailing wasn't sorted properly. The word "Sisyphean" is misleading, since we never pushed our rock anywhere close to the top, but it's a fair evocation of the enterprise.

Sometimes, at a forum or board meeting, I would look around at the dozen or so souls who had ventured out into the cold on a weeknight and wonder what made us do it. Why did we spend our lives on this stuff? Some of them were very old— gentle white-haired couples who seldom said much but turned out regularly, so inured to failure after half a century of it that they looked fairly content. No socialism in *their* lifetime: might as well have some coffee and pull up a chair. For them, and for younger members of their temperament, the organization provided the comfort of belonging, a mix of social club, night school, and church group. They seemed to me examples of Keats's negative capability—able to go on being and believing without any certainty to sustain them.

But most members under fifty still nursed restless ambitions. They got up and demanded that we "define a sharper vision," as if vagueness were all that stood between us and triumph. At one meeting a former New Leftist who worked for the city government announced that all the socialists in Boston could fill Fenway Park. Why weren't we reaching them? We should launch a recruitment drive, reorganize, hire a staff-person! And yet, year after year, our ranks dwindled; the evenings spent phoning snappish people who barely seemed aware that they were still listed as members brought in less and less money; the board exhausted itself trying to stay alive so we could endure another year of fund-raising so that we could stay alive . . . like some ancient organism mindlessly perpetuating its own existence.

The truly ambitious almost inevitably drifted away. As soon as a member had his doctorate or got a political job or began to be heard on NPR, we would stop seeing him at meetings. Before its fragmentation in the Thirties, socialism provided an outlet for talents and drives, but in the Nineties no one was going to get ahead through us. Our core membership was characterized by rare decency and intelligence; among the most durable we could count state legislators and union organizers. But there was a contingent of people who seemed to have nothing else going on—marginal, odd, a whiff of paranoia about them. One member was apparently normal in all respects except that he had an overly loud voice, and somehow this seemed linked to his being a socialist. Another insisted on writing her name with all lower-case letters. And what did they see in my face? Maybe just joining made us odd. Maybe oddness made us join. In friends, I might have found these peculiarities trivial; in comrades, I was hyperalert to every asocial quirk and twitch, for they implicated me. And this seemed to defeat the entire enterprise. I was supposed to be feeling solidarity with my brothers and sisters, and instead I was noticing that someone's navel was exposed.

I never got used to our middle name, never overcame a chronic and shameful sense of embarrassment. Whenever someone said, "As a socialist I . . . ," it made me feel like I had joined a twelve-step group: recovering capitalists. What could it mean to call yourself by a name that has passed not only into popular disrepute but almost out of contemporary speech? It means either (1) you're old enough to have been around when it was a living, breathing idea that animated people around the world; (2) you've studied economic and political theory and have some hypothetical proposals for worker self-management; or (3) you have a good heart. In any case, the word didn't travel well between our airless little office and the outside world.

This was brought home to me most vividly on the softball field. The forerunner of our organization was the Democratic Socialist Organizing Committee, or DSOC, which had picked itself up from the ruins of the Socialist Party ("the defeated remnant of an already defeated remnant," its founder, Michael Harrington, called it). So our team was the DSOX, with the fist and rose stenciled across our jerseys. Once, when we were playing the Shattuck mental hospital guards, a team of large-bodied sadists who liked to take opponents out in the base path, I let a pitch go by. "Strike," their catcher muttered. "High and inside," I said. He answered, "Maybe in *Moscow*." There wasn't time before the next pitch to tell him the history of the anti-Stalinist left and how *our* brand of socialism had nothing to do with Moscow. This was before the fall of Communism: later, teams responded more with amusement or blank stares than with contempt. But there's no real answer to being laughed at.

Whenever a new team joined the league there would always come a moment when I was playing third and their third-base coach would ask in all innocence, "What does the D in DSOX stand for?" "Democratic," I would answer. "We're a political group." Sometimes she was willing to leave it at that, but if absolutely pressed I would tell her our full name and then get into my crouch before she had a chance to ask anything more. Even a team called Peace Action felt a right to snicker. Between the pacifists and the socialists, play was especially aggressive. The softball games provided my most intense moments in the organization, which suggests something worrisome about the limited appeal of rational discourse and a cooperative model for society. In recent years the number of actual members on our roster has dropped, and we've improved greatly.

Our left-fielder, a cabdriver named Glenn, launched a campaign to attract more mainstream people to the organization. Our old recruitment brochure put us at a disadvantage: printed on red paper, it was highlighted by the recurring phrase "We are Democratic Socialists . . ." So we designed a new brochure on white paper that affiliated us with Thomas Jefferson and portrayed us as champions of the ordinary beleaguered American against the likes of Donald Trump. Glenn kept a stack in his briefcase, but the brochures somehow failed to win new recruits. Deciding that the problem lay in the word "socialism," he launched a new campaign to change our name. This plunged us into months of meetings, with arguments and counterarguments in the *Yankee Radical.* Glenn's proposal came before our national convention, where it went down to defeat in committee. So we remained the Democratic Socialists of America. Some members argued that our middle name was the only identity we had.

From the walls of the Workmen's Circle meeting room, grave, bearded, Yiddish-speaking socialists stared down on us. Their pictures haunted me with a sensation of unworthiness. How could we—laboring through another sparsely attended forum on the latest crisis in foreign policy or the organization's mission and vision, before repairing to a local bar for nachos and beer—carry the torch that had once been the light of hope for millions of people? We were linked in solidarity with great names, and one of them was still alive when I joined the organization. I had written for Irving Howe's magazine, *Dissent,* and revered him as a writer and an intellectual. But there was something daunting in his kind of politics, the kind he'd been practicing since Truman was president. His elegiac and severe voice, which after a lifetime of defeats qualified nearly every assertion, made a terrible demand: we had to "grapple with fragments of a tradition," he wrote in *Socialism and America,* while engaging "with the needs of the moment, struggling for betterment in matters large and small, reforms major and modest"; at the same time we had to keep alive an idea of "utopia," which he described in an article just before his death as "run[ning] like a bright thread through American intellectual life . . . a claim for the value of desire, the practicality of yearning—as against the deadliness of acquiescing in the 'given' simply because it is here."

So we had to be passionate and sober, pragmatic and visionary, skeptical and resilient. We had to endure our own insignificance without the prospect of a millennium. It was a very hard faith.

At least Howe's mix of dyspepsia and utopia came out of a period, the Thirties, when socialism meant something more than Victor Berger Night, our holiday beer-tasting fund-raiser named after the co-founder of the Social Democratic Party and first socialist congressman. I read Howe's 1982 autobiography, *A Margin of Hope* (which offered, as always, some hope but more margin), and wrote him to express my envy of his radical youth. He wrote back (he always did; it was part of the faith), "Since you know what I'm going to say, what can I say? Only this: We have to make do with the best we can. We all know DSA isn't what it should be . . . but we have to stick it out for the long haul. Yes, some passion would be good, but the passion of the Thirties was often of the wrong kind. . . . We have to stick to it as long as we can."

Once I heard him speak at a DSA national convention. The Berlin Wall had fallen that week; party chairman Michael Harrington had died a few months before, and whether the organization he led would meaningfully survive his death was a real question. Howe, stooped and white-maned and weary, gave a gloomy, chiding speech in which he told the gathered democratic socialists that they had two years to reconstruct their organization, two years of hard work to turn themselves into the experts on social policy, the tireless activists and writers that

Harrington had been, or else DSA would become a collection of nice, irrelevant people who liked to get together once a year or so. Then he took questions. I had one. I pointed out that socialism had been in decline since before I was born—since before *he* was born. Why did it have only two more years to decline?

"You know," Howe replied with a sly smile, "I ask the same thing about myself. You decline, and decline, and then one day you just stop."

Every year I announced that someone else would have to put out the newsletter. But no one came forward, and I would find myself doing it for another year. This was my contribution: calling Comrade Tom on Wednesday to remind him that I needed his article on post–Cold War foreign policy by the weekend; then Sunday evening trying to lay the thing out on a borrowed or rented Macintosh; a trip to the printer, who was always angry about something and sounded like a Limbaugh ditto-head but whom we were stuck with because there were no other union printers left in Boston; and then a long evening of folding and labeling with the other die-hards, hoping that the membership got the mailing in time for our next forum on single-payer health care.

We moved out of our small office near the train station to an even smaller corner of a room near Fenway Park. Then we moved again to a desk in a Cambridge church basement. Each time we moved, we had to haul halfway across town boxes and file drawers loaded with multiple copies of reasonable and enlightened position papers on the Panama Canal and the Reagan tax cuts. During one move, I put down the box I was carrying up a flight of stairs and started to laugh. The failure of socialism was killing my back. Then I thought of throwing some of the papers out. But that would have meant more work, and there would have to be a discussion first.

Still, I couldn't bring myself to quit. One voice told me that the flame had gone out and I was wasting my years; another told me that quitting would be a betrayal of—something . . . the just society, a century of belief, Irving Howe, my "comrades."

There's an odor of opportunism in such calculations. It's difficult to be an American and not worship success, to accept a permanent place on the losing side. Sometimes I suspected that in Howe's and others' stoicism the lonely dissenter was made into a fetish, his chore glamorized. I might even have shared this fetish (the honor of noble defeat in such company!), but I didn't care to spend my whole life in the margin. I wanted to be on the side of history at least for a while, and when Clinton was elected I and others in the organization wondered if the moment hadn't come.

One member wrote in *Dissent* that the new President was quite possibly "a stealth social democrat." This suspicion became increasingly difficult to entertain, but when you've spent your adult life with your eyes trained on the long distance, vision suffers. These dilemmas aren't easy to negotiate. You don't want to be seduced into vulgar accommodation: you don't want to stiffen into an opposition that's indistinguishable from death.

Our hard-earned irony sustained us and also crippled us. Ardor has seen generations of revolutionaries through seasons of obscurity and, worse, has fostered the delusion that they were the vanguard of historical necessity. The Maoist cashier sits behind the register of Revolution Books waiting for the dictatorship of the proletariat to arrive, like the shtetl Jew who's hired to keep watch for the Messiah and who, when asked how he can tolerate the low pay, replies that at least the work is steady. We had no messianic delusions. We kept our faith at the pace of gradualism, helped defeat a state tax rollback, joined a picket line of hospital workers. But anything that burns low and slow risks going out. And one winter evening, as a board meeting in the church basement bogged down over the question of roast chicken versus Indonesian noodles for our Debs-Thomas fund-raising dinner, I looked at the faces of my comrades around the table and knew I was going to leave them.

"Our solidarity is not great enough," Isaac Rosenfeld wrote in "The Party," his 1947 story about his generation of socialists. "Again I should like to feel it strong about me, embracing us all with a love that is not in politics."

An organization becomes its own reason: what its members have in the end is one another. Maybe this was why we exhausted ourselves trying to prolong our existence for another year: we didn't want to lose what bound us together. Thinking back on the oddities and futilities, I also remember the bonds. I still send in my dues and sometimes ask myself whether I should go back. Unbelievably, what I miss most are the meetings.

The longing persists—call it socialism, community, the Beloved Republic. For Irving Howe it was "as needed by mankind as bread and shelter." Orwell felt the same way: "[E]specially since the French Revolution, the Western world has been haunted by the idea of freedom and equality. . . . Nearly everyone, whatever his actual conduct may be, responds emotionally to the idea of human brotherhood."

We are learning to live without the word. Born in the eighteenth century, did the idea die in the twentieth? Or has it only been suppressed, deformed in our time into the motivational speaker, the cyber-community, the fact that we all watch *Seinfeld* at the same hour? In the age of capitalism's triumph over every other ism, we see its excesses and failings, we might even object to its injustices, but we no longer have any idea to set against it. People all over the world now cling to personal hope in the market's power to change their lives without a larger hope of collective transformation. If we're going to be saved, we will be saved separately, at a profit.

The end of the socialist idea, which endured for almost two centuries, has not been much remarked on in this country, where it never burned as brightly as elsewhere. But taking that idea in its broadest meaning, as a vision of human brotherhood and a just society—in this sense we are all the poorer for its death. With nothing to replace it, each of us is left alone to acquiesce in the given—or else find the will to answer in a new way the old question, What are we to do?

Apprenticeships

Andre Dubus

Digging

That hot June in Lafayette, Louisiana, I was sixteen, I would be seventeen in August, I weighed 105 pounds, and my ruddy, broad-chested father wanted me to have a summer job. I only wanted the dollar allowance he gave me each week, and the dollar and a quarter I earned caddying for him on weekend and Wednesday afternoons. With a quarter I could go to a movie, or buy a bottle of beer, or a pack of cigarettes to smoke secretly. I did not have a girlfriend, so I did not have to buy drinks or food or movie tickets for anyone else. I did not want to work. I wanted to drive around with my friends, or walk with them downtown, to stand in front of the department store, comb our ducktails, talk, look at girls.

My father was a civil engineer, and the district manager for the Gulf States Utilities Company. He had been working for them since he left college, beginning as a surveyor, wearing boots and khakis and, in a holster on his belt, a twenty-two caliber pistol for cottonmouths. At home he was quiet; in the evenings he sat in his easy chair, and smoked, and read: *Time, The Saturday Evening Post, Collier's, The Reader's Digest,* detective novels, books about golf, and Book-of-the-Month Club novels.

He loved to talk, and he did this at parties I listened to from my bedroom, and with his friends on the golf course, and drinking in the clubhouse after playing eighteen holes. I listened to more of my father's conversations about politics and golf and his life and the world than I ever engaged in, during the nearly twenty-two years I lived with him. I was afraid of angering him, seeing his blue eyes, and reddening face, hearing the words he would use to rebuke me; but what I feared most was his voice, suddenly and harshly rising. He never yelled for long, only a few sentences, but they emptied me, as if his voice had pulled my soul from my body. His voice seemed to empty the house, too, and, when he stopped yelling, the house filled with silence. He did not yell often. That sound was not part of our family life. The fear of it was part of my love for him.

I was shy with him. Since my forties I have believed that he was shy with me too, and I hope it was not as painful for him as it was for me. I think my shyness had very little to do with my fear. Other boys had fathers who yelled longer and more often, fathers who spanked them or, when they were in their teens, slapped or punched them. My father spanked me only three times, probably because he did not know of most of my transgressions. My friends with harsher fathers were neither afraid nor shy; they quarreled with their fathers, provoked them. My father sired a sensitive boy, easily hurt or frightened, and he worried about me; I knew he did when I was a boy, and he told me this on his deathbed, when I was a Marine captain.

My imagination gave me a dual life: I lived in my body, and at the same time lived a life no one could see. All my life I have told myself stories, and have talked in my mind to friends. Imagine my father sitting at supper with my mother and two older sisters and me: I am ten and small and appear distracted. Every year at school there is a bully, sometimes a new one, sometimes the one from the year before. I draw bullies to me, not because I am small, but because they know I will neither fight nor inform on them. I will take their pushes or pinches or punches, and try not to cry, and I will pretend I am not hurt. My father does not know this. He only sees me at supper, and I am not there. I am riding a horse and shooting bad men. My father eats, glances at me. I know he is trying to see who I am, who I will be.

Before my teens, he took me to professional wrestling matches because I wanted to go; he told me they were fake, and I did not believe him. We listened to championship boxing matches on the radio. When I was not old enough to fire a shotgun he took me dove hunting with his friends: we crouched in a ditch facing a field, and I watched the doves fly toward us and my father rising to shoot, then I ran to fetch the warm, dead and delicious birds. In summer he took me fishing with his friends; we walked in woods to creeks and bayous and fished with bamboo poles. When I was ten he learned to play golf and stopped hunting and fishing, and on weekends I was his caddy. I did not want to be, I wanted to play with my friends, but when I became a man and left home, I was grateful that I had spent those afternoons watching him, listening to him. A minor league baseball team made our town its home, and my father took me to games, usually with my mother. When I was twelve or so, he taught me to play golf, and sometimes I played nine holes with him; more often and more comfortably, I played with other boys.

If my father and I were not watching or listening to something and responding to it, or were not doing something, but were simply alone together, I could not talk, and he did not, and I felt that I should, and I was ashamed. That June of my seventeenth year, I could not tell him that I did not want a job. He talked to a friend of his, a building contractor, who hired me as a carpenter's helper; my pay was seventy-five cents an hour.

On a Monday morning my father drove me to work. I would ride the bus home and, next day, would start riding the bus to work. Probably my father drove me that morning because it was my first day; when I was twelve he had taken me to a store to buy my first pair of long pants; we boys wore shorts and, in fall and winter, knickers and long socks till we were twelve; and he had taken me to a barber for my first haircut. In the car I sat frightened, sadly resigned, and feeling absolutely incompetent. I had the lunch my mother had put in a brown paper bag, along with a mason jar with sugar and squeezed lemons in it, so I could make lemonade with water from the cooler. We drove to a street with houses and small stores and parked at a corner where, on a flat piece of land, men were busy. They were building a liquor store, and I assumed I would spend my summer handing things to a carpenter. I hoped he would be patient and kind.

As a boy in Louisiana's benevolent winters and hot summers I had played outdoors with friends: we built a clubhouse, chased each other on bicycles, shot air rifles at birds, tin cans, bottles, trees; in fall and winter, wearing shoulder pads and helmets, we played football on someone's very large side lawn; and in summer we played baseball in a field that a father mowed for us; he also built us a backstop of wood and chicken wire. None of us played well enough to be on a varsity team; but I wanted that gift, not knowing that it was a gift, and I felt ashamed that I did not have it. Now we drove cars, smoked, drank in nightclubs. This was French Catholic country; we could always buy drinks. Sometimes we went on dates with girls, but more often looked at them and talked about them; or visited them, when several girls were gathered at the home of a girl whose parents were out for the evening. I had never done physical work except caddying, pushing a lawn mower, and raking leaves, and I was walking from the car with my father toward working men. My father wore his straw hat and seersucker suit. He introduced me to the foreman and said: "Make a man of him."

Then he left. The foreman wore a straw hat and looked old; everyone looked old; the foreman was probably thirty-five. I stood mutely, waiting for him to assign me to some good-hearted Cajun carpenter. He assigned me a pickaxe and a shovel and told me to get into the trench and go to work. In all four sides of the trench were files of black men, swinging picks, and shoveling. The trench was about three feet deep and it would be the building's foundation; I went to where the foreman pointed, and laid my tools on the ground; two black men made a space for me, and I jumped between them. They smiled and we greeted each other. I would learn days later that they earned a dollar an hour. They were men with families and I knew this was unjust, as everything else was for black people. But on that first morning I did not know what they were being paid, I did not know their names, only that one was working behind me and one in front, and they were good to me and stronger than I could ever be. All I really knew in those first hours under the hot sun was raising the pickaxe and swinging it down, raising it and swinging, again and again till the earth was loose; then putting the pick on the ground beside me and taking the shovel and plunging it into dirt that I lifted and tossed beside the trench.

I did not have the strength for this: not in my back, my legs, my arms, my shoulders. Certainly not in my soul. I only wanted it to end. The air was very humid, and sweat dripped on my face and arms, soaked my shirts and jeans. My hands gripping the pick or shovel were sore, my palms burned, the muscles in my arms ached, and my breath was quick. Sometimes I saw tiny black spots before my eyes. Weakly I raised the pick, straightening my back, then swung it down, bending my body with it, and it felt heavier than I was, more durable, this thing of wood and steel that was melting me. I laid it on the ground and picked up the shovel and pushed it into the dirt, lifted it, grunted, and emptied it beside the trench. The sun, always my friend till now, burned me, and my mouth and throat were dry, and often I climbed out of the trench and went to the large tin water cooler with a block of ice in it and water from a hose. At the cooler were paper cups and salt tablets, and I swallowed salt and drank and drank, and poured water onto my head and face; then I went back to the trench, the shovel, the pick.

Nausea came in the third or fourth hour. I kept swinging the pick, pushing and lifting the shovel. I became my sick and hot and tired and hurting flesh. Or it became me; so, for an hour or more, I tasted a very small piece of despair. At noon in Lafayette a loud whistle blew, and in the cathedral the bell rang. I could not hear the bell where we worked, but I heard the whistle, and lowered the shovel and looked around. I was dizzy and sick. All the men had stopped working and were walking toward shade. One of the men with me said it was time to eat, and I climbed out of the trench and walked with black men to the shade of the tool shed. The white men went to another shaded place; I do not remember what work they had been doing that morning, but it was not with picks and shovels in the trench. Everyone looked hot but comfortable. The black men sat talking and began to eat and drink. My bag of lunch and jar with lemons and sugar were on the ground in the shade. Still I stood, gripped by nausea. I looked at the black men and at my lunch bag. Then my stomach tightened and everything in it rose, and I went around the corner of the shed where no one could see me and, bending over, I vomited and moaned and heaved until it ended. I went to the water cooler and rinsed my mouth and spat, and then I took another paper cup and drank. I walked back to the shade and lay on my back, tasting vomit. One of the black men said: "You got to eat."

"I threw up," I said, and closed my eyes and slept for the rest of the hour that everyone—students and workers—had for the noon meal. At home my nineteen-year-old sister and my mother and father were eating dinner, meat and rice and gravy, vegetables and salad and iced tea with a leaf of mint; and an oscillating fan cooled them. My twenty-two-year-old sister was married. At one o'clock the whistle blew, and I woke up and stood and one of the black men said: "Are you all right?"

I nodded. If I had spoken, I may have wept. When I was a boy I could not tell a man what I felt, if I believed what I felt was unmanly. We went back to the trench, down into it, and I picked up the shovel I had left there at noon, and shoveled out all the loose earth between me and the man in front of me, then put the shovel beside the trench, lifted the pick, raised it over my shoulder, and swung it down into the dirt. I was dizzy and weak and hot; I worked for forty minutes or so; then, above me, I heard my father's voice, speaking my name. I looked up at him; he was here to take me home, to forgive my failure, and in my great relief I could not know that I would not be able to forgive it. I was going home. But he said: "Let's go buy you a hat."

Every man there wore a hat, most of them straw, the others baseball caps. I said nothing. I climbed out of the trench, and went with my father. In the car, in a voice softened with pride, he said: "The foreman called me. He said the Nigras told him you threw up, and didn't eat, and you didn't tell him."

"That's right," I said, and shamefully watched the road, and cars with people who seemed free of all torment, and let my father believe I was brave, because I was afraid to tell him that I was afraid to tell the foreman. Quietly we drove to town and he parked and took me first to a drugstore with air-conditioning and a lunch counter, and bought me a 7-Up for my stomach, and told me to order a sandwich. Sweet-smelling women at the counter were smoking. The men in the trench had smoked while they worked, but my body's only desire had been to stop shoveling and swinging the pick, to be with no transition at all in the shower at home, then to lie on my bed, feeling the soft breath of the fan on my damp skin. I would not have smoked at work anyway, with men. Now I wanted a cigarette. My father smoked, and I ate a bacon and lettuce and tomato sandwich.

Then we walked outside, into humidity and the heat and glare of the sun. We crossed the street to the department store where, in the work clothes section, my father chose a pith helmet. I did not want to wear a pith helmet. I would happily wear one in Africa, hunting lions and rhinoceroses. But I did not want to wear such a thing in Lafayette. I said nothing; there was no hat I wanted to wear. I carried the helmet in its bag out of the store and, in the car, laid it beside me. At that place where sweating men worked, I put it on; a thin leather strap looped around the back of my head. I went to my two comrades in the trench. One of them said: "That's a good hat."

I jumped in.

The man behind me said: "You going to be all right now."

I was; and I still do not know why. A sandwich and a soft drink had not given me any more strength than the breakfast I had vomited. An hour's respite in the car and the cool drugstore and buying the helmet that now was keeping my wet head cool certainly helped. But I had the same soft arms and legs, the same back and shoulders I had demanded so little of in my nearly

seventeen years of stewardship. Yet all I remember of that afternoon is the absence of nausea.

At five o'clock the whistle blew downtown and we climbed
out of the trench and washed our tools with the hose, then put
them in the shed. Dirt was on my arms and hands, my face and
neck and clothes. I could have wrung sweat from my shirt and
jeans. I got my lunch from the shade. My two comrades said, See
you tomorrow. I said I would see them. I went to the bus stop at
the corner and sat on the bench. My wet clothes cooled my skin.
I looked down at my dirty tennis shoes; my socks and feet were
wet. I watched people in passing cars. In one were teenaged
boys, and they laughed and shouted something about my helmet.
I watched the car till it was blocks away, then took off the helmet
and held it on my lap. I carried it aboard the bus; yet all summer
I wore it at work, maybe because my father bought it for me and
I did not want to hurt him, maybe because it was a wonderful
helmet for hard work outdoors in Louisiana.

My father got home before I did and told my mother and
sister the story, the only one he knew, or the only one I assumed
he knew. The women proudly greeted me when I walked into
the house. They were also worried. They wanted to know how I
felt. They wore dresses, they smelled of perfume or cologne,
they were drinking bourbon and water, and my sister and father
were smoking cigarettes. Standing in the living room, holding my
lunch and helmet, I said I was fine. I could not tell the truth to
these women who loved me, even if my father were not there. I
could not say that I was not strong enough and that I could not
bear going back to work tomorrow, and all summer, anymore
than I could tell them I did not believe I was as good at being a
boy as other boys were: not at sports, or with girls; and now not
with a man's work. I was home, where vases held flowers, and
things were clean, and our manners were good.

Next morning, carrying my helmet and lunch, I rode the
bus to work and joined the two black men in the trench. I felt
that we were friends. Soon I felt this about all the black men at
work. We were digging the foundation; we were the men and the

boy with picks and shovels in the trench. One day the foundation was done. I use the passive voice, because this was a square or rectangular trench, men were working at each of its sides. I had been working with my comrades on the same side for weeks, moving not forward but down. Then it was done. Someone told us. Maybe the contractor was there, with the foreman. Who dug out that last bit of dirt? I only knew that I had worked as hard as I could, I was part of the trench, it was part of me, and it was finished; it was there in the earth to receive concrete and probably never to be seen again. Someone should have blown a bugle, we should have climbed exultant from the trench, gathered to wipe sweat from our brows, drink water, shake hands, then walk together to each of the four sides and marvel at what we had made.

On that second morning of work I was not sick, and at noon I ate lunch with the blacks in the shade, then we all slept on the grass till one o'clock. We worked till five, said goodbye to each other, and they went to the colored section of town, and I rode the bus home. When I walked into the living room, into cocktail hour, and my family asked me about my day, I said it was fine. I may have learned something if I had told them the truth: the work was too hard, but after the first morning I could bear it. And all summer it would be hard; after we finished the foundation, I would be transferred to another crew. We would build a mess hall at a Boy Scout camp and, with a black man, I would dig a septic tank in clay so hard that the foreman kept hosing water into it as we dug; black men and I would push wheelbarrows of mixed cement; on my shoulder I would carry eighty-pound bags of dry cement, twenty-five pounds less than my own weight; and at the summer's end my body would be twenty pounds heavier. If I had told these three people who loved me that I did not understand my weak body's stamina, they may have taught me why something terrible had so quickly changed to something arduous.

It is time to thank my father for wanting me to work and telling me I had to work and getting the job for me and buying me lunch and a pith helmet instead of taking me home to my mother and sister. He may have wanted to take me home. But he knew he must not, and he came tenderly to me. My mother would have been at home that afternoon; if he had taken me to her she would have given me iced tea and, after my shower, a hot dinner. When my sister came home from work, she would have understood, and told me not to despise myself because I could not work with a pickaxe and a shovel. And I would have spent the summer at home, nestled in the love of the two women, peering at my father's face, and yearning to be someone I respected, a varsity second baseman, a halfback, someone cheerleaders and drum majorettes and pretty scholars loved; yearning to be a man among men, and that is where my father sent me with a helmet on my head.

Thomas Beller

Portrait of the Bagel as a Young Man

I like bagels, but I have never felt in their thrall. I never craved them, never viewed them as something special, out of the ordinary, or exotic. They were a fact of life, personified, when I was growing up, by the local store that baked and sold them, B&T Bagels, on Eightieth Street and Broadway, which was open twenty-four hours a day, seven days a week. Besides selling bagels, the store performed a kind of community service by perfuming the air in its vicinity with the smell of baking bread, which gave the chaotic stretch of Broadway north of Seventy-ninth Street a neighborly, friendly feel. There is something about the smell of baking bread, in its diffuse form, that civilizes people.

Once, during one autumn college break, I was walking along Broadway late at night on the way home from a party when an unexpected early snow began to fall. It was exhilarating and beautiful, and I rhapsodized about the beauty of the city and of the snow, paid careful attention to the little clumping sounds of my feet on the whitening sidewalk, and scarcely noticed that I was cold.

Then, after a few blocks, I noticed. I progressed very

quickly through the various stages of cold until I felt on the verge of freezing to death. I walked faster. I had no money in my pocket for a cab, just a couple of quarters, and with each block the distance home seemed to increase.

And then, amid dark and shuttered Broadway, there appeared an oasis of light and warmth—B&T Bagels.

A lone cashier stood behind her register, white paper cap atop her head.

"What's hot?" I asked.

Behind the cashier was the oven, and just then one of the bakers in his white uniform slid a wood platter into the maw of the oven and removed a squadron of steaming plain bagels, which he dumped into a wire bin. My two cold coins were enough for a hot bit of sustenance. The bagel burned my numb fingers. I walked the rest of the way home with the warm dough permeating my senses.

It was this kind of memory—vague, nostalgic, innocent—that had sprung to mind that day in early September of 1992, when, amid a bleak session of scanning the *New York Times*'s help wanted ads, I came across an ad placed by a bakery that identified itself as being located on "the Upper West Side."

I looked up and thought, What other bakery is located on the Upper West Side? And then I ran to a fax machine with my résumé.

At that time I was a fledgling writer with a graduate degree, a couple of publications and a couple of bum jobs under my belt—bike messenger, gallery assistant, office temp. I took these jobs to make money, but there was also an aspect of penance to them. I don't know exactly for what sin I was repenting. Maybe the sin of having gone to graduate school for writing. On some level I saw these jobs as a kind of karma insurance. It was a way of testing myself: you want to be a writer? Can you handle this? How about this?

I wasn't so noble and pure-minded about literature that it was my only interest. I also played drums in a rock band, and I took these temporary jobs because it seemed that, on any given week, everything could change—we could sign a deal, record, go on tour. I wanted to pay the bills, take things a week at a time, and be ready for the big break. I was still high from a two month road trip/tour the band had taken two years earlier. When that was over I only wanted to do it again. At the time it seemed inevitable, but two years later it was fading in the gauzy haze of fantasy, and I was descending into a panic.

I don't want to romanticize this panic. I think the breaking wave of the present tense is always accompanied by a whitecap of panic, as true of the moment of this writing as it was then, when I was looking for a job to pay the rent, and wondering what the hell was going to happen next with everything that was important to me.

I got the job. It didn't have a title, but I knew right away that it was special. I was to be in charge of inventory, which seemed a position of considerable gravity as it included all sorts of items out of which the bagels were made (poppy seeds, raisins, sesame seeds, sourdough), and I was to be paid ten dollars an hour, which I intuited was at the very high end of the pay scale at B&T. I was also to function as a kind of right-hand man to Mr. B., which meant, among other things, that I had to arrive at eight in the morning and call a series of automated voice-mail systems belonging to several different banks and get that day's balance on several different accounts and write it all out for him so it was there as soon as he sat down at his desk at nine.

My immediate superior was a young man named Rick, a lapsed classical trumpet player from Buffalo, whose blond hair was cut short and whose glasses had small, round rims that made him seem efficient and fastidious. Rick was in the midst of an extremely gradual exit from the bagel factory. He had begun exiting, as far as I could tell, almost as soon as he got there. He'd been there three years. Rick showed me around the upstairs, where the bagel-making took place, and the downstairs, a dungeon-like space illuminated by bare lightbulbs dangling from the ceiling. There was one long hallway, which led to a series of crevices that were used for storage, for locker rooms, for the mechanic's room.

Descending the stairs from the ground floor to the basement felt like entering another world. Each stair had a rounded edge, worn down from years of use. At the bottom of the stairs was a long passageway, and one was immediately in full view of Mr. B., sitting behind his desk, way at the other end. The first time I went down those stairs I was brought up short by a very peculiar image: a pipe leading straight down from the ceiling spewing water into a white porcelain sink. The water splashed into the sink, careened around the white porcelain, and disappeared down the drain.

"What the hell is that?" I asked Rick.

"It's water from the oven, to cool the engines. It just pours down twenty-four hours a day, seven days a week. It never stops." This was a metaphor. For something. I hoped not for my time at B&T Bagels.

Rick taught me the ropes.

Concerning perks: all the bagels you want, for free.

Concerning theft: you cannot steal money, but you can steal food (tunafish, lox, orange juice, soda, ice cream).

Concerning Mr. B.: Sporadically bighearted but for the most part a hardass in the mold of a boss who has worked his way up from the bottom. He was from the Bronx, a Vietnam vet. The youngest of eight kids. He had his own route for a bakery after the war, went to work for the previous owners of B&T, and managed to buy them out with the help of a city-backed loan to help minority businessmen. He couldn't read very well, so when he asked you to "take a look at" some document, it didn't mean he wanted your expert opinion, it meant he wanted you to tell him what it said. But you had to do it with sufficient subtlety so that it wasn't totally obvious he couldn't read it in the first place.

I liked Rick, but I also found him disturbing—there was an itchy, twitchy quality to him, a certain impatience that manifested itself in even the smallest movements, that seemed to scream: I've wasted so much time! He had the air of a man who had just awoken from a nap that had lasted much too long. I could relate to it. Not from experience so much, but as I roamed the complex physical world of B&T Bagels and imagined all the other complexities, grudges, anxieties, and hierarchies that the place must surely hold, I could feel its chaos lulling me some-how, entrancing me; it was that Alice in Wonderland feeling of falling out of one reality into another. I didn't want to be like Rick and awake three years later, shuddering with regret. And yet I could feel myself falling, gleefully falling B&T Bagels, into its reality, the beautiful, sensuous, arduous world of bagel-making.

And nothing entranced me more than the huge, ancient ledger in which all the inventory details were recorded, a book that would come to dominate my days and, eventually, my nights as well.

When I saw that huge, decrepit, almost biblical-looking ledger in Rick's hands, filled with tiny numerical entries, my heart leapt with recognition. The ledger became my domain. I studied it. In the mornings I wandered around the factory with the thing open in my arms, a pencil behind my ear, counting. All around me was chaos—the roar of the oven and, at the other end of the floor, the dough mixer, the hilarious machine that swal-lowed huge globs of dough and then spat out measured dough sausages which ran, via a conveyor belt, to the other machine, which grabbed these dough sausages and rolled them into a loop. A team of men stood at the end of the conveyor belt and, with expertly Chaplinesque gestures, plucked them off one at a time and placed them on a wood platter.

Other men took the platters to a boiling caldron and dumped the dough loops in. Still other men fished them out with a wire scoop the size of a shovel. They flung them down a moist steel gully, a bit like shuffleboard, where another crew took the boiled rings and placed them on wood slats. Then another group of men took the slats and expertly shoved them into the oven, which held a continuously rotating carousel onto which slats were pushed, or flipped, and from which bagels were removed and dumped into large wire bins. The bins were then placed next to an open side entrance where a huge industrial fan blew on them to cool them off. Thus: the bagel smell on Broadway.

Most of this activity took place in full view of the store. While the customers waited in line for bagels, they watched these proceedings with the entranced expressions of people viewing the inner workings of a watch. And having an audience added a tiny spice of theatrical energy to the proceedings.

Amid all this was the sane, specific, and essential world of my ledger, on whose large, swanlike pages was written the information that made all this possible. Amid the craziness I counted.

I counted the fifty-pound bags of poppy seeds, of sesame seeds, of sourdough, of pretzel salt and regular salt. I counted boxes of cinnamon, and raisins. I counted the number of whitefish salads, the kippered salmon salads, the tunafish salads. I counted the number of sliced lox packages, Nova packages, and the whole whitefish (complete with its head and the one dead golden eye that stared at me while I counted).

I counted the Tropicana Orange Juice (Original, Homestyle, Grove) and the grapefruit juice, and the sodas. I counted the frozen fruits and Häagen-Dazs in the freezer up front. I counted the number of mop heads, broom handles, Brillo pad boxes and Ajax. I counted coffee cup lids, coffee cups, and the little plastic sticks people used to stir their coffee (a thousand to a box). I counted plastic forks and spoons and knives. I counted napkins, paper towels, and rolls of toilet paper. I counted the number of white paper bags, the ones that held two bagels, and the ones that held four, six, and a dozen (plus the free extra one). I put on a coat and a scarf and a hat and entered the walk-in freezer, which held a galaxy of cream cheese products so diverse my mind reeled. I searched out the smallest, most minute things and counted them, entered the number in the ledger, and later compared the current number to the one a few days earlier to determine our rate of use and to figure out how much more to order. These long periods of contemplating the ledger were probably the closest I've ever come to Talmudic study.

And then there was the brown sugar. Right in the middle of the bakery, behind the cashiers, was a huge stack of fifty-pound bags of brown sugar. It sat there like a monument to its own importance.

The recipe for a B&T bagel is, Mr. B. informed me with a wink, top secret. But I feel, given the size and visibility of this sugar monument, that I would not be betraying any trust in saying that each and every one of the bagels made here has a dollop (a smidgen? a teaspoon?) of brown sugar in it. Twice a week a truck arrived and workers rebuilt that four-sided column of sugar from its diminished status to a magnificent, proud height. When the sugar stack was low, I felt a pang of fear in my heart; after a delivery, I could stare at it for ten straight minutes and feel all was well with the world.

Downstairs, in a small crevice off to the side of the main office, was a row of desks. I was given one. To my left was Jay, another new hire. He was a slightly built Hispanic man with a thin and neatly groomed mustache, and for the first few days he arrived at work in a long black leather coat, black pants, pointy black cowboy boots, and a huge black cowboy hat. He played trombone. He played in a Latin band that performed regularly at S.O.B.'s and other dance halls around the city. His band was famous, he told me, and I tried to be respectful of that fact, though I had never heard of it. During the first weekend of his job at B&T, he had flown down to Miami to play in Gloria Estephan's support band at the Orange Bowl. As though reading my mind—"If you are so famous, then why are you here?"—he added, "I've got two kids." His voice was reedy and thin. I couldn't imagine him playing trombone.

I respected his outfits, though. They obviously meant a lot to him. He came all the way down from the Bronx, first on a bus and then a subway, and though he spent his days hunched next to me making calls to various delis and grocery stores around the city, asking after unpaid bills, he seemed intent on retaining his image as a star trombonist.

But after the first week he started showing up in sweatpants and sweatshirts. It was not a question of self-esteem, but rather of flour.

Behind us, a few feet away, was a huge flour silo. Twice a week fifty thousand pounds of flour was pumped into it from a truck that drove down from somewhere in Pennsylvania, and several times a day an engine revved up to pump flour upstairs to the dough-mixing machine. The pipes leading upstairs often sprang a leak. A fine mist of flour would fill the air of that small space very quickly. Sometimes it was so fine we would work through it, and after ten minutes all of us would be very lightly frosted with white powder. Sometimes the leaks would be more serious, and we would suddenly be engulfed in a blizzard. On these occasions everyone would jump up from their seats and run into the adjoining office, slam the door, and stand there huddled together for ten minutes while a tiny air conditioner gasped away in the corner.

Jay's outfits were getting killed. And so he gave up wearing them and surrendered his identity, during that eight-hour stretch, to being an accounts receivable guy at a bagel factory. Jay approached his task with such vigorous energy, such upstanding earnestness, such righteousness (he was right after all; these people owed us money!) that I sometimes got a little misty-eyed listening to him press whoever was on the other end of the line for back payments, his voice lowered a bit for extra gravity.

Shortly after I had begun working, Mr. B. called me into his office and handed me a black canvas money belt, instructed me to put it on, and, seeing it was well fastened around my waist, handed me a wad of cash totaling seven thousand dollars. He instructed me to walk the six blocks down Broadway to his bank with the cash and a deposit slip. It was as though the green ink of the dollars had some chemical property that briefly stunned me, because for a moment I just stood there on the black and white tiles, staring abstractly at the cash in my hand.

"Take Jay with you," he said.

"Are you worried I'll get robbed?" I asked. Mr. B. gave me one of those penetrating stares through his wire-rimmed glasses. He was always in such a swirl of papers and phone cords that when he stared right at you for more than a second it seemed significant. Now it seemed clear that he had understood the true content of my question: You don't trust me?

"It's about insurance," he said. "My insurance says you gotta have two people if you're moving more than five thousand dollars."

Broadway was bright with sun and people, traffic careening down the avenue, and Jay and I bopped down the street with the bounce of truant school kids. The pouch of the money belt was nestled near my groin, in that soft private place between the bottom of my stomach and my hip.

These bank deliveries were a frequent occurrence. Sometimes I took Jay, once in a while Rick, and on occasion one of the workers upstairs. The tight bulge of the money belt under my shirt became familiar. Mr. B. trusted me with his cash.

More and more, I came to feel this was a mistake.

My lunch came from the store. A toasted bagel with whitefish salad and an orange juice was typical. I ate on a bench on one of the traffic islands of Broadway with a paper in my lap. I took leisurely hour-long lunches sitting in the sun, noshing and reading the paper, enjoying the open air and periodically lecturing myself that this lunch was not, not, *not* some fantastic moment to be cherished in later years.

Now, years later, I cherish those lunches. The autumn sun was bright and elegiac, the air was crisp, the street bustled with activity, and the respite from my busy morning of inventory and phone orders and cash counting and delivering was sweet. The truth, which I understood but hated at the time, but which I feel a bit more resigned to now, was that the hard work made the respite sweeter.

One day, shortly after Thanksgiving, when I had been on the job nearly three months and the novelty was long gone, I arrived at the factory at an unusually early hour. During the previous weeks I had been on a few dates with a woman named Cathy. In addition to all the more familiar anxieties, I was careful to monitor her for her feelings about my current job. She seemed to think my bagel career was amusing and temporary. She thought it was an interlude, a funny story in the making. I kept my panic that this was no interlude to myself. I liked her attitude. And I liked her. And she liked me. And on the morning in question, I had woken up at her house.

On that chilly November morning I had emerged from the subway into the cold air in great spirits, feeling triumphant, looking forward to the calm stretch of time when I had the office mostly to myself. It was early, and I bought a paper, prepared a cup of coffee, grabbed a bagel, and headed downstairs, where I gleefully sat down at Mr. B.'s desk and prepared for a pleasant half-hour interlude contemplating the previous night and reveling in the quiet of the place before everyone showed up and all hell broke loose (The only thing between me and my half-hour respite were the bank calls. I had developed a weird attachment to the soft, mellifluous female voice on Marine Midland's automated account information line, and had come to look forward to starting my days with the sound of her automated voice). This placid image was so fixed in my imagination that I burrowed toward it single-mindedly, not pausing for my customary glance around the bakery floor to make sure all was well.

I had barely flattened the paper on the desk and taken a sip of coffee when Alberto, the night foreman who was just now coming to the end of his eight-hour shift, entered the room and, with the grave manner of a sergeant reporting bad news to an officer, removed the pointed paper cap he and everyone else upstairs had to wear. He stared at me with his black, sad eyes that were always touched with a hint of violence.

I had underestimated the holiday rush. The ever-fluctuating but always formidable pillar of sugar had been vanquished.

Alberto had worked as the night foreman for ten years and earned only a tiny bit more than I. Like most of the workers upstairs, he was Puerto Rican. He understood my role at the company, my prerogatives and my perks, just as he understood his role, its limits and responsibilities. There was no sympathy in his eyes. I stared at them anyway.

"We ran out around five o'clock," he said. "I've had thirty guys sitting on their asses for two and a half hours." He ran a hand slowly over his slicked-back hair, as though this bit of information might have, in the very telling, unsettled it, put his paper cap back on, and went back upstairs.

I sprang into action. I called Rick, my sugar guy, and begged him to let me have some of the inventory he had already loaded onto a truck headed for other destinations in Manhattan. Then, having been promised enough to get me through the day, I sank into a numb state of dread. Mr. B. would be upset when he heard about the sugar. I could only watch the clouds gather.

The gale was of hurricane force. Mr. B. just happened to arrive a bit late that day, so it took place in view of the whole office. Mr. B. was a hands-on manager. Every one of the myriad details concerning the production and shipping and selling of his bagels was in his head—he delegated with reluctance. And now his worst fears had come true. As he screamed at me and yelled at me and waved his arms around—all this with his coat still on, his paper still in his hand, his scarf still wrapped around his neck—I could see in his red, scrunched-up features another, quieter and more complicated exasperation—One day I come in twenty minutes late and all hell breaks loose! he seemed to be thinking. He had a family, but his business was his baby. It consumed him even as it fed him.

He raged on until I pointed out that it was Tuesday. Tuesday was the day I did a massive inventory of the cream cheeses, and the order had to be in by ten-thirty. I put on my coat, my scarf, my gloves, and retreated into the cold, humming silence of the freezer with the old ledger in which all the figures were kept and began the process of counting, and penance.

Following the sugar disaster I redoubled my efforts to get out of the bagel factory. I had been focusing my money-making energies on what was meant to be my profession—writing. I would make numerous phone calls from my desk to magazine editors, trying to scrounge up some freelance work. There were two obstacles to success in this endeavor. One was that other than a short story I had published, I had very little in the way of credentials—even if all I wanted to do was interview some starlet in exchange for what, compared to my B&T salary, would have been a treasure chest of cash.

Besides my meager credentials there was the problem of the flour silos and the pipes leading up to the dough mixer. With some regularity the enormous engine would switch on, making a sound similar in texture and volume to a big airplane getting ready to ascend. This tended to have an adverse effect on my phone conversations with editors.

"What's that?" they would say when the engine kicked in.

I'm at the airport? I'm at the heliport? I'm at the hairdresser's?

"I'm at work," I would reply and usually, thinking that offense is better than defense, I would add, "I'm working at a bagel factory."

"Oh, how wonderful!" was the usual reply.

It was not wonderful. After three months it was downright miserable. After the sugar incident, my anxiety about the inventory grew exponentially. I overcompensated and placed a mammoth sugar order. A crew of men carried it in from the truck on their shoulders. They made the stack in its customary place, but there were still more bags. They found a place for them in the stairway. But there were still more bags. By the time they were done, the entire factory looked like a World War I trench. A bunker. The staircase, the hallways downstairs, every available space was lined with bags of sugar, as though we were sandbagging a river that threatened to flood. Getting to work meant that everyone now had to turn their shoulders sideways to fit through what little space remained. The complaints were endless, though, curiously, the only person who did not chastise me was Mr. B. himself. His was a tunnel vision, and I suspected that the space his body was now compelled to move through was no larger than the space through which his mind always moved, so he hardly noticed it. All he registered was that we had enough sugar; and perhaps he wanted to give me a break.

The momentum of the holiday season coincided with the momentum of my desperation to escape the bagel factory. For reasons I couldn't fully grasp, the holidays and bagels were weirdly connected, and the store overflowed with customers, not just single-bagel snackers but three-dozen buyers. It was at the height of the holiday season, when the lines for bagels were stretching out the front door even with all the cashiers fully manned, that Mr. B. turned to me during a lax moment and said, "Put on a hat and go upstairs."

"A hat?"

"And a white shirt. Everyone has to wear a hat and a white shirt. You don't need to wear the pants. Go to register one."

My eyes bulged. But after the sugar thrashing I had, in some perverse way, developed an odd servility to go along with my ever-increasing desire to disappear on one of my money belt errands and escape forever. So up I went. I set the white paper cap at a jaunty angle and began to rattle off orders in the manner of a carnival barker trying to drum up business.

"Two poppy and a dozen sesame for the lady in the white fur hat!" I would yell, while the guy next to me grabbed the appropriate bagels and I punched the register's keys and took the money. At the end of each transaction I would belt out a thunderous and rather cathartic "NEXT!" and the long line would inch forward a notch. I got into the flow. I was really enjoying myself.

And then I spotted a couple standing off to the side and staring at me. After a moment I recognized them both, and ninth grade came rushing back. I had slept over at his house a number of times. This was his mother. Our conversation was brief and friendly. The cliché would be for them to be mean and snooty, but they were very nice and, though slightly surprised to see what I was up to, there was no condescension.

For all its non-nasty aspects, this encounter had a strong effect on me. It brought the lurking shame into the open, and once exposed it would not go away. The odd thing was that my sense of shame at my bagel factory job increased right alongside a certain kind of weird pleasure I took in it. I felt, in the tumult of the place, that I was connected to life more intensely than I would be were I in a more suitably professional job. The fact that this exhilarating life was so lacking in comfort just added to my confusion and sense of distress.

One Friday I went alone to Club Broadway, a fancy Latin place above the Ninety-sixth Street subway where Jay's band was playing. The interior was lit with dim purple lights, and there were mirrors on the walls and ceilings. I came late. The dance floor was packed and the band was punching out its marimba rhythms. I arrived just in time to see Jay step forward from the large band, his trombone shiny under the lights. I took in the scene in one huge gulp, the purpleness, the dancing, the size of the band and the brightness of the spotlight reflecting off Jay's huge, unwieldy instrument. I thought of his reedy voice harassing deli owners for their bagel payments and had a stage-fatherish pang of anxiety on his behalf. Poor Jay! I thought. What now?

He unleashed a trombone solo that shook me to my bones. It seemed to shake him, too. The crowd cheered him when he finished, a wild cheer. The band played on. Everyone kept dancing. And in the back of the room was a solitary figure jumping up and down, clapping and screaming like a lunatic.

By December I was miserable in a way I had never been, grasping in some visceral way for the first time in my life the power money has to shape the course of events. I don't know why it took until age twenty-seven to understand this. I began to look on those business majors in college in a new light. They had understood choices, and money, and consequences. I had held crappy jobs before. But somehow I had been able to keep my ego and sense of self apart from them. I felt a bit invulnerable. I possessed a certain kind of money fat. All those years of private school had made being a bike messenger, an office temp or a bagel worker seem bearable and inevitably temporary.

At last I pulled my ace in the hole, an ace so far down it had never occurred to me to use it—I called my editor at the magazine where I had published my first story. The flour silo's engine did not turn on. The call was brief. I told him about the bagel factory. He didn't seem to think it was such a bad thing. He was perilously close to joining the ranks of the Oh How Wonderfuls! I asked if the magazine needed someone to lick stamps or sweep the floor. He said they had those bases covered.

He suggested that perhaps I could do a piece of nonfiction, something short, and asked if I had any ideas. As a rule I never have ideas, which is to say I don't think in terms of proposals, a fact that did more to hinder my freelance activities than any flour silo.

I blurted out the name of Esteban Vicente, an old painter with whom I was acquainted who had a ninetieth birthday coming up and an exhibition to go along with it. Vicente had shared a studio with de Kooning and had become famous along with all the other New York School painters, but his star had waned and now he was obscure. But he had continued to paint, oblivious to his professional fluctuations, or at least not unmoored by them, and was now having something of a revival.

It was agreed that I would write a very short profile—more like a long blurb—to go along with a full-page reproduction of one of Vicente's paintings.

Suddenly Esteban Vicente became the focus of my existence, along with Euro-Disney, which had placed a mammoth order for our bagels. Every day I drove a truck packed to the brim with four dozen boxes of bagels, each about fifteen pounds, to a warehouse in a desolate section of Long Island City, where I would throw each box into the arms of a scrawny kid who stood on the loading dock and stacked them on a platter, which then wrapped them in a giant roll of Saran Wrap. They were finally driven by forklift into a monstrous freezer in which they would be shipped to France for the consumption by European people looking at Goofy. It was arduous physical labor. My back was a mess. I kept thinking, I'm throwing my back out for Euro-Disney!

I went to Vicente's studio on West Forty-second Street to interview him. We sat and talked for a long time—I had called in sick, not entirely a lie because my back could not take another day of throwing boxes—and the longer I talked, the more I began to feel that it was a strange coincidence that I should be coming to know this man at this particular time.

There was something wonderfully impervious about him, and resilient. He had a self-worth which in someone else could become vanity, but vanity is always defining itself against the appreciation of others. The only compass Vicente was watching was his own. His commitment to the idea of art, and of being an artist, amazed me in its lack of irony. Vicente was an education in how much single-mindedness is necessary if you want to survive as an artist.

These rather grand emotions did not, however, mitigate my rather craven ambitions to get my piece in print, to see my name published somewhere besides a B&T paycheck, and when the day of the birthday exhibition arrived, I haunted it desperately for anything useful to stick in the piece, eavesdropping voraciously and guzzling white wine.

I faxed the article from the bagel factory the following Monday morning, having not slept the previous night, and went about my business with considerable energy in anticipation of my release. I returned home that evening and submerged in my bed, but not before, just on cue, as my eyes closed heavily, the phone rang. It was my editor, who in his typical measured tones told me "we" liked the piece. He said he would call me later in the week. I slept deeply.

The next day was Tuesday, cream cheese day, and I went about my duties in the walk-in freezer in a state of elation. Wednesday was good. Thursday, disaster struck. I received a call from my editor saying that there was a problem with the art department. Apparently someone somewhere had raised an objection to reprinting a full page of abstract art, and the whole piece was in jeopardy. Vicente had been asked for a self-portrait.

The man had been an abstract painter for over forty years, and this after a huge principled decision to stop painting and exhibiting figurative work. I didn't think he was a prime candidate for a self-portrait. I amused myself with a mock speech I could deliver about how—maybe just a few dots with a mouth beneath it—it would mean so much to . . . me! To everyone! Hey, it's exposure! But if there was ever a non-pragmatist, it was Vicente. He didn't give a damn about exposure, and for this I admired him.

I drove my truck full of bagels out to Long Island City, parked it, and crawled back to lay among the boxes, warm and fragrant (they were all sesame bagels that day) and fell asleep. By now my job had thoroughly infiltrated my dreams: every other night I had anxiety dreams about running out of whitefish salad. I had another anxiety dream amid the boxes of bagels, and when I opened my eyes the dream/nightmare just continued. This was my life. The fact that it was this beautiful moment of comfort and peace—all those boxes of bread around me muffling the outside world, warming me, the consoling smell—just made it more complicated. My career at the bagel factory was indefinite. Vicente would never do a self-portrait.

Later that day I returned from Long Island City, called my answering machine, and was informed that Esteban Vicente had done a self-portrait. I floated through the flour-saturated air. I ran my hands through huge vats of poppy seeds and watched them pour through my fingers as though they were treasure and I their owner. I went to an out-of-the-way crevice and pummeled a sack of sourdough as if it was a heavy bag. Never have I known such elation! The piece was on! Esteban was going to do a self-portrait!

But gradually this elation gave way to something else. How could Vicente agree to such a thing? My elation turned to a kind of mild, sour grief. Had he been bullied into doing something for pragmatic reasons? Had the voice of commerce lulled his artistic integrity? Did he whip off lots of self-portraits all the time and not tell anyone?

And as I contemplated this, I came to realize that inter-twined with all my admiration for the man was a weird little strand of resentment. This is a weird thing that accompanies one's appraisal of the virtuous—I had regarded his integrity ever so slightly as a reproach. But now, as I considered that it might have faltered, I missed it. I was rooting for it and lamenting it. As much as I wanted the piece to run, I did not want Esteban Vicente to sell out.

The next day, clutching the phone as the flour silo roared in the background, I was told that Vicente had in fact handed in the self-portrait. The magazine had the self-portrait. It was a . . .

The roar of the flour silo drowned out the words. I waited twenty seconds and asked the person at the other end of the line to repeat herself. "The self-portrait was a splotch of red," she said.

The interesting thing was that these seven hundred words landed on the magazine's new editor in chief's desk entirely by accident, and found there a receptive audience. The article did in fact make it into the magazine—though the splotch of red did not. The magazine ended up running a photo of Vicente instead. And I in turn made it out of the bagel factory. A couple of years after I left, Mr. B., riding the nation's growing appetite for bagels, moved his operation into a huge factory just across the street from the Intrepid on the West Side Highway, and the teeming operation on Eightieth Street fell silent, except for the ovens, to which already-rolled dough was shipped from the main plant, to be baked fresh and perfume the surrounding blocks. Esteban Vicente is still very much around. Five years after the events described above he is still painting.

I gave Mr. B. my leave. He responded coolly but did not seem too upset. Later that afternoon he had a heart attack. The place was in an uproar as we watched the paramedics load him into the ambulance with an oxygen mask on his face. I helped carry him up the stairs. Among the white-suited workers upstairs, the men whom I had watched Mr. B. positively brutalize in all sorts of hard-nosed ways (primarily by paying them about five dollars and change an hour and not giving them any vacation time until they had worked there nine months), there was a surge of genuine grief. Everyone spilled out of the side entrance as the paramedics loaded him into the ambulance.

Downstairs, we had to deal with the fact that, at the time he had the heart attack, Mr. B. was counting out a huge sum of cash, which lay unattended on his desk. About five different people volunteered to be responsible for it. I prevailed. In my dreamy fantasies about theft and revenge I could not have conjured up a more enticing scenario, but I counted the money out scrupulously, totaled it, and put it back in the safe.

Characteristically, Mr. B. was back at his desk two days later, a bottle of pills in his shirt pocket, his demeanor and habits otherwise unchanged, except that he periodically repeated a new mantra about taking it easy and now had salad and cottage cheese for lunch instead of pizza. Maybe the heart attack changed the dynamic of my departure, or maybe now that I was on the way out he could entertain nostalgic thoughts about me. But whatever the reason, we had a pretty warm last couple of weeks. I watched my replacement be interviewed. He had graduated from Deerfield, then Dartmouth. He was an aspiring actor. I informed him that when Mr. B. asked you to read something, it didn't mean your expert opinion was being asked, you were just supposed to paraphrase. The rest was up to him to figure out.

I found myself on Tuesday morning, shortly before my last day, standing in the walk-in freezer wearing a suit. I had an important appointment at the magazine that morning, and I was racing through the cream cheese inventory so I would be on time. And then, for the first time since I had been working there, someone bumped the heavy metal door to the freezer, and the ancient metal bolt clicked shut. I carefully put the ledger on some boxes of olive and pimento cream cheese (six-ounce) and commenced to bang hysterically on the inside of the door, screaming at the top of my lungs to be let out. I was screaming in fear—that I would miss my appointment, that my big chance at my new job would be squandered because I was locked in the cream cheese freezer—but I was also laughing. The bagel factory was clutching me for one last moment in its absurd embrace. And when the door was pulled open at last and I was free to rise up and out of that place forever, I felt a tiny pang of intuition, at once thrilling and mortifying, that somehow, in some way or another, I would be back.

Religion

Jonathan Rosen

The Talmud and the Internet

Not long after my grandmother died, my computer crashed and I lost the journal I had kept of her dying. I'd made diskette copies of everything else on my computer—many drafts of a novel, scores of reviews and essays, and hundreds of articles—but I had not printed out, backed up, or copied the diary. No doubt this had to do with my ambivalence about writing and where it leads, for I was recording not only my feelings but also the concrete details of her death. How the tiny monitor taped to her index finger made it glow pink. How mist from the oxygen collar whispered through her hair. How her skin grew swollen *and* wrinkled, like the skin of a baked apple, and yet remained astonishingly soft to the touch. Her favorite songs—"Embraceable You" and "Our Love Is Here to Stay"—that she could no longer hear but that we sang to her anyway. The great gaps in her breathing. The moment when she was gone and the nurses came and bound her jaws together with white bandages.

I was ashamed of my need to translate into words the physical intimacy of her death, so while I was writing it, I took comfort in the fact that my journal did and did not exist. It lived in limbo, much as my grandmother had as she lay unconscious. My unacknowledged journal became, to my mind, what the Rabbis in the Talmud call a *goses:* a body between life and death, neither of heaven nor of earth. But then my computer crashed and I wanted my words back. I mourned my journal alongside my grandmother. That secondary cyber loss brought back the first bodily loss and made it final. The details of her dying no longer lived in a safe interim computer sleep. My words were gone.

Or were they? Friends who knew about such things assured me that in the world of computers, nothing is ever really gone. If I cared enough about retrieving my journal, there were places I could send my ruined machine where the indelible imprint of my diary, along with everything else I had written, could be skimmed off the hard drive and saved. It would cost a fortune, but I could do it.

The idea that nothing is ever lost is something one hears a great deal when people speak of computers. "Anything you do with digital technology," my Internet handbook warns, "will leave automatically documented evidence for other people or computer systems to find." There is, of course, something ominous in that notion. But there is a sort of ancient comfort in it, too.

"All mankind is of one Author and is one volume," wrote John Donne in one of his most beautiful meditations. "When one man dies, one chapter is not torn out of the book, but translated into a better language; and every chapter must be so translated." I'd thought of that passage when my grandmother died and had tried to find it in my old college edition of Donne, but I couldn't, so I'd settled for the harsher comforts of Psalm 121—more appropriate for my grandmother in any case. Donne's passage, when I finally found it (about which more later) turned out to be as hauntingly beautiful as I had hoped. It continues:

> God employs several translators; some pieces are trans-
> lated by age, some by sickness, some by war, some by
> justice; but God's hand is in every translation, and his

hand shall bind up all our scattered leaves again, for that
Library where every book shall lie open to one another.

At the time I had only a dimly remembered impression of
Donne's words, and I decided that as soon as I had the chance, I
would find the passage on the Internet. I hadn't yet used the
Internet much beyond e-mail, but I had somehow gathered that
universities were all assembling vast computer-text libraries and
that anyone with a modem could scan their contents. Though I
had often expressed cynicism about the Internet, I secretly
dreamed it would turn out to be a virtual analogue to John
Donne's heaven.

There was another passage I wished to find—not on the
Internet but in the Talmud, which, like the Internet, I also regard as a kind of terrestrial version of Donne's divine library, a
place where everything exists, if only one knows how and where
to look. I'd thought repeatedly about the Talmudic passage I
alluded to earlier, the one that speaks of the *goses,* the soul that
is neither dead nor alive. I suppose the decision to remove my
grandmother from the respirator—despite her "living will" and
the hopelessness of her situation—disturbed me, and I tried to
recall the conversation the Rabbis had about the ways one can
and cannot allow a person headed toward death to die.

The Talmud tells a story about a great Rabbi who is dying.
He has become a *goses,* but he cannot die because outside his
hut all his students are praying for him to live, and this is dis-
tracting to his soul. A woman climbs to the roof of the Rabbi's
hut and hurls a clay vessel to the ground. The sound diverts the
students, who stop praying. In that moment, the Rabbi dies and
his soul goes to heaven. The woman, too, says the Talmud, will
be guaranteed her place in the world to come.

This story, suggesting the virtue of letting the dead depart,
was comforting to me, even though I know that the Talmud is
ultimately inconclusive on end-of-life issues, offering, as it always
does, a number of arguments and counter-arguments, stories and
counter-stories. Not to mention that the Talmud was codified in
the year 500 A.D., long before certain technological innovations

complicated questions of life and death. Was I retelling the story in a way that offered me comfort but distorted the original intent? I am far from being an accomplished Talmud student and did not trust my skills or memory. But for all that, I took enormous consolation in recalling that the Rabbis had in fact discussed the matter.

"Turn it and turn it for everything is in it," a Talmudic sage (who never said anything else the Talmud deemed worth recording) famously declared. The phrase, a sort of verbal Ouroboros, describes the Talmud and appears in the Talmud, a tail-swallowing observation that seems to bear out the truth of the sage's comment. The Talmud is a book and is not a book, and the Rabbi's phrase flexibly found its way into it because, oral and written both, the Talmud reached out and drew into itself the world around it, even as it declared itself the unchanging word of God.

Though it may seem sacrilegious to say so, I can't help feeling that in certain respects the Internet has a lot in common with the Talmud. The Rabbis referred to the Talmud as a *yam,* a sea—and though one is hardly intended to "surf" the Talmud, there is something more than oceanic metaphors that links the two verbal universes. Vastness, a protean structure, and an uncategorizable nature are in part what define them both. When Maimonides, the great medieval commentator, wanted to simplify the organization of the Talmud and reduce its peculiar blend of stories, folklore, legalistic arguments, anthropological asides, biblical exegesis, and intergenerational Rabbinic wrangling into simplified categories and legal conclusions, he was denounced as a heretic for disrupting the very chaos that, in some sense, had come to represent a divine fecundity. Eventually, Maimonides was forgiven, and his work, the Mishnah Torah, is now one of the many sources cross-referenced on a printed page of Talmud. It has been absorbed by the very thing it sought to replace.

The Mishnah itself—the legalistic core of the Talmud—is divided into six broad Orders that reflect six vast categories of

Jewish life, but those six categories are subdivided into numerous sub-categories called tractates that range over a far more vast number of subjects that are often impossible to fathom from the name of the Order in which they appear. The Hebrew word for tractate is *masechet,* which means, literally, webbing. As with the World Wide Web, only the metaphor of the loom, ancient and inclusive, captures the reach and the randomness, the infinite interconnectedness of words.

I have often thought, contemplating a page of Talmud, that it bears a certain uncanny resemblance to a home page on the Internet, where nothing is whole in itself but where icons and text-boxes are doorways through which visitors pass into an infinity of cross-referenced texts and conversations. Consider a page of Talmud. There are a few lines of Mishnah, the conversation the Rabbis conducted (for some five hundred years before writing it down) about a broad range of legalistic questions stemming from the Bible but ranging into a host of other matters as well. Underneath those few lines begins the Gemarah, the conversation *later* Rabbis had about the conversation *earlier* Rabbis had in the Mishnah. Both the Mishnah and the Gemarah evolved orally over so many hundreds of years that even in a few lines of text, Rabbis who lived generations apart give the appearance, both within those discrete passages as well as by juxtaposition on the page, of speaking directly to each other. The text includes not only legal disputes but fabulous stories, snippets of history and anthropology, and biblical interpretations. Running in a slender strip down the inside of the page is the commentary of Rashi, the medieval exegete, on the Mishnah, the Gemarah, and the biblical passages (also indexed elsewhere on the page) that inspired the original conversation. Underneath Rashi, and rising up on the other side of the Mishnah and the Gemarah, are the tosefists, Rashi's descendants and disciples, who comment on Rashi's work, as well as on everything Rashi commented on himself. The page is also cross-referenced to other passages of the Talmud, to various medieval codes of Jewish law (that of Maimonides, for example), and to the Shulkhan Arukh, the great sixteenth-century codification of Jewish law by Joseph Caro. And one should add to this mix the student himself, who participates in a conversation that began about fifteen hundred years ago.

Now all this is a far cry from the assault of recipes, news briefs, weather bulletins, library catalogues, pornographic pictures, Rembrandt reproductions, and assorted self-promotional verbiage that drifts untethered through cyberspace. The Talmud was produced by the moral imperative of Jewish law, the free play of great minds, the pressures of exile, the self-conscious need to keep a civilization together, and the driving desire to identify and follow the unfolding word of God. Nobody was trying to buy an airline ticket or meet a date. Moreover, the Talmud, after hundreds of years as an oral construct, was at last written down, shaped by (largely) unknown editors, masters of erudition and invention who float through its precincts offering anonymous, ghostly promptings—posing questions, proposing answers, offering refutations. One feels, for all the Talmud's multiplicities, an organizing intelligence at work.

And yet when I look at a page of Talmud and see all those texts tucked intimately and intrusively onto the same page, like immigrant children sharing a single bed, I do think of the interrupting, jumbled culture of the Internet. For hundreds of years, *responsa,* questions on virtually every aspect of Jewish life, winged back and forth between scattered Jews and various centers of Talmudic learning. The Internet is also a world of unbounded curiosity, of argument and information, where anyone with a modem can wander out of the wilderness for a while, ask a question, and receive an answer. I find solace in thinking that a modern technological medium echoes an ancient one.

For me, I suppose, the Internet makes actual a certain disjointed approach that I had already come to understand was part of the way I encounter both books and the world. I realized this forcefully when I went looking for the John Donne passage that comforted me after the death of my grandmother. I'd failed to find it in my Modern Library edition of Donne's *Complete Poetry and Selected Prose.* I knew the lines, I confess, not from a college course but from the movie version of *Eighty-Four, Charing Cross Road,* starring Anthony Hopkins and Anne Bancroft. The book, a 1970 best-seller, is a collection of letters exchanged over twenty years by an American woman and a British book clerk who sells her old leather-bound editions of Hazlitt and Lamb and Donne, presumably bought up cheap from the libraries of great houses whose owners are going broke after the war. I suppose the book itself is a comment on the death of a certain kind of print culture. The American woman loves literature, but she also writes for television, and at one point she buys Walter Savage Landor's *Imaginary Conversations* so she can adapt it for the radio.

In any event, I checked out *Eighty-Four, Charing Cross Road* from the library, hoping to find the Donne passage, but it wasn't in the book. It's alluded to in the play that was adapted from the book (I found that too), but it isn't quoted. There's just a brief discussion of Donne's Sermon XV (of which the American woman complains she's been sent an abridged version; she likes her Donne sermons whole). So I rented the movie again, and there was the passage, read beautifully in voice-over by Anthony Hopkins, but without attribution, so there was no way to look it up. Unfortunately, the passage was also abridged, so when I finally turned to the Web, I found myself searching for the line "All mankind is of one volume" instead of "All mankind is of one Author and is one volume."

My Internet search was initially no more successful than my library search. I had thought that summoning books from the vasty deep was a matter of a few keystrokes, but when I visited the Web site of the Yale Library, I discovered that most of its books do not yet exist as computer text. I'd somehow believed the whole world had grown digital, and though I'd long feared and even derided this notion, I now found how disappointed and frustrated I was that it hadn't happened. As a last-ditch effort, I searched the phrase "God employs many translators." And there it was! The passage I wanted finally came to me, as it turns out, not from the collection of a scholarly library but simply because someone who loves John Donne had posted it on his home page.

(At the bottom of the passage was the charming sentence "This small thread has been spun by . . ." followed by the man's name and Internet address.) For one moment, there in dimensionless, chilly cyberspace, I felt close to my grandmother, close to John Donne, and close to some stranger who, as it happens, designs software for a living.

The lines I sought were from Meditation XVII in "Devotions upon Emergent Occasions," which happens to be the most famous thing Donne ever wrote, containing, as it does, the line "never send to know for whom the bell tolls; it tolls for thee." My search had led me from a movie to a book to a play to a computer and back to a book. (The passage was, after all, in my Modern Library edition, but who could have guessed that it followed from "No man is an island"?) I had gone through all this to retrieve something that an educated person thirty years ago could probably have quoted by heart. Then again, these words may be as famous as they are only because Hemingway lifted them for his book title. Literature has been in a plundered, fragmented state for a long time.

Still, if the books had all been converted into computer text, and if Donne and Hemingway and *Eighty-Four, Charing Cross Road* had come up together and bumped into each other on my screen, I wouldn't have minded. Perhaps there is a spirit in books that lets them live beyond their actual bound bodies.

This is not to say that I do not fear the loss of the book as object, as body. Donne imagined people who die becoming like books, but what happens when books die? Are they reborn in some new ethereal form? Is it out of the ruined body of the book that the Internet is growing? This would account for another similarity I feel between the Internet and the Talmud, for the Talmud was also born partly out of loss.

The Talmud offered a virtual home for an uprooted culture, and it grew out of the Jews' need to pack civilization into words and wander out into the world. The Talmud became essential for Jewish survival once the Temple—God's pre-Talmud home—was destroyed, and the Temple practices, those bodily rituals of blood and fire and physical atonement, could no longer be performed. When the Jewish people lost their home (the land of Israel) and God lost his (the Temple), then a new way of being was devised, and Jews became the people of the book and not the people of the Temple or the land. They became the people of the book because they had no place else to live. That bodily loss is frequently overlooked, but for me it lies at the heart of the Talmud, for all its plenitude. The Internet, which we are continually told binds us all together, nevertheless engenders in me a similar sense of Diaspora, a feeling of being everywhere and nowhere. Where else but in the middle of Diaspora do you *need* a home page?

The Talmud tells a story that captures this mysterious transformation from one kind of culture to another. It is the story of Yochanan ben Zakkai, the great sage of the first century, who found himself living in besieged Jerusalem on the eve of its destruction by Rome. Yochanan ben Zakkai understood that Jerusalem and the Temple were doomed, so he decided to appeal to the Romans for permission to found a yeshiva outside Jerusalem. In order to get him out of Jerusalem without being killed by the Zealots—the Jewish revolutionaries—Yochanan's students hid him in a coffin and carried him outside the city walls. They did this not to fool the Romans but to fool the Zealots, who were killing anyone who wasn't prepared to die with the city.

Yochanan wasn't prepared to die with the city. Once outside its walls, he went to see the Roman general Vespasian and requested permission to set up a yeshiva in Yavneh. Vespasian consented, and it is thus in Yavneh that the study of the oral law flourished, in Yavneh that the Mishnah took shape, and in Yavneh that Talmudic culture was saved while Temple culture died. In a sense, Yochanan's journey in his coffin is the symbolic enactment of the transformation Judaism underwent when it changed from a religion of embodiment to a religion of the mind and of the book. Jews died as a people of the body, of the land, of the Temple service of fire and blood, and then, in one of the greatest acts of translation in human history, they were reborn as the people of the book.

I think about Yochanan ben Zakkai in his coffin when I

think about how we are passing, books and people both, through the doors of the computer age, and entering a new sort of global Diaspora in which we are everywhere—except home. But I suppose that writing, in any form, always has about it a ghostliness, an unsatisfactory, disembodied aspect, and it would be unfair to blame computers or the Internet for enhancing what has always been disappointing about words. Does anyone really want to be a book in John Donne's heaven?

A few weeks after my computer crashed, I gave in and sent it to a fancy place in Virginia, where—for more money than the original cost of the machine—technicians were in fact able to lift from the hard drive the ghostly impression of everything I had written on my computer during seven years of use. It was all sent to me on separate diskettes and on a single inclusive CD-ROM. I immediately found the diskette that contained my journal and, using my wife's computer, set about printing it out.

As it turns out, I'd written in my journal only six or seven times in the course of my grandmother's two-month illness. Somehow I'd imagined myself chronicling the whole ordeal in the minutest recoverable detail. Instead, I was astonished at how paltry, how sparse my entries really were. Where were the long hours holding her hand? The one-way conversations—what *had* I said? The slow, dreamlike afternoons with the rest of my family, eating and talking in the waiting area? Where, most of all, was my grandmother? I was glad to have my journal back, of course, and I'd have paid to retrieve it again in a second. But it was only when I had my own scant words before me at last that I realized how much I'd lost.

Kathleen Norris

Annunciation

My only rule: If I understand something, it's no mystery.
  —Scott Cairns, "The Translation of Raimundo Luz: My Good Luck"

Annunciation" means "the announcement." It would not be a scary word at all, except that as one of the Christian mysteries, it is part of a language of story, poetry, image, and symbol that the Christian tradition has employed for centuries to convey the central tenets of the faith. The Annunciation, Incarnation, Transfiguration, Resurrection. A Dominican friend defines the mysteries simply as "events in the life of Christ celebrated as stories in the gospels, and meant to be lived by believers." But modern believers tend to trust in therapy more than in mystery, a fact that tends to manifest itself in worship that employs the bland speech of pop psychology and self-help rather than language resonant with poetic meaning. For example, a call to worship that begins: "Use this hour, Lord, to get our perspectives straight again." Rather than express awe, let alone those negative feelings, fear and trembling, as we come into the presence of God, crying "Holy, Holy, Holy," we focus totally on ourselves, and arrogantly issue an imperative to God. Use this hour, because we're busy later; just send us a bill, as any therapist would, and we'll zip off a check in the mail. But the mystery of worship, which is God's presence and our response to it, does not work that way.

The profound skepticism of our age, the mistrust of all that has been handed to us by our grandfathers and grandmothers as tradition, has led to a curious failure of the imagination, manifested in language that is thoroughly comfortable, and satisfyingly unchallenging. A hymn whose name I have forgotten that cheerfully asks God to "make our goals your own," a so-called prayer of confession that confesses nothing, but whines to God "that we have hindered your will and way for us by keeping portions of our lives apart from your influence." To my ear such language reflects an idolatry of ourselves, that is, the notion that the measure of what we can understand, what is readily comprehensible and acceptable to us, is also the measure of God. It leads all too many clerics to simply trounce on mystery, and in the process say remarkably foolish things. The Annunciation is as good as any a place to start.

I once heard a Protestant clergywoman say to an ecumenical assembly, "We all know there was no Virgin Birth. Mary was just an unwed, pregnant teenager, and God told her it was okay. That's the message we need to give girls today, that God loves them, and forget all this nonsense about a Virgin Birth." A gasp went up; people shook their heads. This was the first (and only) gratuitously offensive remark made at a convention marked by great theological diversity. When it came, I happened to be sitting between some Russian Orthodox, who were offended theologically, and black Baptists, whose sense of theological affront was mixed with social concern. They were not at all pleased to hear a well-educated, middle-class white woman say that what we need to tell pregnant teenagers is, "It's okay."

I realized that my own anger at the woman's arrogance had deep personal roots. I was taken back to my teenaged years, when the "de-mythologizing" of Christianity that I had encountered in a misguided study of modern theology had led me to conclude that there was little in the religion for me. In the classroom, at least, it seemed that anything in the Bible that didn't stand to reason, that we couldn't explain, was primitive, infantile, ripe for discarding. So I took all my longing for the sacred, for mystery, into the realm of poetry, and found a place for myself there. Now, more than thirty years later, I sat in a room full of Christians and thought, My God, they're still at it, still trying to leech every bit of mystery out of this religion, still substituting the most trite language imaginable. You're okay, the boy you screwed when you were both too drunk to stand is okay, all God chooses to say about it is, it's okay.

The job of any preacher, it seems to me, is not to dismiss the Annunciation because it doesn't appeal to modern prejudices, but to remind congregations of why it might still be an appealing story. I once heard a Benedictine friend who is an Assiniboine Indian preach on the Annunciation to an Indian congregation. "The first thing Gabriel does when he encounters Mary," he said, "is to give her a new name: 'Most Favored One. It's a naming ceremony,' he emphasized, making a connection that excited and delighted his listeners. When I brood on the story of the Annunciation, I like to think about what it means to be "overshadowed" by the Holy Spirit; I wonder if a kind of overshadowing isn't what every young woman pregnant for the first time might feel, caught up in something so much larger than herself. I think of James Wright's little poem, "Trouble," and the wonder of his pregnant mill-town girl. The butt of jokes, the taunt of gossips, she is amazed to carry such power within herself. "Sixteen years, and/And all that time, she thought she was nothing/but skin and bones." Wright's poem does, it seems to me, what the clergywoman talks about doing, but without resorting to ideology or the false assurance that "it's okay." Told all her life that she is "nothing," the girl discovers in herself another, deeper reality. A mystery; something holy, with a potential for salvation. The poem has challenged me for years to wonder what such a radically new sense of oneself would entail. Could it be a form of virgin birth?

Wondering at the many things that the story of the Annunciation might mean, I take refuge in the fact that for centuries so many poets and painters have found it worthy of consideration. European art would not have been enriched had Fra Angelico, or Dante Gabriel Rossetti for that matter, simply realized that the Annunciation was a form of negative thinking, moralistic nonsense that only a modern mindset—resolutely intellectual, professional, therapeutic—could have straightened out for them.

I am glad also that many artists and poets are still willing to explore the metaphor (and by that I mean the truth) of the virgin birth. The contemporary poet Laurie Sheck, in her poem "The Annunciation," respects the "honest grace" that Mary shows by not attempting to hide her fear in the presence of the angel, her fear of the changes within her body. I suspect that Mary's "yes" to her new identity, to the immense and wondrous possibilities of her new and holy name, may provide an excellent means of conveying to girls that there is something in them that no man can touch; that belongs only to them, and to God.

When I hear remarks like the one made by the pastor at that conference, I am struck mainly by how narrow and impoverished a concept of virginity it reveals. It's in the monastic world that I find a broader, and also more relevant grasp of what it could mean to be virgin. Thomas Merton, in *Conjectures of a Guilty Bystander,* describes the true identity that he seeks in contemplative prayer as a "point vierge" at the center of his being, "a point untouched by illusion, a point of pure truth . . . which belongs entirely to God, which is inaccessible to the fantasies of our own mind or the brutalities of our own will. This little point . . . of absolute poverty," he wrote, "is the pure glory of God in us."

It is only when we stop idolizing the illusion of our control over the events of life and recognize our poverty that we become virgin in the sense that Merton means. Adolescents tend to be better at this than grown-ups, because they are continually told that they don't know enough, and they lack the means to hide behind professional credentials. The whole world confirms to them that they are indeed poor, regrettably laboring through what is called "the awkward age." It is no wonder that teenagers like to run in packs, that they surround themselves with people as gawky and unformed as themselves. But it is in adolescence that the fully-formed adult self begins to emerge, and if a person has been fortunate, allowed to develop at his or her own pace, this self is a liberating force, and it is virgin. That is, it is one-in-itself, better able to cope with peer pressure, as it can more readily measure what is true to one's self, and what would violate it. Even adolescent self-absorption recedes as one's capacity for the mystery of hospitality grows: it is only when one is at home in oneself, that one may be truly hospitable to others—welcoming, but not overbearing, affably pliant but not subject to crass manipulation. This difficult balance is maintained only as one remains virgin, cognizant of oneself as valuable, unique, and undiminishable at core.

What may trouble modern people most about this concept of virginity, and the story of the Annunciation itself, is what I find most inspiring; there's no room in the story for the Catch-22 of sexual liberation. It was not uncommon, in the 1960's, for young men to insist that their girlfriends seek medical treatment for "frigidity" if they resisted sexual intimacy. In many cases the young women were reasoning in a mature fashion, doubting that they were ready for sex, at 14 or 17 years of age, and wondering if their boyfriends were as ready as they pretended to be. In doing so, they were regarding sexual intercourse as a major rite of passage, one that would foster but also require a deepening maturity and emotional commitment, and they had the good sense to wonder if it might not be a good idea to become more their own person before sharing themselves so intimately with another. The remedy for this pathology? Birth control pills, of course. These girls were not well served by doctors, or well-meaning clergy who told them not to worry, it's okay.

We all need to be told that God loves us, and the mystery of the Annunciation reveals an aspect of that love. But it also suggests that our response to this love is critical. A few verses before the angel appears to Mary in the first chapter of Luke's gospel, another annunciation occurs; an angel announces to an old man, Zechariah, that his equally aged wife is to bear a son who will "make ready a people prepared for the Lord." The couple are to name him John; he is known to us as John the Baptist. Zechariah says to the angel, "How will I know that this is so?" which is a radically different response than the one Mary makes. She says, "How can this be?"

I interpret this to mean that while Zechariah is seeking knowledge and information, Mary contents herself with wisdom, with pondering a state of being. God's response to Zechariah is to give him a pregnancy of his own. During the entire term of his son's gestation, he is struck dumb and does not speak again until after the child is born, and he has written on a tablet what the angel has said to him: "His name is John." This confounds his relatives, who had expected that the child would be named after his father. I read Zechariah's punishment as a grace, in that he could not say anything to further compound his initial arrogance when confronted with mystery. When he does speak again, it is to praise God; he's had nine months to think it over.

Mary's "How can this be?" is a simpler response than Zechariah's, and also more profound. She does not lose her voice, but finds it. Like any of the prophets, she asserts herself before God, saying, "Here am I." There is no arrogance, however, but only holy fear and wonder. Mary proceeds—as we must do in life—by making her commitment without knowing much about what it will entail, or where it will lead. I treasure the story because it forces me to ask: when the mystery of God's love breaks through into my consciousness, do I run from it? Do I ask of it what it cannot answer? Shrugging, do I retreat into facile clichés, the popular but false wisdom of what "we all know"? Or am I virgin enough to respond from my deepest, truest self, and say something new, a "yes" that will change me forever?

Sexualities

Siri Hustvedt

A Plea for Eros

A few years ago a friend of mine gave a lecture at Berkeley on the *femme fatale,* a subject he has been thinking about for years. When I met him, he was a graduate student at Columbia University, but now he is a full-fledged philosopher, and when it is finished, his book will be published by Gallimard in France and Harvard University Press in America. He is Belgian but lives in Paris, a detail significant to the story, because he comes from another rhetorical tradition—a French one. When he finished speaking, he took questions, including a hostile one from a woman who demanded to know what he thought of the Antioch Ruling—a law enacted at Antioch College, which essentially made every stage of a sexual encounter on campus legal only by verbal consent. My friend paused, smiled, and replied: "It's wonderful. I love it. Just think of the erotic possibilities: 'May I touch your right breast? May I touch your left breast?' " The woman had nothing to say.

This little exchange has lingered in my mind. What interests me is that he and she were addressing exactly the same problem, the idea of permission, and yet their perspectives were so far apart that it was as if they were speaking different languages. The woman expected opposition, and when she didn't get it, she was speechless. Aggressive questions are usually pedagogic—that is, the answer has already been written in the mind of the questioner, who then waits with a reply. It's pretend listening. But by moving the story—in this case, the narrative of potential lovers—onto new ground, the young philosopher tripped up his opponent.

It is safe to assume that the Antioch Ruling wasn't devised to increase sexual pleasure on campus, and yet the new barriers it made, ones which dissect both sexual gestures and the female body (the ruling came about to protect women, not men), have been the stuff of erotic fantasy for ages. When the troubadour pined for his lady, he hoped against hope that he would be granted a special favor—a kiss perhaps. The sonnet itself is a form that takes the body of the beloved apart—her hair, her eyes, her lips, her breasts. The body in pieces is reborn in this legal drama of spoken permission. Eroticism thrives both on borders and on distance. It is a commonplace that sexual pleasure demands thresholds. My philosopher made quick work of demonstrating the excitement of crossing into forbidden territory— the place you need special permission to trespass into. But there is distance here, too, a distance the earnest crusaders who invented the ruling couldn't possibly have foreseen. The articulation of the other's body in words turns it into a map of possible pleasure, effectively distancing that body by transforming it into an erotic object.

Objectification has a bad name in our culture. Cries of "Women are not sexual objects" have been resounding for years. I first ran into this argument in a volume I bought in the ninth grade called *Sisterhood Is Powerful*. I carried that book around with me until it fell apart. Feminism was good for me, as were any number of causes, but as I developed as a thinking person, the truisms and dogmas of every ideology became as worn as that book's cover. Of course women are sexual objects; so are men. Even while I was hugging that book of feminist rhetoric to my chest, I groomed myself carefully, zipped myself into tight jeans, and went after the boy I wanted most, mentally picking apart desirable male bodies like a connoisseur. Erotic pleasure, derived from the most intimate physical contact, thrives on the paradox that only by keeping alive the strangeness of that other person can eroticism last. Every person is keenly aware of the fact that sexual feeling is distinct from affection, even though they often conspire, but this fact runs against the grain of classic feminist arguments.

American feminism has always had a puritanical strain, an imposed blindness to erotic truth. There is a hard, pragmatic aspect to this. It is impolitic to admit that sexual pleasure comes in all shapes and sizes, that women, like men, are often aroused by what seems silly at best and perverse at worst. And because sexual excitement always partakes of the culture itself, finds its images and triggers from the boundaries delineated in a given society, the whole subject is a messy business.

Several years ago I read an article in *The New York Times* about a Chinese version of the Kinsey Report, the results of which suggested that Chinese women as a group experienced *no* sexual pleasure. This struck me as insane, but as I began to ponder the idea, it took on a kind of sense. I visited China in 1986 to find a place still reeling from the Cultural Revolution, a place in which prerevolutionary forms appeared to have been utterly forgotten. Maybe there can't be much erotic life, other than the barest minimum, without an encouraging culture—without movies and books, without ideas about what it's supposed to be. When I was fifteen, I remember watching *Carnal Knowledge* at the Grand movie theater in Northfield, Minnesota, my hometown. Jack Nicholson and Ann-Margret were locked in a mystifying upright embrace and were crashing around the room with their clothes on, or most of them on, banging into walls and making a lot of noise, and I had absolutely no idea what they were doing. It had never occurred to me in my virginal state that people made love *like that*. A friend had to tell me what I was seeing. Most teenagers today are more sophisticated, but only because they've had more exposure. I was thirteen before I stumbled over the word *rape*—in *Gone with the Wind*. I walked downstairs and asked my mother what it meant. She looked at me and said, "I was afraid of that." Then she told me. But even after I knew, I didn't really understand it, and I couldn't imagine it.

My point is this: a part of me has real sympathy for the Chinese couple, both university professors, who married, went to bed with each other faithfully every night, and, after a year, visited a doctor, wondering why no child had come from their union. They thought sleeping *beside* each other was enough. Nobody told them that more elaborate activity was necessary. Surely this is a case of an erotic culture gone with the wind. (In China among the class that could afford to cultivate it, the female body had become a refined sexual art form. In Xi'an I saw a very old woman with bound feet. She could no longer walk and had to be carried. Those tiny, crippled feet were the gruesome legacy of a lost art. Binding feet made them small enough to fit into a man's mouth.) The famous parental lecture on the birds and the bees, the butt of endless jokes and deemed largely unnecessary in our world, never took place in the lives of the two puzzled professors. *But where were their bodies?* We imagine that proximity would be enough, that *natural* forces would lead the conjugal couple to sexual happiness. But my feeling is that it isn't true, that all of us need a story outside ourselves, a form through which we imagine ourselves as players in the game.

Consider standard erotic images. Garter belts and stockings, for example, still have a hold on the paraphernalia of arousal—even though, except for the purpose of titillation, they have mostly vanished from women's wardrobes. Would these garments be sexy if you'd never seen them before? Would they mean anything? But we can't escape the erotic vocabulary of our culture any more than we can escape language itself. There's the rub. Although feminist discourse in America understandably wants to subvert cultural forms that aren't "good" for women, it has never taken on the problem of arousal with much courage. When a culture oppresses women, and all do to one degree or another, it isn't convenient to acknowledge that there are women who like submission in bed or who have fantasies about rape. Masochistic fantasies damage the case for equality, and even when they are seen as the result of a "sick society," the peculiarity of our sexual actions or fantasies is not easily untangled or explained away. The ground from which they spring is simply too muddy. Acts can be controlled, but not desire. Sexual feeling pops up, in spite of our politics.

Desire is always between a subject and an object. People may have loose, roving appetites, but desire must fix on an object even if that object is imaginary, or narcissistic—even if the self is turned into an other. Between two real people, the sticky part is beginning. As my husband says, "Somebody has to make the first move." And this is a delicate matter. It means reading another person's desires. But misreading happens, too. When I was in my early twenties in graduate school, I met a brilliant, astoundingly articulate student with whom I talked and had coffee. I was in love at the time with someone else, and I was unhappy, but not unhappy enough to end the relation. This articulate student and I began going to the movies, sharing Chinese dinners, and talking our heads off. I gave him poems of mine to read. We talked about books and more books and became *friends* (as the saying goes). I was not attracted to him sexually at all, nor did I glean any sexual interest in me from him. He didn't flirt. He didn't make any moves, but after several months, our friendship blew up in my face. It became clear that he had pined and suffered, and that I had been insensitive. The final insult to him turned on my having given him a poem to criticize that had as its subject the sexual power of my difficult boyfriend. I felt bad. Perhaps never in my life have I so misinterpreted a relation with another person. I have always prided myself on having a nearly uncanny ability to receive unspoken messages, to sense underlying intentions, even unconscious ones, and here I had bollixed up the whole business. No doubt we were both to blame. He was too subtle, and I was distracted—fixated on another body. Would the Antioch Ruling have helped us? I doubt it. A person who doesn't reach out for your hand or stroke your face or come near you for a kiss isn't about to propose these overtures out loud. He was a person without any coarseness of mind, much too refined to leap. He thought that dinner and the movies meant that we were on a "date," that he had indicated his interest through the form of our evenings. I, on the other hand, had had lots of dinners and movies with fellow students, both men and women, and it didn't occur to me that the form signified anything in particular; and yet the truth was, I should have known. Because he was so discreet, and because I lacked all sexual feeling for him, I assumed he had none for me.

Nineteenth-century conventions for courtship have been largely disassembled in the latter half of this century, bending the codes out of shape. People marry later. The emphasis on virginity for women has changed. Single women work and are not expected to give up their jobs once they marry. Men have been digesting a set of new rules that are nevertheless colored by the old ones. People still court each other, after all. They are still looking for Romance of one kind or another—short or long—and each one of them is alone out there reading and misreading the intentions of others. The Antioch Ruling was clearly a response to the chaos of courtship—a way of imposing a structure on what seemed to have collapsed—but ambiguity remains, not just in interpretation but even in desire itself. There are people, and we have all met them, who can't make up their minds. There are people who say no when they mean yes, and yes when they mean no. There are people who mean exactly what they say when they say it, and then later wish they had said the opposite. There are people who succumb to sexual pressure out of a misplaced desire to please or even out of pity. To pretend ambiguity doesn't exist in sexual relations is just plain stupid.

And then there are moments of interruption—those walls that block desire. I was absolutely mad about a boy in high school, but there was something about his nose when he kissed me, something about its apparent softness from that angle that I disliked. To my mind, that nose needed more cartilage. I kept my eyes shut. I know of a woman who fell for a man at a party. She fell hard and fast. They returned to her apartment in an erotic fever, kissing madly, throwing their clothes off, and then she looked across the room and saw his underwear. If I remember correctly, it was some male version of the bikini bottom, and her

attraction vanished suddenly, irrevocably. She told the poor man
to leave. An explanation was impossible. What was she to say? I
hate your underpants?

Sexual freedom and eroticism are not identical; in fact,
freedom can undermine the erotic, because the no-holds-barred
approach is exciting only if you've just knocked down the door.
And despite the fact that dinner, a movie, and a kiss at the door
have taken a beating in recent years, seduction is inevitably a
theater of barriers, a playing and replaying of roles, both conscious and unconscious. Sincerity is not at issue here; most of us
play in earnest. Through the language of clothes and gesture and
through talk itself, we imagine ourselves as the other person will
see us, mirroring our own desire in them, and most of what we
do is borrowed from a vocabulary of familiar images. This is not a
territory of experience that is easy to dissect legally.

Apparently, there is a new law in Minnesota against staring.
It has been duly mocked in newspapers all over the world, but
according to my sister, it came about because of the increase in
the number of construction sites around Minneapolis, and
women were weary of walking past them. Most women have
experienced these painful, often humiliating excursions in front
of an ogling, jeering crowd of men, and I don't know of anybody
who likes them. This event—the construction crew whooping
and hooting at a passing woman—is a convention, a thing these
guys do in a group and only in a group, to liven up the job, to
declare their masculinity to the world *safely*. It's the pseudo-
sexual invitation. Not a single one of those men expects the
woman to say, "Yes, I'm flattered. Take me, now."

But staring, even staring in this crude form, does not seem
criminal to me. "Officer, he's staring. Arrest him," has a feeble
ring to it. And I say this despite the fact that twice in my life I
found myself the object of what would have to be described as
aggressive staring. For several years, when I was in high school
and then attending college in the same town, a young man I
knew only slightly would appear out of nowhere and stare. He
did not stare casually. He stared wholeheartedly and with such
determination, he made me nervous and uncomfortable, as if he

did it to satisfy some deep longing inside him. Without any warning, I would find him stationed outside the restaurant where I worked or outside the student union at my college, his eyes fixed on me. They were enormous pale eyes, ringed with black, that made him look as if he hadn't slept in weeks. "I've been standing here since eight o'clock this morning," he said to me once at three in the afternoon, "waiting for you." One night after work he followed me through the streets. I panicked and began to run. He did not pursue me. The problem was that he acted in ways that struck me as unaccountable. He would make abrupt changes in his appearance—suddenly shaving his head, for example. He walked all the way to my parents' house to deliver a gift, badly packed in a cardboard box. Filled with dread, I opened the box, only to find an ugly but innocent green vase. Not long before I received the vase, this young man's twin brother had killed himself in a cafe in a nearby town. He had gone there for breakfast and then after finishing his meal, took out a gun and blew his brains out. I am sure I associated the actions of the twin with the one who survived, am sure that the staring frightened me because I imagined potential violence lurking behind those eyes. The looks he gave me were beyond anything I had ever encountered, but I also honestly believe he meant me no harm. Perhaps in his own way he was in love. I don't know. But the crux of the story is that I think I brought it on myself without meaning to. Once, when I was in high school, I hugged him.

I worked at a place called the Youth Emergency Service, and the staring boy used to hang out there. I don't know where he lived or how he managed. He didn't go to school. He was sad that day, as he probably was most days, and we talked. I have no recollection of that conversation, but I know that in a fit of compassion, I hugged him. I am convinced that the whole staring problem hinged on this hug, and to this day when I think of it, I am mortified. Acts cannot be retrieved and, sometimes, they last. This is not a simple story. I often wonder if any story is, if you really look at it, but I carry his face around with me and when I think of him and the former me, I feel sorry for both of us.

The other staring man was a student of mine at Queens College. I taught freshman English there and an introductory literature class. My teaching was passionate, occasionally histrionic, but I was a young woman on a mission to educate, and sometimes I did. This student was clearly intelligent, although he had profound and jarring diction problems. His papers were written in a gnarled, convoluted style that was meant to be elevated but was often merely wrong. Eventually, I came to recognize that there had been signs of schizophrenia in the writing, but that wasn't until later. I had private sessions with all my students. These meetings were required, and when I met with him, I urged simplicity and hiding his thesaurus forever. The trouble began when he was no longer my student. He would barge into my office unannounced and throw unwanted gifts onto my desk—records, perfume, magazines. He, too, had a penchant for inexplicable transformations, for flannel shirts one day and silky feminine tops the next. On a balmy afternoon in late April, he visited me wearing a fur coat. Another time, I looked up to find him standing in my little graduate-assistant cubicle, his fingers busily unbuttoning his shirt. This story rings with comedy now, but I was aghast. In my best schoolteacher voice, I shouted, "Stop!" He looked terribly hurt and began stamping his foot like a three-year-old, whining my *first* name, as though he couldn't believe I had thwarted him. After that, he would park himself outside the classroom where I taught and stare at me. If I looked a little to the right, I would see him in my peripheral vision. The staring unnerved me, and after several days of it, I was scared. When I crossed campus, he would follow me—an omnipresent ghost I couldn't shake. Talking to him did no good. Yelling at him did no good. I went to the campus police. They were indifferent to my alarm. No, more than that, they were contemptuous. I had no recourse. In time, the student gave up, and my ghost disappeared, never to bother me again. The question is, What does this story exemplify? Would it be called sexual harassment now, because of that shirt episode? Is it stalking? What he actually *did* to me was innocuous. The fear came from the fact that what he did was unpredictable. He did not play by the rules, and once those rules had been broken, I imagined that anything was possible.

Neither of these staring experiences was erotic for me, but they may have been for the two young men who did the staring. Who I was for either of them remains a mystery to me, a blank filled with my own dread. They have lasted inside me as human signs of the mysteries of passion, of emotional disturbance and tumult, and despite the unpleasantness they caused me, I am not without compassion for both of them. I have stared myself. Looking hard is the first sign of eros, and once when I was fourteen, I found myself staring very hard at a house. I had fallen in love with a boy who was fifteen. He cared nothing for me and was involved with a girl who had what I didn't have: breasts. She fascinated me almost as much as he did, because, after all, she was his beloved, and I studied her carefully for clues to her success. One Saturday in the fall, I walked to his house, stood outside on the sidewalk, and stared at it for a long time. I'm not sure why I did this. Perhaps I hoped he would walk out the door, or maybe I thought I might gain the courage to ring the bell. I remember that the house looked deserted. Probably no one was home. It was a corner house on a beautiful street in Northfield, lined with elms. The elms are all dead now, but I remember the street with trees. That house, which once was his house, is still suffused with the memory of my terrible ache for him, a longing I found almost unbearable and which was never requited. Years later, when I was grown (much taller than he ever grew) and I saw him in a local bar, he remembered my "crush" and said he regretted not acting on it. As silly as it sounds, this confession of his gave me real satisfaction, but the fact is he didn't want the fourteen-year-old I had been, but the twenty-two-year-old I had become—another person altogether.

Ogling should be legal. Looking is part of love, but what you see when you look is anybody's guess. Why that skinny ninth-grade boy with glasses sent me into paroxysms of longing, I couldn't tell you, but he did. Feelings are crude. The ache of love feels remarkably like the ache of grief or guilt. Emotional pain isn't distinguishable by feeling, only by language. We give a name to the misery, not because we recognize the feeling but because we know its context. Sometimes we feel bad and don't know why or don't remember why. Mercifully, love is sometimes equal, and two people, undisturbed by the wrong underwear or the wrong nose, find each other inside this mystery of attraction and are happy. But why?

Contentment in love usually goes unquestioned. Still, I don't think enduring love is rational any more than momentary flings. I have been married to the same man for fifteen years, and I can't explain why he still attracts me as an erotic object. He does, but why? Shouldn't it all be worn out by now? It is *not* because we are so close or know each other so well. That solidifies our friendship, not our attraction. The attraction remains because there's something about him that I can't reach, something strange and estranging. I like seeing him from a distance. I know that. I like to see him in a room full of people when he looks like a stranger, and then to remember that I do know him and that I will go home with him. But why he sometimes strikes me as a magical being, a person unlike others, I can't tell you. He has many good features, but so do other men that leave me cold as a stone. Have I given him this quality because it is efficient for me, or is it actually in him, some piece of him that I will never conquer and never know? It must be both. It must be between us—an enchanted space that is wholly unreasonable and, at least in part, imaginary. There is still a fence for me to cross and, on the other side of it, a secret.

Love affairs and marriages stand or fall on this secret. Familiarity and the pedestrian realities of everyday life are the enemies of eros. Emma Bovary watches her husband eat and is disgusted. She studies maps of Paris and hopes for something grander, more passionate, unfamiliar. A friend of mine told me about evenings out with her husband, during which they seduce each other all over again, and she can't wait to get home and jump on his beautiful body; but if on the way into the house he pauses to straighten the lids on the garbage cans, the spell is broken. She told him, and he now resists this urge. These interruptions disturb the stories we tell ourselves, the ready-made narratives that we have made our own. A combination of biology, personal history, and a cultural miasma of ideas creates attraction. The fantasy lover is always hovering above or behind or in front of the real lover, and you need both of them. The problem is that the alliance of these two is unpredictable. Eros, after all, was a mischievous little imp with arrows, a fellow of surprises who delighted in striking those who expected it least. Like his fairy reincarnation, Puck in *A Midsummer Night's Dream,* he makes madness of reason. He turns the world upside down. Hermia prefers Lysander to Demetrius for no good reason. Shakespeare's young men, Demetrius and Lysander, as has often been pointed out, are as alike and interchangeable as two pears. When Theseus points out to Hermia that Demetrius is just as good as Lysander, he isn't lying. It's just that Demetrius is not the one she likes. After much confusion and silliness, the lovers are set right by magic. Demetrius is never disenchanted. The flower juice remains in his eyes and he marries Helena under its influence, the point being that when we fall in love, we've all got fairy juice in our eyes, and not one of us gives a jot about the sane advice of parents or friends or governments.

And that's why legislating desire is unwieldy. A child rushes over and kisses another child in school in New York City, and he's nabbed by the authorities for "sexual harassment." Maybe it was an aggressive act, a sudden lack of control that needed the teacher's attention. Maybe the kissed child was unhappy or scared. And maybe, contrary to the myth of childish innocence, it was *sexual,* a burst of strange, wild feeling. I don't know. But people, children and adults, do bump up against each other. Everywhere, all the time there are scuffles of desire. We have laws against molestation and rape. Using power and position to extract sexual favors from an unwilling employee is ugly and shouldn't be legal. But on the other side of these crimes is a blurry terrain, a borderland of dreams and wishes. And it isn't a landscape of sunshine only. It is a place streaked with the clouds of sadism and masochism, where peculiar objects and garments are strewn here and there, and where its inhabitants weep as often as they sigh with pleasure. And it is nothing less than amazing that we should have to be reminded of this. All around us, popular singers are crooning out their passion and bitterness on the radio. Billboards, advertisements, and television shows are playing to our erotic weaknesses twenty-four hours a day. But at the same time, there is a kind of spotty cultural amnesia in particular circles, a block-headed impulse to crush complexity and truth in the name of right-thinking.

Once when I was attending a panel discussion on the fate or the state of "the novel," at the 92nd Street Y, because my husband had been roped into moderating this discussion, I listened to a novelist, an intelligent and good writer, berate Kafka for his depictions of women. They were bad, she said, wrongheaded. But in Kafka's world of dreams and claustrophobia, a world of irreducible images so powerful they shake me every time I remember them, what does it mean to second-guess its genius, to edit out the women who lift their skirts for the wandering K? When I read Kafka, I am not that housemaid who presents herself to the tormented hero anyway. I am the hero, the one who takes the pleasure offered, as we all do when we sleep.

This is my call for eros, a plea that we not forget ambiguity and mystery, that in matters of the heart, we acknowledge an abiding uncertainty. I honestly think that when we are possessed by erotic magic, we don't feel like censoring Kafka or much else, because we are living a story of exciting thresholds and irrational feeling. We are living in a secret place we make between us, a place where the real and unreal commingle. That's where the young philosopher took the woman with the belligerent question. He brought her into a realm of the imagination and of memory, where lovers are alone speaking to each other, saying yes or no or "perhaps tomorrow," where they play at who they are, inventing and reinventing themselves as subjects and objects; and when the woman with the question found herself there, she was silent. Maybe, just maybe, she was remembering a passionate story of her own.

Wayne Koestenbaum

Masochism

To rail against Disney is to say the obvious.

First I will rant about computers. Later I will discuss Times Square and masochism.

I hate computers, even though I am using one. Computers make people stupid.

I advocate the agrarian.

I telephone a chain bookstore. "What books by Harold Robbins do you have in stock?" I ask the salesclerk.

"Let me check the computer," he says, and puts me on hold.

Why not check the shelves?

The clerk comes back on the line to say that the computer only lists initials of first names. H. Robbins. There are hundreds of H. Robbins titles.

He says, *"Descent from Xanadu.* Is that by Harold Robbins?"

"I don't know," I say. "It doesn't sound like Harold Robbins."

"What about *Spellbinder. The Lonely Lady. Goodbye, Janette."*

Things are looking up.

The clerk puts me on hold.

The clerk comes back to say *"Where Love Has Gone. Never Love a Stranger."*

Happiness.

I'd like to register a complaint, however.

I expect quick service and I expect clerks to know their stock.

I want to defame chains.

"You sound like a Marxist," a writer said to me at a cocktail party. I was complaining about chains. I said, "I'm not a Marxist. I'm too ignorant of Marx to be a Marxist." She said, "You sound like a Marxist. That's refreshing."

Moments earlier in the conversation I'd offended her by complaining about elites. Turned out she belonged to the very elite I was criticizing.

Accidentally I'd spit a bit of smoked salmon onto my palm, and when I shook her hand, I think she could feel the fish fleck.

Yesterday I met a rich man. He moved slowly, though he is only forty. He moves slowly not because he is arthritic or tired, but because he is rich. He didn't wiggle his head nervously in every direction while he spoke. When I talk, I wiggle my head. This is because I am not rich. I am upper-middle class, the lower end.

Do you understand?

Times Square.

The men who walk into the few remaining porn shops are sometimes handsome. I want to engage them in conversation.

I am depressed to see the sexual history of Times Square erased.

I won't claim that Times Square was a utopia, but it was certainly important. See George Chauncy's *Gay New York*. See Sal Mineo's *Who Killed Teddy Bear?* See Joseph Cornell's diaries.

Alas, the Eros has closed, and the Adonis.

The Gap takes up some of the slack, but not enough.

The Disney Store takes up none of the slack, unless you

bring your direst sexual fantasies into the store, or unless you adopt the following style: he or she who verbalizes the sexualized advances that commodities make on our imaginations and actions.

Dumbo is a sexualized commodity.

Other commodities that haunt me are books and countries: I have been alphabetizing my books and I have been planning trips to Florida and Sicily. In Miami I want to become more of a guy by getting a tan and relaxing. In Taormina I will seek echoes of the boys that Baron Wilhelm von Gloeden photographed. See Emmanuel Cooper's *Fully Exposed: The Male Nude in Photography*. See the turn of the century.

I have been thinking seriously about prostitutes. My favorite porn star is Max Grand. In a free gay mag he advertised: "Pornstar. Max Grand. In NYC 11/6–11/18. Nationwide Pager 310–298–3951." I may avail myself of his services and write at great length about the experience.

Max Grand is not a commodity. He is a male escort from El Salvador. His films include *Latin Tongues, Hot Springs Orgy, Leather Confessions, Chicago Meat Packers* and *Cut vs. Uncut*. He is a superstar.

In *Wet Warehouse* #2 he has a lovely speaking voice and a desk job.

Last night I dreamed my students complained about my pedagogy. I was trying, in a huge lecture course, to discuss the difference between cleanliness and filth. I was faultily explaining the co-existence of dirty and clean in the work of Marianne Moore and Elizabeth Bishop. I said incoherently, "Moore's forms look clean but her metaphors are filthy." I was projecting slides of Renaissance paintings—closeups of fabric.

So what if I made my students cry?

Everything quickly devolved into a textbook case of sexual harassment, and the dream ended.

I have been thinking about sadomasochism. I have not been practicing it.

The difference between praxis and mimesis, my old favorite, is not a crux I shall belabor today.

A few leatherfolk I've recently met are among the nicest people in my circle. I feel at home with them. They wear interesting clothes. They talk casually about gear: "I'm wearing a cock ring today."

They don't talk about identity: "I am a sadist." They talk about scenes: "I did an interesting scene."

I did an interesting scene today. I stood in the vicinity of a commodity and ignored it.

I pretended a person was a commodity. I stared at the person, once my friend, and ignored his soul.

I imagined him dead.

I smiled at him while picturing him evacuated.

It is difficult to think outside the lure of commodities.

I mean clothes and books and prostitutes and photographs and neighborhoods and corporations.

This is not a lecture about commodities. I am hardly qualified.

See Guy Hocquenghem's *Homosexual Desire,* especially the chapter on the anus, capitalism and the family.

See the Guess ad campaign.

See Celine Dion.

See me. After class. For tips. On how to ignore commodities.

It is beginning to snow. I am beginning to remember the first short story I wrote, in 1976. I am beginning to forget my body.

My father saw Disney's *Fantasia* in Caracas, 1940. Or was it 1941? I romanticize the moment of him watching it. He saw it several times. It inspired him to want to become a musician. He took piano lessons. He conducted an orchestra, at least once, in college. He conducted the overture to *Don Giovanni.* Or so I remember him telling me. The memory is crucial yet vague.

In Caracas my father wanted to play Monopoly. He couldn't find it in the stores, or his father wouldn't buy it for him. I can't remember. So my father fabricated his own Monopoly board game. This proves his ingenuity. He was a self-starter.

I played Monopoly obsessively in fourth and fifth grade.

My favorite color group contained Marvin Gardens. I loved owning cheap, easily conquered territories: Baltic Avenue.

For every lost tooth I received a silver dollar under my pillow.

I wanted to be rich and French. I called myself "Pierre."

I've nearly given up telling stories about myself.

I don't advocate the self. I advocate the body, an envelope for practices and impulses: a switchboard.

The switchboard contains soul.

Sometimes I man my switchboard. Sometimes my various replacements man it. Sometimes no one mans it.

Sometimes New York City mans it.

Those are exciting moments, though they also resemble drowning.

A person is a style.

I'm waging war against the homogenization of styles.

Get your hands off my switchboard.

I shall now talk about my brother.

I have many brothers.

Five of them visited this morning. I took them shopping. We bought veal stew meat and eggs and Windex.

Keep your heart clean.

That is what I tell my five.

It is Xmas and time to buy gifts for my five.

This is a year for bookbuying. I want to support the independents.

For Brother #1, I will buy *Valley of the Dolls*.

For Brother #2, Jamaica Kincaid's *My Brother*.

For Brother #3, a wine encyclopedia.

For Brother #4, *Discipline and Punish*.

For Brother #5, *The Elements of Style*.

Where shall we dine for Xmas supper?

Downtown.

On the river.

Porridge for the first course, the second and the third.

I want to starve the brothers.

Let them read but do not let them eat.

When we were young we had a tinsel Xmas tree. It came folded in a box. We unfolded it and surrounded it with gifts. Red balls hung from the fake silvery branches. I am certain that it was a fire hazard. It glittered in the room, beside the Heidegger.

We almost ate the Heidegger.

The wind whips through my room. The wind has a mission. It wants to cleanse my thought.

The wind is rattling through my brain. Do you hear? It whistles in the rafters, near the murder mysteries. I bought them at a chain.

Give fifty dollars to Children's Aid.

Don't mention it.

This Xmas, figure out why I'm in love with the aesthetic of autism, the aesthetic of incommunicado.

I admire writing that doesn't communicate, or that communicates blockage.

At the kosher deli the sight of a fat man eating a triple-decker sandwich dissuaded me from ordering a side dish of chopped liver.

Today I have listed the impediments to embodiment.

I do not want to stop.

I enjoy suspense. Harmonic suspension in Wagner, Strauss and Chopin is a history of masochism.

Wagner keeps your body distant from completion, so you may have the pleasure of interminable waiting.

The divergence between the left and the right hands, in a Chopin *morceau,* is an agent of masochism. The right hand's melodic figuration moving separately from the pulsations of the left is a catalyst of masochistic experience in the listener.

The right hand lags behind.

You want it to speed up, but it can't.

The first time I experienced the masochistic oscillation, I was listening to "Siegfried's Idyll."

Wrong. The first time I experienced a pulsation I'd call masochistic, I was observing a cut on a local thumb. The thumb was mine, but also not mine. The wound was the most beautiful object in the kitchen. The wound came from a juice glass, near the medicine bottle. Either the glass had a rough, broken edge, or another, veiled object, in the vicinity, ripped my skin.

The room around the cut on the thumb was dulcet and nonverbal.

The kitchen of the cut was off the dark dining room.

The cut was a sign of greatness.

If I could only live up to the cut—if I could only equal it!

See Gaston Bachelard's *The Poetics of Space.*

My hands are cold from trills.

When I trill, my fingers grow numb.

This is a trill, from C to C-sharp.

It sounds like a razor. It sounds like Emily Dickinson's "firmament."

To warm my fingers, I will stop writing.

My neurosystems' disturbed minutiae are the logical consequence of a shattered worldview.

If I could name the worldview and the cause of its shattering, I would be the master of my style.

As matters stand, I am merely its personal shopper.

Sports

Vijay Seshadri

My Pirate Boyhood

In October 1960, the month the Pirates beat the Yankees in a World Series that ended with a legendary home run, my parents and I were living on Electric Street, in Ottawa. My father, after being awarded his American Ph.D., in physical chemistry, had returned to India to collect my mother and me and move us to Canada, where he took up a postdoctoral fellowship with that country's National Research Council. I have a tape of that last, and most famous, game of the 1960 Series, the first World Series that I have a memory of. The tape was given to me by a friend of mine at work after he heard me lamenting over the fate of the Jim Leyland Pittsburgh Pirates—a team that allegorized certain dementias of our era by winning three straight division titles in the early Nineties, only to fall short of the pennant each time, and then to see itself decimated by the economics of contemporary sports. I've played this tape many times over the last three years, rehearsing its rhythms and anticipating, with a tension that familiarity only intensifies, the famous home run—second baseman Bill Mazeroski's solo shot that opened and closed the Pirate ninth, beating the Yankees 10–9, still the only home run to decide a championship in the bottom of the ninth of the seventh game of a Series. My interest in this game has something to do with the satisfaction it provides: it must be one of the most spectacular baseball games ever played. But it has much more to do with the fact that this game marks a point in time when my life pivoted, when what I might have become began to be subsumed by what I became—half-alienated and half-assimilated, a hyphenated American and a Pirate fan.

My father maintains that he decided to leave India when he did because to do the kind of work he wanted to do he would have had to go to the North (we come from Bangalore, deep in the South, where the culture resembles the culture of North India as little as Italy's culture resembles Sweden's) and that he felt if he had to go north he might as well go all the way. I happen to know for a fact that my parents' desire to see me have a great academic career in science was crucial to their setting out on their long journey to another civilization, but I've never challenged this explanation my father gives for his motives. Not having had a great academic career in science—not having had a career in science at all—I'm naturally uncomfortable when I think about what they gave up. Bangalore must have been a hard place for my parents to go so far from when they did—not the megalopolis of today, where a lot of the world's computer software is being written, and where the newborn, capitalist, high-tech India chafes against the India whose problems seem intractable, but a gracious garden city, one of Asia's most beautiful. My parents were born into a community with deep roots in that region. They had only just stepped out of the old Indian world, the world that antedates the arrival of the British, and even of Islam, to the Subcontinent.

Considering how far they stepped, it's surprising how sure-footed they were. In the mythology of my family, those years in Ottawa are described as filled with possibility. My mother is the keeper of this myth. She was pregnant through much of that first year, giving birth to my sister just before the Kennedy Inauguration—an event greeted in Canada with the same hopefulness as elsewhere (including India, where you can still go into a sweet shop in an out-of-the-way village and find a framed photograph of the thirty-fifth American President hanging in a place of honor and garlanded with marigolds). The Inauguration, my sister's birth, her own strength and youth, and a new life in the New World have combined in my mother's memory to weave a powerful aura around those years. To this day, she will walk out of a room if anything bad is being said about the older members of the Kennedy clan.

The Kennedy years. Our Ottawa neighborhood was bounded on one side by my school, my fifty-cent barbershop, and the Parliament buildings near the river; and on the other by a little commercial strip with an I.G.A. and a fifty-cent movie theater. The people who lived around us were named Matherson, Campbell, Jones. Their religion was nonconformist and their game was ice hockey. I never took to the hockey, though I played a lot of it. I possessed a talent for the religion, though. My parents had the residual piety that characterizes even the most agnostic Indians of their generation, and a God-is-a-diamond-with-many-facets attitude toward doctrine. When the mother of a friend of mine asked if I could accompany him to Sunday school, they said yes, and I became a valued member of a Christian congregation. I might have been valued because I was seen as a heathen ripe for conversion, but I doubt it. Those people were generous and unintrusive and enlightened. They had a reticence and dignity appropriate to their climate and dispensation. I'm sure they liked me as much as they did because I was a loud and contented hymn-singer, and almost letter-perfect in learning the Bible stories. My favorite story was the one about Joseph, who was depicted in our Bible reader wearing his coat of many colors while his jealous brothers circled around him, getting ready to throw him into the pit. My favorite hymn was "O God Our Help in Ages Past," whose first stanza,

> O God our help in ages past,
> Our hope for years to come,
> Our shelter from the stormy blast,
> And our eternal home,

still calls up for me an image of stick-like, barely discernible human figures toiling over an immense, featureless landscape.

My parents' attitude toward Christianity was refreshingly nonsectarian: they also sent me to Mass occasionally with our next-door neighbors, a Québecois family that had moved to Electric Street about the same time we did, from Hull, on the Québec side of the Ottawa River. I squirmed through Mass, but the children of that family were my best friends, and they and their father were the ones who introduced me to the pagan worship of baseball. Of all the people I knew in those years, their father's is the only face I can recollect without an effort of memory. A decade and a half later, my mother, who keeps in touch with everyone she has ever been close to, told me that he had recently committed suicide, a piece of news that gave what I remembered of him a strong, graphic, permanent clarity.

His face was long, saturnine, and classically Gallic-looking, with bushy, emphatic eyebrows and a heavy forehead, which contributed to the image I have of him as always scowling, even when he smiled. I was never afraid of him—he was extremely kind to us children—but he clearly had an uncontrollable nature. He coached a pee-wee baseball-league team that I played on with two of his sons, and drilled us mercilessly. Long after we were expected home for dinner, he had us out on the field chasing fungoes or learning to slide away from the bag. He gave elaborate lectures about baseball history, and about the game's finer points: the position and function of the cut-off man, the proper procedure for a run-down, when to bunt and when to swing away. And he was competitive to the point of instability. During a game in the spring of 1961, while disputing a call at second base, he abused the umpire with such sclerotic profanity that our team was not only made to forfeit the game but was kicked out of the league entirely.

I don't know whether his being a Québecois among British-Canadians contributed to his volatility, but his family was set apart from the social life around them. His children didn't go to public school with the rest of us, but to a parochial school nearby. Other than myself, their playmates were exclusively

French-speaking kids from beyond our street—kids who were perceived, unfairly but inevitably, as tougher and more unruly and less hygienic than the rest of us. In October 1960, I spent a lot of time in their back yard, playing catch with my first mitt and shinnying up the smaller of their two maple trees. It was there that I first heard about a city called New York, the mighty Yankees who lived there, and the great contest then taking place to the south. The whole family were Pirate fans. Their father listened to the games in the afternoon and told us the results around dinnertime. And when the Yankees were brought to ruin at the hands of their improbable opponents, he had us rake up the fallen maple leaves in a pile, which he lighted to make a bonfire so that we could dance around it in joy and vindication.

The next August we moved to Columbus, Ohio, where my father joined Ohio State's chemistry department. When asked where I come from these days by people who expect to hear the name of a place in India, I say I come from Ohio and go on to describe my classic Ohio boyhood—tree-fort building, crawdad-hunting, fishing for bluegills with dough balls—and the streams and woods and railroad tracks near where we lived.

Actually, my Ohio boyhood was classic only in its over-all unhappiness. Disastrously for my athletic and social development, I had exhibited while in Canada a degree of intellectual precocity and had been skipped two grades. This led to my being forced to play with kids who were larger and more coördinated than I was, and I became one of those forlorn, bench-warming children who are a source of pity and terror to their peers. Baseball was the worst, because I always had dreams of baseball glory. (Well into my twenties, in fact, I would fantasize miraculous trains of circumstance that led me to the pitcher's mound in a big-league game.) When I got to bat, it was usually because I was small, and could be relied on to draw a walk; when I was sent out to field, it was usually way out, to left or right.

There were more complicated problems, too. Small, brown, bespectacled, alien, and saddled with a name that others thought was unpronounceable, I was an easy target for the casual cruelties of childhood. It was on a baseball diamond during a game at the lunch recess in the spring of 1964 that I was informed, by a kid half again my size, that I was, if I remember his words correctly (and I do), "nothing but a nigger." (About a year later, this same kid did me another injury. While fooling around on the railroad tracks near our house, I fell and gashed my leg to the bone on a spike protruding from a railroad tie. Coming across me as I hobbled home, he half-carried me the rest of the way, robbing me of the satisfaction of my contempt for him and prematurely introducing me to the hopeless complexities of experience.)

I didn't respond well to the social pressures I was encountering. I began to do badly in school, which was upsetting, to say the least, to my father. I became delinquent and secretive. The sport I excelled in was pyromania. One day, while playing with candles and Ohio Blue Tip matches—which I liked because you could light them on the seat of your jeans, the zipper of your fly, even your teeth—I accidentally set my bed on fire. Firecrackers were illegal in Ohio, but I used my paper-route money to buy them from Ohio State students who smuggled them in from Kentucky and carried on a brisk contraband business. The ones I liked best were the big ones—the cherry bombs and, best of all, the M-80s. My soul still thrills horribly when I see an M-80, with the evil little fuse sticking out of its side. I threw them like depth charges into unpeopled swimming pools and on the weekends staged elaborate, solitary pyrotechnics at the vacant construction sites near where we lived. When I was ten, after weeks of pleading, I persuaded my mother—a soft touch when it comes to her children—to buy me a BB gun. My father made her take it back the next day. I mourned that gun for years, and it was a long time before I recognized how shocking it must have been for my father, who grew up in an intellectual climate imbued by the presence of Gandhi, to come home and see his son cradling a not-lethal but nevertheless dangerous replica of a Winchester repeating rifle.

Apart from interdiction and incarceration, my parents—disciplined, hardworking exemplars of immigrant virtue—didn't

know what to do with me. Life had become more complicated
for them, too. It is somewhere in these years of the mid-Sixties
that I date the beginning of my mother's long return to the
religion of her people. My father was wrapped up in his work.
He wasn't neglectful—he would regularly descend from his nim-
bus of equations and try to guide my education. My tastes in
reading (this was when I was nine and ten and eleven) ran to
Hardy Boys mysteries, sports biographies of people like Red
Grange, and a book that I can't recall the title of but that I read
again and again, which told the story of a girl and a boy who had
various adventures on a tropical island and who eventually grew
up to become Queen Liliuokalani, the last native ruler of Hawaii,
and her prince-consort. My father would try to tempt me with
more edifying material, chiefly the American naturalist fiction
that he had read when in college—*The Grapes of Wrath, Studs
Lonigan,* Dreiser's Frank Cowperwood trilogy. Mostly, though,
he preached the gospel of science to me, telling me stories that
revealed the human side of figures like Einstein and Fermi, and
describing the careers of renowned twentieth-century Indian
mathematicians and physicists such as Ramanujan, Bose, and
C. V. Raman.

In those years before the immigration act of 1965 abolished
the rigid quotas imposed on Asian immigration, there were
hardly any other Indians around. Dressed in her sari, with her
bangles and with the bindhi that signified her married status
placed carefully on her forehead, my mother could be spotted a
mile off. These days the smell of Indian spices—of cardamon,
asafetida, fenugreek, black mustard seed, and turmeric—makes
me ecstatic with expectation. In those days these same smells,
emanating from our kitchen and wafting through the corridor of
our apartment building, made me wince with an immediate, intimate, olfactory awareness of how different we were. At a parents'
day at Crestview Junior High School, I pretended not to notice
my mother when she came to look in on one of my classes—an
act for which she has never forgiven me, which she still holds up
to me as an example of my ingratitude.

❖　❖　❖

Columbus was (and still is) a football town. But it also had a Triple A farm club, the Jets, at that time a part of the Pirate farm system. It was understood that we orbited the Pirate sun, and in the summer of 1967, when we were preparing to leave Columbus and move to Pittsburgh itself—my father was advancing professionally, which seemed to involve an ongoing nomadism—my Pirate boyhood began in earnest. By this time, my isolation had become as much a state of mind as a social fact. I had two friends, classmates of mine, but I was twelve and they were fourteen. The gap between a slightly chubby, indistinct, prepubescent twelve-year-old boy and a teenager of fourteen is enormous. I still had a fetish about my firecrackers, while my friends had moved on to *Playboy* centerfolds and shoplifting. They performed, or claimed they performed, secret acts with the girls of their acquaintance. I tried to keep up, but the hormones just weren't there yet, so I resigned myself to circling our neighborhood endlessly on my bike and spending hours learning how to do a back flip, a full gainer, and a half gainer from the diving board of the public pool a block away.

The strongest memories I have of that last summer in Columbus center on the passionate identification I developed with the Pirates' great rightfielder, Roberto Clemente. Clemente was flirting with a .400 average through the first half of the 1967 season, and getting the kind of national attention that he always craved. I watched him on TV whenever I could, and he was the first performer from whom I derived a satisfaction I would call aesthetic. He was a compact, elegant, laconic presence on the diamond, spare and geometric, with a sprinter's legs. His fielding and throwing were legendary—even then he was recognized as one of the very best ever at his position. Among his peers, only Willie Mays, from whom he had picked up the famous basket catch when the two of them played winter ball in 1954 for Puerto Rico's Santurce club, possessed a comparable grace and aplomb in the field. He didn't have the marvelous Mays liquidity—everything about Clemente was angular and emphatic—but as with Mays, his movements left you with the impression that he lived outside his body and commanded it effortlessly from a great distance. He was a bad-ball hitter—about as far as you could get, in the realms of greatness, from a student of the art like Ted Williams or a street-smart opportunist like Pete Rose—and a fierce, feral protector of the plate. With two strikes on him, he could foul off ball after ball, driving the pitcher crazy, until he got a pitch he could work with.

I used to follow the fluctuations of his batting average with an arithmetic intensity. Not content with the meagre statistics that the paper provided, I built my own landscape of numbers around him, topographically dense and various, with interesting declivities and elevations. I waited every day for the afternoon paper, the *Dispatch*, to arrive. When I got my hands on the sports pages, I took them to the table in our dining alcove, where I had pencil and paper ready. I divided his at-bats into his hits myself and calculated his average out to six digits. Then I determined what his average would be if he went five-for-five the next game, or three-for-four, or three-for-three. I'd do this five, sometimes even ten, games into the future. I projected almost inhuman final averages for him—Rogers Hornsby's modern-day record of .424, for example—and then calculated backward, on the basis of four at-bats a game, the number of times he had to hit safely in the remaining games to reach it. If my sister disturbed me in the middle of my insane projects, I pounced on her with a fury.

This numbers mania subsided after a while, but my identification with Clemente went on deepening. I had to turn off the radio or the TV if he struck out. His successes transported me. I was at once shocked and satisfied when, in a game that August, he lined a drive back to the pitcher's mound and broke the leg of the awesome Cardinal right-hander Bob Gibson. (Through the rest of Gibson's career, I felt toward him the solicitude we reserve for people whom we've injured without meaning to.) The game that has pleased me the most in my years of following baseball was one between the Pirates and Cincinnati, a game that the Reds won 8–7. Clemente batted in all seven Pittsburgh runs, going five-for-five, with a triple and two home runs. I thought that this effort was incredibly poignant in its doomed and solitary heroism.

The only thing I relished about our move to Pittsburgh, which otherwise did not make me happy, was the fact that now I was in the Pirate home world. For the next three years, until I went to college in 1970, I was familiar with pretty much every game they played. I didn't get to the ballpark often. My father couldn't tolerate more than four or five excursions a season, and I couldn't rely on friends because all through high school I refused to make friends. I was fed up with my parents' wanderings and sick of my ambiguous social status, and had decided to go it alone. So through those springs and sweltering summers, when the country was experiencing race riots, assassinations, and the divisions arising from the war in Vietnam, I could be found either in our basement, watching the one or two games that were broadcast weekly on TV, or lying on the floor in our living room, next to our Grundig radio, listening to the play-by-play relayed by Bob (the Gunner) Prince, the gravelly voice of the Pirates, and his sidekick Nellie King.

Clemente had an arthritic back—the result of a car accident in the fifties and the source of the physical frailty that became one of the causes of bad feeling between him and the baseball world—and after each pitch he would step out of the batter's box and whip his neck to the side, as if trying to realign his vertebrae. Though he could hit home runs, he was known for line drives, high averages, and two-hundred-hit seasons. This was upsetting to him, I believe, and to me as well. I used to curse Forbes Field, that beautiful, vanished old park, where the game was played the way it should be, because its spaciousness had forced him to relinquish power for the sake of average, and to resist the temptation to swing for the distant fences. I also felt that his teammates let him down, although they were all fantastic ballplayers. Some of them—Willie Stargell, Matty Alou, Mazeroski—were stars in their own right, but nothing they could do was enough for me. I felt a general animus toward the Pittsburgh pitching staff, and a particular one toward Bob Veale, the gifted but wild Pirate fastballer, because he didn't have the control to be the stopper the Pirates needed. Clemente deserved better; he deserved Gibson or Ferguson Jenkins or Denny McLain.

I found his character as compelling as his play. Much of what I remember about him has been interwoven over the years with the things I have read or heard. But the aura he projected was unmistakable even then, and even to my relatively uninformed adolescent faculties. Moody, sensitive, forbidding, his coal-black, faintly Aztec features usually scowling, he walked the earth feeling aggrieved and misunderstood. He had volatile relations with his managers, and his relations with journalists were bad until his very last years. I remember clearly that he was vocal about the effects of racism on his career—and vocal at a time when there were far fewer blacks in the major leagues than there are now, and when the reserve clause gave management enormous power over players. I found out later, when I read Phil Musick's biography, that he was convinced he had finished so low in the balloting for the 1960 M.V.P. trophy because of the color of his skin, and so refused to wear the 1960 World Series ring. He had a running war with the press over the physical ailments that regularly kept him out of games. The local press was unsympathetic, and he would make matters worse by his response to their provocations. When the broadcaster Dick Stockton suggested that he wasn't a team player, Clemente threatened to kill him if he came into the clubhouse. He had an inimitable way of giving ammunition to his detractors. Asked once how he was feeling before a game, he replied, "My bad shoulder is good, but my good shoulder is bad"—this in that thick Puerto Rican accent of his, which people were not above making fun of in those days, and which always gave me a pained sense of his vulnerability when I heard it in a postgame interview after he'd done something marvelous on the field. I interpreted him in a way that harmonized with my own social isolation, nursing a bitter private grief for him, and projecting onto him not only my dreams of glory but the feelings I had about my complicated social circumstances. I remember reading a story which left me with the impression that his social circle didn't extend

any farther than the other Hispanics in baseball—Orlando
Cepeda, the Alou brothers, Juan Marichal—and I was indignant.

My Pirate boyhood ended with Clemente's death, in 1972,
in a plane crash off Puerto Rico while he was helping ferry sup-
plies to victims of that year's earthquake in Nicaragua. By that
time, other obsessions had come to join, and largely replace,
baseball. I was eighteen, a junior in college, and deeply into the
counterculture. I had all sorts of revisionist explanations of experience, some of which I applied to his abrupt departure from the
world. Though I mourned him when he died, I didn't share the
widespread opinion that his death was heroic. I thought it was
unnecessary, even absurd. I suspected compensatory impulses at
work in his disastrous humanitarian gesture, impulses that I
ascribed to his social awkwardness. I now saw vanity as a driving
force in his character (he was vain, but no more so than other
players at his level of achievement). He had had a splendid
World Series against the Orioles in 1971, finally becoming famous in the way Mays and Hank Aaron and Frank Robinson
were, and I imagined that this grand justification of his talent had
led him to commit an act of hubris, with attendant consequences. He had come to see himself not just as a baseball hero
but as someone with a mission to the world.

All this was unfair to him—he'd grown up poor and wanted
to give something back; it was as simple as that—but I'd been
robbed of maybe two or three more .300 seasons and four or five
hundred more hits. It took quite a while for me to recognize how
perfect he had been for my peculiar, Indian adolescent romance
of hero-worship—complex, human, uncomfortable in the world
he lived in but nevertheless astonishing and unequaled—and
how much I had got from him. Recently I saw in the news that
they were demolishing an old skyscraper in Pittsburgh to make
way for urban redevelopment—a skyscraper that had a gigantic
mural of Clemente, along with other greats of Pittsburgh sports,
on one side. On TV, the building was there, with the mural
visible, and then it imploded in a column of dust that itself collapsed and spread out into the surrounding streets.

There's another gigantic mural of Clemente on a wall of a housing project at the edge of Harlem which is named after him. You can see it from the West Side I.R.T. local after it emerges briefly from its tunnel and runs on elevated tracks between the 116th and 137th Street stations. There he is, the Pride of Puerto Rico, with his bat cocked, facing the city. When I find myself on that subway line, I sometimes stand up in the car near the 125th Street station and look at him as long as I can.

Gerald Early

Ali, the Wonder Boy

1.

Such latter-day disfigurements leave out
All mention of those older scars that merge
On any riddled surfaces about.
—Weldon Kees, "A Good Chord on a Bad Piano"

Muhammad Ali, as a result of his touching, or poignant, or pathetic, or tragic (take your pick) appearance at the torch-lighting ceremony at the 1996 Olympics Games in Atlanta, has become, for new generations that did not grow up with him and for the older generations that did, the Great American Martyr, our new Lincoln, our new Martin Luther King. Our Father Abraham. Our Father Martin. Our Father Muhammad: the man whose hands, once unerring pistons of punishment in the prize ring, tremble from boxing-induced Parkinson's disease: the man whose voice is such a slurred whisper that he, who was once called the Louisville Lip because he loved talking so much, does not like to speak in public and rarely does: the once-uncompromising black nationalist now reduced, like Orson Welles at the end, to performing magic tricks for the crowd as if he were parodying his own pop-culture greatness, exposing it as an illusion, just as his nationalism had been, just as his cultist/ religious self had been. Everything in popular culture throbs with impermanence, its significance threatened by the triteness it cannot hide, by the banality it bloats into eminence through a personality that blends the public and the private. And no one embodied American popular culture, its excesses, its barbarities, and its disarming densities, more than Muhammad Ali.

The public rarely responds to the demise of a great popular performer with anything approaching good sense or objectivity, and almost certainly with nothing approaching gracious humor, something that, in this case, the subject himself seems to be trying to instruct us in how to achieve. This is even less likely to happen when the figure in question is a black man, a cunning archetype who is already so burdened by the baggage of both sentimentality and taboo as to be likely to be virtually a walking expression of the culture's irrationality, as he would be even if his old age had been a bit less marked by illness.

To be sure, Ali has been a lightning rod for the culture's irrationality all his life, sometimes provoking it purposely, sometimes being a veritable representation of it himself. This was, after all, the man who not only brilliantly playacted a combination panic attack/nervous breakdown at the weigh-in of his first championship fight with the dreaded Sonny Liston in 1964: served as the redoubtable black trickster to Howard Cosell's liberal Jewish straight man: had a highly publicized religious conversion to a strange, if influential, cult that disliked whites but wanted to be a perfect imitation of them, aggrandizing its importance while humanizing its stark doctrine; and who said that no Vietcong ever called him "nigger." He also believed for some several years that a mad scientist named Yacub invented white people by grafting them from blacks, that satellites from Allah circled the earth and would imminently destroy the United States, and that blacks who dated or married whites should be killed. Like any true believer, Ali's truth was mixed with a great deal of nonsense. Unlike most religious believers, he was not converted by revelation but convinced by polemics.

*   *   *

Now the public, because of Ali's illness, wants to drown him in sainthood and atone for its guilt. This is principally true of whites, who spend a good deal of their time, when they think about race (and to think about Ali is to think about race because Ali made it a prominent subject in his public rantings and sermons—so successfully that he, in fact, managed to make over his most inner-city-like black opponents, the blackest of the black, into white men), either denying that it is a problem they caused or confessing that they have committed such atrocities against blacks that only the most abject deference toward them now can make up for it all. For a black person to experience this is to be caught between benign neglect and affirmative action, between tough love and a comforting paternalism, between the amputation of virulent racism and the gangrene of liberal racism. Ali, our racial alpha and omega, the object of absolute scorn and absolute pity.

This white guilt arises largely from Ali's position against the Vietnam War, a war we have come to see as at best misguided and at worst evil, and his subsequent three-and-one-half-year exile from boxing; that somehow, we, the American public, or the white American public (as blacks see themselves as playing no part in the rather capricious application of the Selective Service Act that abused him), are the cause of his current affliction. And we did this to him because he became a Black Muslim and spoke out frankly against racism and white double-dealing, something no black athletic hero had ever done before (or since, really). He was severely maimed by and for our racial sins, our racist use of the system against him.

Thus it seems no accident at all that Muhammad Ali should be reawakened in the public's mind, largely as the subject of the Academy Award–winning documentary *When We Were Kings*, along with the celebration of Jackie Robinson in 1997, the fiftieth anniversary of his breaking the color line in Major League baseball with the Brooklyn Dodgers. Yoked together in the public's consciousness this year were, arguably, the two most influential American athletes of the twentieth century, the American century, the first and maybe not the last, hallowed nearly as handsome, transcendent, boyish American angels hovering over our leveled playing fields of dreams, sacrifices on the altar of our hypocritical democracy, emblems of the double V, the victory on two fronts, the real world of social relations and the fantasy world of athletics; the noble black American male as inventor of an heretical Americanism, demonstrating what\it cost a black to have democratic ideals and to force whites to live up to them. Ironically, Robinson did this by insisting he was an American and Ali by insisting he was victimized because he was never considered an American, but both paid the price. What do we remember most about Robinson but that he suffered, he endured insults and provocation, that he died at fifty-two, prematurely aged, we feel, from the abuse he took as a player in order to integrate the Great American Game?

It is no slight schizophrenia that troubles us when in today's society young black men are so often represented in popular culture as buffoonish thugs or coon-like clowns, and in our collective imagination as real, certifiable thugs and rapists. When the police mistreat a black man like Rodney King or when a sports hero like O. J. Simpson falls from grace people hardly know whether to be outraged or relieved. Yet when it comes to Jackie Robinson and Muhammad Ali these days, the public, especially whites, nearly weeps. James Baldwin was right: that a certain type of black male figure of social protest elicits this contradiction, of blunting the very effects that his social protest was meant to induce. The white response to Ali and Robinson may be a reflection of racism but it seems more profoundly to be a sign of some organic confusion, a mythic yet turbulently defective pietism at the very heart of our perception of ourselves. We cannot see in the way Captain Delano, in Melville's *Benito Cereno,* could not see, in all our tragic innocence.

Muhammad Ali, in truth, does not make a very good martyr, as Wilfrid Sheed once observed, or cannot quite be taken seriously as one. Doubtless, as Sheed has pointed out, Ali had a martyr's complex, which is why he became a member of the

Nation of Islam, not because he felt the slings and arrows of outrageous racism (Ali had an indulged life, from boyhood on) but because he wanted "to [take] on the scars of his brothers." For a man with as great a sense of public mission and public consciousness as Ali had, an act of such solidarity with the most bitter blacks on the bottom was a theatrical and vividly condensed bit of risk-taking. What Ali had, in this regard, is exactly what Malcolm X claimed to have near the end of his life, not truth, not vision, not wisdom, but sincerity.

This counts for a great deal in an age of relativism and cynicism, in an age when we have given ourselves over to the adolescent's version of reality, instead of the Hemingwayesque version: one's measure of authenticity was not how one lived one's life in the face of what made it impossible but how deeply one felt about something. Intensity of feeling equaled real experience. Ali always had a portion of something Hemingwayesque but he had more than a bit of sheer adolescent emotionalism. His reasons for not wanting to join the army were never terribly convincing but they had a potency because he was so sincere, movingly and petulantly so. He had the strength of a simplistic, unreal orthodoxy for which he seemed prepared to die in an age when the simplistic, unreal orthodoxy that held this country together was beginning to unravel, violently and quickly.

But Ali cannot be taken seriously as a martyr because: first, athletes such as Jackie Robinson, Joe Louis, Ted Williams, Bob Feller, Hank Greenberg, Christy Mathewson, and others lost several years of their athletic prime serving in the armed forces during World War I, World War II, or the Korean War. No one seems to think this was tragic. Granted, we have a different view of those wars but Ali did not pay anything more for his dissent, in relation to his career as an athlete (as a citizen, he paid more than he should), than other star athletes in the past have paid for not dissenting. Plus, he had the luxury of not being in danger in combat, although he was always open to the crazed assassin's bullet.

And Ali never went to prison for his pacifist beliefs, like his leader Elijah Muhammad, or like Bayard Rustin. He wasn't

killed for his beliefs like his one-time mentor Malcolm X or his
admirer Martin Luther King. For instance, when Ali appeared at
Randolph-Macon College for Men in Virginia on April 17, 1969,
to give a speech, one of 168 campuses he was planning to visit
that year in order to raise funds for his defense against the draft,
although there was some considerable outcry from the alumni
and the locals about his visit, there was virtually no protest when
he arrived on campus. He gave his speech, largely a kind of rote
Nation-of-Islam homage to Elijah Muhammad, answered questions at some length, rather tactlessly asked the dean of men for
his check when he was through, and, despite being worn out, was
talked into appearing at an inner-city school in the vicinity. According to the account given in *The Catholic World,*

> The content of the speech itself was standard Black
> Muslim rhetoric, but the presentation was pure Cassius
> Clay entertainment. . . . Perhaps one might, in fact,
> criticize Ali for making his address so entertaining and
> amusing that the seriousness of his subject was some-
> what obscured.

It was this quality of Ali's, his ability to attach a certain humor
and thus a profoundly human face, as well as a kind of pop-
culture sheen, to black anger and indignation, that, I think, saved
his life. Much as the Marxist or deconstructionist critic reveals
the workings of ideology in ordinary words and actions, so did Ali
unmask the racism behind the complacency of white Americans.
But he seemed more amused by his discovery than belligerent,
more deeply struck by its wondrous expression of a benighted
humanity than outraged by its expressions of unjustified power
and dominance. This is the full dimension of the simplistic
sincerity that protected him rather like an amulet or a juju.

So, in fact, after his exile, he went on to make an astonishing amount of money, to star in a movie of his life, and to become one of the most famous people, and surely the most
famous Muslim, in the world. By the mid-1970s, after redeeming
himself and regaining the title by defeating the fearsome, sullen

George Foreman, Ali had become such an accepted figure in the American mainstream that DC Comics put out a special edition of *Superman* where "that draft dodger," as he had been called in the 1960s, beat the Man of Steel, the Great White American Hero, in a prizefight to save humanity from an alien invasion. Martyrdom, where is thy sting? No black man, except Martin Luther King, ever imposed his *Weltanschauung,* such as it was, with such romantic and compelling force.

Second, there is no indication that Ali would have left boxing sooner, would not have suffered the brain damage he did or anything of the kind, if he had not been exiled, very unfairly, from boxing between the ages of twenty-five and twenty-eight. It is a rare boxer, especially one as good as Ali and as eager for and as needy of public attention, who quits before he is literally beaten into retirement. What Ali had was an irresistible combination of talent, showmanship, a vast conceit that bordered on both the heroic and the insufferable. He not only believed in God, but, to paraphrase the lyric from the musical *Hair,* he believed that God believed in him. Though Ali makes a poor saint, he makes a very good fallen prince, which is exactly what he is: the weary, enigmatic sovereign of our time, of our realm, of our racialized imagination.

What unnerves us now about Ali and brings out the insipidness of victimology is that he has wound up like an old, broken-down prizefighter. The guilt we feel is that we used him as a commodity and that he used us to create great dramas of his fights, dragon-slaying heroics, extraordinary crises of our social order. It mattered greatly whether he won or lost and we are guilty about having been conned into believing a prizefight means much of anything in this world, guilty about what our being conned did to the confidence man. But Ali, far from being a victim, is perhaps one of the most remarkable examples of triumph over racism in our century. It is not surprising that so many white people hated him; it is surprising that before his career ended a good many had come to love him.

Ali has been compared to a number of famous people, from

Oscar Wilde to Jack Johnson, from Elvis Presley to Jay Gatsby. I think he bears no small resemblance to our two finest jazz musicians, Louis Armstrong and Duke Ellington, and perhaps his genius might be best understood in relation to theirs. Like both of them, Ali was a Southerner. Like Ellington, he came from the border South and so did not experience the most brutal sort of racism, but like Armstrong he came from a mythic Southern place, Kentucky, with its thoroughbreds, its bluegrass, its mint juleps, its colonels, so he experienced a deeply self-conscious white South, which may explain why he felt the oppression of racism so deeply without having had to endure a great deal of it. Being a Southerner, I think, explains his showmanship. Like Armstrong, Ali was essentially a comic. This is why, although he was deeply hated by many whites at one point in his career, he was able to come back. He rarely said anything without a certain kind of mocking quality, and his rage, like his incessant bragging and egoism, was often that of the teenager. Ali offered the public the contradictory pleasure of having to take him seriously while not having to take him seriously. He was deeply aware of this himself and played a game of public relations deceit as cleverly as anyone else.

In retrospect, Ali struck intense chords of ambiguity as a black public figure, though somewhat different ones, just as Armstrong did. Joe Louis might have seemed an Uncle Tom to many compared to Ali but Ali laughed and smiled more in public in a week than Louis did in his entire life. Ali actually seemed to like white people (which he did; he liked everyone); whereas Louis never seemed comfortable around them and never much appeared to like them. He simply contained himself in their presence. How was it that a black man could openly show how much he enjoyed white people and yet not be branded an Uncle Tom by his own people? What Ali did with sheer brilliance was to make himself the center of laughter but never the object of it. He controlled what his audiences laughed at when he made himself a source of humor.

Ali's laughter was meant to signify something different from Armstrong's, not exactly an expression of deference to his audience (although Ali certainly wanted to please his audiences, even as he may have exasperated them) but rather an expression of boyish joy in his own freedom and strength, a casual astonishment at the refulgence of his own extraordinary gifts, which seemed to strike him simultaneously as both miraculous and absurd.

Like Ellington, Ali had a certain charm and elegance, both in and out of the ring, a need to baby himself and to womanize. Both men were highly photogenic. Like Ellington, Ali loved to hear himself talk, and he loved having people around him, not because they were the best possible people at what they did, but because they did one or two things that amused or intrigued or that he admired and felt he could use, much as Ellington saw his musicians, some of whom were not the best possible players Ellington could have had on those instruments. They did well something Ellington had a great need of for his orchestra, and Ali lived his life largely as if he were conducting a very large orchestra.

Ali did this for his opponents, too. He brought out the best of what they had. He was enormously generous and this touches us deeply. Ali, like Armstrong and Ellington, had magnetism, inventiveness, a heroism that did not evade using the devices of the trickster of black folklore or those of the minstrel black of the nineteenth-century American stage. But he embodied both images as the antithesis as well as the fulfillment of himself, not as a person but as his own individualized archetype. That is why Ali is loved so much today. Like all great heroes he showed us the enormous possibility of true self-determination.

2 .

And is this then (said I) what the
   author calls a man's life? . . .
Only a few hints, a few diffused
   faint clews and indirections. . . .
   —Walt Whitman, "When I Read the Book"

Muhammad Ali could barely read. Yet his was the religion of the book. Not only the Koran but Elijah Muhammad's *Message to the Blackman in America.* (He was a fervent advocate of the book *One Hundred Years of Lynching,* a popular book among certain knowing coves in the black community, as I remember from my boyhood, used to convince those who were casual or apathetic about the Unspeakable Negro Massacres that they had better get with the truth and quit having the white man brainwash them with the white Jesus and movies like *King Solomon's Mines.*) What fascinated Ali, like many of the poorly educated, was the authority of books or their failure as authority. When I met Ali a few years ago, he went on at some length about the contradictions in the Bible. As a devout Muslim, he seemed greatly pleased by this: he must have felt he was deflating the power of that text. I told him that as a Christian I hardly expected the Bible to be anything more than a messy and messed-up book. "Now, you see how tough it is to be a Christian," I said. He smiled at that.

Ali scored a 78 on the army intelligence tests, indicating that he had a low IQ. He was, at first, declared mentally unfit to serve in the army. "I have said I am the greatest," Ali said in 1964, "ain't nobody ever heard me say I was the smartest." A man of his wit and quickness could not be that dumb, we protest. Yet I think the score was an honest reflection of Ali's mental abilities. Ali was not literate, nor was he analytical. When he was younger he could successfully debate people who were much smarter because he had the zealot's set of answers to life's questions. His mind worked through formulas and clichés. His personality gave them a life and vibrancy that they would otherwise have lacked. He was intuitive, glib, richly gregarious, and intensely creative, like an artist. He would have scored better on the test had he been better educated but still he would never have had a score that reflected the range of his curiosity or his humanity. But it is perhaps no surprise for a man so taken by the authority of the book that he would be so attractive to people who wrote books for a living or that a book itself may possess some small authority in telling us about him.

The first piece of sportswriting that ever struck me, and that I still remember vividly, was Red Smith's November 16, 1966, account of Ali's fight against Cleveland "Big Cat" Williams, a fight Ali won in three rounds. I am not quite sure why I was so impressed by this article; to Smith I am sure it was probably just another fight assignment, except that the exuberance of Ali seemed to have affected the writer in such a way as to make the reading a deeper experience than it had any right to be. It was this piece of writing, not actually watching the fight on television, that convinced me that Ali was truly a great fighter, a once-in-a-lifetime performer. I was a freshman at Penn when I read Norman Mailer's "Ego," about the first Ali–Frazier fight, in *Life* magazine. The sheer propulsion of the prose, the relentless brinkmanship of the rhetoric, the dizzying intellectual mixology of history, sociology, and journalism in the cocktail of Mailer's own omnipresent ego nearly took the top of my head off and, oddly, made it possible for me to write a paper on Spenser's *The Fairie Queene,* on something called "the psychological body," a straight steal from Mailer. I realized even then, as a teenager, that there was something special about much of the writing about Ali, as if a writer were thinking that he or she might be writing for both the ages and for the disposable present for there was something so indispensable and so perishable about the subject.

It is amazing that Ali has managed to fascinate so many first-rate writers for so long, nearly forty years. "When he isn't performing," Wilfrid Sheed wrote, "he is not so much dull as non-existent. There is an awesome blankness about him." And perhaps it is this blankness that has attracted writers, a need, with such a fabulously burnished surface, to create or fill in a depth that can, simultaneously, never be reached while being easily filled. After all, Ali was not a particularly difficult person to understand because what he may have been hiding was probably no more complex or real than anything he chose to reveal at any given moment, although, on the other hand, he may have been very difficult to penetrate because, for so public a man, he did choose to hide something, did serve as his own most effective psychic gatekeeper. Hunter Thompson spoke, melodramatically and self-mockingly, of having to pass nine moats to get to the real Ali. Budd Schulberg spoke of Ali's Chinese boxes. Mailer called him the psychology of the body. Larry Neal called him "body bebop" who "understands the mysteries of the circles and the squares." Garry Wills thought of him as having the awesome vacuity of utterly self-absorbed celebrity. Choose whatever metaphor of inscrutability you wish!

All of this, one supposes, represents the writer's challenge: to explain a man who perhaps did not deserve so much explanation but who seemed to serve a need in writers to explain. Great writers may have been challenged because they wanted to find the angle on the subject that other great writers hadn't found in a figure who was known to everyone. Writing about anyone in popular culture becomes, for any good writer, the quest for the holy grail, a mission to supply texture where it has been washed clean by cliché and obliterated by too many tramping feet. Besides, it was fun to write about Ali, largely because it made two otherwise dreary, ponderous subjects—race and boxing—seem irreverent and comic, lively and vital, while still giving the writer a sense that writing about them granted him access to some esoteric knowledge of the grimmer side of life.

To write about someone whose like is not to be seen again in our lifetime has brought out an urgent brilliance in some of the writers who have tackled Ali as a subject. We might classify the writers who wrote most notably about Ali in this way: the professional sportswriters such as Smith, Lipsyte, Mark Kram, John Schulian, Pat Putnam, and Pete Axthelm who did straight reporting and character studies; the highbrow journalist/chroniclers like George Plimpton, A. J. Liebling, and Norman Mailer who did longer literary and sociological analyses and were the self-conscious reincarnations of Paul Gallico, Pierce Egan, and William Hazlitt, respectively; the other intellectual boxing aficionados like Budd Schulberg and Joyce Carol Oates who resemble the highbrow journalist/chroniclers except they don't pretend to be Boswell to Ali's Johnson. We also find the boxer/intellectual like Jose Torres, who has the authority of the insider; the fan-as-disciple like Davis Miller, who reminds us that any celebrity can become a religious cult because any celebrity is, in the end, not like you and me; and black intellectuals like Ishmael Reed and Amiri Baraka, although, in the end, one is surprised that so few black intellectuals wrote about Ali, and fewer still wrote about him memorably, although dutiful homage was paid to him by black writers as disparate as Harry Edwards, Nikki Giovanni, Quincy Troupe, and Samuel Yette. No black writer of note who wrote about him, except Gordon Parks, tried to get to know Ali in the way many of the white writers who wrote about him did or tried to.

There is a reason for this that is related to how hero worship of a black subject is a somewhat different exercise, depending on where you are along the fault lines of race. Put another way: Charlie Parker and Jimi Hendrix became white heroes as did Ali, but what made any of these men heroes for whites was not quite what made them heroes for blacks. Still the fact that they were heroes for whites added a complex dimension to the meaning of their heroism for blacks, and therein lies the tale. For blacks, Ali represented determination, pride, defiance, religious commitment, excellence, physical beauty; all of which became synonymous with being black. For whites, Ali may have represented these qualities as well but they were all quite apart from his blackness, which, whether seen as prosaic or mysterious, as an essence or an artifice, as a social condition or a state of mind, was something that had to be plumbed for its own sake. Also, Ali was an athlete, and blacks feel a great deal more uneasy than whites about the meaning of athletic heroics and race politics. For more than a few black folk hate connecting black achievement to athletics.

3 .

But you, a new brood, native,
    athletic, continental, greater
    than before known,
Arouse! for you must justify me.
    —Walt Whitman, "Poets to Come"

If you told me I could go back in my life and start over healthy
and that with boxing this would happen—stay Cassius Clay and it
wouldn't—I'd take this route. It was worth it.
    —Muhammad Ali on his Parkinson's illness, 1988

"I'm just a typical American boy from a typical American town,"
folk singer Phil Ochs sang in his "Draft Dodger Rag," and perhaps I was or thought I was, once. The summer of my fourteenth
year was the last that I played baseball regularly. It was that
spring that a Jewish friend gave me Bernard Malamud's novel
The Natural to read. I am not sure why he gave it to me because
he did not care much for baseball. I didn't think that he cared
much for novel reading either. But he liked *The Natural* a lot. I
guess he just liked the story. He thought it was funny and said a
lot about losing and life. I so loved the novel that I wanted to
make a bat like the Roy Hobbs's Wonderboy, for I loved the
name of it, the splendor of omniscient innocence it carried. I
told all the boys, all the fellas, as we all read comic books together (and little else), that Batman's ward, Robin, was mis-
named. "He's not the boy wonder. He's the Wonder boy!" And
they all agreed for they had never heard of a boy wonder but
everyone, everyone knew about the Wonderboy.

I was no good at woodworking and the like, so I saved my
paper route money and simply bought a bat, the best bat I could
find, a genuine Louisville Slugger, the first one I ever owned. I
sanded that bat, restained it dark, retaped the handle, and decided to give it a name. I carefully carved, scratched, really, into

the bat the word "Ali." I tried to carve a lightning bolt but my limited artistic skill would not permit it. I wanted to carry it in a case but I didn't have one. I just slung it on my shoulder like the great weapon it was, my knight's sword. And I felt like some magnificent knight, some great protector of honor and virtue, whenever I walked on the field with it. I called the bat "the Great Ali."

I used that bat for the entire summer and a magical season it was. I was the best hitter in the neighborhood. I had a career year. There was no pitch I couldn't hit. At the plate, I could do no wrong. Doubles, triples, home runs. I could hit at will. This probably would have happened with any bat I might have used. I had grown bigger and stronger over the last year and had practiced a great deal over the winter. My hand-eye coordination was just superb at that moment in my life. Once I won a game in the last at-bat with a home run and the boys just crowded around me as if I were a spectacle to behold. O wondrous boy was I!

In any case, the bat broke. Some kid used it without my permission. He hit a foul ball and the bat split, the barrel flying one way, the splintered handle still in the kid's hands. It was the end of the Great Ali.

It was 1966 and Ali seemed not simply the best boxer of the day but the best boxer who could ever possibly be imagined. He was so good that it was an inspiration to see him fight on TV, to see even a picture of him. My body shivered when I saw him as if an electric shock had pulverized my ability to feel. It was the good feeling of boyish hero worship I had. He was the Wonderboy. Nothing could touch him. He so filled me with his holy spirit that whenever, late in a game, our side needed a rally, I would chant out loud to my teammates, "Float like a butterfly, sting like a bee. Rumble, young man, rumble!" That made little sense metaphorically in relation to baseball but it seemed to work more often than not. It was for me, this 1966, Ali's absolute moment of black possibilities fulfilled. And I wanted that and for a moment, too, had it, perhaps, among the neighborhood fellows, the touch and glory of the Wonderboy.

When the bat broke, it seemed as if a certain spell was broken, too. I still continued to hit in the little time that was left that season before school started but I was not as interested in baseball anymore. I drifted away from baseball after that summer by steps and bounds. The next summer, 1967, Ali was convicted of draft dodging. Martin Luther King came out against the Vietnam War. Baseball did not seem very important. Something else was. For you see, I could never be sure, before that spring when Ali refused to be drafted, if he really would, really would actually refuse to go, refuse to take that step. Maybe Ali would turn out to be another Roy Hobbs. Maybe he was just some miserable, talented hick who would sell out and strike out.

So when he refused I felt something greater than pride: I felt as though my honor as a black boy had been defended, my honor as a human being. He was the grand knight, after all, the dragon slayer. And I felt myself, little inner-city boy that I was, his apprentice to the grand imagination, the grand daring. The day that Ali refused the draft, I cried in my room. I cried for him and for myself, for my future and his, for all our black possibilities. My poor broken bat, the evaporating memories of my great season, all ghostly in the well-lighted reflections of the fires of some politics and principles that I did not understand but I felt as if I had a new nervous system, as if my cerebral cortex had become a new antenna for a newer reality. If I could sacrifice like that, I thought. If I could sacrifice my life like Ali! You see, it was, I was sure then, the end of the Wonderboy, the utter and complete end, the final breaking of the bat. But it was, as things turned out, only the end of the beginning. It wasn't even that the best was yet to come, or the grand second act, but rather— everything that was to give 1967 meaning was to come. Nineteen sixty-seven was only the first death, the germinal crisis. The grand knights always live twice. Nothing breaks the Wonderboy.

Rediscoveries

George Orwell

Some Thoughts on the Common Toad

Before the swallow, before the daffodil, and not much later than the snowdrop, the common toad salutes the coming of spring after his own fashion, which is to emerge from a hole in the ground, where he has lain buried since the previous autumn, and crawl as rapidly as possible towards the nearest suitable patch of water. Something—some kind of shudder in the earth, or perhaps merely a rise of a few degrees in the temperature—has told him that it is time to wake up: though a few toads appear to sleep the clock round and miss out a year from time to time—at any rate, I have more than once dug them up, alive and apparently well, in the middle of the summer.

At this period, after his long fast, the toad has a very spiritual look, like a strict Anglo-Catholic towards the end of Lent. His movements are languid but purposeful, his body is shrunken, and by contrast his eyes look abnormally large. This allows one to notice, what one might not at another time, that a toad has about the most beautiful eye of any living creature. It is like gold, or more exactly it is like the golden-coloured semi-precious stone which one some times sees in signet-rings, and which I think is called a chrysoberyl.

For a few days after getting into the water the toad concentrates on building up his strength by eating small insects. Presently he has swollen to his normal size again, and then he goes through a phase of intense sexiness. All he knows, at least if he is a male toad, is that he wants to get his arms round something, and if you offer him a stick, or even your finger, he will cling to it with surprising strength and take a long time to discover that it is not a female toad. Frequently one comes upon shapeless masses of ten or twenty toads rolling over and over in the water, one clinging to another without distinction of sex. By degrees, however, they sort themselves out into couples, with the male duly sitting on the female's back. You can now distinguish males from females, because the male is smaller, darker and sits on top, with his arms tightly clasped round the female's neck. After a day or two the spawn is laid in long strings which wind themselves in and out of the reeds and soon become invisible. A few more weeks, and the water is alive with masses of tiny tadpoles which rapidly grow larger, sprout hind-legs, then forelegs, then shed their tails: and finally, about the middle of the summer, the new generation of toads, smaller than one's thumb-nail but perfect in every particular, crawl out of the water to begin the game anew.

I mention the spawning of the toads because it is one of the phenomena of spring which most deeply appeal to me, and because the toad, unlike the skylark and the primrose, has never had much of a boost from the poets. But I am aware that many people do not like reptiles or amphibians, and I am not suggesting that in order to enjoy the spring you have to take an interest in toads. There are also the crocus, the missel-thrush, the cuckoo, the blackthorn, etc. The point is that the pleasures of spring are available to everybody, and cost nothing. Even in the most sordid street the coming of spring will register itself by some sign or other, if it is only a brighter blue between the chimney pots or the vivid green of an elder sprouting on a blitzed site. Indeed it is remarkable how Nature goes on existing unofficially, as it were, in the very heart of London. I have seen a kestrel flying over the Deptford gasworks, and I have heard a first-rate performance by a blackbird in the Euston Road. There must be some hundreds of thousands, it not millions, of birds living inside the four-mile radius, and it is rather a pleasing thought that none of them pays a halfpenny of rent.

As for spring, not even the narrow and gloomy streets round the Bank of England are quite able to exclude it. It comes seeping in everywhere, like one of those new poison gases which pass through all filters. The spring is commonly referred to as "a miracle", and during the past five or six years this worn-out figure of speech has taken on a new lease of life. After the sort of winters we have had to endure recently, the spring does seem miraculous, because it has become gradually harder and harder to believe that it is actually going to happen. Every February since 1940 I have found myself thinking that this time winter is going to be permanent. But Persephone, like the toads, always rises from the dead at about the same moment. Suddenly, towards the end of March, the miracle happens and the decaying slum in which I live is transfigured. Down in the square the sooty privets have turned bright green, the leaves are thickening on the chestnut trees, the daffodils are out, the wallflowers are budding, the policeman's tunic looks positively a pleasant shade of blue, the fishmonger greets his customers with a smile, and even the sparrows are quite a different colour, having felt the balminess of the air and nerved themselves to take a bath, their first since last September.

Is it wicked to take a pleasure in spring and other seasonal changes? To put it more precisely, is it politically reprehensible, while we are all groaning, or at any rate ought to be groaning, under the shackles of the capitalist system, to point out that life is frequently more worth living because of a blackbird's song, a yellow elm tree in October, or some other natural phenomenon which does not cost money and does not have what the editors of left-wing newspapers call a class angle? There is no doubt that many people think so. I know by experience that a favourable reference to "Nature" in one of my articles is liable to bring me abusive letters, and though the key-word in these letters is usually "sentimental", two ideas seem to be mixed up in them. One is that any pleasure in the actual process of life encourages a sort of political quietism. People, so the thought runs, ought to be discontented, and it is our job to multiply our wants and not simply to increase our enjoyment of the things we have already. The other idea is that this is the age of machines and that to dislike the machine, or even to want to limit its domination, is backward-looking, reactionary and slightly ridiculous. This is often backed up by the statement that a love of Nature is a foible of urbanised people who have no notion what Nature is really like. Those who really have to deal with the soil, so it is argued, do not love the soil, and do not take the faintest interest in birds or flowers, except from a strictly utilitarian point of view. To love the country one must live in the town, merely taking an occasional week-end ramble at the warmer times of year.

This last idea is demonstrably false. Medieval literature, for instance, including the popular ballads, is full of an almost Georgian enthusiasm for Nature, and the art of agricultural peoples such as the Chinese and Japanese centres always round trees, birds, flowers, rivers, mountains. The other idea seems to me to be wrong in a subtler way. Certainly we ought to be discontented, we ought not simply to find out ways of making the best of a bad job, and yet if we kill all pleasure in the actual process of life, what sort of future are we preparing for ourselves? If a man cannot enjoy the return of spring, why should he be happy in a labour-saving Utopia? What will he do with the leisure that the machine will give him? I have always suspected that if our economic and political problems are ever really solved, life will become simpler instead of more complex, and that the sort of pleasure one gets from finding the first primrose will loom larger than the sort of pleasure one gets from eating an ice to the tune of a Wurlitzer. I think that by retaining one's childhood love of such things as trees, fishes, butterflies and—to return to my first instance—toads, one makes a peaceful and decent future a little more probable, and that by preaching the doctrine that nothing is to be admired except steel and concrete, one merely makes it a little surer that human beings will have no outlet for their surplus energy except in hatred and leader worship.

At any rate, spring is here, even in London N.1, and they

can't stop you enjoying it. This is a satisfying reflection. How many a time have I stood watching the toads mating, or a pair of hares having a boxing match in the young corn, and thought of all the important persons who would stop me enjoying this if they could. But luckily they can't. So long as you are not actually ill, hungry, frightened or immured in a prison or a holiday camp, spring is still spring. The atom bombs are piling up in the factories, the police are prowling through the cities, the lies are streaming from the loudspeakers, but the earth is still going round the sun, and neither the dictators nor the bureaucrats, deeply as they disapprove of the process, are able to prevent it.

Derek Walcott

The Antilles

Felicity is a village in Trinidad on the edge of the Caroni plain, the wide central plain that still grows sugar and to which indentured cane cutters were brought after emancipation, so the small population of Felicity is East Indian, and on the afternoon that I visited it with friends from America, all the faces along its road were Indian, which, as I hope to show, was a moving, beautiful thing, because this Saturday afternoon *Ramleela,* the epic dramatization of the Hindu epic the *Ramayana,* was going to be performed, and the costumed actors from the village were assembling on a field strung with different-coloured flags, like a new gas station, and beautiful Indian boys in red and black were aiming arrows into the afternoon light. Low blue mountains on the horizon, bright grass, clouds that would gather colour before the light went. Felicity! What a gentle Anglo-Saxon name for an epical memory.

Under an open shed on the edge of the field, there were two huge armatures of bamboo that looked like immense cages. They were parts of the body of a god, his calves or thighs, which, fitted and reared, would make a gigantic effigy. This effigy would be burnt as a conclusion to the epic. The cane structures flashed a predictable parallel: Shelley's sonnet on the fallen statue of Ozymandias and his empire, that "colossal wreck" in its empty desert.

Drummers had lit a fire in the shed and they eased the skins of their tablas nearer the flames to tighten them. The saffron flames, the bright grass, and the hand-woven armatures of the fragmented god who would be burnt were not in any desert where imperial power had finally toppled but were part of a ritual, evergreen season that, like the cane-burning harvest, is annually repeated, the point of such sacrifice being its repetition, the point of the destruction being renewal through fire.

Deities were entering the field. What we generally call "Indian music" was blaring from the open platformed shed from which the epic would be narrated. Costumed actors were arriving. Princes and gods, I supposed. What an unfortunate confession! "Gods, I suppose" is the shrug that embodies our African and Asian diasporas. I had often thought of but never seen *Ramleela,* and had never seen this theatre, an open field, with village children as warriors, princes, and gods. I had no idea what the epic story was, who its hero was, what enemies he fought, yet I had recently adapted the *Odyssey* for a theatre in England, presuming that the audience knew the trials of Odysseus, hero of another Asia Minor epic, while nobody in Trinidad knew any more than I did about Rama, Kali, Shiva, Vishnu, apart from the Indians, a phrase I use pervertedly because that is the kind of remark you can still hear in Trinidad: "apart from the Indians."

It was as if, on the edge of the Central Plain, there was another plateau, a raft on which the *Ramayana* would be poorly performed in this ocean of cane, but that was my writer's view of things, and it is wrong. I was seeing the *Ramleela* at Felicity as theatre when it was faith.

Multiply that moment of self-conviction when an actor, made-up and costumed, nods to his mirror before stopping on stage in the belief that he is a reality entering an illusion and you would have what I presumed was happening to the actors of this epic. But they were not actors. They had been chosen; or they themselves had chosen their roles in this sacred story that would

go on for nine afternoons over a two-hour period till the sun set.
They were not amateurs but believers. There was no theatrical
term to define them. They did not have to psych themselves up
to play their roles. Their acting would probably be as buoyant
and as natural as those bamboo arrows crisscrossing the afternoon pasture. They believed in what they were playing, in the
sacredness of the text, the validity of India, while I, out of the
writer's habit, searched for some sense of elegy, of loss, even of
degenerative mimicry in the happy faces of the boy-warriors or
the heraldic profiles of the village princes. I was polluting the
afternoon with doubt and with the patronage of admiration. I
misread the event through a visual echo of History—the cane
fields, indenture, the evocation of vanished armies, temples, and
trumpeting elephants—when all around me there was quite the
opposite: elation, delight in the boys' screams, in the sweets-
stalls, in more and more costumed characters appearing; a delight of conviction, not loss. The name Felicity made sense.

Consider the scale of Asia reduced to these fragments: the
small white exclamations of minarets or the stone balls of temples in the cane fields, and one can understand the self-mockery
and embarrassment of those who see these rites as parodic, even
degenerate. These purists look on such ceremonies as grammari-
ans look at a dialect, as cities look on provinces and empires on
their colonies. Memory that yearns to join the centre, a limb
remembering the body from which it has been severed, like
those bamboo thighs of the god. In other words, the way that the
Caribbean is still looked at, illegitimate, rootless, mongrelized.
"No people there," to quote Froude, "in the true sense of the
word." No people. Fragments and echoes of real people, unoriginal and broken.

The performance was like a dialect, a branch of its original
language, an abridgement of it, but not a distortion or even a
reduction of its epic scale. Here in Trinidad I had discovered that
one of the greatest epics of the world was seasonally performed,
not with that desperate resignation of preserving a culture, but
with an openness of belief that was as steady as the wind bending
the cane lances of the Caroni plain. We had to leave before the

play began to go through the creeks of the Caroni Swamp, to catch the scarlet ibises coming home at dusk. In a performance as natural as those of the actors of the *Ramleela,* we watched the flocks come in as bright as the scarlet of the boy archers, as the red flags, and cover an islet until it turned into a flowering tree, an anchored immortelle. The sigh of History meant nothing here. These two visions, the *Ramleela* and the arrowing flocks of scarlet ibises, blent into a single gasp of gratitude. Visual surprise is natural in the Caribbean; it comes with the landscape, and faced with its beauty, the sigh of History dissolves.

We make too much of that long groan which underlines the past. I felt privileged to discover the ibises as well as the scarlet archers of Felicity.

The sigh of History rises over ruins, not over landscapes, and in the Antilles there are few ruins to sigh over, apart from the ruins of sugar estates and abandoned forts. Looking around slowly, as a camera would, taking in the low blue hills over Port of Spain, the village road and houses, the warrior-archers, the god-actors and their handlers, and music already on the sound track, I wanted to make a film that would be a long-drawn sigh over Felicity. I was filtering the afternoon with evocations of a lost India, but why "evocations"? Why not "celebrations of a real presence"? Why should India be "lost" when none of these villagers ever really knew it, and why not "continuing," why not the perpetuation of joy in Felicity and in all the other nouns of the Central Plain: Couva, Chaguanas, Charley Village? Why was I not letting my pleasure open its windows wide? I was entitled like any Trinidadian to the ecstasies of their claim, because ecstasy was the pitch of the sinuous drumming in the loudspeakers. I was entitled to the feast of Husein, to the mirrors and crêpe-paper temples of the Muslim epic, to the Chinese Dragon Dance, to the rites of that Sephardic Jewish synagogue that was once on Something Street. I am only one-eighth the writer I might have been had I contained all the fragmented languages of Trinidad.

Break a vase, and the love that reassembles the fragments is stronger than that love which took its symmetry for granted when it was whole. The glue that fits the pieces is the sealing of its original shape. It is such a love that reassembles our African and Asiatic fragments, the cracked heirlooms whose restoration shows its white scars. This gathering of broken pieces is the care and pain of the Antilles, and if the pieces are disparate, ill-fitting, they contain more pain than their original sculpture, those icons and sacred vessels taken for granted in their ancestral places. Antillean art is this restoration of our shattered histories, our shards of vocabulary, our archipelago becoming a synonym for pieces broken off from the original continent.

And this is the exact process of the making of poetry, or what should be called not its "making" but its remaking, the fragmented memory, the armature that frames the god, even the rite that surrenders it to a final pyre; the god assembled cane by cane, reed by weaving reed, line by plaited line, as the artisans of Felicity would erect his holy echo.

Poetry, which is perfection's sweat but which must seem as fresh as the raindrops on a statue's brow, combines the natural and the marmoreal; it conjugates both tenses simultaneously: the past and the present, if the past is the sculpture and the present the beads of dew or rain on the forehead of the past. There is the buried language and there is the individual vocabulary, and the process of poetry is one of excavation and of self-discovery. Tonally the individual voice is a dialect; it shapes its own accent, its own vocabulary and melody in defiance of an imperial concept of language, the language of Ozymandias, libraries and dictionaries, law courts and critics, and churches, universities, political dogma, the diction of institutions. Poetry is an island that breaks away from the main. The dialects of my archipelago seem as fresh to me as those raindrops on the statue's forehead, not the sweat made from the classic exertion of frowning marble, but the condensations of a refreshing element, rain and salt.

Deprived of their original language, the captured and indentured tribes create their own, accreting and secreting fragments of an old, an epic vocabulary, from Asia and from Africa, but to an ancestral, an ecstatic rhythm in the blood that cannot be subdued by slavery or indenture, while nouns are renamed and the given names of places accepted like Felicity village or Choiseul. The original language dissolves from the exhaustion of distance like fog trying to cross an ocean, but this process of renaming, of finding new metaphors, is the same process that the poet faces every morning of his working day, making his own tools like Crusoe, assembling nouns from necessity, from Felicity, even renaming himself. The stripped man is driven back to that self-astonishing, elemental force, his mind. That is the basis of the Antillean experience, this shipwreck of fragments, these echoes, these shards of a huge tribal vocabulary, these partially remembered customs, and they are not decayed but strong. They survived the Middle Passage and the *Fatel Rozack,* the ship that carried the first indentured Indians from the port of Madras to the cane fields of Felicity, that carried the chained Cromwellian convict and the Sephardic Jew, the Chinese grocer and the Lebanese merchant selling cloth samples on his bicycle.

And here they are, all in a single Caribbean city, Port of Spain, the sum of history, Trollope's "non-people." A downtown babel of shop signs and streets, mongrelized, polyglot, a ferment without a history, like heaven. Because that is what such a city is, in the New World, a writer's heaven.

A culture, we all know, is made by its cities.

Another first morning home, impatient for the sunrise—a broken sleep. Darkness at five, and the drapes not worth opening; then, in the sudden light, a cream-walled, brown-roofed police station bordered with short royal palms, in the colonial style, back of it frothing trees and taller palms, a pigeon fluttering into the cover of an eave, a rain-stained block of once-modern apartments, the morning side road into the station without traffic. All part of a surprising peace. This quiet happens with every visit to a city that has deepened itself in me. The flowers and the hills are easy, affection for them predictable; it is the architecture that, for the first morning, disorients. A return from American seductions used to make the traveller feel that something was missing, something was trying to complete itself, like the stained concrete apartments. Pan left along the window and the excrescences rear—a city trying to soar, trying to be brutal, like an

American city in silhouette, stamped from the same mould as Columbus or Des Moines. An assertion of power, its decor bland, its air conditioning pitched to the point where its secretarial and executive staff sport competing cardigans; the colder the offices the more important, an imitation of another climate. A longing, even an envy of feeling cold.

In serious cities, in grey, militant winter with its short afternoons, the days seem to pass by in buttoned over-coats, every building appears as a barracks with lights on in its windows, and when snow comes, one has the illusion of living in a Russian novel, in the nineteenth century, because of the literature of winter. So visitors to the Caribbean must feel that they are inhabiting a succession of postcards. Both climates are shaped by what we have read of them. For tourists, the sunshine cannot be serious. Winter adds depth and darkness to life as well as to literature, and in the unending summer of the tropics not even poverty or poetry (in the Antilles poverty is poetry with a V, *une vie,* a condition of life as well as of imagination) seems capable of being profound because the nature around it is so exultant, so resolutely ecstatic, like its music. A culture based on joy is bound to be shallow. Sadly, to sell itself, the Caribbean encourages the delights of mindlessness, of brilliant vacuity, as a place to flee not only winter but that seriousness that comes only out of culture with four seasons. So how can there be a people there, in the true sense of the word?

They know nothing about seasons in which leaves let go of the year, in which spires fade in blizzards and streets whiten, of the erasures of whole cities by fog, of reflection in fireplaces; instead, they inhabit a geography whose rhythm, like their music, is limited to two stresses: hot and wet, sun and rain, light and shadow, day and night, the limitations of an incomplete metre, and are therefore a people incapable of the subtleties of contradiction, of imaginative complexity. So be it. We cannot change contempt.

Ours are not cities in the accepted sense, but no one wants them to be. They dictate their own proportions, their own definitions in particular places and in a prose equal to that of their detractors, so that now it is not just St. James but the streets and yards that Naipaul commemorates, its lanes as short and brilliant as his sentences; not just the noise and jostle of Tunapuna but the origins of C.L.R. James's *Beyond a Boundary*, not just Felicity village on the Caroni plain, but Selvon Country, and that is the way it goes up the islands now: the old Dominica of Jean Rhys still very much the way she wrote of it; and the Martinique of the early Césaire; Perse's Guadeloupe, even without the pith helmets and the mules; and what delight and privilege there was in watching a literature—one literature in several imperial languages, French, English, Spanish—bud and open island after island in the early morning of a culture, not timid, not derivative, any more than the hard white petals of the frangipani are derivative and timid. This is not a belligerent boast but a simple celebration of inevitability: and this flowering had to come.

On a heat-stoned afternoon in Port of Spain, some alley white with glare, with love vine spilling over a fence, palms and a hazard mountain appear around a corner to the evocation of Vaughn or Herbert's "that shady city of palm-trees," or to the memory of a Hammond organ from a wooden chapel in Castries, where the congregation sang "Jerusalem, the Golden." It is hard for me to see such emptiness as desolation. It is that patience that is the width of Antillean life, and the secret is not to ask the wrong thing of it, not to demand of it an ambition it has no interest in. The traveller reads this as lethargy, as torpor.

Here there are not enough books, one says, no theatres, no museums, simply not enough to do. Yet, deprived of books, a man must fall back on thought, and out of thought, if he can learn to order it, will come the urge to record, and in extremity, if he has no means of recording, recitation, the ordering of memory which leads to metre, to commemoration. There can be virtues in deprivation, and certainly one virtue is salvation from a cascade of high mediocrity, since books are now not so much created as remade. Cities create a culture, and all we have are these magnified market towns, so what are the proportions of the ideal Caribbean city? A surrounding, accessible countryside with leafy suburbs, and if the city is lucky, behind it, spacious plains.

Behind it, fine mountains; before it, an indigo sea. Spires would pin its centre and around them would be leafy, shadowy parks. Pigeons would cross its sky in alphabetic patterns, carrying with them memories of a belief in augury, and at the heart of the city there would be horses, yes, horses, those animals last seen at the end of the nineteenth century drawing broughams and carriages with top-hatted citizens, horses that live in the present tense without elegiac echoes from their hooves, emerging from paddocks at the Queen's Park Savannah at sunrise, when mist is unthreading from the cool mountains above the roofs, and at the centre of the city seasonally there would be races, so that citizens could roar at the speed and grace of these nineteenth-century animals. Its docks, not obscured by smoke or deafened by too much machinery, and above all, it would be so racially various that the cultures of the world—the Asiatic, the Mediterranean, the European, the African—would be represented in it, its humane variety more exciting than Joyce's Dublin. Its citizens would intermarry as they chose, from instinct, not tradition, until their children find it increasingly futile to trace their genealogy. It would not have too many avenues difficult or dangerous for pedestrians, its mercantile area would be a cacophony of accents, fragments of the old language that would be silenced immediately at five o'clock, its docks resolutely vacant on Sundays.

This is Port of Spain to me, a city ideal in its commercial and human proportions, where a citizen is a walker and not a pedestrian, and this is how Athens may have been before it became a cultural echo.

The finest silhouettes of Port of Spain are idealizations of the craftsman's handiwork, not of concrete and glass, but of baroque woodwork, each fantasy looking more like an involved drawing of itself than the actual building. Behind the city is the Caroni plain, with its villages, Indian prayer flags, and fruit vendors' stalls along the highway over which ibises come like floating flags. Photogenic poverty! Postcard sadnesses! I am not recreating Eden; I mean, by "the Antilles," the reality of light, of work, of survival. I mean a house on the side of a country road, I mean the Caribbean Sea, whose smell is the smell of refreshing possibility as well as survival. Survival is the triumph of stubbornness, and spiritual stubbornness, a sublime stupidity, is what makes the occupation of poetry endure, when there are so many things that should make it futile. Those things added together can go under one collective noun: "the world."

This is the visible poetry of the Antilles, then. Survival.

If you wish to understand that consoling pity with which the islands were regarded, look at the tinted engravings of Antillean forests, with their proper palm trees, ferns, and waterfalls. They have a civilizing decency, like Botanical Gardens, as if the sky were a glass ceiling under which a colonized vegetation is arranged for quiet walks and carriage rides. Those views are incised with a pathos that guides the engraver's tool and the topographer's pencil, and it is this pathos which, tenderly ironic, gave villages names like Felicity. A century looked at a landscape furious with vegetation in the wrong light and with the wrong eye. It is such pictures that are saddening rather than the tropics itself. These delicate engravings of sugar mills and harbours, of native women in costume, are seen as a part of History, that History which looked over the shoulder of the engraver and, later, the photographer. History can alter the eye and the moving hand to conform a view of itself; it can rename places for the nostalgia in an echo; it can temper the glare of tropical light to elegiac monotony in prose, the tone of judgment in Conrad, in the travel journals of Trollope.

These travellers carried with them the infection of their own malaise, and their prose reduced even the landscape to melancholia and self-contempt. Every endeavor is belittled as imitation, from architecture to music. There was this conviction in Froude that since History is based on achievement, and since the history of the Antilles was so genetically corrupt, so depressing in its cycles of massacres, slavery, and indenture, a culture was inconceivable and nothing could ever be created in those ramshackle ports, those monotonously feudal sugar estates. Not only the light and salt of Antillean mountains defied this, but the demotic vigour and variety of their inhabitants. Stand close to a waterfall and you will stop hearing its roar. To be still in the nineteenth century, like horses, as Brodsky has written, may not be such a bad deal, and much of our life in the Antilles still seems to be in the rhythm of the last century, like the West Indian novel.

By writers even as refreshing as Graham Greene, the Caribbean is looked at with elegiac pathos, a prolonged sadness to which Lévi-Strauss has supplied an epigraph: *Tristes Tropiques*. Their *tristesse* derives from an attitude to the Caribbean dusk, to rain, to uncontrollable vegetation, to the provincial ambition of Caribbean cities where brutal replicas of modern architecture dwarf the small houses and streets. The mood is understandable, the melancholy as contagious as the fever of a sunset, like the gold fronds of diseased coconut palms, but there is something alien and ultimately wrong in the way such a sadness, even a morbidity, is described by English, French, or some of our exiled writers. It relates to a misunderstanding of the light and the people on whom the light falls.

These writers describe the ambitions of our unfinished cities, their unrealized, homiletic conclusion, but the Caribbean city may conclude just at that point where it is satisfied with its own scale, just as Caribbean culture is not evolving but already shaped. Its proportions are not to be measured by the traveller or the exile, but by its own citizenry and architecture. To be told you are not yet a city or a culture requires this response. I am not your city or your culture. There might be less of *Tristes Tropiques* after that.

Here, on the raft of this dais, there is the sound of the applauding surf: our landscape, our history recognized, "at last." *At Last is* one of the first Caribbean books. It was written by the Victorian traveller Charles Kingsley. It is one of the early books to admit to Antillean landscape and its figures into English literature. I have never read it but gather that its tone is benign. The Antillean archipelago was there to be written about, not to write itself, by Trollope, by Patrick Leigh-Fermor, in the very tone in which I almost wrote about the village spectacle at Felicity, as a compassionate and beguiled outsider, distancing myself from Felicity village even while I was enjoying it. What is hidden cannot be loved. The traveller cannot love, since love is stasis and travel is motion. If he returns to what he loved in a landscape and stays there, he is no longer a traveller but in stasis and concentration, the lover of that particular part of earth, a native. So many people say they "love the Caribbean," meaning that someday they plan to return for a visit but could never live there, the usual benign insult to the traveller, the tourist. These travellers, at their kindest, were devoted to the same patronage, the islands passing in profile, their vegetal luxury, their backwardness and poverty. Victorian prose dignified them. They passed by in beautiful profiles and were forgotten, like a vacation.

Alexis Saint-Léger Léger, whose writer's name is Saint-John Perse, was the first Antillean to win this prize for poetry. He was born in Guadeloupe and wrote in French, but before him, there was nothing as fresh and clear in feeling as those poems of his childhood, that of a privileged white child on an Antillean plantation, *"Pour fêter une enfance,"* *"Eloges,"* and later *"Images à Crusoe."* At last, the first breeze on the page, salt-edged and self-renewing as the trade winds, the sound of pages and palm trees turning as "the odour of coffee ascends the stairs."

Caribbean genius is condemned to contradict itself. To celebrate Perse, we might be told, is to celebrate the old plantation system, to celebrate the *bequé* or plantation rider, verandahs and mulatto servants, a white French language in a white pith helmet, to celebrate a rhetoric of patronage and hauteur; and even if Perse denied his origins, great writers often have this folly of trying to smother their source, we cannot deny him any more than we can the African Aimé Césaire. This is not accommodation, this is the ironic republic that is poetry, since, when I see cabbage palms moving their fronds at sunrise, I think they are reciting Perse.

The fragrant and privileged poetry that Perse composed to celebrate his white childhood and the recorded Indian music behind the brown young archers of Felicity, with the same cabbage palms against the same Antillean sky, pierce me equally. I feel the same poignancy of pride in the poems as in the faces.

Why, given the history of the Antilles, should this be remarkable? The history of the world, by which of course we mean Europe, is a record of intertribal lacerations, of ethnic cleansings. At last, islands not written about but writing themselves! The palms and the Muslim minarets are Antillean exclamations. At last! the royal palms of Guadeloupe recite *"Eloges"* by heart.

Later, in *Anabase,* Perse assembled fragments of an imaginary epic, with the clicking teeth of frontier gates, barren wadis with the froth of poisonous lakes, horsemen burnoosed in sandstorms, the opposite of cool Caribbean mornings, yet not necessarily a contrast any more than some young brown archer at Felicity, hearing the sacred text blared across the flagged field, with its battles and elephants and monkey-gods, in a contrast to the white child in Guadeloupe assembling fragments of his own epic from the lances of the cane fields, the estate carts and oxens, and the calligraphy of bamboo leaves from the ancient languages, Hindi, Chinese, and Arabic, on the Antillean sky. From the *Ramayana* to Anabasis, from Guadeloupe to Trinidad, all that archaeology of fragments lying around, from the broken African kingdoms, from the crevasses of Canton, from Syria and Lebanon, vibrating not under the earth but in our raucous, demotic streets.

A boy with weak eyes skims a flat stone across the flat water of an Aegean inlet, and that ordinary action with the scything elbow contains the skipping lines of the *Iliad* and the *Odyssey,* and another child aims a bamboo arrow at a village festival, and another hears the rustling march of cabbage palms in a Caribbean sunrise, and from that sound, with its fragments of tribal myth, the compact expedition of Perse's epic is launched, centuries and archipelagos apart. For every poet it is always morning in the world. History a forgotten, insomniac night; History and elemental awe are always our early beginning, because the fate of poetry is to fall in love with the world, in spite of History.

There is a force of exultation, a celebration of luck, when a writer finds himself a witness to the early morning of a culture that is defining itself, branch by branch, leaf by leaf, in that self-defining dawn, which is why, especially at the edge of the sea, it is good to make a ritual of the sunrise. Then the noun, the "Antilles" ripples like brightening water, and the sounds of leaves, palm fronds, and birds are the sounds of fresh dialect, the native tongue. The personal vocabulary, the individual melody whose metre is one's biography, joins in that sound, with any luck, and the body moves like a walking, a waking island.

This is the benediction that is celebrated, a fresh language and a fresh people, and this is the frightening duty owed.

I stand here in their name, if not their image—but also in the name of the dialect they exchange like the leaves of the trees whose names are suppler, greener, more morning-stirred than English—*laurier canelles, bois-flot, bois-canot*—or the valleys the trees mention—*Fond St. Jacques, Mabonya, Forestièr, Roseau, Mahaut*—or the empty beaches—*L'Anse Ivrogne, Case en Bas, Paradis*—all songs and histories in themselves, pronounced not in French—but in patois.

One rose hearing two languages, one of the trees, one of schoolchildren reciting in English:

> I am monarch of all I survey,
> My right there is none to dispute;
> From the centre all round to the sea
> I am lord of the fowl and the brute.
> Oh, solitude! where are the charms
> That sages have seen in thy face?
> Better dwell in the midst of alarms,
> Than reign in this horrible place . . .

While in the country to the same metre, but to organic instruments, handmade violin, chac-chac, and goatskin drum, a girl named Sensenne singing:

> Si mwen di 'ous' ça fait mwen la peine
> 'Ous kai dire ça vrai.
> (If I told you that caused me pain
> You'll say, "It's true.")
> Si mwen di 'ous ça pentetrait mwen

'Ous peut dire ça vrai
  (If I told you you pierced my heart
  You'd say, "It's true.")
Ces mamailles actuellement
Pas ka faire l'amour z'autres pour un rien.
  (Children nowadays
  Don't make love for nothing.)

It is not that History is obliterated by this sunrise. It is there in
Antillean geography, in the vegetation itself. The sea sighs with
the drowned from the Middle Passage, the butchery of its ab-
origines, Carib and Aruac and Taino, bleeds in the scarlet of the
immortelle, and even the actions of surf on sand cannot erase the
African memory, or the lances of cane as a green prison where
indentured Asians, the ancestors of Felicity, are still serving
time.

    That is what I have read around me from boyhood, from
the beginnings of poetry, the grace of effort. In the hard mahogany of woodcutters: faces, resinous men, charcoal burners; in a
man with a cutlass cradled across his forearm, who stands on the
verge with the usual anonymous khaki dog; in the extra clothes
he put on this morning, when it was cold when he rose in the
thinning dark to go and make his garden in the heights—the
heights, the garden, being miles away from his house, but that is
where he has his land—not to mention the fishermen, the foot-
men on trucks, groaning up mornes, all fragments of Africa originally but shaped and hardened and rooted now in the island's
life, illiterate in the way leaves are illiterate; they do not read,
they are there to be read, and if they are properly read, they
create their own literature.

    But in our tourist brochures the Caribbean is a blue pool
into which the republic dangles the extended foot of Florida as
inflated rubber islands bob and drinks with umbrellas float towards her on a raft. This is how the islands from the shame of
necessity sell themselves; this is the seasonal erosion of their
identity, that high-pitched repetition of the same images of service that cannot distinguish one island from the other, with a

future of polluted marinas, land deals negotiated by ministers, and all of this conducted to the music of Happy Hour and the rictus of a smile. What is the earthly paradise for our visitors? Two weeks without rain and a mahogany tan, and, at sunset, local troubadours in straw hats and floral shirts beating "Yellow Bird" and "Banana Boat Song" to death. There is a territory wider than this—wider than the limits made by the map of an island—which is the illimitable sea and what it remembers.

All of the Antilles, every island, is an effort of memory; every mind, every racial biography culminating in amnesia and fog. Pieces of sunlight through the fog and sudden rainbows, *arcs-enciel*. That is the effort, the labour of the Antillean imagination, rebuilding its gods from bamboo frames, phrase by phrase.

Decimation from the Aruac downwards is the blasted root of Antillean history, and the benign blight that is tourism can infect all of those island nations, not gradually, but with imperceptible speed, until each rock is whitened by the guano of white-winged hotels, the arc and descent of progress.

Before it is all gone, before only a few valleys are left, pockets of an older life, before development turns every artist into an anthropologist or folklorist, there are still cherishable places, little valleys that do not echo with ideas, a simplicity of rebeginnings, not yet corrupted by the dangers of change. Not nostalgic sites but occluded sanctities as common and simple as their sunlight. Places as threatened by this prose as a headland is by the bulldozer or a sea almond grove by the surveyor's string, or from blight, the mountain laurel.

One last epiphany: A basic stone church in a thick valley outside Soufrière, the hills almost shoving the houses around into a brown river, a sunlight that looks oily on the leaves, a backward place, unimportant, and one now being corrupted into significance by this prose. The idea is not to hallow or invest the place with anything, not even memory. African children in Sunday frocks come down the ordinary concrete steps into the church, banana leaves hang and glisten, a truck is parked in a yard, and old women totter towards the entrance. Here is where a real fresco should be painted, one without importance, but one with real faith, mapless, Historyless.

How quickly it could all disappear! And how it is beginning to drive us further into where we hope are impenetrable places, green secrets at the end of bad roads, headlands where the next view is not of a hotel but of some long beach without a figure and the hanging question of some fisherman's smoke at its far end. The Caribbean is not an idyll, not to its natives. They draw their working strength from it organically, like trees, like the sea almond or the spice laurel of the heights. Its peasantry and its fishermen are not there to be loved or even photographed; they are trees who sweat, and whose bark is filmed with salt, but every day on some island, rootless trees in suits are signing favourable tax breaks with entrepreneurs, poisoning the sea almond and the spice laurel of the mountains to their roots. A morning could come in which governments might ask what happened not merely to the forests and the bays but to a whole people.

They are here again, they recur, the faces, corruptible angels, smooth black skins and white eyes huge with an alarming joy, like those of the Asian children of Felicity at *Ramleela;* two different religions, two different continents, both filling the heart with the pain that is joy.

But what is joy without fear? The fear of selfishness that, here on this podium with the world paying attention not to them but to me, I should like to keep these simple joys inviolate, not because they are innocent, but because they are true. They are as true as when, in the grace of this gift, Perse heard the fragments of his own epic of Asia Minor in the rustling of cabbage palms, that inner Asia of the soul through which imagination wanders, if there is such a thing as imagination as opposed to the collective memory of our entire race, as true as the delight of that warrior-child who flew a bamboo arrow over the flags in the field at Felicity; and now as grateful a joy and a blessed fear as when a boy opened an exercise book and, within the discipline of its margins, framed stanzas that might contain the light of the hills on an island blest by obscurity, cherishing our insignificance.

Capturing Nature

Gordon Grice

Mantid

From my second-floor apartment I could see across the parking lot to the creek, and I used to step out on the landing at dusk to watch the fireflies lighting up against the backdrop of the darkening pines and maples and Osage orange trees. One night the miller moths were especially thick around the light fixture on the landing, and I was about to go inside because the furry, knuckle-sized creatures kept bumping me, leaving iridescent streaks of dusty scales on my sweating skin. That's when I noticed one of them jerk from the arc of its flight and buzz like a disgruntled bee.

There was a beige-painted wood banister along the landing, and a piece of it had grabbed the moth and was chewing its head off. As I looked closer, the carnivorous piece of banister adjusted its grip slightly, and I recognized it as a praying mantis, or mantid, as the entomologists prefer. She held the moth, wings down, before her face and turned to stare at me. She looked like a person wiping her face with a napkin.

The mantid was two and a half inches long and exactly the color of the banister. Her triangular head came to a point in mandibles like two tiny pairs of pruning shears; they were surrounded by four fingerlike palps. She walked on four legs. The front pair of legs, the ones she didn't use for walking, were covered with spikes and ended in boat hooks, and she held these up before herself. The odd position of mantid forelegs has suggested contemplation or wisdom to many people in different parts of the world. The Greek root of *mantid* means "prophet." In Africa and the Middle East, legends of religious and prophetic significance adhere to the mantid. In the United States, its common names include *soothsayer*. And, of course, it is accused of "praying."

I trapped the mantid in a gallon pickle jar and brought her inside, adding a few twigs and leaves for her to climb on. By morning she had turned green to match the leaves.

I caught a few miller moths and tossed them in. The mantid climbed halfway up a thick twig and clung there with her middle and hind legs, her big forelegs folded close to her chest. A moth flew near. Her head swiveled to watch its erratic, glass-bumping flight.

She snatched it from the air. I didn't see it happen; her strike was too fast to see, even as a blur. Scientists say an entire strike lasts one twentieth of a second. I only sensed some startling occurrence, and then the moth was trapped in her spiky arms. She was already biting it in the furry scales just behind its bald head. Mantids generally bite in just this spot, severing the prey's major nerve, the equivalent of a spinal cord. This surgical technique, which mantids somehow instinctively apply to a wide range of prey, breaks the connection between an insect's limbs and brain. It's not necessarily a fatal wound, but it leaves the insect powerless to defend itself.

The moth flapped its wings into a buzzing blur every few seconds while the mantid unhurriedly ate it, starting from the head. The pruning-shear mouthparts worked away, biting out chunks of moth and lapping the juices. The moth's scales, which had broken into particles of dust when they smeared my hand, looked like little brown feathers when they were whole, and they drifted down in a steady snow.

I kept the mantid for a week or so, frequently feeding it

moths. The twig it perched on was unsteady. Sometimes it spun out of place when the mantid struck at a moth. The mantid's strike, missing its target as the mantid lost her footing, would hang in the air for an instant, giving me a rare look at the process—the arms unfurled, reaching, like a model showing evening gloves.

I had read that mantids eat almost anything, from hornets (they leave the stinger uneaten) to hummingbirds to frogs. One mantid seized a mouse and ate it alive, starting from the nose. (That mantid was five inches long.) I myself had seen them eating black widow spiders; as the mantid devours what passes for the spider's brain, one spider leg moves up and down as if keeping time to music. I fed this mantid whatever crawled across the landing: a spotted white caterpillar, which held to the grass stem from which the mantid plucked it, bending the stem almost double on its way to death. House flies—she ate only the larger ones. Field crickets that walked up to her boldly like paunchy men in tuxedos. A huge orb-weaving spider with legs striped in silver and gold. She would eat anything she could see moving; I watched her watch the movement before she made the kill.

The mantid is a visual animal, far more so than almost any other arthropod. Her two huge eyes form a human-style face: gaze at her and she seems to be gazing back, as cats and monkeys do. Try the same trick with most insects and, if you can even discover any eyes, you'll find they don't give the same impression.

The mantid's two big eyes, arranged so that both can see forward, give her stereoscopic vision. That means she can see two images of the same thing and, by combining the two, judge depth. That's the same trick we humans use. The mantid can also see a little bit of color. But her specialty is seeing motion: in order to eat, she has to detect animal motion among wind-stirred leaves. When she sees prey moving, she freezes until it comes close; then she launches her invisibly fast strike. She can see in light or near-dark, but, like many predominantly visual animals, she prefers to hunt by day.

The mantid has a feature unique among insects: the ability

to turn her head. A mantid can actually look over her own "shoulder." This combination of traits—swiveling head, stereoscopic vision, depth perception, and motion detection—causes mantid behavior to resemble that of cats and people more than it does typical insect behavior, at least in matters of food and self-defense. For example, what happens if you thrust your hand toward a person's face, stopping just short of contact? The first reaction is a flinch. What happens if you try the same thing with a cockroach, a close cousin of the mantid? It runs, changing directions frequently to confuse you. And what if you try the same thing with a mantid? She flinches. Mantids react like people because they see the world in basically the same way.

Visual talents of this sort usually go with a predatory lifestyle. We're not pure predators like the mantid, but we have the equipment to be. We also have grasping appendages, another frequent predator trait, just as cats have grasping claws and mantids have what scientists call *raptorial* arms. "Raptorial" is biologese for "grasping." Few insects can hold prey items as the mantid can.

All of our similarities to the mantid result from convergent evolution, which means that unrelated animals develop similar features because they've adapted to similar environmental challenges. The killer whale, a warm-blooded animal built on a frame of bones, is shaped like the white shark, a cold-blooded animal with a cartilaginous skeleton. That's because they both live in the ocean and eat seals: convergent evolution. Our similarities to the mantid are subtler.

To start with, we both have weak senses except for sight. If you want an illustration of the weakness of your ears and nose, follow a dog around outdoors and try to figure out what he's alerting to every time he cocks his head or stops to stare. You'll soon believe yourself deaf and blunt-nosed. If you tried the same thing with a mantid, you would understand her better, even though the dog is, relatively speaking, your first cousin and the mantid a stranger.

The metaphors reveal our visual nature. When we English-speaking humans want to show that we understand something, we say "I see." But "I hear" is the language of rumor; it means something is possible but unproved. I'm told many languages have analogous sensory metaphors. They reflect the epistemology our bodies teach us.

The mantid is pretty useless when it comes to hearing. Of the approximately two thousand mantid species in the world, many lack ears altogether. In only a few species are both genders equipped with ears. The remaining species—over half the total—exhibit sexual dimorphism. The male has an ear, and the female doesn't. The mantid ear is unique; each male has only one, which is in the center of his chest. Most animals can tell the direction of a sound because of subtle differences in reception between their two ears, but the mantid lacks this talent. He cannot use his ear to locate food or mates. His vision is, of course, all he needs to hunt prey. He finds receptive females by scent: the females emit pheremones.

To follow this scent, the male flies by night. This fact accounts for his longer wings. The females of most mantid species don't fly at all. This is where the male mantid's ear reveals its function. It detects only high frequencies, so it is useless for most defensive purposes, but it does pick up the echo-locating screams of bats. Insectivorous bats eat mantids on the wing. A mantid that hears a bat's call power-dives to avoid being taken. Since this tactic doesn't require the mantid to know where the bat is, the single ear suffices. Scientists believe the mantid's ear, for which no other function has yet been discovered, evolved in response to predation by bats.

The mantid as meal: that brings us to another important trait we share. We're both predatory animals in the middle of the food chain. The mantid is built to kill, but she can also be killed, and often is.

We sat talking on the porch, and out in the grass at the edge of the light the black cat continually pulled himself into a tight ball and then sprang at some insect floating by. We saw him miss a few moths, and we saw him leap at things we couldn't see.

After a while he came trotting up to the porch with something in his mouth. The something was thrashing its legs in the fur of the cat's cheeks.

The cat crouched to play with his captive, dropping it on the sidewalk and pinning it with one paw. It was a big green mantid. When the cat raised the paw and looked, the mantid rose on his hind legs, throwing his formidable front limbs into the air to show their red and yellow undersides, and staggered toward the cat, as if to intimidate the feline with its size. Scientists call that a *threat display*. The cat clapped his paws together on the mantid.

A second later the mantid slipped free and burst into buzzing flight, making a swift, clumsy are before the cat's face. The cat sprang to catch the mantid in midair. And when he had his captive wrestled to the cement, he was through playing. He bit and pulled his head back, breaking the mantid in half. The fight went on for another five minutes or so, the black cat eating, the green mantid still waving his limbs in protest. The cat left the spiny forelimbs and a tangle of winged thorax.

The human animal, too, is in the middle of a predatory chain. This idea ticks off a lot of people who, generally because of some religious or cultural bias, think we ought to be the bosses of the animal kingdom. ("Kingdom": even that bit of taxonomic apparatus shows a human bias toward thinking in hierarchies.)

A skeptical reader may point out that, as he sits in the comfort of his den in the middle of his town reading this book, he's in virtually no danger of being eaten by anybody. Good for you, sir; you rank with the termite. We humans are safe in our own shelters and towns, just as termites are safe in their mounds.

Another reader remarks that her shotgun elevates her to the status of top predator. You're right, ma'am; our talent with projectile weapons is a powerful one, and puts us on a par with the rock-chunking baboons. If, however, you encountered any of the predators that really see us as food—not your flimsy North American predators like the coyote or the cougar (though each of those has killed a human or two), but, say, a saltwater crocodile or a white shark—your gun would stand only a slim chance of winning the day for you.

But, a third reader murmurs sullenly, we can kill anything if we team up on it. True, and we often use this trick to eradicate troublesome tigers. They become troublesome by eating a few people—in some cases, a few hundred people. Similarly, baboons pack-hunt leopards, but this doesn't change the fact that leopards are serious baboon-eaters.

The leopard is adept at shaking the anthropocentrist in all of us, at making us rethink our preconceptions of hierarchies in the natural world and especially our sense of sitting at the top of the heap. The fossil skull of an early man shows the puncture wound characteristic of death by leopard. This cat is far smaller than the lion or the tiger, but he kills far more people. He's been with us, in Asia and Africa, since before we wrote histories; he was there before we came out of the jungle to walk the savannas, and he's never shared our conceit that we're fundamentally different from other apes and monkeys. Today he eats our close relatives, chimpanzees and baboons, just as he ate our ancestors. He still eats us—hundreds of us every year. Some single leopards have killed hundreds of humans. The Panar leopard of northern India, for example, took more than four hundred people. That's the Indian government's official death toll, which strictly excludes uncertain cases. Leopards share our enjoyment of sport killing. One in Tanzania killed twenty-six people without eating any of them.

There's a theory that lions and tigers eat people only after they learn to like the taste of human flesh by scavenging battlefields and plague-ridden villages. Whether that's true of lions and tigers or not, it certainly doesn't apply to the leopard, which needs no prompting to add some protein-rich primate to its diet. It's also claimed that the big cats resort to human-eating when they are too old and feeble to catch their "natural" prey. But among human-eating leopards, healthy, exceptionally large males are common.

The lion and tiger kill by seizing the throat or nose and

closing down the flow of air with a patient vise of a bite. This strategy is well suited to hoofed animals, which, once brought down, have little defense. The leopard rarely suffocates his prey. He is used to hunting animals that can scratch and grab at his eyes—baboons, chimps, humans. He has no patience for a caught animal. He bites through the skull for a quick kill.

Like the mantid's, his strategy aims to break the nervous system. He is built to kill us.

Our mythic prototype of a creature from another planet has round luminous eyes on a face whose other features seem atrophied. That's the face of a mantid.

Things that are really alien don't look alien. Look at diatoms under a microscope and you don't have the feeling of looking at once-living things; the creatures more nearly resemble wallpaper. Do you empathize with a trout, a sparrow, or a lobster? Forms of life that are relatively different from us cause us little or no visceral response. Animals that resemble us more closely—cats and dogs, for example—make some of us feel sympathy, friendship, even love. We understand some of these animals' motives, because we share them—the visceral pleasure of eating, games based on instinctive hunting and fighting habits, and so on.

The things that scare or repulse us are those that are sympathetically human in some respects, but markedly alien in others. For example, apes appear in a disproportionately large number of horror fantasies, from "The Murders in the Rue Morgue" to *King Kong*. Apes disturb us with their imperfect humanity. So do dolls. In talking with people about their childhood fears, I have heard many mentions of dolls and mannequins, and the fear seems to center on the eyes: the rest is passably human, but the dead eyes make the thing terrible, at least in the dark. Of course, the human body itself becomes an object of terror as soon as it dies, because it is still human, but not in the way we want it to be.

That archetypal image of the extraterrestrial—bilaterally symmetrical, bipedal, visual—is an unlikely choice if you want to imagine what might really live on other planets. After all, what are the chances of an alien looking almost exactly like *any* earth animal, and us in particular? But the image makes sense psychologically, for it is us touched up with a few strokes of strangeness.

The mantid spends most of her time looking like a reasonable enough, if slightly sinister, character. She walks along poised to grab something; she reacts visibly to prey; she will try to avoid anyone who offers to step on her. If you persist in threatening her, she will throw her arms in the air and wave them, as if to say, "See how big I am? You'd better think twice about dogging me, buddy." But sometimes the mantid will show you that, however understandable most of her actions may be, she also has a side alien to us.

The female is the color of jade, her abdomen thick and fleshy. She is mostly still, her feet hooked into the texture of the elm tree's bark. When I first glimpsed her, I mistook her abdomen and wings for the chrysalis of a monarch butterfly. But as my eyes picked her shape out of the relief map of bark and beetle-chewed leaves, I saw the long stretch of her thorax ending in a plow-share head, at the upper corners of which her amber eyes bulge like beaded water, each of them punctuated with a black period in the middle that resembles a pupil but is not.

The male approaches, angling away from her face to avoid being too easy a target. He is more slender, and holds his hind wings slightly ruffled beneath his green forewings; his angular looks could help him pass for a twig. His eyes are different too, duller, more ascetic. He lacks her mass but is almost as long, perhaps two inches. He walks down the trunk toward her, his body held away from the bark by his four hind legs, which jut out to the sides of his body from his thorax, then turn right angles to meet the bark. His head swivels as he comes, keeping her in view. She watches him, and her mouth-parts work idly.

When he is perhaps an inch away, he stops and begins to sway on his bent legs like a sumo wrestler in warm-up. Her forelegs unfurl slightly, then stop in midair, one slightly ahead of the other. She, too, begins to sway. He walks from side to side before her, sometimes stopping to sway, his wings unfolding slightly and trembling. She watches him walk. Her own movements stop, or perhaps continue too subtly for me to see. He edges around to her side.

Suddenly he runs a good six inches and lunges into the air, his blunt forewings flicking forward to let the transparent hind wings fan out into buzzing flight. She turns her head to follow him with her full-yellow-moon eyes. He lands in the grass, then flaps back to repeat his flying leap. This time he returns and begins to slap the female with his antennae. His head moves from side to side like that of a playful dog fighting his master for a toy. The slender antennae lash her like the proverbial wet noodle, failing to even ruffle her antennae.

She strikes.

Now she is standing still, her blur of motion over so quickly it might seem unreal, except that she is slowly eating the right half of his head.

He stands swaying, his actions only slightly interrupted by the amputation of half his head.

Then, while she is still eating, he crawls onto her back. He seems in this semiheadless state to have found a renewed vigor and sense of purpose. There will be no more showy stunts. His pale penis emerges from the rear of his body, extruded between the plates of his exoskeleton. His abdomen snakes around beside hers and forms a painful-looking curve. They begin to copulate.

Turning her face almost 180 degrees, she regards him for a moment, as if his attentions were a distasteful surprise. Then, twisting with some difficulty, she brings her raptorial forelimbs into position and strikes again. This time she retrieves the remainder of his head and a scrap of his thorax, from which one foreleg dangles.

He doesn't seem to mind. He stays on her back like some undersized Headless Horseman. I recall my grandfather once showing me a big female mantid and calling it a "devil-horse."

The copulation continues. It lacks the aerobics of a mammalian encounter. After the insertion it involves, besides the cannibalism, merely clinging and a slight pulsing in the male's soft abdomen. It may go on for a long time; some couplings have outlasted my patience for watching. The genitals fit so tightly that, if you try to separate the pair, their bodies will tear apart before they disengage.

The female hasn't finished her meal. She strikes again, removing everything forward of his middle pair of legs. She eats rapidly. His raptorial forelimbs lie on the bark like discarded hand tools. She walks out from under what's left of his body and stands a few inches away, cleaning her forelimbs with her mouth. The male's remains crabwalk a few steps. The abdomen pulses faintly. The female picks her steps on the rough bark as she goes away. He stays there, wiggling his abdomen obscenely, staggering in sideways arcs. He will do so until something else comes along to eat him.

Males die a few days after copulation, even if the female hasn't harmed them. The female will lay eggs in a day or two. She lays them in a gluey substance she squeezes out of her abdomen, all the while moving herself in a spiral like a cake decorator's bag of icing. Special appendages at her rear end whip the substance into a froth. One egg case takes her a whole morning, and by afternoon the gluey stuff has set like cement. She usually gets at least three cases built before she dies, each containing up to two hundred eggs. Each one looks like a little army barracks. A case is impervious to just about everything except the teeth of rodents and the mandibles of parasitic wasps.

The hardwiring for the entire mating ritual lies in a cluster of nerves in the floor of the thorax. The brain is not involved, except to inhibit the mantid from constantly going through the mating motions. That's why the male not only can finish without a head, but even performs with more gusto once he's decapitated. The female can mate headless as well, though that's rarely necessary. The female can even lay her eggs after she loses her head. The cockroach, a cousin to the mantid, has the same peculiar wiring. It has long been known that roaches are capable of learning; they can run mazes and can even be conditioned to flee darkness and love light. This latter exercise has been replicated with headless cockroaches. They first learn the experiment after their heads have already been removed, and they repeatedly show that the learning has taken. Their learning ability is not in the head.

Perhaps you wonder how the roach can survive without a head. Well, it does need its head for eating. After a few weeks, a headless roach starves to death.

The mantid, which depends on her eyes and specializes in severing a prey animal's brain from the rest of its nervous system, can survive the devastation of her nervous system and the amputation of her eyes.

Alien, indeed, from the human perspective. Yet, some of the control mechanisms for human lovemaking are low in the spine, not in the brain.

In France, folklore has the mantid pointing lost children toward home. Zulu legend depicts the mantid as a stealer of children. Those two opposite characterizations show how readily we attach motives to the creature whose moves so often resemble our own.

Of course, those two legends also show how silly our anthropomorphic explanations can be. Early entomologists often described the mantid as a hypocrite because she acts as if she's praying while she's really plotting the murder of some hapless bug. This is exactly the sort of foolishness contemporary scientists hope to forestall when they advise us not to anthropomorphize at all. Other animals may or may not have mental processes like thought and emotion, the biologists say; it's best not to assume, and of course we can't observe such phenomena directly. This position too often gets oversimplified, so that a lot of people recite the "fact" that animals have nothing like human emotion. This idea, common as it is among educated people, is a misreading of the attempt at scientific objectivity, which merely asks that we suspend judgment on the question until we have proof.

We may not have proof, but we do have good evidence of emotional lives in mammals. Apes trained to use sign language sometimes overflow with emotion, saying things along the lines of "You are an unpleasant excrement-head." Of course, any lover of cats or dogs takes an emotional empathy with these mammals for granted. The theory among some scientists these days is that the emotions of unity—love and the like—developed with the mammal brain, and that the more primitive reptile brain is limited to aggression and other simple feelings.

But what about animals even more alien to us—more "primitive," as our egos would have it—than reptiles? Do they feel? Science tends to treat these creatures as electrochemical machines. I have had a hint or two of something deeper in my dealings with arthropods. One particular incident made me wonder all over again where the lines are drawn. It also reminded me of a certain overworked quotation—Hamlet to Horatio, about the things in heaven and earth.

It was the rain that drove them up into the daylight world.

In the semiarid region where I live, these beasts must be plentiful underground, but I rarely see them, even when I'm looking under rocks and boards for interesting creatures. The beast's shape marks it a relative of the cricket, but its back is humped, its forelegs are thicker. There are many such creatures—camel crickets, mole crickets, Jerusalem crickets, all burrowing, seldom-seen inhabitants of the soil. The Jerusalem cricket has a bulbous, disturbingly humanoid head that accounts for the common name *child-of-the-earth*. But the beast I'm talking about doesn't completely match the looks and behavior of any of these well-documented insects. Doubtless some entomologist has cataloged it, but I have never found it in a book.

The beast is a gleaming red-brown—it looks as if it might be made of the kind of plastic used for tortoiseshell combs and brushes. I had seen them at the bottom of water meter wells three or four feet underground, and I had seen small specimens above ground a few times, always in wet weather. But I had never seen anything like this.

It was late summer in the wettest year I could recall. Much of the country was under flood. We weren't flooded in our semidesert, but the black earth had grown a leprous infection of white mushrooms, and every outdoor thing seemed transformed by the wetness into a refractor of rainbows. The world stank with rot and rebirth—a smell delirious and nauseous.

As I pulled my car into the wet driveway one afternoon, I saw the beast crossing the cement. While I was still in the car twenty feet away, I recognized it as the species I'd seen a few times before, but I hardly believed it. The thing was larger than some adult mice I've seen. It was the third one I had seen during that wet spell, but the other two had been much smaller. It moved slowly, walking like some deliberate beetle, not jumping as a true cricket would. The proximity of my car disturbed it not at all. I had been hunting rattlesnakes and had several jars in the car for collecting the snakes' heads and tails. I used one of these to catch the cricket-beast, which walked agreeably into the jar with no urging from me.

I had no special plan for the cricket-beast. I didn't even know what it was. After checking a reference book, I tentatively decided it must be a type of camel cricket that eats rotting vegetation.

I transferred the thing to a gallon jar half-filled with dirt. I threw in some wet leaves for food. It moved its slow body, heavy as a brass bullet, through the leaves. My family came to the consensus that it was one of the most disgusting things I had ever brought in. Having nothing better to do with it, I figured I would keep it around to look at for a day or two, then feed it to one of the tarantulas that occupied terraria on my utility room counter.

That evening, the rain was at it again, and a mantid squeezed in the back door. He was about two inches long, and gray. I decided to see whether this thin, perfect predator could handle something as large as the cricket-beast. I dropped the mantid into the gallon jar.

The mantid did something I had never seen before. He looked at the cricket-beast and began to run away sideways, keeping his face toward the beast at all times. He seemed scared. Of course, even as I thought this, I accused myself of anthropomorphizing. I still thought the cricket-beast was an eater of plant rot. I recalled dangerous situations in which I had seen mantids—tangled in a black widow's web, battered by a cat, swarmed by ants, shoved into a jar by yours truly. In none of these situations had I seen a mantid use this body language of apparent fear.

I made chicken noises at the mantid.

The cricket-beast, waving its long antennae, turned toward the mantid. The mantid froze. The beast held its position in the center of the round jar. This is the top-predator position—a tarantula placed in a similar environment will, after a little exploration, take up this same spot in the middle of a container. I said as much to my wife, her sister, and her sister's husband, explaining that the cricket-beast must be an idiot not to realize what danger it was in.

The mantid took another step away. The cricket-beast, which had been sluggish up to now, leaped. The mantid was knocked wings over teakettle, landing a few inches away. As he tried to regain his "feet," the beast pounced again. This time it landed squarely on the mantid and bear-hugged him. Then it began to eat the mantid in a leisurely but methodical way, its many mouth parts wiggling like fingers. It chewed the mantid's face off first, and continued downward, not even pausing at the thick carapace. The four of us watching were amazed and repulsed. The others were not avid bug-watchers, as I am, but the spectacle was so intense in its microcosmic way that no one could stop looking.

In ten minutes the mantid was gone. Nothing remained but his transparent wings. The cricket-beast crawled sluggishly to the center of the jar.

Anne Fadiman

Collecting Nature

The net was green. The handle was wood, and the grip was uncomfortably thick, like that of a tennis racket borrowed from an older player. The mesh bag was long enough that if we caught a tiger swallowtail—or a spicebush swallowtail, or a mourning cloak, or a European cabbage, or a common sulphur, or a red admiral, or a painted lady, or a monarch, or a viceroy—we could, with a twist of the wrist, flip its tapered tip over the wire rim and trap the butterfly inside.

Then, being careful not to scrape off the colored scales, we pinched the wings shut and transferred the butterfly to the killing jar. (Our bible, *A Field Guide to the Butterflies of North America, East of the Great Plains,* by Alexander B. Klots, recommended a more complicated method of transfer that involved holding the handle between one's thighs, grasping the bag just below the butterfly, slipping the jar into the net, and coaxing the butterfly inside it. But this technique demanded a prodigious level of coordination—on the order, say, of that displayed by the Cat in the Hat when he balanced a goldfish bowl on an umbrella while standing on a rubber ball—and we were never able to master it.) My brother and I had started with a shallow plastic container, like a petri dish, which came in the children's butterfly kit that we had rapidly outgrown, but because the hindwing projections of the swallowtails tended to get crushed against the perimeter, we graduated to a large glass jar from which our mother had scrubbed the last traces of strawberry jam. At the bottom of the killing jar was a piece of cotton saturated with carbon tetrachloride.

"Carbon tet," we called it, not because it was easier to pronounce—we collected long words as eagerly as we did butterflies—but because the nickname suggested that we and it were on familiar terms, as was indeed the case. Thirty years later a friend of mine dabbed some spot remover on a sofa, and I instantly recognized the smell of the killing jar. During the fifties, when my brother and I started chasing butterflies, potassium cyanide was still in use as well, but because it is a deadly poison, Professor Klots recommended liquid carbon tetrachloride, which is "not very poisonous unless inhaled deeply," and which we persuaded our parents was as innocuous as smelling salts. The butterfly would flutter for a few moments, sink to the bottom of the jar, and slowly expire.

The murder was less grisly than it would have been in, say, 1810, when insect specimens were dispatched by pinching the thorax, stabbing them with a pin, asphyxiating them over the flame of a sulphur match, or skewering them with a red hot wire. Around 1820, the vogue in Europe was the "stifling box," a sealed container submerged in boiling water. The killing jar was introduced in the 1850s, after the royal physician used chloroform to ease the delivery of Queen Victoria's seventh child, and net-wielding country vicars across Great Britain realized they could amass their collections of marbled whites and Camberwell beauties without overt violence; they could simply anesthetize their specimens to death.

The problem with chloroform, as with potassium cyanide and carbon tetrachloride, is that these poisons freeze the butterfly's muscles into an extreme version of rigor mortis, and the wings cannot be spread. My brother and I therefore popped the corpse into a "relaxing jar"—now there's a euphemism right up there with Orwell's Ministry of Peace—that dampened it into pliancy, whereupon it could be pinned to the spreading board, a balsa rectangle with a groove down the center that allowed the wings to be flattened without squashing the thorax and abdomen. Caught, killed, relaxed, and spread, the butterfly was laid to rest in a Riker mount, a shallow glass-topped box filled with absorbent cotton—a sort of mass grave for soldiers who had given their lives on the battlefields of suburban Connecticut.

When did we realize that this was horrible? My brother, Kim, and I had started collecting butterflies when he was eight and I was six. Shame set in about two years later. I remember a six-month period of painful overlap, when the light of decency was dawning but the lure of sin was still irresistible. Like alcohol, nicotine, or heroin, lepidoptery is hard to renounce. A tiger swallowtail is an unbelievable thing to find in your back yard: a *big* butterfly, five inches across, striated with yellow and black, with blue splotches on the hindwings rendered iridescent by light-diffracting scales—"like the colors," wrote Professor Klots in a memorably lyrical passage, "produced by a glass prism, the blue of the sky, the spectrum of the rainbow, and an oil film on water." Who would not wish to take such a creature home? To glimpse something so gaudily tropical, more like a quetzal than a sparrow, on your own home ground; to pursue it across the lawn, down the stone steps, around the two topiary peacocks that stood guard over the wading pool, and along the flower border, until it lit on a snapdragon or a delphinium; to swoop your net through the air and see something fluttering inside; to snatch that bit of life from the rich chaos of nature into your own comparatively lackluster world, which it instantly brightened and enlarged; to look it up in Klots and name it and *know* it—well, after you did that a few times, it was hard to muster much enthusiasm for Parcheesi.

"The next two days were so wet and windy that there was no going out," wrote Alfred Russel Wallace in 1869, about a collecting trip to the Aru Islands north of Australia:

[B]ut on the succeeding one the sun shone brightly, and
I had the good fortune to capture one of the most magnificent insects the world contains, the great bird-
winged butterfly, Ornithoptera poseidon. I trembled
with excitement as I saw it coming majestically towards
me, and could hardly believe I had really succeeded in
my stroke till I had taken it out of the net and was
gazing, lost in admiration, at the velvet black and brilliant green of its wings, seven inches across, its golden
body, and crimson breast. It is true I had seen similar
insects in cabinets at home, but it is quite another thing
to capture such oneself—to feel it struggling between
one's fingers, and to gaze upon its fresh and living
beauty, a bright gem shining out amid the silent gloom
of a dark and tangled forest. The village of Dobbo held
that evening at least one contented man.

Few people read Wallace any more, even though he
founded the science of island biogeography and, independent of
Darwin, evolved a theory of natural selection. A few years ago I
borrowed a 1902 edition of one of his books from a large university library and noticed that it had last been checked out in 1949.
But he has long been a favorite of mine, in part because no one
has ever done a better job of capturing the febrile excitement
one feels on netting a really beautiful specimen. And unlike the
editor of a 1975 book on butterflies—who, when he quoted this
passage, squeamishly omitted the phrase "to feel it struggling
between one's fingers"—Wallace made no bones about how crucial the violence was to the thrill.

While Wallace was chasing butterflies in the Malay Archipelago, thousands of his compatriots back home in England were
doing the same thing. A special butterfly net was even invented
that, when folded, looked exactly like an umbrella, so that one
could take it on a stroll without attracting undue attention. (As
the British historian David Elliston Allen has pointed out, one
did look rather a fool if it started to rain and one's umbrella
remained obstinately furled.) Sunday afternoons, after church,

were a favorite time for entomology, which was considered a highmindedly Christian pursuit. An 1843 pamphlet entitled *Instructions for Collecting, Rearing, and Preserving British & Foreign Insects*—it now reposes in an envelope in the Library of Congress, as fragile as a sheaf of butterfly wings—begins with the following words:

> The contemplation of the works of the CREATOR is the highest delight of the rational mind. In them we read, as in a volume fraught with endless wonders, the unlimited power and goodness of that BEING, who, in the formation of Atoms, and of Worlds, has alike displayed unfathomable Wisdom. There are few objects in Nature which raise the mind to a higher degree of admiration, than the Insect creation. Their immense numbers—endless variety of form—astonishing metamorphoses—exceeding beauty—the amazing minuteness of some, and the complex and wonderful organization of others, far exceeding that of the higher animals—all tend to prove an Almighty artificer, and inspire astonishment and awe!

I sympathize with these views. When I was in high school, an evangelical Christian friend attempted to rouse me from my agnosticism by asking, "Isn't there *anything* that seems so miraculous it simply has to be by design?" I answered, "Butterfly metamorphosis." I knew it was explainable by rational principles, but it still seemed to hold an irreducible spark of divinity. When Brahma watched the caterpillars in his vegetable garden change into pupae, and thence into butterflies, he was filled with the certainty that he, too, would attain perfection in a future incarnation. Brahma, however, was content to observe the works of the CREATOR, whereas the author of the 1843 pamphlet (using methods he detailed in a thirteen-page chapter called "On killing and preserving Insects in general") believed he could appreciate them most fully only if he did them in.

Any parent of a small child is familiar with the ineluctable impulse to own that which one admires. It is why my husband

and I used to tell our daughter, before she was old enough to be so easily duped, that F.A.O. Schwarz was a toy *museum.* When we were very young, my brother and I could not yet divorce our ardor for butterflies from our desire to flatten them in Riker mounts and hang them on the wall. Distinguishing the two required an unchildlike conjunction of self-control and guilt: the sort of moral conversion, for example, that might transform a trophy hunter into a wildlife photographer. We threw away our killing jar not because we wished to stop causing pain—crushing an ant or a cockroach, which presumably had a nervous system similar to that of a tiger swallowtail, stirred few qualms—but because, unlike Alfred Russel Wallace, we grew uneasy with the pleasure it gave us.

During the period of withdrawal, when we still caught butterflies but were ashamed of enjoying it, a luna moth settled on the grille of the air conditioner that was bolted into the window of our father's dressing room, on the second floor of our house. If you have ever seen a luna moth—pale green, hindwings tapering to long slender tails, antennae like golden feathers—you have not forgotten it. It was a hot, humid, firefly-filled summer night, and Kim and I were sitting outside on the front lawn. The light from the house illuminated the moth with a spectral glow. We could not reach it from the ground. We could not open the window from inside. I cannot remember ever desiring anything so much.

All children collect things, of course, but the difference between collecting stamps and collecting butterflies is that you do not have to kill the stamps. Also—and this casts lepidoptery in a slightly more favorable light—the rarity of certain species of insects can be naturally experienced, whereas the rarity of stamps must be looked up in a book. A child knows that a common sulphur is less precious than a luna moth because she has seen thousands of the former and only one of the latter, but how could she guess that an 1856 British one-penny rose is worth a dollar and an 1856 British Guiana one-penny magenta is worth $935,000?

I once read a book on collecting that included photographs of collectors of toilet paper, Weetabix boxes, and airsickness bags. They were all male and all nerdy-looking. My father's first cousin, William James Sidis—a child prodigy who knew Greek and Latin at three, entered Harvard at eleven, and ended up an ill paid back-office clerk—collected streetcar transfers, of which he eventually accumulated more than two thousand. Billy Sidis was nerdy, too, as well as deeply unhappy. Surely the desire to collect inanimate objects with no intrinsic beauty or meaning, as opposed to paintings or books or antique Chinese snuff bottles, reflects a yawning lack of self-confidence. All collecting is a form of spuriously easy mastery, but it is almost unbearably pathetic that a man of Sidis's ability was so incapable, in either his work or his hobby, of picking something anywhere near his own size.

Collecting insects is less pathetic than collecting streetcar transfers, but most people would consider it more sinister. Is it surprising that the revolutionist Jean-Paul Marat, the author of a 1790 pamphlet advocating that "five or six hundred heads be cut off," was an amateur lepidopterist? Is it entirely a coincidence that Alfred Kinsey, before he collected 18,000 sexual histories (along with innumerable nudist magazines, pornographic statues, and pieces of sadomasochistic paraphernalia), collected tens of thousands of gall wasps? Was it not inevitable that John Fowles should have made Frederick Clegg, who collected a beautiful art student and imprisoned her in his cellar, a collector of butterflies as well? I read *The Collector* when I was sixteen, and I got a perverse insider's thrill when Frederick drugged Miranda with chloroform and carbon tetrachloride, both of which he had previously used in his killing bottle to drug fritillaries and blues.

But on the other side of the scale—and I believe he carries enough weight to outbalance an entire army of lepidopteran weirdos—there is Vladimir Nabokov. It is my view that if you have never netted a butterfly, you cannot truly understand Nabokov. This, of course, may be merely a rationalization, the ignoble offspring of my desire to believe that the tiger swallowtails of my misspent youth did not die in vain. Only Nabokov, eloping at age ten with a nine-year-old girl in Biarritz, would have taken, as the sum total of his luggage, a folding butterfly net in a brown paper bag. Nabokov chased butterflies on two continents for six decades; spent seven years as a Research Fellow in Entomology at Harvard; discovered several new species and subspecies, including *Cyclargus erembis* Nabokov and *Neonympha maniola* Nabokov; and wrote twenty-two articles on lepidoptera, including a 1951 review of my own Alexander B. Klots in the *New York Times Book Review*. (He called it "wonderfully stimulating.")

In a 1931 story called "The Aurelian"—an archaic term for butterfly collector—Nabokov describes a butterfly shop in Berlin whose windows are full of "eyed wings wide-open in wonder, shimmering blue satin, black magic." To the right of the shop there are a tobacconist, a delicatessen, and a fruit seller. To the left there are stores that sell soap, coal, and bread. This is how Nabokov viewed butterflies. One may progress through life surrounded on all sides by drabness, but if there are butterflies at the center, there will never be a want of beauty or romance. What more appropriate passion could a writer have? Lepidopterists, more than naturalists of any other stripe, have long inclined toward the literary, as one can tell from looking at the names they have given the objects of their study. There are butterflies named after Homer, Catullus, Martial, Juvenal, Propertius, and Persius; after dozens of characters in Greek and Roman mythology; and even after several marks of punctuation—the question mark, the long dash, and the comma. (Nabokov described the comma in a famous passage about listening to his governess read French classics on the veranda of the family estate outside St. Petersburg, while his imagination was joyfully diverted by the comma-like markings on a butterfly that had settled on the threshold.)

Many of the themes in Nabokov's fiction—metamorphosis and flight, deception and mimicry, evasion and capture—are lepidopteran. And to my ear, his very language is too. The first canto of *Pale Fire* contains, within its four-and-a-half-page compass, the words *torquated, stillicide, shagbark, vermiculated, preterist, iridule,* and *lemniscate.* Nabokov collected rare words, just as he collected rare butterflies, and when he netted one, especially in the exotic landscape of his second language, his satisfaction is as palpable as if he had finally captured the brown and white hair-streak that once eluded him when he was a boy. Nabokov's style is not just poetic; it is taxonomic. He mentions with something close to hatred the village schoolmaster who, taking his charges for a nature walk, used to quash young Vladimir's hunger for precision by saying "Oh, just a small bird—no special name." And what scorn Nabokov bears for *us,* his clueless audience, when he writes, "I had found last spring a dark aberration of Sievers' Carmelite (just another gray moth to the reader)."

Phase Two of my life as a collector—again, one shared with my older and wiser brother—was an intemperate, catholic, and nonmurderous surrender to the urge to identify the small bird and the gray moth. If catching was the central theme of our childhood, curating—classifying, labeling, sorting, arranging, displaying—was the central theme of our adolescence. Butterflies were the slender wedge that opened up something much larger: an earnest attempt to stuff the entire natural world, down to the last kingdom, phylum, class, order, family, genus, and species (I can still rattle these off in the proper sequence, having learned the mnemonic "King Philip, Come Out For God's Sake" at age twelve) into our spare bedroom. It never occurred to us that it would not fit.

The spare bedroom, on the southwest corner of the second floor of our house in Los Angeles, to which we had moved when I was eight and Kim was ten, had a sign on the door that read:

THE SERENDIPITY MUSEUM OF NATURE
NO SMOKING, PLEASE

The sign was embossed in blue with a Dymo Labelmaker, than which there was no more perfect gift, circa 1963, for a pair of children who were crazy about naming things. I am not quite sure why our parents turned over this room to us, nor why they let us hammer pieces of whale baleen into the striped tan wallpaper, nor why they permitted us to fill the bathroom with dirt in order to accommodate our pet California king snake. All I can say is that I am profoundly grateful that they did.

In *Our Mutual Friend,* Silas Wegg visits a shop belonging to "Mr. Venus, Preserver of Animals and Birds, Articulator of human bones." Mr. Wegg is there because—could anyone but Dickens ever come up with this one?—he wishes to retrieve his leg, which Mr. Venus purchased, for potential inclusion in a skeleton, from the hospital in which it was amputated. "I shouldn't like," says Wegg, "to be what I may call dispersed, a part of me here, and a part of me there, but should wish to collect myself as a genteel person." (Mr. Wegg may thus be the only collector who has ever collected himself. He does get his leg back, though not until later in the book; it arrives under Mr. Venus's arm, carefully wrapped, looking like "a sort of brown paper truncheon.") Mr. Venus shows Mr. Wegg around the shop. "Bones, warious," he explains.

> Skulls, warious. Preserved Indian baby. African ditto. Bottled preparations, warious. Everything within reach of your hand, in good preservation. The mouldy ones a-top. What's in those hampers over them again, I don't quite remember. Say, human warious. Cats. Articulated English baby. Dogs. Ducks. Glass eyes, warious. Mummied bird. Dried cuticle, warious. Oh, dear me! That's the general panoramic view.

The general panoramic view of the Serendipity Museum of Nature was similarly warious. It bore a far closer resemblance to Mr. Venus's shop, or to a seventeenth-century *Wunderkammer* crammed from top to bottom with miscellaneous natural curiosities, than it did to any museum we had actually seen.

We displayed not only things that had once been alive but things that had once held life: the discarded skin of a garter snake, the exoskeleton of a cicada, the speckled egg of a scrub jay, the pendant nest of a Baltimore oriole. Blowfish were suspended from the ceiling on strands of dental floss. In the south-east corner, pinned to the wall, were scraps of fur—leopard, tiger, polar bear, rabbit, otter, nutria, mink—left over from coats tailored by a local furrier. Next to them was a man-size piece of styrofoam into which we had stuck hundreds of feathers. On the west wall we had nailed a desiccated sand shark, which looked like a crucified demon. Shelves and card tables held, among other things, a stuffed mouse, a stuffed bat, the skeleton of a pit viper, a hornet's nest, a mounted ostrich egg, a hunk of petrified wood, the fossils of ammonites and foraminifers, several dried salamanders, a dead tarantula, three dead scorpions, a sperm whale tooth, a box of our own baby teeth, the foot of an egret, a pickled squid, a pickled baby octopus, and a pickled human tapeworm, about which I am said to have exclaimed, when I received it on my tenth birthday, "Just what I always wanted!" There were also about a dozen bird and mammal skulls that we had retrieved from road kills and cleaned with Clorox. (Pending their Clorox baths, our mother permitted us to wrap the corpses in aluminum foil and store them in the freezer, as long as we labeled them clearly enough to prevent her from confusing them with dinner.)

Our old Riker mounts hung on the south wall, but the tiger swallowtails were fading. Our new passion was shells, which we housed in a huge metal cabinet, typing the genera on little slips of paper and gluing them to the drawer fronts. In conchology, as a mid-nineteenth-century British magazine observed, "there is no cruelty in the pursuit, the subjects are so brightly clean, so ornamental to a boudoir." It is true that on the Florida island where we spent our spring vacations, we did occasionally collect live king's crown conchs, boil them, extract the animals, and clean the shells with muriatic acid. (Being trusted with dangerous substances was a continuing theme throughout our childhood.) But it was more sporting, and more fun, to walk along the beach and, among the jetsam of broken cockles and clams, to spot a banded tulip, an alphabet cone, an apple murex, or (great find of my youth!) an angulate wentletrap.

Last week I was reminiscing about our museum with my brother, who is now a natural history teacher in Wyoming. Kim said, "When you collect nature, there are two moments of discovery. The first comes when you find the thing. The second comes when you find the name." Few pleasures can equal those of the long summer afternoons we spent sitting on the floor in a patch of sunlight, our shell guides spread out before us, trying to identify a particular species of limpet or marginella—and finally, with a whoop of delight, succeeding. Without classification, a collection is just a hodgepodge. Taxonomy, after all—and I think we unconsciously realized this, even as teenagers—is a form of imperialism. During the nineteenth century, when British naval surveys were flooding London with specimens to be classified, inserting them into their proper niches in the Linnaean hierarchy had strong political overtones. Take a bird or a lizard or a flower from Patagonia or the South Seas, perhaps one that has had a local name for centuries, rechristen it with a Latin name, and presto! It has become a tiny British colony. That's how Kim and I felt, too. To name was to assert dominion.

"You're like a miser," Miranda says to her captor in *The Collector*. "You hoard up all the beauty in these drawers. . . . I hate people who collect things, and classify things and give them names." That's the popular notion, all right. Even my husband finds it a wee bit pathological when he finds me taking the shells *he* has collected and arranging them in rows, by species. But I believe it is no accident that the three greatest biological theorists of the nineteenth century—Alfred Russel Wallace; Henry Walter Bates, who developed the theory of mimicry; and Charles Darwin—were all, at their cores, collectors. Wallace, who collected plants as a boy, returned from the Malay Archipelago with 125,660 "specimens of natural history," mostly insects. Bates, who collected bugs as a boy, returned from the Amazon with 14,712 different *species*, again mostly insects, of which eight thousand were previously undiscovered. When he was a boy, Darwin collected coins, postal franks, pebbles, minerals, shells, birds' eggs, and, above all, in the days when "to beetle" was an infinitive, hundreds of specimens of the order Coleoptera. His zeal was such that once, with a rare beetle in each hand, he spied a third species, and popped the beetle in his right hand into his mouth. He later sent home from South America box after box of specimens—birds, mammals, reptiles, insects, fish—that he had skinned and stuffed and pickled while fighting terrible seasickness in the *Beagle*'s poop cabin. It was not enough just to *see* the Galapagos finches; he had to *collect* them, and get help classifying them, and compare their beaks back home in England, before he was able to develop the theory of the origin of species.

All nature collectors share a particular set of tastes and skills: pattern recognition; the ability to distinguish anomaly from norm; the compulsion to order experience. A few of them also have brilliant imaginations, as well as what Darwin called the capacity for "grinding general laws out of large collections of facts." *Collections* of facts. Those of us who lack the latter two abilities will never change the course of science, but when we invite a new shell or butterfly into our lives, we are doing a part of what Darwin did. And lest the primacy of the collecting instinct be underestimated, let us reflect that Darwin was never able to remember for more than a few days a single date or a line of poetry, but at age sixty-seven, he wrote, apropos the beetles of his youth, "I can remember the exact appearance of certain posts, old trees and banks where I made a good capture."

We sold the Serendipity Museum of Nature. My brother and I were off to college, our parents were moving to a smaller house, we thought it was time to grow up, and . . . well, we just did it. We put an ad in the *Los Angeles Times,* and over the course of a weekend, a stream of strange people walked underneath the blowfish and took away the pit viper skeleton and the desiccated sandshark and the pickled human tapeworm. The things we prized most, because we had found them ourselves, were worthless. I remember jamming dozens of birds' nests into plastic garbage bags. I was almost seventeen; it was the last day of my childhood.

Thank heavens, we kept the shells, because they were small and easily stored. Today they rest inside a wooden cabinet in the home of our elderly parents, who surprised us a few years ago by moving to the Florida island where we had collected the shells in the first place. When I visit, I still cannot resist picking up the odd murex or limpet when I walk along the beach. They do not have the same meaning they once did, but, as Swann said in *Remembrance of Things Past,* "even when one is no longer attached to things, it's still something to have been attached to them."

Three years ago, I found a 1951 edition of *A Field Guide to the Butterflies of North America, East of the Great Plains,* by Alexander B. Klots, in a secondhand store in upstate New York. There was a stamp on the school library bookplate that said DISCARDED. Discard *Klots*? How could anyone do that? I suppose for the same reason that I once discarded Klots myself: because there wasn't room. When I was younger, I didn't know what I wanted from life, so I wanted everything—new experiences, tiger swallowtails, egrets' feet. Now that I have collected a family, a home, a profession, and a few thousand books, my New York City apartment and my life are full. Before my husband's last birthday, I sent for a copy of the Carolina Biological Supply Company catalogue so I could buy him a flower press. I felt the old thirst when I read about the tarantula spiderling kit, $49.95; the owl pellets, "fumigated and individually wrapped," $3.20; the live salamander larvae, $11.45 a dozen; the slime mold box, "preferred by professional slime mold collectors" (a lovely phrase, as I had never thought of it as a profession), $5.80. I knew, however, that I would never order these things. There isn't room.

My favorite Nabokov story, "Christmas," is about a man named Sleptsov who has recently lost his son, a butterfly collector. In an agony of suicidal grief, Sleptsov looks through his son's belongings—spreading boards, specimen files, a net that still smells of summer and sun-hot grass. Suddenly, from the biscuit tin in which it had been stored, the dormant cocoon of a great *Attacus* moth, stirred into life by the unaccustomed heat, bursts open. A wrinkled black creature the size of a mouse crawls out and starts slowly unfurling its wings. As soon as he witnesses this miracle, Sleptsov knows he must stay alive. This is a story about lepidoptery, but it is also a story about parenthood. One reason we have children, I think, is to experience through them the miracle of the *Attacus* moth: to learn that parts of ourselves we had given up for dead are merely dormant, and that the old joys can re-emerge, fresh and new and in a completely different form, from their chrysalis.

I have two children. Henry, who is three, owns three rubber caterpillars—a black swallowtail, a pipevine swallowtail, and a zebra heliconian. I know their species because he likes to match them up with the pictures in Klots, which now sits on a shelf in his bedroom. Henry is at an age when anything seems possible, and the other night, having just looked at a diagram of metamorphosis, he saw a housefly crawling across the ceiling and said, with dreamy excitement, "Maybe that fly will turn into a stag beetle!"

Susannah is eight. When she was six, we gave her a kit containing five painted lady caterpillars. She watched them pupate. After they broke out of their chrysalises as fully formed butterflies, she carried them in a net enclosure from our cramped apartment to a nearby garden. Then she loosened the net and let them go.

Fathers

Bliss Broyard

My Father's Daughter

There is a particular type of older man I like. He must be at least twenty years my senior, preferably thirty years or more. Old enough to be my father, it's fair to say. This man is handsome, stylish, a connoisseur of women, intelligent, cultured and witty, old-fashioned and romantic. He has male friends whom he loves as brothers. He knows how to dance the old dances: the lindy, the cha-cha, the samba, even the tango. He's vain about his appearance and is unabashedly delighted any time I tell him he is looking trim or healthy or particularly handsome. When I compliment his fedora, he tilts it to an even more jaunty angle. He reads the romantic poets and can quote their lines in a way that doesn't sound corny. He has fought in wars, has traveled a good bit of the world and has a reputation of being a ladies' man in his day. He tells me stories about girls he knew overseas: geishas and lonely nurses. He notices what I am wearing; he notices if I have changed my hair style or done my makeup in a new way. Each time I see him, he tells me I've never looked better. Our conversation is playful, mischievous, saucy. He sometimes makes pronouncements about women that make me blush and often also make me angry—things I would object to from a man my own age. Many of the traits in my favorite type of older man I would find foolish, affected, or tiresome in a younger man, but with you, old sport, I am always charmed.

Our relationship is not intimate, though our conversations often are. I tell this older man about whom I am dating and make not-so-subtle innuendos about my sex life: this one didn't understand that conversation is a necessary part of seduction, that one had the eagerness of a boy and a boy's lack of self-control; another one clutched his machismo between the sheets like a security blanket. We both shake our heads and mourn the shortage of decent young men out there these days. We both secretly believe that my charms belong to another era, a better and more refined world, his world. In his day, no doubt, I would have been a smash. At least this is my fantasy of what he is thinking.

Where do I meet these men? Mostly they are my father's friends. And since he died six years ago at the age of seventy, I have been transfigured from being my father's daughter into a young woman friend of these men in my own right.

Vincent, the oldest of my father's friends, lives in Greenwich Village, still carrying on the same sort of life he and my father led when they were young there together. There is Davey, the youngest of my father's friends, who over the years was his summer playmate for touch football and volleyball and beach paddle and who is now a father himself. Mike was the closest to my dad, serving as his primary reader during his long career as a writer and book critic. When Mike and I talk on the phone, he seems to miss my dad as much as I do. Finally there is Ernest, my father's most contentious friend. My dad used to say that he had to befriend Ernest, otherwise Ernest wouldn't have any friends at all, although I think he secretly took pride in being able to tolerate his pal's notorious crankiness.

Though the ages of these men span more than twenty-five years and they come from a variety of backgrounds, I think of them as natives of a singular world, a world belonging to the past and a particular place: Greenwich Village, where my father's friendships with these men—if not actually born there—were consummated. Like any world, it has its own language and culture. There is a hip, playful rhythm to the conversation and an angle of the observations that makes everything appear stylized, either heroically or calamitously. In this world, folks don't walk, they swagger; they don't talk, they declaim. Women are crazy, beautiful, impeccably bred, tragic. They are rarely boring. No one has much money, but happiness, as my father liked to say, could be bought cheaply. A man's status is determined by his wit and intelligence and, most of all, his successes with women. A woman's status is a product of her beauty and her novelty, not a fresh kind of novelty because that would imply innocence—and you couldn't have too much innocence if you were with this crowd—but the kind of novelty that places you on the cutting edge of things. To be described as modern is a high compliment.

Of course, nostalgia has smoothed out these memories to make them uniform and sweet, and the world that I know from my father's stories is pristinely preserved in my mind as though it were contained in one of those little glass spheres that fills with snow when you shake it. I imagine, though, that by stepping in I can unsettle this scene with my presence and make it come back to life; then I will find a world that is more cozy than the one I live in, a world that is as reassuring and familiar as those winter idylls captured under glass.

Vincent has lived in the same apartment on Perry Street for over forty years, and as I walk up the five flights to visit him, the years slip away behind me. Everyone lived in four- and five-floor walk-ups in the old days, Vincent has told me. All cold-water flats.

"Your father and I once went to a party at Anaïs Nin's, and I rang the bell and flew up the five flights as fast as I could. Your dad had briefed me that Anaïs gauged her lovers' stamina and virility by how long it took them to reach her floor without puffing."

This is a story I heard from my father, though many of the

stories Vincent tells me about the old days I have not. Those are the ones I have come to hear.

Vincent's apartment is decorated with souvenirs from his years traveling the world as a cruise director on ships. Geometric Moroccan tiles and bits of Persian carpet and copper-colored patches of stucco cover every inch of the walls. Through a beaded curtain is his bedroom, where tapestries form a canopy over a daybed heaped with Turkish pillows. The tub located in the entrance hall is concealed by day with a sort of shiny green lamina which, when you gaze upon it, is reminiscent of an ancient Roman bath. Also off the entrance hall is the toilet, concealed only with a thin strip of fabric. Once, after I'd used it, Vincent asked me if I noticed how the base was loose. I hadn't.

"Well, it's been like that for almost forty years," he explained. "Once I loaned the apartment to your dad so he could take a girl he'd met somewhere private. Afterward, the toilet was a little rocky. I asked him what the hell he was doing in there, and he told me they were taking in the view." Vincent took me back into the bathroom and pointed out the Empire State Building, barely visible between two other buildings. "I won't have the toilet fixed," he said, "because I love being reminded of that story." I headed down the stairs with Vincent's laughter trailing behind me.

Should a daughter know such things about her father? Should she have an image of him that she must rush past, one that is a little too vivid and too private to be promptly forgotten? It is easy to become embarrassed by such stories, to let my own paternal memories sweep them under some psychic rug, but my father's past is like a magnet I can't pull myself away from. This is my history too, I argue to myself. I've had my own sexual adventures, my own versions of making love on a shaky toilet, an aspect of my life that I have been sure to share with my father's friends. I have paraded past a host of boyfriends past them, have brought along young men to their apartments, or out to dinner, or for an evening of dancing. When the fellow gets up to fetch another round of drinks, I might lean back in my chair and watch him walk off.

"So," I'll say offhandedly, "I'm not sure I'm going to keep this one. He's bright and successful too, but maybe not quite sexy enough."

"You are your father's daughter," the man answers, laughing, which is just what I'd hoped to hear.

Of course, with my own contemporaries I am never so cavalier. I have argued on behalf of honesty and respect in relationships. I have claimed to believe in true love. I will even admit that I am looking for my own version of a soulmate (although I can confess to this only in an ironic tone of voice, all too aware of its sentimental implications). Nevertheless, this desire runs in me alongside a desire for a successful writing career, children, and a house in the country with dogs and flower beds and weekend guests visiting from the city—a lot like the kind of life my father left New York to build with my mother, a move that shocked many of his friends.

All of my father's friends share a boyish quality, one that is often delightful with its playfulness and vitality but that contains an underside, too: a sort of adolescent distrust of any threat to the gang. A silent pact was made never to grow up. And though I wouldn't be here if my father, at the age of forty, hadn't managed finally to break free of this hold to marry my mother, I carry on this pact with his friends in spite of myself.

Some of these men eventually did marry and have children now themselves, have daughters who one day, no doubt, they hope to see married. If I would let them, they would probably wish for me a similar simple and happy fate. But I don't want to be seen in the same light as their daughters. Just as they knew my father as a friend first, rather than a dad or husband, I want them to view me as their friend rather than my father's daughter. Otherwise, I would never learn anything about him at all. I search out these men to discover the man behind my father, that is who I've come to meet.

Besides all this, these men are exceptional, and to be accepted by them, my aspirations must be sophisticated, more rarefied and imaginative than my dreams of a husband and house in the country.

Once out for dinner with the contentious friend, Ernest, we argued about the value of monogamy in relationships. Over the years, Ernest has taken me to some of New York's finest restaurants. Everywhere the maître d's know him by name, probably because he is the worst kind of customer: he demands special dishes which he then complains about, is rude to the waiters, and usually leaves a shabby tip. I put up with his behavior for the same reason a parent puts up with a misbehaving child in a restaurant—to challenge Ernest would only egg him on. What I had forgotten was that in conversation he is the same way.

His expression grew increasingly pitying and snide while he listened to my argument for monogamy, which—best as I can recall—went something like this: monogamy in a relationship engendered trust and trust was the only means to a profound intimacy, not the kind of combustible sexual intimacy that Ernest favored (I added pointedly), but the kind that requires a continual commitment of faith, not unlike the effort to believe in God. And the rewards of this type of intimacy—the compassion, the connection—were infinitely greater. Trust was the only route to a person's soul!

I was only about twenty-five at the time, and while my line of reasoning was hardly original and smacked somewhat of piteous posturing, I remember being pleased that I was able to unfold my rationale in a composed, yet passionate manner. Sometimes when I was talking with my father or his friends, I would grab panic-struck for a word only to find it out of my reach. By the end of my speech, Ernest looked amused. He dabbed at his mouth with his linen napkin and sat back in his chair. "I had no idea you were so bourgeois," he said. "How in the world did your father manage to raise such a bourgeois daughter?"

"Bourgeois" was one of those words that floated through the air of my childhood, occasionally landing on a dinner guest or neighbor or the parent of one of my friends. I wasn't sure when I was young what it meant, but I didn't miss how efficiently the term dismissed the person as though he or she had been made to vanish into thin air.

For weeks after that dinner with Ernest, I carried on an internal debate with myself about the value of monogamy and, more fundamentally, wondered from what source I had formed my opinions on it: Was this something that my father believed, if perhaps not in practice, then in theory? Was I falling into a conventional, clichéd way of thinking? Or did I actually believe the stance I'd taken with Ernest for the very reason that it was not my father's position. This was not the first time I had tried to locate myself behind his shadow.

Although my father was a critic of books by profession, he could be counted on to have an opinion on just about anything. At a gathering back at my house following his cremation, I sat around the dining room table, reminiscing with a group of family friends. We began listing all the things my father liked, and after one trip around the table, we ran out of things to say. The someone offered up "thick arms on a woman," and someone else jumped in with "kung fu movies and cream sauces," starting us on a long and lively conversation about all the things my father disliked. What surprised me during this discussion (besides the welcome relief it provided to that bleak day) was how many of my own opinions were either my father's—or the exact opposite. I remember thinking that rather than having a unique personality, I was merely an assemblage of reactions, a mosaic of agreements and disagreements with my dad—a feeling that has reoccurred intermittently since. I keep hoping to find the line where he stops and I begin.

Vincent keeps scrapbooks. He has scrapbooks from his travels, scrapbooks from his days in Cuba where he first encountered the Afro-Cuban music that became his and my father's passion, scrapbooks from his youth with my dad in New York City. Sometimes before heading out to dinner or to a club to hear some salsa band, Vincent and I will have a drink in his apartment—we always drink champagne or sherry—and flip through these books. One evening I pointed out the pictures of people I didn't recognize. Vincent became irritated when I didn't know their names. Machito. Milton. Willie. You must know who these people are! How can you have not heard these stories? You should have paid more attention to your father when he was alive, he scolded. Are you listening to what I am telling you? Your father was a beautiful man! He lived a beautiful life!

Nostalgia made us quiet when we were out on the street. Vincent was nostalgic for a past that seemed in danger of being forgotten, and me—I was nostalgic for a history that both was and wasn't mine.

Vincent has worked as a tour guide on and off for most of his life and he walks very fast. That evening, I let him lead me around by my elbow. He rushed me across the intersections, hurrying me along in a variety of foreign languages: *vite, rapido,* quick-quick-quick. He began to talk as we twisted and turned through the labyrinth of streets, pointing out various buildings and explaining their significance: *there was an illegal nightclub here where we went to hear Machito drum, you had to know the code word to be let inside; this was where your dad had his bookstore and Milton and Willie hung out talking, talking, talking about books.* We turned a corner to arrive on a quiet, tree-lined street. He pointed out the top floor of a brownstone. *Your dad lived there for a while. He had a girlfriend in the next house over, and rather than walk down the five flights to the street and then up another five flights to her apartment, he would climb across the roof to her window like a cat burglar.*

I pointed out the steep pitch of the roofs and said that my dad must have really liked the girl to put himself at such risk. "Oh, he wasn't afraid of risks," Vincent answered knowingly, and I had no idea at that moment whether this assessment was true or not, a realization that brought tears to my eyes. After a moment, I remarked quietly that men didn't do that anymore—climb over rooftops for a woman—at least none that I'd ever met.

Only when a parent dies does it seem that a child gains a right to know that parent's life. While my father was alive, his life, as it should have, belonged to him. Besides, we were too involved with each other for me to step back and gain some objective view. But now that his life contains both a beginning *and* an end, it seems possible to shape some complete picture. I can't help regretting, though, that so much of my information must come secondhand. Perhaps Vincent is right. I should have paid more attention to my father when he was alive. Perhaps if I had asked him more questions about his past, I could have learned these things from him myself. Perhaps if he had lived longer, if we had moved on from being father and daughter to being friends, we would have arrived at some understanding of each other, or rather I would have arrived at some understanding of him that would allow me to incorporate such anecdotes like a splash of color into the portrait I held of him rather than their changing the portrait completely.

But when my father was alive, I was too busy trying to figure out what he thought of me—another question that I now lay at the feet of his friends, as though he had handed off his judgment like a baton in a relay race.

At another, earlier dinner with Ernest, I watched him as he studied my face. I hadn't seen him in a few years, and I knew that since our last encounter I had evolved from looking like a girl to looking like a woman.

"You've grown up to be attractive," he finally decided. "For a while there it seemed that you wouldn't. Your features were so sharp and you were always frowning. You should keep your hair long, though. It softens your face."

I wish I could say that if my father had been present he would have reprimanded Ernest for this cold comment, but I know that he wouldn't have. Over the years I came to learn that being my father didn't limit his ability to assess me critically. He had opinions about my hairstyle, he picked out the clothes that he thought best brought out what he referred to as my "subtle appeal"; he noticed anytime I gained a few pounds. And while I realize now that in his world a woman was as powerful as her beauty, that doesn't lessen the hurt caused by such impartial opinions.

At times with these friends I have felt like an impostor or a spy, trying to lure them into a conversation where they will unwittingly reveal some assessment of me my father had shared with them, or that, since they knew him and his tastes and were able to observe us with the clarity of a spectator's view, they will reveal some insight about our relationship that remained hidden from me. On occasion, I have just asked point-blank what it is I want to know.

Recently I had a wedding to go to in the Long Island town where my dad's youngest friend, Davey, now lives with his wife, Kate, and their three teenage children. Davey has been in my life for as long as I can remember. And my father was in Davey's life as long as Davey can remember. They first met in the summer of 1950 on Fire Island. Davey was a chubby, cheerful boy of four, and my father was a trim, athletic bachelor of thirty. It's hard for me to picture the start of this friendship; nevertheless, during the ensuing summers on Fire Island, the man and boy became friends. They would remain close friends until my father's death. Davey spoke at my father's memorial service, recalling how when he was sixteen he helped move my parents from one five-story walk-up in Greenwich Village to another a few blocks away. Theirs was a friendship sealed by carrying books, he said. Throughout my childhood, Davey visited us each summer on Martha's Vineyard, and he and my father would write in the mornings (Davey eventually became a successful playwright) and then the two men would head to the beach for an afternoon of touch football or beach paddle, or they would just stroll and talk.

During this recent visit, Davey and I strolled on the beach ourselves and talked about *our* writing. He had been feeling discouraged recently about the unsteady progress of his career. I had just finished a graduate school degree in creative writing and was nervous about reentering the world with this new label of *writer*. We had walked a short distance when Davey mentioned that his back was bothering him and asked if we could sit down. We lay on the sand, a bit damp from the previous night's rain, and looked out over the choppy ocean.

A few days before, TWA flight 800 had crashed not far from where we lay, and earlier that day bits of fuselage and an airline drinking cup were found on a neighboring beach. Groups of people searched along the shoreline—airline officials, family members, curiosity seekers. Davey talked about his own kids, how well they were all doing, how different they were from one another and from him and Kate. It was clear in listening to him how much he respected and loved them, but I was surprised at how objectively he was able to assess their talents and weaknesses. I asked him what my father thought of me.

"Well, of course he loved you," he said, and then looked away toward the beachcombers. I could see that my question had upset him. Perhaps he was wondering if his children would ever ask such a thing. I was searching too, there on that beach, but my debris was not the result of some tragic, sudden accident; rather, my father had died slowly from the common illness of cancer when I was twenty-three, an age when most children are letting go of their parents in order to establish their own independence. I was lost somewhere between missing my father and trying to move past him. Davey looked back at me and said again with a surprising urgency in his voice that I must believe my father loved me. And I do, but in an abstract way, believing in my father's love the same way that I believe that all parents must love their children. What I am searching for is the shape of that love. These men are bright men, observant and persuasive. They are my father's friends, after all. I want them to make elegant arguments, peppered with indisputable examples and specific instances of the how and why and where of that love.

When all this searching makes me too weary, I call Mike. He is a psychologist and a writer too. Besides his interest and insight into human nature, he has most of Western literature for reference at his fingertips, which makes him wonderful to talk with. Over the years, even when he and my father lived in separate states, my dad would read to him the first drafts of almost everything he wrote. I can remember my father stretched out on his bed for an hour at a time, laying in the dark room, telephone in hand, chatting with his pal. Their talk was filled with elegant phrasing, animated starts and stops, black humor, and the sort of conversational shorthand one develops with an old, close friend.

When signing off, my father would say, "All right, man, work hard and I will too."

I called Mike up recently with some gossip about the size of an advance for a book written by one of his colleagues. Mike is working on a new book and with one kid about to enter college and another following closely behind, he's hoping for a sizable advance himself. Before long we have moved on to the subject of his new book: how difficult and necessary it is to console yourself to the disappointment of life and the world. Doesn't scream best-seller, I joked, since no one likes to admit to this truth. I talked about how this disappointment often feels like a large white elephant in the corner of the room that no one will acknowledge, and how that denial makes you feel like you're crazy. Given the choice between feeling crazy and feeling disappointed, I don't understand why more people don't opt for the latter.

"You're exactly right, Blissie," Mike agreed. "That's just what I am trying to get at."

I was stretched out on my own bed now, watching the afternoon shadows lengthen down my wall. Talking with Mike was like walking down a familiar path that leads toward home. Here is the oak tree; around the bend is the stone wall. Talking with Mike was almost like talking with my father.

Both men shared a predilection for cutting through hypocrisy and looking past denial. They viewed the world with a bittersweet affection, appreciating the shadows of life's events as much as the events themselves. I once asked my dad why all the great stories were sad ones. Most good stories are mysteries, he said. The author is like a detective trying to get to the bottom of some truth, and happiness is a mystery that can come apart in your hands when you try to unravel it. Sadness, on the other hand, is infinitely more resilient. Scrutiny only adds to its depth and weight.

I don't ask Mike what my father thought of me. Mike's a shrink, after all, and he knows that I'm the only one who could answer that question.

What I realize when I am with the older men in my life is that the older man I want most is my father, and no amount of colorful anecdotes, no amount of recreating the kind of outings he might have had with his pals, can conjure him up in a satisfying way. Grief, like sadness, is too resilient for such casual stand-ins.

After I finished talking with Mike, I remained lying on my bed. Outside my window it was dark, and I hadn't bothered to turn on the light. I was thinking about how it is an odd time to get to know your father, after he has died. And it is odd to get to know him through his friends. I wondered why I should assume that they knew him any better than I did? If some aspects of his life before I knew him were mysterious to me, certainly the reverse was true as well: there are parts that only I know about. Would his friends be surprised to learn that when I was a baby, after my bath, my father would carry me around the house seated naked in the palm of his hand, holding me high up over his head like a waiter with a tray. Or that he would spend afternoons tossing my brother and me, torpedo-like, from the corner of the bedroom onto my parents' bed, the far wall piled high with pillows. Before each toss, he would inspect our teeth to make sure they were clenched so we wouldn't bite our tongues. Would his friends be surprised to know that when I was in college he would sometimes call me up in the middle of the day because he was feeling lonely in the empty house. Or when standing over him in his hospital bed, my throat choked with all the questions I realized there wasn't time to ask, and, his mouth filled with a pain beyond articulation, he suddenly seized my hand and raised it to his lips. "You're my daughter," he assured me. "You're my daughter."

When my father and I went out dancing together, we didn't dance the old dances, as Vincent and I tried to do when we went to hear a salsa band. Vincent had great hopes for my talent as a dancer, since my father was such a good one, but as he attempted to lead me across the floor, I kept overanticipating his moves. The slightest pressure of his hand would send me off in a new direction.

My dad relied on me to introduce him to the new music, the new dances. Competitive as always, he wanted to be sure that he could keep up with the times. In our living room, the rug pulled back and the coffee table pushed aside, I cranked *Word Up* by Cameo. I led the way across the smooth wooden floor, shouting out the lyrics, my hands waving in the air, my hips bumping left and right. I can still hear his encouragement as he followed along behind me. With my eyes closed, in the quiet of my dark bedroom, his hoots rise out of the silence.

M. G. Stephens

Meditations on the Harp

I suggest to Joe that we go out to do something for the rest of the afternoon. The next day we would be locked into the funeral service all day, and the day after that would be the mass and then the service at the cemetery. He agrees. He mentions visiting the Salvador Dali museum in Saint Petersburg, the next town over.

I remember that, when he painted, Joe's sense of color was sublime, very delicate and light. The colors were pastel and feminine, even "beautiful." These are not, normally, concepts I associate with the life of my brothers, who tend to be rougher at the edges, tougher, more hardened at the core. That is probably why I get along with Joe so well. We are the creative types in the family, though it might be said that each one of my brothers and sisters had some kind of artistic streak. Some played music; others danced. I wrote; Joe painted. I often thought that our oldest brother, Jimmy, might have made a good actor with his deep, booming voice and his huge, operatic body. Peter seemed to have some kind of penchant for the stage, too. The girls were, like Joe, more visually oriented. Tom played a guitar. I know that Brendan was a jock, mostly baseball, but I'm sure he had some kind of creative urges. Like Joe, he was into beautiful objects, in Brendan's case, blue glass bottles.

But of all my siblings, I am most comfortable around Joe. His sense of humor is dark and bizarre. He likes to be irreverent. As we walk from one surreal painting to the next, he comments. At a painting entitled "Portrait of My Sister," he says, "It kind of looks like Kaitlin," our own sister. "The Disintegration of the Persistence of Memory," with its melting clocks, oyster-colored non-human figures, fish, and rhino horns, reminds him of our childhood home where the juxtaposition of object was, as I just said, surreal.

Joe takes the extravagant imagery of Dali's painting and applies them to our personal lives.

Did I remember the time our mother left a plastic dish on the hot stove and it melted? The plate flapped over the porcelain top of the stove.

"It was like a Dali," Joe says.

I laugh, though I do not recall this event. Perhaps it never happened. Joe was merely story telling, spinning out a tale. The point is, it could, should, might have happened. Anything was possible in that household, that fallen domain we grew up in on Long Island. Is that why Dali's paintings look so realistic to us?

When I laugh at Joe's comments, I realize that why I'm there is really far from my mind. Being in Florida lends an unreality to everything. This could not be explained away by the fact that I am more familiar with oaks and elms than palm trees or robins and bluejays more than pelicans and herons. The orange is one of my favorite fruits. I prefer the blue-green water of the Gulf to the dark gray-green color of the North Atlantic Ocean.

But I also realize that when people first die, nothing but unreality surrounds the circumstances, particularly the lives of the survivors. There really is no adequate vocabulary to explain what happens. No amount of education prepares one for the ontological moment. That I did not get along with this parent does not matter. In fact, it makes the situation worse. I must feel bad for someone I did not particularly like. I must mourn for the dead in the way that others do for their loved ones. And I am not talking about a friend or acquaintance. I refer to my own father. He is the corpse that none of us has dealt with yet. One moment you are alive, if not well, and the next, you are gone, the life force flown out of you, dead, as they say, as a doornail. Kaput!

I find myself becoming quiet. Joe goes off in one direction, and I walk the other way. The main room in the museum is quite large, with paintings all around it. I see him on the other side of this large room, admiring the smaller paintings like "Morphological Echo" and "Paranonia," works I had admired moments earlier. I stand in front of a fourteen-foot high painting entitled "The Discovery of America by Christopher Columbus," overwhelmed by its sheer volume as it towers over me. It is a kind of homage to Velazquez, Columbus the possible Catalonian (not the Italian), and even Pop Art. Though I have never been a great fan of Dali's, I admire this painting, the same way I admired the smaller, more intimate paintings across the room.

Nearly all his titles affect me. One painting is called "Autumn Sonata," and it renders, in the quintessential dreamlike landscape of a surreal painting, a basilica, an arch, cripples, men fighting on horseback, boats, low-slung mountains, all of it meticulous and slightly larger than a postcard. But since I am a writer, not a painter, I think of words, not images. I am not thinking about my father. Perhaps I am too consciously not thinking about him. I focus on that word "surrealism." How often it is misused to describe more journalistic events. Something "weird" is called "surreal," when, looking at these paintings by Dali, it is plain to see that the surreal is not weird so much as dreamy. In that sense, the dead become surreal, not weird but dreamy themselves. All that remains of them are the shadows they cast inside of us, just like the ominous shadows cast across the theatrical boards of some of these paintings and their landscapes. A dead father is like a melting clock.

"Puzzle of Autumn" contains a Turneresque sky gone a jaundiced yellow. But the one that really catches my attention is entitled "Meditation on the Harp." A man and woman posed, the woman naked. In front of them stands a deformed, cone-headed figure with big feet. The painting instantly brings to mind some dark relationship I might have with my own parents, the attraction and repulsion, the shame and guilt. Also, I cannot help but think of how the term "harp" is often used as a derogatory name for Irish people, and that my father was nothing if he was not a harp.

This seems right, in fact, it is inspired, even brilliant. You would not look at Rembrandts, thinking about my clan; you did not search out the impressionists. Picasso or Matisse made no sense in this world. Salvador Dali did.

If I were looking for a movement to characterize my family, I'd choose Surrealism. A writer friend once described it as the juxtaposition of two or more objects in a way that they were not ordinarily perceived. I think he meant literary surrealism, but the definition was fine for my blood relations. A fish rains down on a man in a bowler hat dressed like a banker. A clock melts across a tree. A couple who should not have had any children—have sixteen of them, and nine live. Surrealism is born.

Take our childhoods. A lawnmower might be found in a closet, a yard rake in the kitchen. That textbook for history, the one you could not find the entire school year, shows up on a pantry shelf. Laundry was found in the garage. Tools for the car were in the refrigerator. A bed might be piled sky-high with clothing. Therefore, you slept in the closet.

I had gone along on this excursion, partly as a joke, partly as an homage; the Chief, I thought, and nearly all his children agreed, was an absurd man. It was a quality that he bequeathed to his children whole-cloth, with no strings attached. Each of us, to various degrees, had a weird sense of humor, all of it fueled by the ridiculous.

Joe's sense of the ridiculous seemed to be in its glory that afternoon as he regaled me with stories about our father, his escapades, his bons mots, his observations, and his saying. One of the more famous incidents—this one made the local papers and then the evening television news—was when he started up his Dodge Dart, got out of it, and went back inside the house for coffee one morning.

Some of the children said he went back inside to finish his breakfast, others said it was to take a shit. Really, it doesn't matter. When he came back outside, the car popped out of Park and went into Overdrive gear, and since the wheel was turned a certain way, the car rolled around in circles, chasing after its driver. The Chief ran in the same arc, though slightly ahead of the car. A saner man might have stepped out of the way; a dumber man might have tried to stop the car. Our father chose to run ahead of it as if in some Buster Keaton moment, the machine personalized and anthropomorphic and out to get the Chief for the way he treated it; the car was going to run him down.

We exit from an interstate highway onto Fourth Street South, turn right at a light, and go six blocks to Eleventh Avenue South, and at Great Explorations, "the Hands On Museum," we turn left. It is downtown, the waterfront of Saint Pete's. We come to the Dali Museum.

My brother parks the car in the lot and we go inside a large, modern room, all of whose walls are covered with Dali paintings.

Joe is not painting now, but he used to be quite a good painter and, I suspect, if he got back to it, he still would be. My younger brother sells furniture at flea markets in New York City. I'm closest to Joe in age, and though we had not done much together as kids, we did become good friends once he moved into the city after high school to attend the School of Visual Arts. It was during this period—I lived in an abandoned building on lower Second Avenue—that Joe lived in his own abandoned building on the western edge of Canal Street. Only Joe was far more ingenious than I was; all I managed to finagle was a set of keys that admitted me into my abandoned building. Joe had commandeered his building, borrowing water from one adjacent building, electricity from another. Despite his being a degenerate hippie reeking of herb and zonked on acid, the more working-class elements of the family were drawn to Joe's crash pad, too. Thus on any night one might visit him and find the drunken Chief himself holding court on a flea-bitten couch in the living room when he was transferred from Hell's Kitchen to the piers in Greenwich Village, years before he was exiled to work at Kennedy Airport. To encounter my father in this decrepit location was like meeting Hamm from Samuel Beckett's *Endgame*. Forget about the Pope of Greenwich Village. He was the Emperor of the Waterfront.

A gaping hole in the second floor looked directly down upon the first floor, an empty storefront that Joe used for a painting studio. If my father was not there, you might find our older brother Peter camped out, hiding from the law. The old man's excuse was that he was working the piers below Morton Street, and this was a convenient place to crash instead of taking the train all the way out to Long Island.

This wonderful crash pad reminded me of Gulley Jimson in *The Horse's Mouth*, though others found it to be like Ken Kesey's funny farm in Oregon, only an urban version. Drugs oozed out of every crack in the bare walls; rats and vermin skittered across the rafters. The deafening traffic outside on Canal Street inched its way toward the Holland Tunnel, though usually everyone was too trashed on drugs and booze to notice. Once, visiting Joe on the West Side, he invited me to dinner; he lowered himself through a skylight into the luncheonette next door, the same place from which he boosted his electricity, and came back with ham, eggs, Cokes, lettuce, and tomatoes. Amazingly, the owner never caught on, even when Joe and his friends descended through the skylight, partying all night long, making ice cream sodas, grilling hamburgers, concocting BLTs from heaven above.

But it didn't stop there. After Joe got busted and sent on probation out of the city—the judge told him that he wanted to remove him from the pernicious world of Art which had corrupted his good Catholic mind—he wound up spending the next twelve years on an equally déclassé, though always wonderful and unpredictable, crash farm in rural, northeastern Connecticut, the land complete with hippie garden and old work horse he rode bareback (the horse) and naked (my brother), the endless pack of dogs he owned from Scotties to Russian wolfhounds, his feral animals forever being gunned down by the local farmers and the Ku-Kluxers which unfortunately had a toehold in that part of Connecticut. But eventually the party ended; the piper needed to get paid, and Joe wound up leaving the farm and coming back to Long Island, first to get sober, then to find work, and finally, to settle down with his family. He is married, has two children, and lives in upstate New York, but comes down to the city once a week to sell his antiques.

Being left alone, surrounded by strangers and these oddly beautiful paintings, I reflect upon the past twenty-four hours. It might be more accurate to say that the last twenty-four hours grab and shake me awake. I had not spent any extended time, other than holiday visits with anyone in my family since I was fifteen years old. No one in my immediate family had died yet. My only experience, even in middle age, was to attend the funeral of my grandfather when I was a boy, a grandmother in my adolescence, and more than ten years earlier, my maternal grandmother. My other relatives did not so much die as move to the suburbs, never to be heard from again.

That morning, after I came back from looking around for newspapers to read, we went out for an all-you-can-eat breakfast at another hotel before heading off to see my mother and other family members at the Sunday Mass. This breakfast place, it turned out, was significant. This literally was the last place I had ever seen my father, at least the last place where I saw this man with my father's name. (My real father was last seen that day I took him drinking in my neighborhood bar in New York City.) It was right after their fiftieth wedding anniversary two years earlier. I had come down to Florida for the first time, even though my parents and most of my siblings had been living there for years. I am a bit of a prodigal son, I guess, although no one was going to lose sleep over whether I was at their family gatherings or not.

The family book on me goes like this: Michael was considered odd, even in this very odd family. He wrote books, lived a separate life from theirs. In essence, he betrayed the working-class covenants by presuming to be something other than what the family had thought he would become, perhaps a cop, a fire-man, or more probably a high school English teacher after he graduated from the state teachers' college. His becoming a writer did not make him any different, though. After all, this was a truly outcast bunch, none of them fitting into the mainstream.

We sat eating breakfast, looking at the Gulf outside the windows. Pelicans and herons dove for fish. The sky remained overcast and gray. No sun shone. It was as cold outside as it had been in New York City the day before. I watched as a pelican climbed ponderously skyward, paused in the air, then dove, bullet-like, into the water below, catching a fish in its oversized bill.

The room was a bright pastel and it had an airy, high-ceilinged quality to it. The customers were the everyday variety of working-class and middle-class tourists and retirees, not an exotic face among them. Off-season drew only those like our-selves, because of family obligations.

Herons stood on the beach outside as still as lawn orna-ments. Occasionally, one might shift a leg; otherwise they did not move at all. I could not think of a more foreign landscape. Yet I could not help thinking about that last time I was here for their fiftieth anniversary, and then seeing my father in this room, eat-ing absentmindedly.

My father smiled, sitting at his table. His smile was vacant, not tossed at anyone. He did not talk. Speech had escaped this grand old schmoozer. He appeared benevolent, even kind. Cer-tainly he was calm, none of his jittery animation existed anymore. If someone entered the room without knowing who he was, one might find him a nice-looking, cheerful old coot, a bit dotty, but otherwise quite okay.

Though my father did not speak, my mother filled in the blank spaces for us.

"He may have lost his memory," she said, "but he never lost his appetite."

My mother said these words as though they were positive signs. Memory was not important, but an appetite was. Memory was a burden, but an appetite that could be fulfilled was the culmination of these Depression Era dreamers. They had not starved, after all. They had survived the Depression and the World War, the Fifties, the Sixties, clear up to the Nineties.

As my mother spoke my father ate oatmeal, slurping and happily making noises. He dunked his toast into the coffee, something he would have smacked us for when we were children. Though our household was chaotic and seemed to have no rules, my father could be unusually strict with us at times. These times were when he was not drinking. Once he was drinking, he might become violent, hitting us liberally, but all the rules had flown to the wind. When he was not drinking, the rules came back.

My father poured ketchup on his eggs and stacked piles of bacon and sausage on the side of his plate as if they were monuments to his hunger. The strokes had taken away his memory, his biography, and the past, but hunger was a lower-brain function, a product of the brain-stem.

Maybe the old man eventually came to an understanding with Florida, but I could not relinquish the thought that what bound us together was that we were both New Yorkers. We loved Manhattan, a borough others in the family were either indifferent or hostile to. Sometimes I would forget and think that my family were New Yorkers, too. But they were not. They were Long Islanders. The accents were similar and, occasionally, the attitudes coincided. But New York is a city—The City. Long Island remains the essence of the American suburb, a place that depends on a car to get around. Suburbanites adored material objects. The grittier spiritual life of a city belied this love of tchotchkas and cars. This might simply mean that life often is cheap in the city; your good looks, your money, your fame mean nothing to a street kid out to cut or shoot you. Sick as it may sound, I liked that kind of edge that the city provided. But Florida was more like Long Island than New York City, and perhaps that is what baffled me most about my father's ultimately coming to terms with it. There was no one more New York than the old man, and no one knew the city as well as he did, not even I who had lived my entire adult life there.

Perhaps that is why I am at the Salvador Dali Museum with my brother Joe. I cannot handle—because I cannot fathom—Florida. Coming to this museum is a compromise. It is not New York City—people in Manhattan might scoff at Dali's paintings—but it is not quite Florida either. I suppose I am still thinking of my literary friend's definition of surrealism. I am willing to settle for an odd juxtaposition in order to get by in Florida. I cannot accept the thing itself, but I am willing to ride along with it if I have these odd paintings to buffer the experience of Florida. Yet probably Florida has nothing to do with it. The paintings act as a buffer between me and death because dreams are about sex and death, and Dali's dreams are everywhere on these canvasses. Procreating and dying remain my family's true gifts, and my father was no exception.

If he did not die with great dignity, then he died fighting all the way. That is something, I guess, fighting being preferable to surrender. When you surrender, you are gone. He gave the good fight, they said. He went out like a trooper. Of course, none of this is true. He did not give a good fight nor go out like a trooper. From what I heard, he died empty-headed, not even knowing if he was alive or dead. The seam between life and death had been erased for him. He went out in a hazy breath of intoxicated fury, fighting ghosts instead of substances. The substances had done him in.

I stand in front of another huge Dali painting, "The Hallucinogenic Toreador." Venus de Milo multiplies herself. She looks like the figure on a Venus pencil, but with her shadows, she appears to turn into a bullfighter. Art and mass reproduction are issues of this century, but in my family reproduction was everything. My mother and father were profligate human beings, throwing themselves into a life of reproduction in a way I have seen nowhere else. I don't know of any human being other than my mother who was pregnant sixteen times. Sixteen is the number she tells me. Perhaps it was even higher. And my parents married when they were considered old for their generation, in their late twenties.

I don't think Yeats had my parents in mind when he spoke

of the "grand gesture," that most Irish of actions, full of grace and dedicated artfulness. But how do I, their son, explain this productivity to a world unfamiliar with such inclinations? Instead of it being grand, perhaps it was simply an enormous gesture. Maybe like Henry Ford grinding out Model T's, it only had to do with mass production. If you make enough children, some of them might prosper and take care of you late in life. Yet I think that my father, especially, would rather die than depend on one of his children for help. Finally, like these Dali paintings, my parents simply were extravagant, overblown, yes, surreal.

What did the others do? I don't know. I imagine that they stayed at my mother's condominium, telling stories to each other for the rest of the day. The stories would be ones everyone was familiar with. They might drink coffee, smoke, eat coffee cake, and talk. My family liked nothing better than talking. Joe and I went to the Dali Museum. I do not think that one choice was better than the other. They did what they had to do in order to survive, to endure the terrible weight of a personal death. We did what we had to do.

I discovered two things: Dali was not, as I had thought for years, a flim-flam artist, but an artist who had a shrewd—even an ingenious—eye for his own time. Andy Warhol and Salvador Dali capture the twentieth century as well as any visual artists I can think of. One sees it as a joke; the other as a preposterous dream. Neither is completely right; more important, neither is completely wrong. The other thing I learned to do was to look at my father without all the venom I had gathered in me for so many years. He was a man, a human being, and he had died.

I often used to hear this old fellow at AA meetings say that alcoholics were like anyone else, only, he said, "We are all more simply human than otherwise."

It was not so much that my father was more simply human than otherwise. I saw that all of us were.

As we walk toward the van in the parking lot, Joe and I are joined in our moment before grief. We laugh. I think that laughter is as good as any emotion to come to terms with the fact that all of us are only here for a blink of the eye, then we are gone.

Driving out of Saint Pete's, I think of Dali and Warhol, and I decide to include Marcel Duchamp in that visual triumvirate that paid lip service to the century. I am in Florida, deep at the ass end of the millennium, waiting to become profound and significant in the next great age, but knowing, too, that insignificance and banality are as likely a destination as great discovery. I realize that no one is going to say anything about my father except me. I am his eulogist in this formal sense outside the family. If I did not praise him, he would be condemned. What a terrible burden, I think.

Like so many other abused children, one part of me is filled with rage and outrage, the other part a mixture of wonder and love. In many respects, our devotion (my siblings', I mean) is greater than children who truly loved their parents; we were so lost, his parental warmth—basically a chilly wind in winter—was all we had. The Dali paintings remind me of this, too, because each of them, being surreal, is about dreams, and we all know that dreams have only two subjects—sex and death. That's just what family is, too, sex and death, procreation and dying, giving birth and burying the dead. Unlike Mediterraneans who would have had the decency to take along a mistress or two, we are puritanical Irish-Catholics; we only know how to make babies from sex. Yet who could deny the erotics of this afternoon? Young women browsed those eerie works, commenting in Spanish, Portuguese, French, and English about the bloody imagery on the sometimes oversized canvasses, particularly those monstrously heroic ones about Columbus and nuclear war. How do you leave the twentieth century? By coming to Clearwater to bury your father and then visiting the Dali Museum.

On the way back to the motel on the beach, I buy a pair of cross-training sneakers at a factory outlet, I eat McDonald's french fries and some chicken fajitas, I wonder why I have yet to taste a good orange or drink some fresh-squeezed orange juice, or why I imagine that I am feeling nothing about being on the Gulf Coast of Florida, and even less about my father's death.

Professional Languages

Marcus Laffey

The Word on the Street

We say "K." It means that a radio transmission is over. The military—and just about everyone else—says "Over," and I don't know if the N.Y.P.D. has any argument for the difference except difference's sake. I'm a patrolman, so I do what I'm told. "You O.K.? K." "A-O.K., K." It is a code, after all, and a code communicates confidentially, which is to say that it's supposed to mean nothing to most people: codes, like good children, don't talk to strangers. But talk they do—so much so that here, behind the vaunted "blue wall of silence," it's often hard to get a word in edgewise.

If the N.Y.P.D. is becoming less and less of a fraternity, it will remain a kind of ethnicity, because ethnicity is defined by language. An arrest is a "collar," but also a "pinch"; a perp can be a "skell" or a "mope," depending on whether he's a bum or a thug. A D.O.A. is someone who's gone E.O.T., end of tour. "Two under" or "Ten under" is an accounting of collars, but in Transit a "man under" is not under arrest but under a train. The police department, perhaps because of its paramilitary nature, has a fondness for acronyms, which vary from the flat-footedly functional to the downright cool: the Robbery Apprehension Module descended from the Robbery Identification Program, which broadened the range of the Senior Citizens Robbery Unit. And thus SCRU begat RIP, and RIP begat RAM, with a certain loss of panache.

There's an oddity to cop talk, coming as it does from the shotgun marriage of street slang and legalese. The raw talk of criminals, victims, and the cops themselves is framed in the jury-rigged particularity of statutory phrases: "The alleged perpetrator called him a 'bitch-ass punk' and mooshed him, causing annoyance and alarm." To moosh is to shove in the face, and is almost more demeaning than a slap, because of the suggestion that there is no need to add injury to insult. Naturally, cops pick up a lot of criminal vocabulary, especially in the drug trade, where the criminal words for things are the only words there are; you can say, "He was holding a deck," or you can say, "He was holding a glassine envelope of a white powdery substance . . . alleged and believed to be heroin." Crack isn't usually packaged in vials anymore but in miniature heat-sealed plastic bags, which the dealers call "slabs." The official and legal term for them is "slabs" as well. To make a rule of this kind of exception would lead to indictments that read, "To wit, defendant did possess one mad fat rock of yayo."

New York cops and robbers used to sound more like James Cagney or the Bowery Boys. In recent decades, the accent has grown softer, but the dialect has got bigger, blockbusted with words and rhythms from the barrio and the 'hood, so that you can hear "Yo! Yo! Yo!" and "Fuhgeddaboudit!" not only in the same conversation but from the same mouth. And the accent is by no means gone. I recently overheard a two-minute conversation between cops which looped around one word:

"He robbed a pawn store."

"A porn store?"

"Yeah, a pawn store."

"Right, porn."

"Pawn."

"Porn . . . o?"

Usually, though, the babel of the city just mixes with police jargon in striking ways as we all strive to express ourselves with bits of a hand-me-down language which don't always fit. I was once working with an informant to obtain a search warrant for a drug dealer's house. She was a strange creature, a dedicated and unapologetic crackhead who now and then felt the inclination to turn in a dealer "for the mood of it." One day when she strolled into the precinct another cop alerted me to her arrival, calling out, "Hey, your girlfriend's here." She then remarked, with neither pride nor shame in the fact that her better days were behind her, "He don't want this twisted ass." And so this confidential informant, or C.I., or Charlie Ida, became known as Twisted Ass, and the successful warrant we executed was dubbed Operation Twisted Ass. There are also times, though, when the clipped neutrality of police jargon sounds weirdly euphemistic, as if the speaker were keeping a lifted-pinky distance from lurid circumstances. I heard a dispatcher revise an assignment for a patrol car: "Be advised, unit, that domestic dispute is now coming over as a severed limb." And I overheard a cop recall, brightly, "Oh, sure, I was the first nonfatal shooting of 1994! In the keister!"

Some cop talk, of course, is too colorful. At the police academy, an instructor once told us, "There's one word that, if cops never used it at all, would do away with eighty per cent of civilian complaints." He paused for a response, and we shouted in cheerful unison, "Asshole!" He smiled. "Correct."

The department now trains its members in "verbal judo," a daylong course in how certain phrases and attitudes can shape interactions with the public. (A cop I know made a happy slip of the tongue, calling it "gerbil voodoo.") Although there shouldn't be any need to tell cops not to be rude, the program expounds on the strategic asset of good manners, advising a conversational stance that is plain, even obvious, and relentlessly polite. You talk through everything, explaining who you are and what you're doing and, when faced with some form of noncompliance, you lay out the good and bad options available to both of you:

"Good afternoon, sir. I'm P.O. Laffey of the N.Y.P.D. I'm

stopping you for running a red light. Is there any reason I should know . . .

"I understand you pay my salary, sir, but I still need to see your license . . .

"Sir, if you give me your license you can be on your way in a minute, but if you don't I'll have to bring you in."

The protocol does work to reduce the stress of such encounters, even if its Robocop. Berlitz seems more suited to traffic stops than to heated domestic disputes. You obviously don't begin a car stop with the phrase "Where's the fire, Grampa?" But you also don't say "You know why I pulled you over, right?" because the driver might think it has something to do with the bank he's just robbed, resulting in an exchange of gunfire instead of information.

If you can talk a good game as a cop, you're halfway there. The police work of action—of confrontation and force, of round-house punches and high-speed chases—is what makes the movies and the news, and both civilian lives and our own sometimes depend on it. But what you say and how you say it come into play far more than anything you do with your stick or your gun, and can even prevent the need for them. I know cops who have talked would-be suicides down from rooftops and convinced raving gunmen to release child hostages. More often, you talk people into talking, just talking, instead of screaming and waving a two-by-four. There are fighting words and the opposite: passwords that most people seem to have—some topic or tone that cuts them short or brings them down, reaches them through reason, decency, or shame. I once watched an eight-year-old boy silence a foul-mouthed drunk in a pizza parlor by barking at him, like a headmaster, "Hey! There's ladies here!"

And talk tactics aren't confined to the street. Most robberies and all drug deals are committed by members of a felony society, from suppliers and fences to all manner of partners in crime. They know people, know things. And, with every arrest, you make the time to persuade them to share that knowledge. The classic interrogation, where the detectives sweet-talk, bluff, and browbeat the perp into an admission of guilt, is seldom a part of what a patrol cop does. But when a perp wants to talk, naturally, you accommodate him.

The first time I read someone the Miranda warnings, I had a hard time keeping a straight face; it sounded like a Joe Friday impersonation. More to the point, in my cases, self-incrimination is rarely an issue. As I tell them, "I don't need anything out of you, I already have you. If you don't want to be had anymore, give me someone better. You're not going anywhere." The methods of persuasion are varied in style and efficiency, as any adman, politician, or whiny child can attest. You might try to create an intense emotional climate that permits a moment of surrender, more frequently, you gain cooperation through the opposite means, by presenting it as the rational choice. You wheedle, enlighten, repeat. I've heard the sum of these techniques referred to as "jerkology."

When I tried to flip Anna (all the names in this piece, including my own, have been changed), a heroin dealer I had arrested, the first ten minutes brought nothing. She was a hard-core junkie, an operator with such mileage on her that the first word that came to me when I saw her was "survivor," though it should have been the last. She didn't look just dirty but dusty, as if she'd been left in an attic, and she had ulcerated limbs that looked as if someone had taken bites out of them. On being questioned about whether she knew anyone who had guns or was doing robberies, she offered a bored denial, and when she was asked about the heroin spot where she worked she just shook her head. I knew she had done state time, and I also knew a bit about the setup where she worked—the brands, the players, the hours. Debriefings are like poker: you have to get the perp to stay in the game, even though it's clear that you're the better player, with the better hand. It's also unlike poker, in that if you play well you both win.

"Anna, there's only one way you can make this go away. You know that, right? It's through us, right? Talking, helping us out? It's not through J.J. We know him, too, and know you work for him. Today, he was hanging on the corner while you were running your ass ragged taking money and handing out bags of dope. And you're in cuffs and he's home, watching 'Oprah.' Yeah, Anna, it's four o'clock already! You moved a couple hundred decks this morning for J.J.—ten bucks each, that's a couple grand. How much did he pay you, fifty bucks? Or did he just throw you a couple of bags for yourself? Is he gonna send a lawyer down for you, is he gonna water your plants while you're away?"

But she didn't reply. I asked her about prison, and she said she didn't like it much. She still owed time for parole, and she'd have to do that even before she did what she'd get for today. She knew that, she told me, but she told me nothing else. My mistake with Anna was to keep pitching appeals to her freedom. She was an addict, whose life was a closed circuit of having it and needing it, and nothing I could offer would affect her truly solitary confinement. But she'd been talking, and I wanted to keep her talking. I asked if she had kids. She flinched, and asked for another cigarette. She nodded.

I changed the subject back to her dealing that day, describing customers, lookouts, and so on—authoritative blather to lead her to believe we had her down. Then I asked her what her kids' names were. As she said them—"Fernando and Lucy"—it was as if she were watching them sleep. Then she breathed deeply, and softly began, "J.J. keeps it in the corner building, on the second floor, the first door on the right. He brings enough for the day, from another stash house in the middle of the block." At that moment, I felt that I had jerkologically *arrived*.

Often the problem isn't getting people to talk but getting them to tell the truth: cops hear lies so often that they're almost background noise—an aggravating fact of the real estate, as if you lived next to the subway or the airport. I've seen liar prodigies, virtuoso liars, thinking man's liars, lowdown liars, and liars from the heart. One enormous woman bellowed at me as I took a crack vial from her open hand, "You planted that there!," which reminded me of the Richard Pryor line about a man whose wife caught him in bed with another woman: "You gonna believe me, or your lying eyes?" (My liar followed up with at least one unassailable truth: "You can't take me to jail, I don't have a bra on. Look!") My favorites are the liars who can provide limitlessly elastic explanations for why things are not the way they seem. When I arrested a heroin dealer named Ray, he explained to me that he was in the building only because he was waiting for his aunt, and that he let serial junkies in because they might know where she was, and that the reason he had more than six hundred dollars in his pocket was, obviously, that his wife just had a baby shower and it was money for a crib. . . . In another instance, a would-be informant confessed, in persuasive detail, to a spree of violent felonies, but my initial thrill at his capture melted away as hours of research failed to produce a scrap of documentary evidence of these crimes. I took consolation in considering the little miracle of his half-dozen putative victims suddenly restored to health and safety, unrobbed, unstabbed, unshot.

Most people who call the police are credible, because their reasons for doing so are obvious: they are hurt, or sick, or have had something stolen. And you encourage them to talk—to ventilate or rant in case they come up with some vital detail (my favorite witness: "He was tall! Five-ten! Maybe even five-twelve!") or, sometimes, give themselves enough rope. Everyone has the right to be heard, but no one has an absolute right to be believed.

When a robbery victim told me that three white men in white suits broke into her apartment, locked her in the bathroom, and made off with her cigarettes, I felt that I had to question her further before I put out an A.P.B. for the Bee Gees. When I first suggested calling for an ambulance, she shook her head.

"Sometimes you don't know if you're hurt right away," I continued. "With the shock of it, and all, it's best to be safe and check. Are you under any kind of treatment right now, do you take any medicine?"

She nodded, and I asked what for.

"For the voices."

You have to ask. The quality of the information you get is only as good as what you ask for, vetted through repetition and playback, prodded along for further detail, probed for the soft spots in the story as if for dry rot in a wall. Even so, you should still expect to get it wrong sometimes. On patrol, you can find yourself embroiled in plotlines that if you saw them in a movie would have you flinging popcorn at the screen. When I went to testify to the grand jury after a rape arrest, I was greeted by the A.D.A. with the eight words I least expected, or wanted, to hear: "You know he has an identical twin, right?" The technical term for that kind of situation is "cluster fuck."

There's a biting old adage favored by cops which I admire, not least because it advises a guarded appraisal of the saying itself: "Believe half of what you see, and none of what you hear." Like a lot of cop talk, its sardonic double meaning says something and denies it at the same time. I don't mean the way cops misspeak to each other for a purpose, like when P.O. Tony tells his partner, P.O. Mike, "Hey, Pete, this guy's O.K." and he's really telling Mike that he isn't—that he has a weapon. You might better understand this ambiguity by looking at the word "buff," which can convey several shades of insult. A buff is a green idealist, and it suits a rookie to be a kind of buff, to have more heart than brains. A buff can also be a too-serious type who looks in the mirror and sees Eliot Ness, and whose ego makes him difficult, and occasionally dangerous, to work with. To say that a veteran cop is a buff can be a compliment—though one best made behind his back—because it means he's found a way to take things seriously and lightly in turn that still allows him to do good and have fun. Or it means he's a bit demented. But if the fact that it's a dig, however affectionate (a cop is entitled to buff out a little after a good collar), seems to say something cynical about cop culture, consider that the opposite of "buff" is "hairbag," which is straight-forwardly bad, and means a bitter and burned-out complainer. A possible inference is that faith and doubt can be equally blind. Or you could say, "My advise is, Don't take my advice."

In this complex private language, a handful of statements remain unambiguous, however, and the radio code "10–13"—for "Officer needs assistance"—is both the plainest speech and the most forceful. Since the code "10–85" is also a call for aid, ranging from administrative assistance ("I need a unit to eighty-five me with an accident report, Central, nonemergency") to certain high levels of urgency ("Eighty-five, Central, forthwith, large crowd with baseball bats, be advised this is a solo unit"), there's an etiquette to calling a 10–13—a respect for its authority of last resort. It has elements of both shouting "Fire!" and saying the Hail Mary.

When you hear it on the radio it shuts you up and raises your heart rate: the air clears, the white noise turns church-quiet, and it's as if the hundreds of cops in a division, in all the precincts and cars and street corners for a few square miles, have gone into a sprinter's crouch. The voice that calls it can be nearly breathless with terror, and the background noise can tell of gunshots or a raving mob, but the number itself, no matter how it's spoken, has an autonomous and radical power.

I would have guessed that this particular code came from misfortune—the superstitions about the number itself—and there's a logic to that, for no one calls a 10–13 on a lucky day. But its association with disaster has given it an equally strong sense of rescue—a "10–13" is also the name for the benefit parties that cops throw for other cops, usually to help with a medical expense—thereby defining it as both the call for help and the help itself. And so I was glad to hear (from a non-cop friend, who is a bit of a buff himself) that the code has its source in a Biblical phrase. Chapter ten, verse thirteen (10:13) of the Epistle of Paul to the Romans reads, "For whosoever shall call upon the name of the Lord shall be saved." The thought of old commissioners slyly encrypting police codes with heavenly messages is hard to resist. But I take it the way I take most everything cops say and hear—that is, everything below the level of lawful orders and sworn testimony, everything that needs to be interpreted instead of obeyed. You believe it if you like, ignore it at your risk, but listen, always, if you hope to understand.

Miroslav Holub

Science and the Corrosion of the Soul

Bryan Appleyard says quite clearly in his 1992 book *Understanding the Present* that science affronts human dignity: "Science is not a neutral or innocent commodity. . . . Rather, it is spiritually corrosive, burning away ancient authorities and traditions."

Appleyard believes that science has developed since Galileo into an autonomous entity, with a life of its own, progressively detrimental to human existence. No wonder, then, that *Understanding the Present* has been quoted in editorials in scientific magazines such as *Nature;* a fundamental misunderstanding of science rarely gets expressed so vigorously—the tone makes one think of parliamentary debates—and seldom achieves such commercial success.

Appleyard, echoing Francis Fukuyama's *The End of History,* thinks that science endangers human survival on the planet despite the positive role it has played, together with technology, in the victory of liberal democracy. Liberal democracy is no triumph either, since it allows too many things that are adverse to what they call "human essence": embryo research, abortion, animal experimentation, environmental destruction, development of uncreated species and unprecedented polymers, nuclear technologies, the human genome map, and other unnatural activities.

At this point, someone should define what would constitute a human triumph in the antiscience conception, but the critics usually don't get around to that.

Of course, the issue is the "natural world" of sense and meaning in which we live as concrete and more or less replicable beings. The difficulty with the natural world is that it is being addressed and handled both by scholars, competent philosophers of the Husserl camp, and by simple minds of the New Age style, for whom Husserl's book on the crisis of Western science is the same kind of trap as molecular genetics. Where the philosopher whispers, the simple mind shouts.

A second difficulty lies in the fact that at the individual level of a thinking and feeling man or woman, the natural world is supposed to be grasped by the human mind as if the mind itself were a thing apart; this is logically impossible. The human cognitive apparatus is a product of biological evolution, and its mission is to guarantee the survival of the species, not "recognition of truth," as the Slovakian biochemist and philosopher Ladislav Kovac has recently pointed out. The recognition of truth can be a recognition of the aspiration toward a supra-individual cognitive system. It's a wonderful idea to imagine somebody or something evolving to the state of real or final wisdom, wisdom for all of us. So far, this hasn't happened to any individual soul or through any spiritual movement. So far, it has only been the trend of the cognitive networks of modern sciences. They are both objectively and subjectively "the reason which owns us," in F. B. Schelling's words.

More surprisingly, in all such argumentation, we never really get a definition of the "human essence." If it is something unchanging, at the core of each man, woman, and child, why get upset with animal experimentation, since we have always survived at someone else's expense and "natural" cultures have so often performed bloody human and animal sacrifice compared to which a surgical intervention on an anesthetized animal is a pastoral procedure? If there was something invariant in us we certainly became alienated from it at the crucial point of self-reflection, in our relationship to death, and at the very beginnings of the cultures and civilizations called "European."

If, on the other hand, this "human essence" is a changing quality, which is the basis of my faith and hope, then changes must also occur in the content of expressions like "human," "being human," "human dignity," and "humanitarian approach." Then there is no point in regretting that ancient authorities and traditions get burned away. It becomes hard to put any trust in the urge to return to fundamentalisms, from religious ones to the ecological fondness for all things visible and sentimental as opposed to things invisible and outside the range of our feelings. We must learn to ask, on a case by case basis, whether a proposed view is a relapse to a more primitive stage of the spirit, soul, or mass mentality, or whether it is a response not only to civilization's problems and to scientific viewpoints, but also to Westernization, which for many societies of the Third World is synonymous not only with economic growth but with survival itself.

In *The End of History and the Last Man,* Francis Fukuyama contends that the historical evolution of liberal democracy is a proof in itself of how human nature has changed over the last couple of millennia. Heidegger took Nietzsche's radical historicism to the conclusion that any traditional ethics or morality sooner or later becomes impossible. In terms of approach and method, Picasso said: "We always stick with the old-fashioned ideas, with outdated definitions, as if it were not the very task of the artist to find new ones." And he was well aware of what he was burning away. But what is all right when it is said by a historian, a philosopher, or an artist becomes outrageous when it is uttered by a geneticist or a physicist.

Ultimately, then, how can we believe that science is an autonomous, aggressive, and oppressive force or power? Are we saying that it's something like a product of mutants from dimension X? The essence of radical historicism is derived from science, and science is, I believe, as integral a part of modern humanity as art (though I won't bet, even if just from professional shyness, as Richard Rorty does, that poetry's evolutionary chances are better than philosophy's). Science is part of our spiritual climate, just as that climate is the consequence of our activities, including scientific ones.

The increase in scientific knowledge, wrote Mario Vargas Llosa, undoubtedly influences history. However, there is no possibility of rationally predicting the development of scientific knowledge.

Was anything wrong with the Viennese atmosphere of the early decades of this century, from which emerged not only new disciplines dealing with the subconscious, with sexuality, and with language, but also new approaches to the demarcation of sciences and pseudosciences? Why would Freud be less corrosive for traditional human values than Karl Popper and Ernst Mach? Doesn't the cultural atmosphere of Vienna, or at other times the climate of Copenhagen, Cambridge, or even Prague, show that science is not an autonomous entity but a natural component of a creative atmosphere and of human progress, or at least of the process of solving the soluble?

Either we respect even what we do not understand or we pretend to understand only what we respect. Unfortunately, respect is not very closely connected to knowledge. Sometimes it is entirely disconnected.

I admit that these are the opinions of somebody who has been trying to do both science and art for a long time. Maybe my soul has been corroded, or it has refused to be inflated by the hot air of group mentality. Maybe my soul has been lost altogether. But I know at least a few artists with an obviously healthy soul who respect science as a way of acquiring knowledge and as an integral part of Western culture.

What corrosive forces or what supportive factors have I experienced thanks to scientific work, at least in terms of self-reflection, and, if possible, without superstitions and illusions? The main limitation I'm aware of is that I'm unable to accept any other mode of acquiring knowledge about the world of nonself than the scientific mode, the one that is acceptable for professional scientific criteria in various disciplines, the one about which I know, from my own experience and from literature.

In other words, I am unable, in principle, to share the axioms—I would call them myths—Milton Rothman exposes in his book *The Science Gap* (1992):

> Nothing is known for sure.
> Nothing is impossible.
> Whatever we think we know now is likely to be
>   overturned in the future.
> All theories are equal.
> Scientists create theories by intuition.
> Advanced civilizations will possess forces unknown to us.
> Etcetera

Neither can I accept the traditional poetic myth that "the scientist doubts, the poet knows," since I know from everyday life and work that poetic knowledge outside a poem is not worth a wooden nickel, and any other teaching of the men of spirit or the men of practice will not last very long, with the exception of several scientific and technical fundamentals with everyday application. In most situations we are like the courtiers from the poem "Seekers after Truth" by Dannie Abse:

> Below, distant, the roaring courtiers
> rise to their feet—less shocked than irate.
> Salome has dropped the seventh veil
> and they've discovered there are eight.

The consequence of the above-mentioned scientific limit is, however, that I am not alone with my private history, my own mental restrictions, my stupidity and ingenuity, my inventiveness and forgetfulness; I share the notions (knowledge and know-hows, as Vilém Laufberger used to say), gained by observation, experiments, judgment, and computations by other trustworthy persons who convince me, correct and complement me, and mostly surpass me by far, which is a pleasant feeling for anyone who does not see himself as Prometheus.

Another limitation is the loss of "the pleasure of transcendence," or more specifically the pleasure of personal transcendence. This pleasure, as Harold Bloom writes in his book *Agon: Towards a Theory of Revisionism* (1982), is "equivalent to narcissistic freedom, freedom in the shape of that wilderness that Freud dubbed 'the omnipotence of thought,' the greatest of all narcissistic illusions."

It is of interest that the omnipotence of thought is demonstrated by predisposed individuals much more readily in the sphere of macrocosms and microcosms than in the sphere of communal hygiene or local administration. In politics, the frontiers of free invention are surprisingly much more tangible than in the treatment of rheumatism and in time-space theory. We limited individuals, less disposed to free invention, understand that the earth is not flat, that the center of the universe is not in our solar system, that Newton with his laws of gravity was more reliable than theoreticians of UFOs, that photons are unchanging and permanent entities, that one cannot exceed the speed of light, that life is based exclusively on biochemical principles such as the self-perpetuating information systems of nucleic acids, that even spiritual existence is based on impenetrable complexity and on the order-out-of-chaos principle, that a swan cannot be crossed either with Lohengrin or with Leda, and that there are only two surpassing, transcendental categories in life: the genome and the extracorporeal heritage that is sometimes called culture and sometimes civilization.

There is, however, the inner circle, the dark world of the Self, located within reach of our knowledge, know-hows, and decision making in the same way as the secretions of glucocorticoids and the reserve of stem cells in the bone marrow are. That is, it is located within reach, but we are not very good at reaching it, although we need not make a virtue out of our difficulty. The darkness of this inner world is demonstrated by the fact that the description Lewis Thomas offered in his 1974 essay on the au-

tonomy of organs also applies to it: "Nothing would save me and my liver if I were in charge. . . . I am . . . constitutionally unable to make hepatic decisions." It is also demonstrated by the fact that, as Thomas says, there are quite a number of selves, and they come one after the other, with others waiting in line for their turn to perform, and the worst moment comes when one wants to be just a single self. Some manage it—at least Thomas does—only when they are listening to music.

As I know from my own experience, there is very little of that singular Self in the dark inner world, but there are a lot of events and images from the outside. A soul expert calls them archetypes and makes them part of some tribal subconscious, when in fact what I have in there is this year's kangaroo from Wilpena Pound in Australia, the frightened face of an elderly lady across the aisle on the plane, tumors in the satin lung tissue of an unknown young man I dreamed about last night, the hardly audible violin music in the garden during sunset yesterday evening, the outline of a girl I once loved, and the figure of my mother, the quiet voice of a girl without a father, who cut her face with a kitchen knife—it's nothing, she says, you just press it to your cheek and slice—obstacles to the publication of this scientific study, ways of surmounting them, the voice of Dana H., melodiously interpreting a film on the sexual habits of ground squirrels . . . In fact, I even have in there—and I don't regret it—the paradox of Schrödinger's cat, several NK cells, a couple of nude mice, the anthropic principle of the universe with Doctor Grygar's profile, and the TNT mice probe with the dark eyes of Doctor Marie L., four unanswered letters, a mess involving my phone bills, the first eight lines of the *Iliad,* and a spot on my beige jacket.

I would not compare my inner world with the transcendent soul, the hypertrophic soul (in Milan Kundera's term), but I'm guessing that each of us has a soul just the right size.

I do not know if my personal myths, feelings, and illogical urges are good for anything. They are here, they are strictly personal, they do for a sort of poetic attitude. They are simply, in

the literary application, private idiosyncratic metaphors, symbiotic plants in the "secret gardens of self," in William Carlos Williams's term.

In view of these secret gardens I have no doubt about the role of poetry (in the broadest sense of the word) in my life, in every life, in the average human inner world governed by principles of uncertainty. I do need poetry as a sort of consolation, a temporary relief and limited hope about my personal future. I do not need poetry or religion to explain anything about Self and non-Self. I need poetry as the last possibility for saying something against gravitation, against the degeneration of nucleic acids and arthrosis, although I know that it does no good.

Limitation as recognized by scientists (as opposed to poets, fundamentalists, New Agers, and other playful minds) is the awareness of what is possible, of the borderline between anarchy of thought and scientific courage.

Ultimately, science limits the spirit (or soul) in the technical sphere. When you are doing something in the laboratory, something mechanical like weighing, or something magical like seeking fluorescent cells in black darkness, you are outside the inspirational sources of art or any other inventiveness and creativity. Your mental activity is focused on digital counting or maneuvering in the dark. You are totally devoted to figures or to darkness. If you do it forty hours a week, there is not much time left for creative mental activity. A soul craving other levels of experience must learn patience and humility. Given those constraints, writing poetry or anything else becomes a kind of recreation. Such a view may appear to be a terrible limitation to some artists, but it does not appear so terrible to me, especially when I consider how many artists have sold their talents for commercial success, how many former researchers have embarked upon careers as entrepreneurs, moneymakers, or, most horrifying of all, political big shots.

Science teaches us some discipline. It forces us to concentrate on a single problem and a single approach to it at the given moment: only then is there hope of achieving some tiny success in any research, including art. In a purposeful activity there is no

room for free floating. Scientific practice has taught me: That there is a big difference between real involvement of the mind and hand and a purely internal "creative" thought. That lengthy social exchange of monologues based on "what I am" cannot replace "what I have done." That ten minutes are ten minutes even at a lecture or a poetry reading. And finally, that criticism is not sublimated violence or a plot by depraved individuals to destroy someone's progress; very often it is a qualified assessment of our work by others, naturally in the conditions of the existing climate or paradigm. Or dogma.

There's a moral component to be derived from science, and most humanists don't like this at all. Alas, most humanists are defined mainly by never having worked in science. They have never read Jacob Bronowski saying that science nowadays requires rigorous thinking and a scrupulous code of conduct in the laboratory, library, or operating theater or at the control panel. A rigorous code of conduct is not very satisfying in terms of the free human soul, but the soul does not have much fun even during the daily routine, for instance, when replacing a fuse or waiting at a traffic light. Today, the scientific mode of conduct and inquiry presents a model of behavior that will gradually become more and more necessary, even in the nonscientific sectors of our dense civilization's time-space.

I don't deny that one can develop habits of rigor in the pursuit of the arts and humanities. But in science and technology you acquire an exacting attitude more quickly, and you learn that deviations will be punished. We know of many cases of fraud, error, and human failure in science and technology, from plagiarism to experiments like Chernobyl. By contrast, I'm not aware of many cases of fraud and failure in the arts, maybe because they are noticed rarely and by very few people.

Sadly, we no longer learn information on the norms of life from philosophy and from poetry; we learn them from technical instructions, which have a linguistic and aesthetic quality that approximates the level of communication among social insects. Their influence on the soul is undoubtedly negligible, but it's better to have some norms than none at all. Science is not to blame; the norms reveal not so much the shortcomings of science as the shortage of it.

And yet, the soul—that dark blossom in a secret garden—does have an impact on science itself. It too is an integral part of the existing atmosphere and genius loci, which I have eulogized elsewhere. Public and private metaphors, fantasies, civilized myths, or myths favored by common sense—all these affect the time and the place, and through them the way we are tuned and our half-conscious affinities for judgments, hypotheses, estimates of probable and possible events. They have contributed to the fact that the evolution of science cannot be assessed by rational methods.

It is something like the zeitgeist, composed of little individual idiosyncrasies and group mentalities and paradigms. "The objective spirit," says Norbert Bischof in a 1993 book on Konrad Lorenz, "has a human dimension in addition to the material dimension, and it has always been known. But we did not like psychology to get too close to the human factor. . . . When searching for hidden motifs of creativity, they were evaluated in terms of morality instead of being analyzed in terms of causality."

If it were true that "the reason is basically just the effector of our emotions," as Ladislav Kovac writes, then the collective mind and reason might be one of the few ways out of the comical state in which the individual reason is able "to transform any common hormonal disorder into a metaphysical concept."

However, it is not desirable for souls or zeitgeists to undermine the self-confidence of entire scientific disciplines, or to influence collective processes of questioning and procedures that lead from the insoluble to the soluble. Why relativize those few scientific certainties we have, and force researchers to apologize for being here and for having achieved something?

I would like to share Mr. Appleyard's complaint, but I have nothing to complain about. Science has taught me to say "although" and "but," and it has made me fall from the symbolic world of language, myth, religion, and art to the "natural world" of physical reality, the immediate reality of man, the most characteristic and highest product of culture.

Anything that opposes the universal tendency of accretion to human knowledge (not simply personal, individual knowledge) is a deviation, an evolutionary deviation and also a moral deviation, says Ladislav Kovac. To doubt organized science in the name of the "natural world" is to endanger the survival of the natural world.

The poet W. H. Auden understood this, as is clear from the definition of art he once gave me: Art is spiritual life made possible by science. I took it very personally.

Seeing

Edward Hoagland

I Can See

The blind eat many a fly," says a fifteenth-century proverb—familiar as recently as fifty years ago, when I was small and blind people were still all over, tap-tapping with their white canes and saddled with dark glasses. The canes, if waved, could bring traffic to a halt, and their rhythmic tapping could part a stream of pedestrians and function for the blind person as a kind of radar besides. Power and pathos: dark glasses were an emblem of the saddest, sharpest handicap. Ostensibly making it harder to see, they signified instead that the person *couldn't* see, and probably had a face so wooden or so profoundly wounded by loneliness that he preferred to go incognito.

Common problems such as cataracts or glaucoma were not often reversible back then, whereas today you need to fly to Third World outposts to encounter blindness on such a scale. This phenomenon of adults who were helpless and pitiable, though in the prime of life, became one of the first moral puzzles children recognized. Old age they knew; jailbirds they knew about; real freaks (like the "waterhead" whom I once visited, painfully imprisoned in an easy chair in a dark cottage, his head bloated to double-size) they might also have some vague acquaintance with. But the blind were ordinary folk, innocent of any crime or grotesquerie, of no specific age, who lived in a crabby or long-suffering perpetual night. A mean individual that I knew snickered when he told me how he'd snuck into a blind man's house when he was a boy—having watched him leave for his weekly tap-tap trip to the grocery store—and shat into the sink where all his dishes were. And I could hear the desolate groan the blind man must have uttered, coming home, smelling the evidence of what had been done to him, and searching for where it was, while he fathomed his impossible position living alone, as the story spread among the children of the neighbourhood.

In the 1950s, when I reached my twenties, however, certain types of people began to adopt dark glasses to convey a different message and as a form of chic. Jazz musicians, for example, could dramatize the underground, persecuted, joky character of their existence and telegraph the idea that even at night they already knew too much about what was going on to want to see any more. Better for the spirit to be self-absorbed, ironically bemused, optionally blind—a "spade" so savvy that he wore shades. Yet highway troopers, too, wore smoked glasses to mask their emotions and thus look formidably impassive as they delivered news as highly charged as jazz. And many of the newsworthy intellectuals of the era, café-based existentialists on both sides of the Atlantic, likewise affected sunglasses as a means of demonstrating that a great deal of the passing parade was better left unseen. Impelled by the atrocities of two world wars and signature books like *Nausea* and *The Stranger*, they seemed to advocate disguising your identity to limit what you let yourself take in of a corrupt, demoralizing world in which the night was better than the day because of what it screened.

I didn't agree with this, and didn't wear dark glasses. Believing in nature and an overshadowing beneficence even in its offshoot, human nature, I wanted to gorge on every waking sight. I loved the city like the country—the hydrants that fountained during the summer like a splashing brook—and wanted to absorb the cruel along with the good. I knew that Americans had responded to the bloody ruination of the Civil War not in a fashion corresponding to Sartre or the Theatre of the Absurd, but by turning West once again to seek the balm of the wild. I saw this because my own solution to a sad spell was also to head outdoors and climb a spruce, find a pond, or hitch-hike West, where I achieved an acquaintance with the frontiers that were left. In the city, my response was to seek the most crowded places, Coney Island, Union Square, the Lower East Side, Times Square, on the same instinctive principle: that life in bulk is good. Embracing the fizz and seethe of a metropolis was safer then, as was hitch-hiking, but my feeling for crowds has never changed. Rubbing shoulders with thousands of people, my spirits surge much in the way that I grin at seeing a one-year-old, or will approach an elderly person, optimistic at the prospect of talking with them; a basic faith kicks in. It's automatic, not ideological. I believe life has meaning; I find diversity a comfort in the wilds and in the city—that there are more species than mine, more personalities than me. I believe in God as embodied in the earth and in metropolises. I believe that life is good.

So, night or day, in Alaska or Africa, Bombay, Rome, Istanbul, New York, I never wore dark glasses. I can remember dazzling long wonderful days out in a boat in alligator refuges in Georgia, bird sanctuaries in Texas or Louisiana, scouting with wildlife experts who had some protection for their eyes. But I wanted to see everything just as it really was, in the full spectrum of colours, as a bird or reptile would. In the desert I was the same, and in Greenwich Village, at Andy Warhol parties, I'd no more shade my eyes from the blitz of strobe lights than put in earplugs. I wrote for the purpose of being read in fifty years, and how could you describe a world whose colours you hadn't honestly seen?

But nature played a trick on me. Sunlight kindles cataracts (which I didn't know), and in my fifties I got them bad, compounded by bad retinas. At about the same juncture a bunch of my writer friends died before their time of lung cancer, emphysema, throat ailments, and the like—Edward Abbey, Donald

Barthelme, Raymond Carver, Frederick Exley, Richard Yates, and several lesser-known good souls—at least partly because they had ascribed to the equally romantic notion that writers ought to smoke, drink, fuck, carouse, and get pie-eyed (whereas I only thought they should fuck). Not all of this chemical imbibery stemmed from the Gallic-Kafka-Beckett idea that life was shitty, which had been in vogue. Nor was it simply macho, though the Hemingway-Mailer axis of behaviour was as influential as the Europeans' despair. The hard-living ethos had its best argument in the idea that the mind, like a pinball machine, may need a bit of slamming to light up. Smoking like a chimney, drinking like a fish, or using pot or stronger dope might rev the mind, dramatize the vertiginous character of life, and wipe out humdrum thoughts for a while.

I didn't disagree with the proposition of slamming one's sensibility around—that's why I walked across the Brooklyn Bridge at dawn sometimes and had driven or hitch-hiked across the country eight times. Strangers and the play of expressions across their faces, by the thousands in a single day—Hausa, Chinese, Irish, Navajo, Polish, Puerto Rican—these were what the city boiled down to for me, just as it was the scores of species in the woods that make the country rich as it is: blackburnian warblers and moccasin-flowers, oyster mushrooms and oakworm moths, bigtooth aspen, squirrel-corn and hop hornbeam. The city hasn't worn quite as well for me in forty years of loving it. I love it more at a distance now, but remind myself that from my twenties to mid-thirties I chose to spend the height of the spring and summer in the midst of New York as often as out in the country. Human nature, if cosmopolitan enough, with bodegas and storefront churches and *kielbasa* eateries and elderly people sitting in folding chairs on the sidewalk and numerous infants, was nature to me. I walked by the Hudson almost daily, when the past night's paroxysm of violence or vomit had abated and the commerce of the day lent the city its terrific thrum—not just the million people, but the million trucks. I had a Bella motor scooter that I'd ride the length and breadth of Manhattan, or I'd go to a Yankee game and walk all the way home from the Bronx to the East Village, 180 blocks, as the daylight darkened. Or nose along the classic portal side-streets—Elizabeth and Forsyth and Mott and Eldridge and Orchard—off of Canal and Delancey, where people were still beginning new American lives. Or amble under the financial towers at Nassau, Whitehall, Pine and Wall Streets, with that wonderful lift the beige and creamy and gray-stone downtown and midtown buildings can sometimes give you at midday, when they're so full of sunlight and strivers that optimism is lent to anybody who strides through. High buildings, high hopes. This was a special place to be and its enhancing identity was catching.

Mute, because of my stutter, I'd wandered Boston's night neighbourhoods with hungry yearning throughout my college years, supposing that maybe just to stare at a single mysterious light in a lonely house with enough longing would cause the woman inside, whoever she was, to sense my presence and slip to the front door and signal me inside. In a sensible world, a just and passionate world, it shouldn't be necessary to be able to talk to find a lover. After all, bad guys tend to be the best talkers of all. But I wasn't bold, I was shy, and such adventures didn't happen to me. I was a walker, a witness, but didn't *close*. One time a waitress in a café near the old North Station, where the trains from Maine came in, left me an extra dessert, but I couldn't bring myself to use this as an entrée to better things. Instead I'd walk for five, six or a dozen miles, feasting my eyes on the lights of the oil refinery in Everett and the half-darkened State Street mini-skyscrapers, and the harbour, where of course the glistening water, like all ocean water, seethed. I loved Boston's sourball sweetness, with its softer darkness, orangey street-lights, miniature but meta-ethnic neighbourhoods—Italians back to back with Irish, blacks with Portuguese, Chinese, North End, South End, West End. The weekend street markets at Faneuil Hall, and Skid Row nearby. During my years in the army, mostly stationed as a lab technician at a hospital in Pennsylvania, I hiked round Philadelphia. After my discharge in 1957, I lived in and explored the hills of San Francisco, the prettiest of cities. And afterwards, for two-and-a-half years in the early 1960s, I walked extensively in Paris, London and Rome, plus wilder environs in Sicily and Greece. In the guise of a wildlife writer, a hook-and-bullet writer for Sports Illustrated, I went south also, to Baton Rouge and beyond. People there might tell me how they had "treed a coon" and not mean a raccoon. A plain old hook-and-bullet writer must likely be a good ole boy too, so I was privy to the sort of blathering that ostensibly political journalists seldom hear.

As a writer, though, I was above all visual: I concentrated on what I could see. My first book had been set in a circus; the second was about the cruel but graceful art of boxing. But now I was beginning to forsake the city for wilderness areas, in pursuit of ideas for books. I continued to live in New York, as Audubon, Frederic Remington, Albert Bierstadt and so many other artists who have made wild places their subject matter have done (you generally accomplish more in the city because of its inexorable thrum). But I did spend three or four months a year drinking from a spring, bathing in a pond, heating with wood and lighting with kerosene in northern Vermont, and this kept me reasonably honest when I went foraging for stories—my husky in the car—in the Far West and Deep South. The dog would jump out the side window and pee and jump right back in when we stopped for gas. "Better than havin' a pistol," one hillsman said, when we were halfway through Tennessee. "A pistol can snap, but a dog like that'll go rightattem."

When an old-timer who lived by a lake would tell me he moved his difficult bowels every morning by wading hip-deep, I knew what he meant; so had I. If he loved the frogs' songs as much as the birds', I could say, "Same here." They were, what, three hundred million years old? I had learned to shoot in the army, so I was up to the tin-can contests we sometimes had; up to scrambling up a mountainside to see an old mine hole. I knew dogs and therefore wolves; goats and therefore deer; parrots and therefore ravens and crows; big exotic wildlife and therefore little homebody wildlife as well. I knew what I wanted—pristine lore—and that is always half the battle.

*   *   *

My eyes were important allies in these endeavours. And in my anti-modernist ebullience I was not, I think, a Pollyanna; I saw the South with a Yankee's acidulous eye and the North with Thoreauvian impatience. (In my teens I'd been more drawn to the Tolstoyan mode, but couldn't sustain such exalted idealism and the literary aspirations to go with it.) Acidulousness is not absurdism, however. Sunshine and drifting water under a shifting mosaic of leaves, with alligators in the bayou and otters in a creek alongside—I mean, what more do you need to believe? In my travels I was seeing so many alligators and otters (once an alligator eating an otter), and waterfowl in flocks of thousands, and whales, seals, walruses, moose, elk, caribou, then African lions and elephants, warthogs, horned toads, striped skunks, black and greenish porcupines, painted turtles, white-tailed deer, ruby-throated hummingbirds, black-throated cliff swallows, blue warblers, red newts, golden eagles, water buffaloes, desert dromedaries, and little swerving brown bats, how could I not believe? So many creatures in a matrix of ethology that when I was out of doors there was never a day I doubted life's divinity. In the city, I went to and loved Beckett's *Krapp's Last Tape, Waiting for Godot,* and Pinter's, Ionesco's, Genet's, and others' plays as brilliant—but didn't actually accept the premises of absurdism. To a naturalist, absurdism is ultimately absurd. It's a subway/sidewalk/basement philosophy, a starless-moonless-cloudless-night philosophy. But there are few real cloudless, starless, moonless nights, and people living in basements and subways for more than a few years have constructed an uncommon life for themselves. Absurdism was like a stopped clock, but time doesn't stop.

Even my sense of divinity was visual. I'd never bothered to learn many of the bird calls in my neck of the woods, and knew my friends by their faces, not their body language or the barometer of the voice. I played great music drawn from several centuries all day long, but didn't focus on it as a radiant expression of humanity's special genius—not as intently as I studied the visual drama of the clouds and sun, the Hudson rushing onward, the pointy firs, fuzzy tamaracks, sheeny willows, generous sweet-sapped maples, or a hawk in a basswood tree.

But as my sight dimmed, from what turned out to be incipient cataracts, I found driving becoming difficult. I began placing sets of binoculars next to the windows I looked out of, or wearing them around my neck and using them a dozen times a day. I focused, too, on bookish pursuits, as if my time were short, but postponing thinking about what was wrong with me because I'd always lived for the sake of my work, and as if I might die before it was finished. Even in my twenties, each night I'd made sure that the day's accretion was legible enough for somebody else to decipher if I kicked off. I've always anticipated a "disaster" (faith in nature implies that you accept death as natural and often proper), and have always had weak eyes. Nature did not expect us to live to be eighty-four, or even sixty-five. Nature did not expect us to *see* so much, either—the daily TV catalogue of scandals and calamities, far-flung tear-jerkers and utter outrages that you'd think some day would end. You'd think that when the massacres of ethnic cleansing are broadcast everywhere, or simpler accidental tragedies like school-buses hit at railroad crossings, they would never happen again. People would see the horror on the screen worldwide, and *never do it again*. Not slaughter thousands of people because of their tribe, nor stop a school-bus on the railroad tracks.

The doctors I went to for my blindness weren't sure what was really wrong because the underlying culprit, beneath the cataracts, was that my retinas were in terrible shape—"pitted and bulging like a bald tire about to burst," as one surgeon put it. He didn't want to operate; the ordinary cataract procedure would be more dangerous because of the pressure that it would engender on the back of the eye. Indeed, the first three doctors that I consulted declined, and they mistook the primary problem I was having with my vision. They thought it must be the retinas, not my clouded lenses, because they could see through my lenses to the back of my eyes so much more clearly than I could see out.

Meanwhile, as my eyes weakened, I began to see the truth of that fifteenth-century proverb, and found myself swallowing flies or other foreign matter that might be swimming in my soup or juice. I quit driving and gave my car away because bicyclists now looked like mailboxes posted beside the road, dogs like cardboard boxes, and pedestrians like poplar trees. I was afraid I wouldn't be able to see a child playing there at all. I was living in the country at the time and thus became a long-distance bus rider. I lived in Vermont, and the local line, called Bonanza, was my carrier when I went to Manhattan. By great good luck, Bonanza happened to have been founded some forty years before by one of my ex-schoolmates, and he still headed the company and was esteemed as a good boss. It was my luck because I'm a shy person and in my previous spates of riding buses for long distances, during my youth, I'd never been able to summon the courage to sit up front and strike up a comfortable conversation with the driver to hear his tales of the road. I'd looked out the window for hours instead, which was its own reward. But now that I couldn't see much of anything I needed an opening to help change my habits, engage the driver's interest in this blindish codger who had difficulty talking because of a stutter.

I hadn't ridden buses much since the cross-country Grey-hounds of my hobo summers when they were still a hardscrabble mainstream means of travel. But with cheap air travel, that's over. Long-distance buses have become the habitat of busted souls who have lost their cars to the finance company or have lost their license for driving drunk; of childless, indigent old people; or frightened new immigrants from Laos, Nigeria or Guatemala City, who have too many kids to manage; of people who have just been released from an institution; or people like me who were legally blind. I did meet several others who couldn't see beyond the end of their nose, and some gently retarded individuals who saw the world as cloudily as I did but by a different process. A woman who carried herself like the Queen of England, but fell down a lot, always smiling; a man with stained pants whose faeces smelt of whisky.

I remember once being seated on the Bennington bus next

to a tough-faced diminutive man who looked to be in his sixties and whom I'd first noticed in the New York terminal because he had been hobbling about with chest pains, suffering agonies in the queues. He turned out to be a racetrack groom, just cashiered from his pick-up job in Florida because of angina attacks, and tossed into the welfare system there. He spoke in muttered bursts, half-collapsed in his seat as he anticipated the stabbing shafts of pain—although of course he was a lean, fit, hardbitten-looking sort of guy in other respects. Now in desperate straits, he was making his way back to Pittsfield, the Massachusetts town which he had left in anger twenty years ago, to throw himself upon the mercy of a son who still lived there, and whom he hadn't seen since then. We arrived in the December chill at ten o'clock at night, but no one had come to meet him.

However, the night was not unlike the day for me, because I couldn't see either the stars or birds, either a plane's lights or a fox ranging a roadside field, or even read with my two eyes at once, because I had to hold a book or magazine so near that I was not able to focus both of them upon the words. I'd close one and rest it for a while, while using the other. But my straits weren't desperate. I had a lifetime of preparation for this, in the sense of jiggering my finances into position for long-term survival and remodelling the furniture of my mind for life's later stages. Goodness knows, I hadn't wanted to be blind, but neither had I wanted to be young forever, and some of the changes I was now undergoing were amusing in their way, or curious, and an adventure. When I reached the city on my trips, I couldn't read street signs or numbers, so had to rely on my memories of its geography and count the blocks I walked from each big two-way cross-street—42nd, 57th, 72nd, 79th, 86th or 96th, or 34th, 23rd, 14th—to find my way, stumbling on the curbs and listening for the lights to change according to the traffic's sound or the lurch of the crowds. Often I took taxis, but even this was complicated because I needed to pretend that I could see the route that we were following in order not to be led round Robin Hood's barn, and also that I could read the meter, after we arrived. "What's it say?" I'd casually ask, dropping my eyes to my wallet, as I chose a bill by its placement, then raise them again and gaze at the numerals I couldn't really make out, at the same time that the cabbie turned toward me and answered.

I couldn't recognize my friends, and when I did know who I was talking to by moving close enough to recognize them by their shape or by the tenor of their body language, I couldn't see if they were attentive or distracted, whether they had had a sleepless night and a saddening day or were feeling effervescent and mischievous. And by the time I leaned right next to somebody's face to distinguish a smile from a scowl, the play of conversation had usually moved on.

My father, when he was first operated on for cancer, was insistent, even a bit frantic, that nobody in his professional life should know exactly what he had. He was afraid that if word got out, he might be written off; that other lawyers would cease to count him as a player or think of him as in the running—a colleague or an opponent of any consequence. Similarly, I felt that as a blind writer I need not be reckoned with. No more reviews, essays or jurying; no more books to come out. I could be politely dismissed, and the good-time Charlies among my friends would depart. With glasses on I was seeing at twenty feet what normal eyes, without eyeglasses, could pick out at four hundred, so the process did resemble being terminally ill. People would visit me ritually once and never again.

The platinum light in the early morning, as a gentle rain fell, nearly broke my heart—the tiers of green, each subtle shade different, ash and cedar, spruce and apple, lilac and dogwood leaves—beauty I was losing. I walked through the timothy and orchard grass, the tangles of vetch, the fireweed stalks and raspberry canes, each registering as friends I might not see again— with what was left of my eyesight standing on tiptoe, or dimly perceived through my binocs, if I stopped. Hearing a toad sing, I would visualize him, along with the chorus of tree frogs in the alder thicket, rejoicing in the rain. My dog I saw because he came to my hands, and birches became my favourite trees (except in July when the basswoods bloomed with that fetching, incomparable scent that was Thoreau's favourite also) because their white bark glowed.

I bought a telescope to gaze at the rising moon, sometimes following its slow-scudding trajectory through much of an evening, and wore field glasses all day, ready to peer through a window if I heard a car turn into the driveway or if the wind blew and I wanted to see the crowns of the trees bob and interlace. But I was generally too late; by the time I located the car, it would be too close to stare at discreetly, and a bird—if I heard a bird sing—would have hopped to another branch or taken flight before I got it into focus. Still, just having these eight-power lenses to clap in front of my regular glasses was a comfort, though already I could feel they'd be no help if I went truly blind.

As the curtain drew tighter, closing my horizon from a hundred to sixty and then thirty feet, I saved my spirits from thoroughly sinking by paying attention to the peculiar details of what was happening to me and how to continue functioning. I hitchhiked to my teaching job and home, thumb-up, like a boy again; I'd done so much of that in my teens. I mapped the seating of my classes, asking the students to sit in the same place each week so I would know who was speaking, and to speak without first raising their hands. Walking to town, I focused upon my lungs and legs, and itemized the feel of the weather, or the menu of colours my eyes still took in, after shadings became a blur. I listened to Dickens and Shakespeare on tape and experimented with radio snacking from *Canadien Français*.

There are fair-weather friends and foul-weather friends, and we need both kinds in our lives, especially so because each is likely to absent himself rather abruptly when the wind shifts. The drama of an emergency may unsettle a fair-weather specialist, uncorking alarming vibrations of vertigo in him, and cause him to make his excuses and discreetly flee. But the same intimations of pervasive catastrophe will give the foul-weather person a bracing sense that life is, indeed, dangerous and interesting. The proverbial social worker, who is an absolute ace at her work but only manages to hold her own hang-ups in check by focusing hard on her clients', is an example. But of course it is she who pulls people through their crises, not your sunnier, more politic soul who avoids the taint of misery. On the other hand, when you bask in good news and things are going fine, an ambulance-chaser may not be your best bet for a drinking buddy. He'll remain rather ambivalent about what it means. He'll be listening for the crump of thunder, the winds of a cyclone just over the horizon, as if your good luck probably cannot last. You want, instead, the comradeship of summer soldiers then.

My summer soldiers were now cancelling lunch dates, quietly dropping me from party lists, and tacitly waiting to see if my eye problems were going to sort themselves out, like other difficulties, financial, legal, personal, that sometimes throw a wrench into a person's career and remove him from circulation for a spell. We were at an age when people we knew were beginning to die off anyway and get dropped from everybody's rolodexes. But unlike other paradoxes that plague us, blindness—to be alive yet be denied the chief measure of enjoying life—is often studied in Sunday school as a kind of paradigm. At least it used to be, because even as kids we could approximate the experience just by closing our eyes. You couldn't do that with cancer, or other unambiguous disasters. But why were people rendered blind, born blind—squeezed into inhabiting only their fingertips and ears? We could not answer this.

The ethic of pity was what we were taught to feel with regard to blind people. The taboo against bumping or cheating or tripping them up was extreme. So wicked a notion could scarcely provoke a titter, it was so terrible; and hearing that story of the boy we knew who'd snuck into the blind man's house and shat in his sink—it was so wild we couldn't believe it, then couldn't restrain our ugly giggles. To imagine his wail of despair and throttled horror, the disgust and dread for the interminable future the man must have felt when he returned, sniffed incredulously, searched and finally ran his hand against the turds, or maybe set his dishes down in them all unawares . . . this lay beyond the bounds of civilization. And the perpetrator remained unusual. The last time I saw him, he was in his fifties and said that he had bought a pair of binoculars to watch a lonesome spinster woman who lived across the road, who he said was "going to hang herself for sure one day." He was waiting for the morning when he would see her stringy body strung from a rafter—her misery having got the best of her.

One rarely hears of anybody suffering some variety of biblical self-loathing because of their past cruelty to others. Mostly they sit in church, vote, shop, and deal in goods or services like anybody else. They're anaesthetized, living well and in denial; and nothing wakes them up. But when I left home for a series of cheap hotels in New York during my twenties, while I was setting my course as a writer, I used to know several blind men and women who'd been stranded in these bleak establishments by the social agencies and their own lack of money. Though generally innocents, they were living like "sinners in the hands of an angry god," squirming upon a griddle of petty fears and pilferage, morning humiliations and afternoon griefs, while the genuine sinners in high-rises along Central Park West a few blocks away lived high off the hog. They'd grope along the walls in the endless shabby corridors or through the lobby, its floor tilting, to get out to the street to feel the sunshine on their faces and buy a can of tunafish and a quart of orange juice.

Tuna is indeed a comfort, if you pay attention to it—tasting of the sea, in fact the very salts of life—and so is orange juice, which opulently personifies the sweet acidity of roots, sunshine and trees. When I was blind I loved to savour juices—grapefruit, apple cider and V-8—all of which, considering the pleasure they give, seemed unbelievably available and inexpensive. But the problem for these blind people was just procuring the food, or going to the common bathroom at the corner of the hall with a gauntlet of other souls eyeing them on the way with the vibrations of satisfaction that come from seeing someone worse off than you are. The women sometimes got manhandled in alcoves off the stairs, the lobby, or the elevator as they made their way down to the coffee shop, by old men who lay in wait along the route they had to follow, and "copped a feel" under the pretext of assisting them over a set of steps or around a pail. Gracious, what despair they must have felt as the months and years ground on—the hopeless tar pit they had fallen into! No end to how precarious their daily position was—and just the jabbering talk-show hosts on the radio for company—except for one tragic and unlucky lady whom I'd known slightly, who was burned alive when the hotel that the Welfare Department had beached her in caught fire, and the various crummy, sighted men who had used to grope her in the corridors when she left her room forgot all about her until the place had become an inferno. They remembered on the sidewalk.

Blind, I could no longer go to museums (would have had to stand so close my glasses scratched the paintings). I couldn't see butterflies and realized that unlike the kingdom of birds these white admirals and tiger swallowtails were totally lost to me. At least I had tapes of bird calls, but this meant only that I was learning to recognize the calls of warblers and other little woods birds that I'd never bothered to track down and actually look at while I still had my sight.

Blindness, as one feels it from inside, is like a shutdown of the front wall of one's head. The ears—at both sides—are left, but one's eyes, useless now, seem to have constituted one's entire forehead and face, north of one's nose. And what wouldn't one sacrifice to get them back! I would have eaten out of garbage cans, gone friendless, given my possessions away or surrendered a leg to be able to see grass wave in the wind, not just hear it— see whose footsteps were approaching, not have to wait until people chose to speak. My regret was so comprehensive that I seldom spoke of it, just as, when you visit a dying person, only seldom do they blurt out, *Oh god, I'm disappointed! I'm losing everything I've loved and cared for, everything important to me!*

Instead I apologized as charmingly as I could when I reached for what I thought was my wine at somebody's dinner party and put my hand into the cranberry sauce, or tripped over a coffee table, spilling the pot and six people's cups. I improvised ways to disguise how sightless I was by keeping my face wisely

turned toward whoever was speaking and recognizing my acquaintances by their morphs and stoops, their irascibility or depression, anxiety or kindness. I learned to listen urgently for the
click of a stop light on the street, and to assign my students only
books that I had read intensively before, staving off the time
when I would be too disabled to teach.

In H. G. Wells's short story, "The Country of the Blind," a
sighted wanderer slides down a mountainside into a precipitous
valley peopled entirely by the congenitally unsighted. At first he
gloats, remembering the folk adage that "In the country of the
blind the one-eyed man is King." But it turns out not to be that
easy. They can trace and chase and capture him by their super-
sense of sound, and after they do so, and have humoured him a
bit in his oddities, they decide to "operate" on him for his own
good to remove the "growths" in his eye sockets that appear to
them to be at the root of his abnormality. Though he's fallen in
love with a young woman who has often mediated for him, she
too wants him normalized. The jelly of his eyes, she realizes, is
the source of what she regards as his hallucinations, and therefore of friction between them. Oddity can never reign; and so he
flees to freeze in the snows above the valley, alone and in the
ecstasy of eyesight, rather than submit to being blinded by them.

Quite so. I discovered that sight was an ecstasy next to
which sex, for example, was small potatoes. Watching raindrops
running down a window and the grey sky's purplish bellying and
the trembling trees, I gorged on what I could still manage to see.
I studied seed-heads through my telescope—and the scrimshaw
on the moon—and a balm-of-Gilead's intricacy of boughs. Lying
down next to a brook, I watched the amber water ripple, the
yellow miracle of moss. I laid my head next to individual rocks,
or underneath a pine whose million needles were a sunburst, and
above them fishbone clouds. Black crows; the greenish-bluish
tawny grasses; a red sweatshirt; or a white birch's beckoning
bark. Nothing else—not speech or smell or hearing—matters
like your eyes. In the city I would try frantically to find an address that I had to get to, but would be unable to read the

numerals on the buildings or the streets, and stutter so badly that the people I asked for help dodged by me as they would a madman.

Walking had always been one of life's centrepieces for me, especially in the city, where it enabled me to pack in enough joy, sensation and exercise to make up for the deficits of living there. Seventy, eighty blocks hadn't seemed a lot, and when younger I had been a whirlwind walker, attentive to developments a hundred yards ahead (this, along with my native New Yorker street smarts, had kept me safe for decades). Good eyes had helped me finesse, too, the more pressing threat of having to speak. My boyhood stutter, which extended well past middle age, made me appear not simply importunate like a bum or beggar but disoriented and deranged—my mouth flabbering, my expression wounded, needy, fatalistic. Thus, for any information I needed, it was imperative that in the second or two I had before a respectable citizen brushed by me assuming I was homeless and a panhandler, I convince him I was handicapped, not one of the legion of beseechers inhabiting the street. And it was so searing to be rebuffed—I *did* feel homeless then—that until I had gone semiblind, I would search and search to almost any lengths to avoid asking directions. But, blind, losing the confident posture and direct, lively eyes of somebody on top of life, I really did begin to look like an alcoholic pleading for a quarter, or flipping out. The experience of being mistaken for a derelict is only briefly beneficial to the soul; and as a stutterer for more than fifty years, I'd been scalded by such episodes often enough already.

My careers as writer and teacher were stalling. I couldn't read my students' essays, and had to stop reviewing books for newspapers. The travel assignments that I coveted dried up because when an editor took me out to lunch he would notice me bumping into hydrants. I thought of reinventing myself as an author of children's stories. Like poems, they'd be short enough to rewrite in my head and dictate later. Otter and muskrat, snake and frog, fox and woodchuck, owl and squirrel, cowbird and warbler, coyote and rabbit, skunk and deermouse—these would be my characters. But, disheartened on the darkening streets where

my thwarted haste was just a mote in New York's pariah population, I simply wept at times—my badge of misery so commonplace. In the country, friends shrunk farther into the haze, as if
in a science fiction novel, though of course it was I who was
shrinking. "Good to see you," I once said, in parting, whereupon
the childhood doggerel echoed in my mind: *I see, said the blind
man, but he didn't see at all.*

Then, curiously, my stutter began to lighten, as if it were at
the far end of a seesaw from this infinitely more serious problem.
Stuttering is probably hereditary, but in degree or severity it's
also the servant of emotions such as self-consciousness, embarrassment, and other low-grade fears and agitations that tend to
feed upon themselves. Yet my mind was thrown out of its accustomed tics and potholes. The downward spiral or vicious circle,
which had worn deep ruts in my synapses over the course of half
a century, was broken by the pitch of urgency of this much worse
emergency. Adrenaline, too, always helpful, kicked in, and instead of getting depressed I could rise to a challenge with a kind
of Battle-of-Britain exuberance, could quit stuttering, crack a
joke and ask for assistance with straightforward good humour. As
I saw less, I felt liberated to chat with strangers because I knew I
wouldn't see their silent laughter if my difficulties aroused their
schadenfreude. Though I hadn't had a chance to tunnel beneath
the wreckage and find the detours that blind people use, such as
a whetted sense of hearing or aggrandized fingers, curiosity pep-
ped my spirits. It's what makes war fun—coping, camouflaging—
and thus at parties I could often speak better under the stress of
not being able to see. But if you can't make out the mood or
identity of the person you are talking to, or discern who is across
the room, and have to cadge a ride somehow in order to get
home, the bravery of blindness remains only a small advantage.

Sex was another story. Touch and imagination, being equal
legs of a tripod, can fill in splendidly for fading eyes. Sex became
an intense focus for me. At fifty-seven, fifty-eight, I was making
love as often as ten times a week, both for solace and to insist to
my partner, *Don't count me out!* This eyelessly frenetic pace was

a survival tactic in every sense—morale, manhood, contact, sanity—and yet, like so much else in life, took a perverse twist. The masochist in me made hay with the fact of my helplessness, and I began to fantasize during lovemaking that I was becoming a love-slave, employed by my tender friend for no purpose except sensuality, that my existence depended upon getting hard and staying hard morning and night. I focused in blind obsession upon giving pleasure, on performance, frequency, reliability—imagining rainstorm, if it was morning, or by the rising of the moon at night. Like a bug's antennae, my hands and ears sought clues, feeling the gusts of wind and hearing them, as I fingered the white flowers of wild-carrot, orange hawkweed, tigerish lilies. I couldn't drive a car, hustle a buck, smile at my good buddies; but I still had these sighted interludes, and days full of Chopin and Schubert, Arrau and Rubinstein. Life for a while could continue to be heaven on earth, as I had always believed, enhanced by telepathy as my eyes flagged.

The important thing was to avoid being deranged by talk-radio and other "hosts" whose egos were like suppurating boils that never popped. Week by week, their garish, chameleon pleas for applause and rancid false laughter, their acrid logic, their make-nice appeals to the ecumenical piety of chuckling greed or boob-ogling, festered like a pus that never seeps away and heals. I knew that the remedy for deep-seated grief is to involve oneself with others and I was doing a bit of that. I'd always been a listener, even an expert listener, because of how hard it was for me to talk. But if you have to walk two miles to get to town and can't read people's faces when you get there, you're less convincing than a more self-centred, sighted person. Your face goes wooden from the lack of give-and-take with other faces, and your companion, distracted by your blindness, cannot seem to lose himself in chatting with you. Also your limited intake of what is current on the streets and on TV and in the newspapers, your wistful indrawn circumscribed concerns and bumbling preoccupation with Memory Lane make you a less engrossing listener than somebody whose problem is just that he can't talk.

❊   ❊   ❊

I was having trouble finding a surgeon who would risk rup-
turing my retinas while operating on my cataracts. One brightly
clever doctor on Park Avenue told me it could be "a Pandora's
box," with multiplying disasters; I should wait till I was so old I
was "coughing and bent over." Another personable physician
with a high reputation, near Fifth Avenue, kept referring to
"technical problems" regarding the prospects for surgery and
would venture no prognosis. Maybe it was better to be content
with a quarter-of-a-loaf, he said. Another only spoke to me with a
tape recorder on—he sat by the microphone—though he took
painstaking photos of my retinas, perhaps as what is called—
"defensive medicine."

Like many writers, I'm a student of catastrophe, and once
turned off the Baton Rouge–New Orleans road in Louisiana to
visit the National Leprosarium, in the hamlet of Carville, a languid, breezy institution next to the levee of the Mississippi where
lepers are warehoused. But eyelessness is worse than leprosy or
the penury of being homeless or my worst experiences when
mute for weeks in the vice of a stutter. Hooded like a hostage, I
examined my dilemma with a teary nostalgia for lesser troubles,
feeling my way along the walls that hemmed me in. Then I heard
about a woman surgeon who was said to be both cautious and
creatively brave. I made an appointment, and, dressing carefully
in a red turtleneck pullover and a blue blazer (and carrying my
best book along as an offering), I went to see her. By this time I
needed to squint in order to look just half a dozen feet ahead.

"You can't see!" she exclaimed immediately, when I sat
down and showed her how close I had to hold a magazine. After
putting in the drops and situating me in the examining chair, she
said, "We ought to operate. How soon can you do it?" Later she
explained that eyes with retinas as frail as mine often fooled
the ophthalmologists because an early-stage cataract's effect on
the patient's already bad vision was cataclysmic, whereas they
could still see in and thus assumed that he or she should be able
to see out, unless retinal deterioration was the real problem.

An active, slim, short-haired woman of medium height and
middling age, she had small confident hands and practical-

looking glasses. After my operations, I thought of her romanti-
cally as Athena, the rescuer of heroes on the plains of Troy, but
at first impression she reminded me of the "A" student at a
university who outperforms the males but disarms their usual
resentment of a woman of studious appearance who does exceptionally well by being attentive, perceptive, efficient, unobtrusive
and sympathetic, avoiding any hint of superiority or grandiosity. I
trusted her, in other words, and could imagine her diminutive
fingers slicing through my corneas and guiding a micro-knife into
my eyes.

With nothing to lose, in any case, I soon found myself lying
under a partial anaesthetic in a crowded mini-operating room in
a New York hospital, hearing conversations but recognizing only
light and dark, as various mechanisms and instruments were lowered over me. A nurse said to another that she had "hit the
jackpot today, doing all eye operations." I wondered if she was
speaking with irony. A surgeon came in, greeted me courteously,
and examined the flawlessly healed incision that he had made in
my throat to extract a parathyroid gland the year before. Then
my physician entered, happily chatting with an ophthalmological
resident whom she was training. Their bubbling reminded me of
sociable hours in my childhood when I'd overheard two women
preparing salad, say, for a church supper—this time, though,
they were at work on the crux of my being. My surgeon even
teased me about not acting macho, knowing I could hear, and
when I tried to mumble a protest, she gaily told me to "just lie
there and keep quiet." The tactful diplomacy with which she
ordinarily negotiated with men evaporated when she had them
on the table.

I was naked under a paper sheet with an anaesthetic needle
taped to a vein in my wrist and oxygen being piped to my nos-
trils; and after an interval I heard her interrupt her companionable chatter to the young resident with a pregnant pause, and
then the joyous words, almost whispered: "It's *breathtaking*, isn't
it, when it goes as perfectly as that? I love it."

"Yes," the student said, having watched her deftly extract
the clouded lens from its filmy capsule in my left eye by a new

technique called *capsulorhexis,* and now insert a plastic one of sculpted specifications that had been manufactured in Bellevue, Washington, delicately into its place. But a minute later the student added, "Oh, the lens fell on the floor."

"That's the old lens. No harm. We don't need that," my saviour answered, mostly for my benefit, as I drifted off to sleep.

Other present methods of operating for cataracts are known as the "can-opener" and the "Christmas tree," according to how they look to the surgeon through the macro-microscope which lowers on to the patient's face from the ceiling. All are outpatient procedures, whereas sixty years ago recovery required lying with one's head between sandbags for several weeks.

I woke up a couple of hours later in a chair in a large room full of hernia patients who were also waking up and about to go home. My doctor, in her bluestocking street clothes, walked through to make sure that I was out of the woods, feeling buoyant because she had performed her morning's string of operations well. She reminded me that she would take the bandage off my eye in her office the next day. With one eye covered and the other still clouded by its cataract, I was led back to our hotel by Trudy, my Significant Other, in a precariously optimistic state of shock.

Trudy was a counsellor at Bennington College in Vermont, where I also taught. She had been raised in Great Neck, Long Island, an expensive, predominantly Jewish suburb of New York City, where her father taught band music in the elementary schools and where some of the parents were paying off the anti-Semitism of other suburbs by giving *goyische* kids a hard time. She had married a law student, later a Vermont state senator, who had come from a newly rich New York family, his father a broker in the petroleum business. Later, one of her sons became a varsity wrestler and then a Navy Seal. Her own parents had leaped to Long Island's suburbia from the coal country in the Scranton area of Pennsylvania, where hardscrabble farming or railroad work were the alternatives to going down in the mines. She'd spent summers and sometimes longer there with a loving but half-crazy aunt, and another year in bed at home because of rheumatic fever—experiences which had marked her. She was upscale, upwardly mobile, yet singed by this knowledge of secret skeletons and vulnerabilities, alcoholism and violence in the family's closet.

One of her sisters had thrust ahead and become an astronaut, helping to launch the Venus probe. And Trudy herself worked a good deal in the midst of a high-tech, genteel kind of violence, in this case the atmosphere of a fancy avant-garde college where designer drugs were rampant, plus old-fashioned beer and booze to lace it with and four-day weekends that the kids could totally obliterate. For some of them the whole term was lived in a perpetual state of emergency, and she as the college therapist was their first handhold if they suddenly panicked and felt that they were falling off the cliff.

At eight o'clock the next morning I was in appropriately groggy pain, half sedated, half elated, when the doctor's maid— who was both pitying and accustomed to the sight of early-morning walking wounded—let me into her brownstone. The second floor was for patients. There was a properly dim, old-fashioned and functional examining office, but the waiting room was her drawing room, with a red-velvet, leathery, sumptuous Persian-rug decor, tall books in a breakfront, silk-screen portraits of falcons, and folding doors and a chandelier.

I was early, as usual—another proof to my teasing surgeon of how unmacho I was—and she left her coffee in the dining room downstairs, which was enlivened with uncaged grey African and green Amazonian parrots, to come and unbind my wounded eye. My stoicism of the pre-op period had evaporated: it felt as though I had run my eye into a stick. I was querulous and flinchy.

My enthusiastic, inspired surgeon mocked and praised me. "What a fussbudget! But *excellent,* excellent. Your eye is excellent," she exclaimed, peering with her powerful mini-light inside. It was her favourite word, as I discovered during the ensuing weeks, overhearing many other people being examined as I sat on the sofa in the waiting room.

She prescribed drops to prevent infection or any glaucoma type of damage to the optic nerve, and gave me an eye-guard for sleeping, in case I accidentally socked or rolled over upon the eye. Though most doctors wait at least six months to remove the cataract in the patient's second eye, she decided we were on a roll and said we should go ahead and do it in three weeks. Under my gimpy, grouchy air of extreme infirmity I was swelling with cheerfulness, and agreed. To amuse me further (knowing my interest in animals), she told me the gelatinous fluid she'd injected underneath my cornea to cushion it during the operation was obtained from roosters' combs.

"And no Pandora's box," she added, in what was becoming a joke with us. She said her husband was reading my book to her in bed at night.

Before that first operation, she had asked if I would prefer to be twenty-twenty without glasses when she was finished, or a bit near-sighted, as I was used to being, which was better for reading. With the implants, she could determine the result. I naturally answered that I'd like to experience perfection, to see like an airplane pilot in my sixties. But now, Athena-like, she told me casually that she had decided not to give me twenty-twenty vision; she had sewn in plastic that would assure me only twenty-forty—"better for readers"—because bookish people "feel confused" if in late middle age they are suddenly endowed with pilots' eyes.

This peremptory decision, overruling my romantic notion of being gifted with eagle eyes, irritated me only slightly because I was so grateful to her and because I remembered with a kind of fond awe the public health nurses I had travelled with as a journalist in Alaska, who often held a life-and-death power in the isolated villages they served. A woman deathly sick was likely to receive urgent sisterly care, but with a man the question was more whimsical. If he was dirty and crude and, whatever his age, had no "cute" aspects, he might languish like a prisoner of war, scarcely attended to until death took him. But if he was appealing in some way, whether by being brave or dignified or funny—if he had either youth or presence—the nurses would exert themselves intensely, even affectionately to help him, while seldom masking the enjoyment that flexing their power gave them.

When the doctor took off my bandage, there was no *Eureka, I can see!* because I'd never been stone-blind. Instead, just an abrupt, astounding discovery of how bright light actually is. Not the beauty—the *brightness* of the world. My eye squinted and winced, shutting out most of the sights now hammering at the door. Limping away from her office, I believed her when she'd said that the vision in my left eye had been restored. Yet the stairs, curbs, cars, and rushing strangers on the sidewalk, and all the lettering or numerals mapping the metropolis were hardly less of a problem. I reeled, I wobbled as I walked. But a bulging though still tentative joy—glimpsing shards of the rich, russet stone of the nearby buildings, and slivers of eggshell-blue above that, speared by shafts of sunlight brighter than metal—threatened to capsize me even more than my staggering gait. I kept the eye four-fifths shut, rather fearfully; yet could begin to see fragments of faces, abbreviated as if by a camera's shutter. Many of these first faces were like catching sight for an instant of an old friend.

I sat recuperating in the darkish two-room apartment on East 19th Street that I'd sub-let for the month of November, glad it was both nondescript and dark, and that the month, as well, was a dark one. White sunshine blazed fitfully through the window bars and venetian slats. But I could take only short doses of such splendour. I made impulsive forays into the street at all hours, grabbing a look at random faces; also the scrumptious colours of food on my plate in a restaurant. Yellow squash, green peas, orange sweet potatoes, vivid chicken livers. Ochre or sandstone apartment buildings were underlined by their staccato storefronts, cherry-red, beige-and-butter, at street level; and the hauntedly nostalgic neon sign of a bar-and-grill bespoke for me more than thirty years of lonely, happy scrambling about this and other New York neighbourhoods for love and sex and conversation, for new sensations and friendship. Trudy had had to go back to her job in Vermont now that I was ambulatory, and without being unfaithful to her I began calling people with real gusto, summoning them to have lunch, supper, coffee or a drink, like Lazarus, formerly "terminal" but now restored to life. Because I couldn't walk far, they came to me, from several periods of my life—first marriage, second marriage, first bachelorhood, second bachelorhood, old classmates, new writers I admired—and we gabbled keenly in one of half a dozen cozy taverns or Japanese or Italian places. My elation was infectious enough that in one meat-loaf-and-gravy establishment which lacked a liquor license, the family kept slipping me complimentary glasses of wine from the kitchen.

I was pleased, too, to come back once or twice a week to have my new friend manipulate my pupils with her magic eyedrops—exclaiming at how "big" they got while gazing in at my retinas and fingering my brows and cheeks—as we talked about our grown children, and her parrots squawked from the floor below. The "crush" or tropism of a patient toward a doctor who has saved that patient's life had occurred in me; and she on her side seemed to indicate that her marriage was in some sort of temporary trouble that agitated her considerably. We lingered, talking like close pals.

The second operation didn't progress quite as famously. My lens capsule tore, and she had to revert to the "can-opener" technique to slip the natural lens out and the plastic lens in. (This one had been manufactured in Fort Worth, Texas.) The procedure took longer, and I twitched with discomfort, needing extra anaesthetic through the needle taped to my fist. Nor was the same note of gaiety present in my surgeon's voice. And the resident apprentice who was observing the operation, a young man, sounded sulky in response. She was displeased with her luck at *capsulorhexis*—she told me later that her average rate of success at doing it was about fifty per cent, which made her performance with my two eyes typical—but that elegance, and not my basic vision, was all that was at stake. The resident, she said, had been sulky because she hadn't allowed him to poke the long main anaesthetic needle into the depths of my eye socket, after the preliminary fist-stuff had taken effect, as student physicians observing an eye operation are usually permitted to do, just as a matter of politesse. She'd told him instead (as I was glad to hear, lying on the table) that "this is a well-known writer." She told me she had finessed the previous resident—the young woman—in this regard by the fact that a charity patient was next in line, whom the resident would have a free hand with. So they'd simply chatted through the moment when she did the deep needle-stick behind my eye (patients are completely un-aware of it) herself.

My neighbourhood at 19th Street, near Gramercy Park, was not a primary part of Manhattan for me. I'd been born in, and till the age of eight had lived in, the East Eighties, near my surgeon's office; and certain blocks there still hold a wet-skinned luminosity for me, when I pass through on foot or even in a taxi: memories greeny-brown, like amphibians, as if linked with my emergence from the sea. Then my parents moved to Connecti-cut, where I acquired a feeling for the woods. After college I returned to the city to make my way as a writer, married and migrated between a series of apartments on the Lower East Side or Upper West Side, neighbourhoods of pungency, drama and character. Afterwards I married my second wife and lived with her and our daughter for two decades beside the Hudson River in Greenwich Village, an area that will always be my spiritual home—until I felt driven to move to Vermont by our divorce.

So here I was, in digs a friend had managed to find for me on short notice, and sorry at first to be recuperating in a locale that was not piquant with important memories. But I was near-ing sixty and, hitting the streets again in this, my natal city, I soon found plenty of personal history near Gramercy Park as well. My daughter's Quaker grammar school was only four blocks off—and there were bakeries that we'd snacked at after her school plays, corners that we'd met on to walk home, the watering hole where we'd had her graduation party. Then of course I remem-bered that St George's, the Episcopal church where I had been christened in 1933, stood across from her school on Stuyvesant Square. I went inside and gazed at the very font—white marble shaped like a seashell—and pictured my parents, both about thirty, standing with their friends, hopes high, in the depths of the Depression. Their hopes for themselves, on balance, had not been steeply disappointed at the time of my father's death in 1967—which reminded me that my mother, who was originally from Aberdeen, Washington, had been courted by him at a residence for young women located right here on Gramercy Park, two blocks from my sub-let. He used to deliver her to the door in the evening after supper and come and have breakfast with her early the next morning, as he walked from the apartment that he shared with another man on 44th Street way downtown to his law firm on Wall Street. A Vassar girl, she had trained a little as a social worker and had worked in personnel at Macy's.

Looking at *that* building then led me to realize with a start that although my own memories of courting my first wife, Amy, were mostly situated uptown at 242nd Street in the Bronx, where she lived in 1959, or else at 103rd Street and Broadway—where I was ensconced—in fact I had proposed to her right in this immediate neighbourhood, in a cheap little hotel on 20th Street at Third Avenue. I was holed up in a gleeful frenzy reading the proofs of my second novel, *The Circle Home,* and excerpting fifty pages of it, "The Last Irish Fighter," for what would be my first fiction in a national magazine (or "The Greatest Boxing Story of Our Time" as *Esquire* billed it). Amy was working at the National Bureau of Economic Research in midtown, and so we met at my fourth-floor room to go out to supper. I may have popped the question earlier in a preliminary way, because we'd looked at rings, but this was the evening that, in the elevator, we made it official. It was a rope elevator, the relic of a quieter, turn-of-the-century era. You pulled yourself up or down with a simple tug, aided by counterweighted pulleys; and aside from the smooth nicety of propelling oneself with a flick of the wrist, you stopped the conveyance by catching hold of the rope, and thus could do so between floors—as I did in order to kiss Amy hard and present her with the Tiffany ring that she had liked.

I was now more than usually fearful of being mugged, or any other violent tumble on the street, because a blow on the head might unstring the back of my eyes; yet forgot this kind of trouble when I looked up to see an aluminum plane banking toward LaGuardia under the ripped, scudding clouds, as dusk began to sparkle. People were suddenly souls, not blurry undersea shapes, and in my gluttony of walking I wandered into a print shop, squinty, stumbly, one rainy day, and saw my first museum art in a year and a half—Titian . . . Tintoretto—literally, heaven on earth. I sang hymns on Sunday at St George's church and sat in various local caravanserais feasting my eyes on the faces, the sunshine spilling over the plane trees outside, a prismatic dry cleaner's sign across the street, the cello curve of a woman's hips. Actual sex, money, fame, advancement meant next to nothing to me compared to what I had gained, and I watched street folk foraging in ashcans with less pity for them just because they could see. The hell with what you had to eat, if you could see.

My well-centred, savvy surgeon told me to lift nothing heavier than five pounds lest the pressure spring my retinas, but I somehow assumed that masturbation wouldn't do this; it was the one "blind" thing I did. Otherwise my mind shouted, *Look at the lights! Look at the sky!* The doctor had warned me I'd eventually lose my sight again, but the tiaraed bridges with their lyre-like cables crossing the East River knocked me over just as they had when I'd lain on my back in my parents' sedan at the age of four or five, going to Oyster Bay on Long Island and treasuring the starry ride. At noontime at Gracie Mansion, near her office, the East River trumpeted with blue and pewter sliding water, curling Hell Gate currents, and muscley clouds filling the sky, all of which upped my exuberance when I went in to see her, and made us sometimes chatter for a while into her lunch hour after the eye exam was over.

I'm amused, when I count back thirty years, by how many of the central women in my life have been registered nurses (three) or social workers (three, counting one of the nurses, all of whom moved on to other fields). They were professional caregivers, in other words, though because neither of my wives was

enrolled in such a category, other affinities, artistic, intellectual
or spiritual, must have appealed to me more powerfully. But that
sure hand and confident eye of a former nurse has been hard to
match if we had other things in common. Since I was shy and
often verged on being clumsy, a woman who had washed and
catheterized a hundred penises, slapped babies' bottoms, tickled
a smile from Alzheimer's patients, performed the Heimlich ma-
noeuvre (I had a secret dread of choking on a piece of meat), or
called Code Red and banged her fists on a heart patient's chest
to bring him back from the River Styx, and stayed by the bed for
many hours while a carcinoma sufferer moaned, vomited, cried,
bled, defecated and died—a woman like that would not find an
ugly stutter like mine off-putting, could fix an unreliable erection
by simply reaching down, and think no commonplace misfortune
insoluble. Men have considered nurses sexy since time began;
and belonging to a healing vocation, they were more likely to
draw close at a party, when they saw me disabled for a moment
by my stammer, than pull away, if that mix of strength with
weakness intrigued them.

However, while blind, I'd discovered all over again how few
people of either sex will tolerate expending many minutes on
the handicapped—they're gripers, needy, uninformed, self-
absorbed, living in the past. The child's game where someone
pretends to be blind is one of the sexiest known and, carried to
the teens, you could feel a buttock or a breast quite innocently
while controlling the girl's progress, making her stumble, then
saving her from a fall, until you gave her permission to open her
eyes and you played at being helpless. But, metaphorically,
"blind" means ignorant of basic facts, a sucker in business, politics, a cuckold in love, the prey of real estate or stock market
sharks, unresponsive to the misery of troubled friends; and in
real life it costs jobs, avocations, the very heart's warmth of seeing faces. Now, abruptly, after paying a clever lady $5,200 to
stick a knife into my eyes (the hospital and anaesthetist tripled
the bill), I was liberated. Not just returned to the *status quo ante*,
as any heart or cancer sawbones may contrive to do in roto-
rootering your plumbing, but given plastic eyes that, too good to

be true, took in more than ever before. Old body, new orbs. I was ebullient, standing straighter, nervous energy alight, paying intense attention as if to make up for lost time.

The blue dawn, the golden noon, the funky neon, riveted and bewitched me, and morning, noon and night now I was gazing at dear acquaintances in Irish pubs and Italian or Chinese restaurants, in wooden booths in nosh-and-schmoozing joints. I positively loved my white potatoes, earthy meat loaf, red ketchup. The colours!—and the foam on the beer, the bubbles in ale, the checkered table cloth—and we could go to a movie!

Yet the enigma was that these familiar friends whom I hadn't accurately observed in several years looked not just older, but sadder, pummelled and beat-up. They looked cudgelled, while I in contrast was feasting my eyes. I was supremely happy, while they who had been window-shopping, movie-going, taking in a thousand sights during my blind times, seemed tacit testimony that the exuberant evidence of joy in the world I saw was wrong-headed and going to be short-lived. Was there something they knew that I didn't; or the other way around? Did the eyes not really matter except as a baseline? Was happiness in the long run entirely internal, grounded in a stew of genes, hormones, childhood "conflict resolution," careerism, and consumerism? Had the visible world, God's greenery, so little to do with it? The sudden elevation of my spirits was obviously because of the freakish salvation I had undergone—but did the eyes have so meagre and ambiguous an input for everybody else? Or was our fate, as far as happiness was concerned, just embedded in our foreheads beforehand?

My effervescence, being infectious, cheered everybody up for the space of a chat. What they generally wanted, when I asked, was a partner to confide in and grow old with, a nest egg in the bank, and a feeling that their lives had registered on other people affectionately and with a watermark of honour: that they had walked a road and not a treadmill. OK and Amen. But Emerson in *Nature* goes beyond that, speaking of becoming "a transparent eye-ball . . . part and particle of God." As my second eye healed, I was beginning to be able to read again, and after the famine of my isolation I gorged on friendship. When I walked, I glanced up the walls of sunstruck buildings, at stone the colour of a pronghorn's skin or of a Bloody Mary, at seething leaves, part green, part russet, in a double crown of trees.

In the same essay, Emerson writes: "In the woods, we return to reason and faith. There I feel that nothing can befall me in life—no disgrace, no calamity (leaving me my eyes), which nature cannot repair." I felt almost that way in the city too, but in due course got one of my former students to carry my suitcase to the bus station and put me, still fragile, on the bus to Vermont. My vivacious benefactor, the surgeon, had indicated that her marriage was righting itself, and for my part, I had remained faithful to the friend I lived with in Vermont despite the fact that my Lazarus charisma had drawn a few sexual invitations my way. Of the women I have lived with, I have only been unfaithful to my second wife, and that was a twenty-five-year marriage in the second half of which I also felt betrayed.

We pulled out of the Port Authority bus terminal on to Tenth Avenue an hour after dusk. Several statuesque black prostitutes were standing shoulder to shoulder in the midst of the stream of traffic like newsboys offering their wares—they had lowered their dresses to their waists. The driver shook his head as we headed for all-white Vermont. The city, the universal city—Dickens's, Balzac's—lent me its last lurid strings of lights: little clusters of stores, bravely carmine, lavender and sunflower-yellow in the dun stretch of Hell's Kitchen blocks. The the brief upscale sparkle of Lincoln Centre and Amsterdam Avenue; and a spell of visual salsa in Spanish Harlem, jeroboam wine bottles glowing amid orange pumpkins, red peppers and yellow squashes under green awnings and Christmas-tree lights. Then blitzed central Harlem, poverty blinking in the higher windows, the lights self-effacing so as not to draw hold-up men, and just beyond that the dark funnel of the highway network sweeping us to Connecticut. The driver told me about another prep school-mate of mine from forty years ago who was now supporting him-self by running up bus schedules on his home computer and occasionally doing some dispatching in the Port Authority terminal. It was probably not what he had dreamed of: which led me to remember another friend of mine, now nearly broke, whom I'd visited recently, a cheery guy I'd crossed the country with in 1953, in a 1936 Model A Ford that overheated during the day, so we drove at night. So many friends . . . none of whom had dreamed of nearing sixty in the particular straits that they were in.

I was delighted to reach Vermont's snowy roads, and to see Trudy standing by her car at Bennington's bus stop. We bumped bodies a few times before we hugged. Trudy hadn't seen me with my new eyes before, but they were still so squinty and tentative that the change wasn't apparent at first. We joked about the fact I was going to have to go for a follow-up to the local eye doctor, whom she happened to have had a passionate affair with for years, so she was afraid that he might find an excuse to poke my fovea out. (In the event, he didn't. A husky, playful sort of guy, he was amused by the phone call that had placed me in his office, but also extremely impressed by what my surgeon had done, which he had only seen illustrated in medical journals. "So that's how they do it in the big city," he murmured, peering in.)

In the days that followed, I groped ecstatically for a realignment with the local scenery I had been missing: with Mount Anthony, the little corrugated, wooded, cavey peak that overlooks the town of Bennington, as well as with the sensuous roll of the field outside my window that runs a way toward it, and the preliminary granite ridge of the spine of the Green Mountains that invigorates my view to the east. And the locust, ash and maple trees, the blue spruces, white birches and red-barked pines, the juncos wintering in the dogwoods, the hungry possum nibbling seeds under a bird-feeder, the startling glory of a skunk's white wedge of fur in a shaft of faint light from the moon—plus things that had always bored me, like moving headlights on a road across the valley or tardy fog at ten a.m.—had become fascinating. An art book could mesmerize me—Michelangelo's "Moses," or a Turner—though I still hadn't been to an actual museum because I'd come home as soon as I was sufficiently strong to risk the jolting of a bus.

The faces in Bennington, including Trudy's, seemed quite new to me. I had no memory of them before I'd become partially blind, so I didn't see them with the perspective of how life had battered them, just the novelty of how they looked. Here was a Daughters of the American Revolution face; there was Mickey Rooney's; and here was W. C. Fields's, or was it slacker, like Charles Laughton's (or maybe Hitchcock's)? It was curious to look at the layout of the town of Bennington, too—the Legion Hall, the Post Office, the taco joint, the rest home, the supermarket mall, all of which I had been driven by a hundred times without seeing a thing. How pretty the old church was where Robert Frost is buried! And down below, the town nestled steeply in the hills like a New England village is supposed to. Only closer could you see the boarded-up red-brick factories and turn-of-the-century careened-over mills, with peeling, boxy frame houses lined in a dingy little cross-grid nearby.

Stumbling with Trudy's two small grandchildren over the snowdrifts on Main Street to get to the Bennington Steak House, a town hangout and bar that is also hospitable to family dinners, with colouring books on the table and more fuss made about the kids who come than about the drunks on the other side of the partition, I felt the twin reactions one has to a New England winter—that it's awfully repetitive, one snowstorm on the heels of another and nowhere new to go; yet what delight to hold the children by the hand, with the pink light of the street lamps spilling on the snow, and Trudy's complexity to grip or grapple with. Tall and forceful but fitful, confident yet insecure, fatalistic though energetic, materialistic but idealistic, she was a handful. A bit of a sense of emergency energized and exhilarated Trudy. She got rolling when somebody's mind went off the rails. Naturally she was alert to signs that I might have sought refuge with her merely while I'd been incapacitated. I did my best to let her see that this was not the case.

Erin McGraw

Bad Eyes

The subject veers almost uncontrollably toward metaphor, but I mean to take it literally: I have unusually poor vision, minus thirteen hundred diopters and still losing ground, ordinary progressive myopia that never stopped progressing. In me, the process by which light is supposed to focus images at the back of the eye has gone berserk, and the point of focus shifts ever closer to the front, like the projection of a movie falling short of its screen.

My eyeballs aren't round, like marbles or baseballs, but are oblong, like little footballs. This awkward shape puts so much strain on the retinas that a rip has developed in my left one, where the tissue gave out like exhausted cloth. Now my ophthalmologist carefully includes a retina evaluation at annual checks, and I have a list of warning signs that would indicate a significant rupture: sudden, flashing lights; floaters showering into my vision like rain.

Mostly, though, nothing about my vision is so fraught or dramatic. I am shortsighted, is all, mope-eyed, gravel-blind, blind-buck and Davy; a squinter, the sort who taps her companions at plays and baseball games: "What just happened? I missed that." I live in a world where objects collapse into haze. Beyond the narrow realm that my contact lenses permit me to see clearly, I navigate by memory and assumption.

Here are some of the things I can't see, even with my contacts in: a baseball in play, birds in trees, numbers and subtitles on TV, roads at night, constellations, anything by candlelight, street signs, faces of people in cars, faces of people twenty feet away. One of my consistent embarrassments comes from snubbing friends who stood more than a shadow's length from me, friends I didn't even nod to because I couldn't tell who they were. So I've adopted a genial half-smile that I wear when I walk around my neighborhood or down the corridors of the department where I work. I have the reputation of being a very friendly person.

Here are some of the things I can find when I narrow my eyes and look: tiny new weeds in the front garden, fleas scurrying across my dog's belly, gray hairs. My mother, watching me struggle before the bathroom mirror for ten minutes while I spray and brush and bobby-pin to hide the worst of the gray, comments, "I don't know why you bother. You don't have much. No one even sees it."

"I see it every time I look in the mirror."

"Well, you see what you're looking for."

She's told me this all my life. I roll my eyes and keep working the bobby pins.

The glasses I remember best and loved most arrived when I was eight years old. They were my second pair; the first were brown with wings at the corners, the eyeglass equivalent to orthopedic shoes. I was delighted when the doctor announced that they needed to be replaced.

My parents didn't share my delight—only a year had passed since we had gotten that first pair. For six months, unconsciously, I had been moving books closer to my face and inching nearer the TV. Nothing was said about it. I think my parents assumed that I must have been aware of a development so obvious to them, but I was a dreamy, preoccupied child and hadn't noticed that the edges of illustrations in my books were no longer crisp. When I was moved to the front row of my classroom, it never occurred to me to ponder why.

I was pleased to be there, though, and preened in my new glasses. Sleek cat eyes, the white plastic frames featuring jaunty red stripes, they were 1965's cutting edge. I often took them off to admire them. When my correction needed to be stepped up again, I insisted on using the same frames, even though by then I had to keep the glasses on all the time, and could only take pleasure in the candy-cane stripes if I happened to pass a window. In my school pictures for three years running I wore these same glasses. By the third year they were clearly too small for my face, and my eyes practically disappeared behind the thick glass.

Every six months my mother took me to the eye doctor, and nearly every visit meant new, slightly heavier lenses. At first I resented only the hours spent in the waiting room, where I was often the only child, but gradually I began to dread the examination itself, the stinging dilation drops and my frustrating attempts to read the eye chart. While I struggled to focus on letters that seemed to slip and buckle on the far wall, fear bloomed in my stomach.

"T," I would begin rashly, remembering that much from the visit before, but then I strained to make out the next wobbly shape. "U, maybe, or C. It could be O." Not bothering to comment, the doctor tilted back my chair, pulled around one of the clicking, finicky machines, and began the measurements for the next set of lenses. Both he and I ignored my quick, anxious breathing and dry mouth, but when he was finished I burst out of the office as if I were making a jail break.

Back in the world, my panic dropped away, and my worsening vision seemed nothing more than an inconvenience. Perhaps if I had been an outdoorsy kind of child, a girl who noticed leaves or clouds or insect life, I might have grieved the first time I was unable to detect a distant, sly animal. But I wasn't especially fond of the natural world, which was too hot or too cold and full of things that made me itch. The steady loss of detail—my inability first to make out the petals of a flower, and before long to discern the flower at all without glasses to help me—felt unimportant. I jammed on my glasses first thing in the morning, took them off after turning out my light at night, now and then remembered to clean them. Easy enough.

Only occasionally did I get the sense that I was hampered. The sisters at my Catholic school made me take my glasses off before games at recess, a sensible precaution; I was a terrible athlete and could be relied on to stop dead in front of almost any moving object. So I was hit in the face by kickballs, tetherballs, basketballs, and once, memorably, by a softball bat that caught me square on the cheek. The sister blew her whistle and bustled toward me, scolding. Why hadn't I gotten out of the way?

I didn't cry when the bat hit me, although it hurt, but her chiding made my lips start to quiver. I hadn't *seen* it, I protested. All of a sudden something had hit my face; the blow came out of nowhere.

It came out of the batter's box, the sister pointed out. *You shouldn't have been standing so close. You know you can't see well, so you have to be cautious.*

She handed me my glasses and I walked off—sulkily, coddling my sense of injustice—to the nurse's office. The nurse said I'd suffered only a bruise, but I couldn't easily dismiss the incident. Up to that point, no one had told me, *You are at risk, you must take precautions.*

Back at home, I took my glasses off and looked at the house across the street. I recognized its shape and details, but that hardly required vision. I saw the house every day, and could have drawn from memory its long, flat roof and the row of bunkerlike windows.

So I walked up the street, turned onto a cul-de-sac that I didn't know well, and took off my glasses again. Instantly, the turquoise stucco bungalow before me smeared into a vague blue box. I could make out windows, but couldn't tell if the curtains were open or closed; could find the front door but not the mail slot; the wrought-iron handrail but not the steps it accompanied.

A shout erupted and I spun around, shoving my glasses

back on to find that the shout had nothing to do with me: a couple of boys were playing catch at the top of the street. Nevertheless, my heart was whapping now, hurting me. I was foolish to stand so publicly, blinking and helpless, right in the middle of the sidewalk. Anyone could have sneaked up, knocked me to the ground, and taken my wallet, if I had had a wallet.

I thought of comic-strip blind beggars on city streets, their canes kicked away, their tin cups stolen. For the first time, my bad eyes took on meaning: they were an invitation to bullies, and the fact that no one had yet taken my glasses and knocked me down was just dumb luck. Pressing my glasses in place, I ran home. This new notion of myself seized my imagination, and I fell asleep for several nights imagining scenarios in which I was unfairly set upon, a lamb before wolves. I saw myself suffering nobly and being remembered reverently.

And then I forgot about my experiment in front of the blue house. I continued to play games without glasses at school, continued to get smacked with kickballs, continued not to be accosted by glasses-snatching bullies. Finally tired of my red-and-white striped glasses, I zipped through half a dozen new pairs, trying out granny glasses in three different shapes, including ones with octagonal lenses that made me look unnervingly like John Lennon.

By the time I was entering junior high, though, I was tired of wearing glasses. More precisely, I was tired of my bespectacled reflection, how glasses made my eyes look tiny and dim, my nose like a tremendous land mass. So I initiated a campaign to get contact lenses, which were just becoming widely available, although not usually for twelve-year-olds. To my astonishment, my cautious, conservative ophthalmologist immediately agreed.

"Contacts help sometimes, with myopia like this," he explained to my skeptical mother. "The theory is that the contact flattens the lens of the eye. It can slow down the disease's progress." I was so elated that I hardly flinched when he called what I had a "disease," a word we usually avoided. And so, a month later, we began a regime that I was in no way ready for.

⁕ ⁕ ⁕

These were the days when the only contact lenses were made of inflexible plastic, thick by today's standards, hard, immovable foreign bodies that had to be introduced to the protesting eyes at gradual intervals. The first day, the wearer put them in for two hours, then took them out for an hour of recovery, then in again, out, in, out. The second day, three hours.

The optometrist guided my shaking hand, showing me how to slip the lens directly in place. Before I could even look up, I had blinked the contact out; it bounced off the counter beneath us and hit the floor. My mother hissed. The optometrist ordered me not to move; he gently dropped to his knees and patted the linoleum until he found the lens and laboriously cleaned it again.

I blinked the lenses out twice more before he could get them centered on my corneas. Then, tentatively, he stepped back and asked, "How's that?" I was too stunned to answer. For all the talk about wearing schedules and tolerance, no one had told me that contact lenses would *hurt*. Each eye felt as though a hair had been coiled precisely on top of it, and hot, outraged tears poured out. Although the optometrist kept telling me to look up so that he could take measurements, I couldn't keep my eyes from snapping shut. Light was like a blade.

"It always takes a little while," he was telling my mother, "but she'll get used to them. Just take it easy. Don't let her overdo."

No fear of that. I was already frantic to take the lenses back out again, and the remaining hour and forty-five minutes of my first wearing period seemed interminable, an eon of torment. My mother had to lead me back out to the car by the hand; even with the sunglasses the optometrist had given me, I had to close my eyes. Light bouncing off of car windows and storefronts was searing.

For the next month, all I could think about was my eyes. As the optometrist had promised, they began to accommodate to the contacts, but accommodation wasn't comfort. My eyes stung, lightly, all the time. Every blink set the lenses shifting, and that slight movement felt as if it were grinding a ridge into the moist corneal tissue. The irritation made me blink again, shifting the contacts some more.

I spent the summer steeped in resentment. I refused invitations to parties and shopping trips because I had to put my contacts in and take them out, in and out, none of which would have happened if I had had reasonable eyes to begin with. Even after I built up some expertise and didn't have to spend ten minutes tugging the corners of my eyes raw to dislodge the lenses, the contacts kept falling out on their own, vaulting away from my eyes, forcing me to freeze in midstep. With slow, scared care I would sink to my knees and begin patting first my clothes, then the ground around me, feeling for a tiny, mean-spirited disk.

For the first year I spent a lot of time apologizing about lost lenses, ones I rinsed down the drain or cracked, one that the dog snuffled up, and ones that simply shot out of my eyes and disappeared. My parents were understandably unhappy, and I became familiar with the dread that curled through me as soon as I felt one of the lenses begin to shimmy, the indicator that it would soon try for a getaway.

But that dread, at least, was practical. Cresting through me like high tide was the other dread, the one I had forgotten about and put off for years. With the contacts ejecting themselves at malicious whim, I was constantly aware that my next breath might leave me marooned, half-blind, vulnerable. The fact that no one ever treated me with anything but solicitude—often strangers got down on their hands and knees with me—did nothing to soften my fear. I started to walk more slowly, to avoid shag carpeting, to sit with my head tilted slightly back, hoping gravity would keep the contacts in place. Outside, I lingered by the sides of buildings.

By now the myopia was at a full gallop, and the world I saw without any lenses was no longer blurry; it was pure blur. If, for some reason, I had to walk across a room without glasses or contacts, I shuffled like a blind girl, groping for handholds, batting at the air in case something—a lamp, a shelf, some pot hanging from the ceiling—might be ready to strike. Smudged, bulging shapes crowded against me. I imagined fists or rocks or sudden, steep edges, threats from dreams that seemed probable in this shapeless landscape.

At visits to the ophthalmologist, I strained and fought to see the eye chart, memorizing E F O T Z and F X I O S C before the doctor caught on. I paid closer attention to the toneless way he informed my mother that I needed, again, a stronger correction, and felt my throat clench. My mother said, "I thought the contacts were supposed to slow this down."

"They might be doing that," he said. "There's no way of telling. She might be going downhill even faster without them." He bent over to write notes on my chart, which was half an inch thick by now. My eyes were good enough to see that.

I could see other things, too. I could see the expression on my friend's face when I came to spend the night and unpacked all my cumbersome equipment: cleansing solution, wetting solution, saline solution, and the heat-sterilization unit that had to be plugged in for two hours. I could also see her expression after I emerged from the bathroom wearing my glasses. "Let me try them on," she said. I handed them over to let her giggle and bang into walls, and tried not to betray how anxious I was to get them back.

In biology class, I saw my teacher's impatient look when I told her that I couldn't draw the cells clustered on the microscope's slide. "Just close one eye and draw what you see," she said, and so, hopelessly, I did, even though I knew no cell ever had such peculiar zigzags. When I got my lab book back, the teacher had written, "You obviously have trouble seeing enough. Or correctly."

Maybe it was that prim, striving-for-accuracy last phrase that caught me. Or the clinical tone. Whichever, instead of feeling embarrassed or crushed, I was relieved. In a voice that didn't whine or tremble, her note offered me an interesting new self-definition. I grabbed it.

With relief, I gave up trying to make out faces across a

football field and stopped straining to read the face of a bell tower clock, tasks I had been using to gauge my vision's deterioration. By this time I was wearing a new, flexible kind of contact lens made out of silicone, far more comfortable and less apt to fall out, so I was confident enough to stroll across parks and thickly carpeted rooms. I started asking the people around me what words were written on the blackboard, what images were flickering by on the TV screen, and people told me. I was a person who had trouble seeing enough, or correctly, so they filled me in on the nuances I would miss on my own.

At a movie, nodding at the screen, my friend whispered, "She keeps noticing that clock. That clock has something to do with the murder." Or, gesturing at the teacher the next day in class: "She's smiling; she's in a good mood. I'll bet she's started smoking again."

I was being given not only facts, but also interpretations. Those who could see sharply gave me shadow as well as object, context in addition to text. Did I resent all of these explanations and asides, pronounced slowly as if for the dimwitted? Not on your life. Friends and family were making things easy for me, and after years of constant unease, I was happy with that.

I drew other people's opinions over me like a blanket. Sight, it seemed, blended right into insight, and to perceive anything was to make a judgment call. Since the people around me had the first kind of sight, I was willing to grant that they had the second. And then the corollary: since I lacked the one, I surely lacked the other.

Anybody with half an eye can see where this story is going: I got lazy. Knowing that many details were going to be lost to me anyway, I stopped trying to see them. I could get the notion of a landscape, but not the trees it contained; I could recognize a skyline, but not the buildings within it. I was all big picture, untroubled by the little stuff.

During my junior year in college, when I was an exchange student in England, I traveled to public gardens and scenic overlooks and took pictures. Only when the pictures were developed did I find out that candy wrappers had clogged the shrubbery, and that across the top slat of the pretty green park bench somebody had carved *BOLLOCKS*. These weren't microscopic flaws; they were clear to anybody, even myopic me. I had been fully able to see the candy wrappers, but hadn't bothered to. My photo album from that year is a catalogue of England's trash, none of which I looked at until the pictures came back. Then I felt outraged and—this is the kicker—betrayed.

Somewhere, at a juncture I couldn't pinpoint, I had made a tactical shift in how I used my bad eyes. Not only had I given up trying to see the actual, physical world, but I had begun to let myself see a better world, one cut to my taste and measure, a world that, just for starters, didn't contain flyaway Snickers wrappers. And I believed in that world firmly enough to feel cheated when the wrappers got caught on the thorns of barberry bushes.

My inability to see the physical world had infected my mind: I had learned to deceive myself using my mind's eye, just as my real eyes had been deceiving me for years. When I came home from that year abroad, I saw myself as English and annoyed the daylights out of my friends for months by calling the place we lived a *flat* (although it was in fact a house), by stowing groceries in the car's *boot*, and by pulling beer out of the refrigerator to let it warm up. Had anyone had a mind's camera in those days, they might have pictured me with highway trash wrapped around my ankles and *BOLLOCKS* scrawled on my forehead.

Permitting someone with so shaky a grasp of reality to enter relationships was just asking for trouble. The catalogue of my romances from those years is unrelievedly dreary—boys taking short vacations from their long-term girlfriends, boys who didn't like girls, boys who needed a place to stay and someone to do the cooking. And then the hurt boys, the ones whose long-term girlfriends had left them, who called their therapists twice a day, who were too depressed to go to class. By this point I hardly need add that I saw nothing inappropriate about any of these choices.

When, at twenty-one, I announced my intention to marry a man I knew only slightly and understood less, dismayed family members and friends ringed around me, trying to make me see how inappropriate the choice was, how poorly we were matched, how little pleasure we took, even then, in each other's company. Their attempts hardened my resolve. I looked into the eyes of my intended and saw a soul misunderstood by the world, whose inability to hold a steady job indicated his need for a supportive wife, whose vague visions of success I could share without quite having to get them into focus.

The marriage lasted seven years—longer than it should have. Even when it finally collapsed, its flimsy walls giving way under disappointment, disillusion, and broken promises on both sides, I still couldn't make sense of the ruin, or understand why it had happened. I couldn't *see,* I wailed to a therapist, week after week.

"If you want to see, you have to look," she told me.

"I do look. But I can't see."

"Then you don't know how to look," she said.

Irritated by the smug shrinkishness of her answer, I said, "Okay. Fine. Tell me how to look."

"This isn't some kind of mystical thing. Just pay attention. Your only problem is that you don't pay attention."

As always when I am handed an accurate piece of information about myself, I was stung. Days had to pass before I calmed down and heard the invitation behind the therapist's words, weeks before I was willing to act on them. Not that I knew how to act. All I knew was that a new world was taking shape at my perceptions' furthest horizons, still distant and faint, but visible just barely.

Five years ago my second husband and I bought a house, the first I had ever owned, and with it came property. The house sits on an ordinary suburban lot; we are not talking about Sissinghurst here. Still, space had to be filled up in gardens and around trees, and I learned, generally by error, about bloom time, soil acidity, shade tolerance, and zone hardiness.

Like most chores, gardening teaches me about myself, and I have learned that I am never going to be a prize-winning gardener whose lilies glisten and whose roses scent the air a block away. But I am a tidy gardener: I make time to stake perennials and deadhead the coreopsis; I struggle to preserve clean edges around the beds.

And I am a heroic weeder, a merciless one, driven. I sometimes come into department stores with dirt under my fingernails from digging out knotweed from planting strips in the parking lot. Many gardening tasks are too heavy for me, or require too delicate a touch, but weeding means the staving off of brute chaos, a task I approach with brio.

A year or so after I started gardening, I visited my mother, who has a garden of her own. Stooping to pluck weeds as we talked, I sought out the infant tufts of Bermuda grass that hadn't yet had a chance to sprawl and colonize. "How can you even *see* those tiny things?" my mother asked, and I was so startled that I paused for a moment, still crouched at plant level.

How *can* I even see those tiny things? I can spot an errant sprig of clover from halfway across the yard, but can't make out the face of a good friend five rows down in an auditorium. I can see my gray hairs as if they were outlined in neon, but can't read a football scoreboard on TV. The college co-ed who didn't notice trash and graffiti has become a woman who scours every scene, vigilant in her pursuit of jarring notes, infelicitous details. She has learned to look, and to pay attention. But she still can't see the picture itself, or the happy accidents it might contain.

Bad eyes pick out the bad—it makes sense. Put like that, the condition sounds dire, requiring corrective lenses for the brain or soul. But my myopia is physical before anything else; I am truly unable to make out the face of my friend in that auditorium, however much I might want to see her. A hinge exists between the literal and the metaphorical reality of my crummy vision. I can bear in mind that my vision is untrustworthy, but I can't change it.

All of which brings me back to my high-school biology

teacher, God bless her, who diagnosed me more accurately than anyone else. I am a person who has trouble seeing enough, or correctly. Knowing this, I must go forth with useful caution, avoiding quick turns and snap decisions.

And, truly, I do all right. I haven't yet stepped off a cliff or driven into a pedestrian, and my judgments in recent years seem little worse than anyone else's. I just have to look, then look again. I have to remember that I am seeing only part of the picture. I have to remind myself to allow for my margin of error, and then bear in mind that the world is, always, more populous and bright and bountifully landscaped than it appears.

Collections

Alexander Theroux

Black

Black is the Stygian well. As a color, truculent, scary, deep and inaccessible, it appears as a kind of abstract unindividualized deficiency, a bullying blot with a dangerous genius to it. There is no ingress. It absorbs and efficiently negates all color—in spite of the fact that Claude Monet once pronounced it of all colors the most beautiful—and with the negative aura of nothing more than itself suggests the sinister, dissolution and the permanence of disease, destruction and death. As Jan Morris says in (and of) *Fisher's Face,* reminding me of black, "One does not like that queer withdrawal into the expressionless." It is a color rightly described in the words of Henry James as portentously "the fate that waits for one, that dark doom that rides." It shocks us in the saccade of its sudden, inky prohibition but becomes as well in the inscrutable deepness of sleep the backdrop of all our dreams, and is sometimes even a comfort. (Dickens wrote, "Darkness was cheap, and Scrooge liked it.") With its syntax of hidden and unverifiable dimension, black has no indexicality but remains for the fat prohibitive hachuring of its drawn drapes a distinct code above all colors that, like espionage, legislates no place signs or particularity. In its relentless boldness, black is both atrociously present and atrabiliously absent.

No one would deny that the color black in its solid vaga-bondage, forgive the paradox, barges into things, and how its bigness booms. There is nevertheless relief, arguably, in seeing the ultimate value of "reality," and it is here, perhaps, that black allows for any continuing comfort.

Is that why Henri Matisse declared, "Black is the color of light," in spite of the fact that in color theory black is the absence of light? No pure colors in fact exist. Black and white, which are banished from chroma, at least in the minds of many if not most people, in the same way 0 and 1 were once denied the status of numbers—solid Aristotle long ago defined number as an ac-cumulation or "heap"—are each other's complements just as they remain each other's opposites. Is this too paradoxical? W. H. Auden wrote,

> Where are the brigands
> most commonly to be found?
> Where boundaries converge.

Weirdly, black *is:* darkness truly is our destiny at both ends of life. And yet it *is not:* "And those wonderful people out there in the dark," declares creepy, decaying, old, self-deluded Norma Desmond, when there is nothing out there at all. If an object absorbs all the wavelengths. We call it black, in the same way, for example, that a leaf that absorbs red light looks green to us or a stained-glass window that absorbs blue looks orange. And yet how can we legitimately call what is so full of other colors, whether white or black, *one* color? There is beyond its almost muscular intensity an irreconcilable force to the sheen of its light and shape of its lutulence, *ut tensio sic uis:* "as the tension, so the power." Black both is and it is not: disguises appear, we use aliases, and silently stand before that unabsorbing wall. The color black is the extreme, high-gravity, bombed-out, cave-blot color of Nox, Rahu, Quashee, Hela, Erebus, Sambo, Maevis and, deader than Dead Sea fruit with black ashes inside, it is the dark side of the Manichean alternative.

More often than not, it is with black as with Gustav Mahler's *Sixth Symphony,* which in its deep complexity, in Bruno Walter's phrase, "utters a decided 'No.' "

It is a color specifically inimical to white, including its thousand shades and tints and tones, along with what is in between. (Technically speaking, *tints* are colors that also contain white; *shades,* colors that contain black; and *tones* are those colors containing gray.) We call an object black if it has absorbed all wavelengths. Ordinary sunlight (or white light) is a mixture of light at all wavelengths—or all colors. A material that we perceive to be colored, of whatever color, has absorbed certain visible wavelengths and not others. Black and white, however, as polar extremes most significantly both embody what Paul Fussell, discussing the nature of enemies, refers to as "the *versus* habit," one thing opposed to another, not, as he explains, "with some Hegelian hope of synthesis involving a dissolution of both extremes (that would suggest a 'negotiated peace,' which is anathema), but with a sense that one of the poles embodies so wicked a deficiency or flaw or perversion that its total submission is called for." In this sharp dichotomy along the lines of "us" versus "them," black *is*—legendarily, has always been—precisely that wickedness. If white is known, safe, open and visible; black, unknown, hostile, closed and opaque, is the masked and unmediated alternative. Is it not clear in the confrontation of chess?

> The board
> detains them until dawn in its hard
> compass: the hatred of two colors

writes Jorge Luis Borges in "Chess."

It has an unholiness all about it, does black. "Your blood is rotten! Black as your sins!" cries Bela Lugosi in the film *Murders in the Rue Morgue* (1932). Doesn't the devout Moslem pray for the Kaaba's return to whiteness, which has turned black by the sins of men? Is not black the color of chaos, witchcraft, black magic, mad alchemy and the black arts? "Some negroes who believe in the Resurrection, think that they shall rise white," writes Sir Thomas Browne in *Christian Morals* (1716). And what of the darkness of bondage? The descent into hell? Evil? The word black is, more often than not, considered somewhat of a rude and insulting adjective, especially in English, serving as a dark, maledroit, prefixal name or term like "Dutch" and "psycho" and "gypsy." What puzzle can ever be worked of the spasmodic record of all it portends? Who in the essence of its ultimate reduction does not disappear? No animal or bird can see in total darkness. What is the color of the Congo? Boomblack! Jew's pitch! Nightmare! The bituminous side of life. Coalblack trolls. Demons. Bats. Moles. Fish alone can live in the unravellable inscrutableness of darkness. Coelacanths, blind as stones! According to the song "Think Pink" in *Funny Face* (1957) what should be done with black, blue and beige, remember? Banish the black, burn the blue and bury the beige! In Saint-Saëns's *Danse Macabre,* the white skeleton may terrifyingly dance in the darkness, but it is Death playing the violin.

After the ominous scriptural caveat "Whoever touches pitch will be defiled" (Sirach 12), the color black has never stood a chance. The rule was writ. Watch, for the night is coming.

Why speak of Cimmeria and unearthly mythologies? Darkness is right above us. Space itself is perpetual night, an atmosphere as black and haunted as the Apocalypse, totipalmate, hovering, suffoblanketing our entire and endless universe in which, crouching in total enigma, we lost inchlings squat in fear with headfuls of questions. How caught we are by its vastnesses. Midnight, according to Henry David Thoreau, is as unexplored as the depths of central Africa. "It is darker in the woods, even in common nights, than most suppose," he wrote in his diary at Walden Pond. "I frequently had to look up at the opening between the trees above the path in order to learn my route, and where there was no cart-path, to feel with my feet the faint track which I had worn." Old-timers in New Hampshire used to say of a winter's blackness, "This is a gripper of a night." But don't we know, by what we fear, what blackness is by the state of our natural condition? Black intimidates us. As the line from the old song "Lovin' Sam (The Sheik of Alabam)," tells us, "That's what it don't do nothin' else, 'cep."

On the other hand, what with any clarity defines whiteness? No, W. B. Yeats is correct: nothing can live at the poles (". . . there's no human life at the full or the dark"). No activity can be discovered there, no incarnations. They are gloomy waste places in the extreme, noncerebral and brainless and uninhabited, recalling for me the phrase by which Laurel and Hardy were once described: "two minds without a single thought." Orthochromatics shock us, before anything else, not only in the insolence of their extremes, but in the way they are part of the same destitution. Schiller asserted, *"Verwandt sind sich alle starke Seele"*—"All strong spirits are related."

Black suggests grief, loss, melancholy and chic. It also connotes uniformity, impersonality, discipline and, often as the symbol of imperial order, jackbooted force and Prussian dominance. It is the color of Captain Mephisto and the dark lunar half of the Zoroastrian puzzle, with the kind of legendarily subterranean and inscrutable, praealtic malignity apposite to it that conjures up the sort of words on which writers like Edgar Allan Poe and Arthur Machen and H. P. Lovecraft constantly relied, like "unutterable," "hideous," "loathsome" and "appalling." It is the color of the contrarian, the critic and the crepe-hanger. It is airless, above all, hermeneutically closed, a larcenous color which in its many morphs of mourning and concomitant glumness is wholly subject, like André Gide's brooding immoralist, to "evasive and unaccountable moods." What could be worse than to be destitute of light and at the same time incapable of reflecting it? Blackness tends to envelop and overwhelm a person by dint of the largeness of volume in which it appears or is presented to one, in the very same way that the faster you walk the more your peripheral vision narrows. The Japanese adjective *usui* means not only thin as to width but light as to color. What other color in the spectrum comes at you point-blank and so directly yet without access? It is immoderate and almost autoerotic in what subrationally but somehow inexorably it suggests of possibility in the theatrical, untiring and even violent depth of its inscrutable vastness. The darkness of black is the part of its brooding deepness inviting dreams. The soul of the color harbors in its holophrastic enigma all sorts of moods, including deliberation and delay. Didn't Rodin tell us, "Slowness is beauty"? There is gravity in the batwing-black of its weight, pull and shocking hue. It is the very medium of stark, rigorous negativity, a storm in Zanzibar, the black cataracts of Stygia, Kanchenjunga and its ferocious clouds, black maelstroms, black goat tents, catafalques, of defeaturing and helmeting shadows, rebellion and revolt, the unforgiving, spectral grimace fetched up in beetling frowns—the color of Spartacus, Robespierre, Luther, Marat, Sam Adams, Marx and Lenin and Mao, intractable Prometheus and defiant Manfred.

> From thy own heart I then did wring
> The black blood in its blackest spring

Mystery doesn't so much surround the color black as it defines it. If color symbolizes the differentiated, the manifest, the affirmation of light—and is not God, as light, ultimately the source of color?—black in turn indicates primordial darkness, the non-manifest, renunciation, dissolution, gravity. Isn't it sadly apposite to the surreptitious ways of man himself? Didn't André Malraux write perspicaciously in *The Walnut Trees of Altenburg* "Essentially a man is what he hides"? Don't we placate by our reliance on black the very color with which we most identify? A wife in Africa to be fertile often wears a black hen on her back. In Algeria, black hens are sacrificed. A black fowl in certain folklores, if buried where caught, is alleged to cure epilepsy. In medieval France, the limbs of black animals when applied warm to the limbs of the body supposedly relieved rheumatism. Chimney sweeps wear black as a totem with the same credulity that bandits in Thailand and Myanmar adorn themselves with protective tattoos. In Ireland, England—even Vermont—black wool to many people provides a cure for earache, just as in Russia it cures jaundice. Who can explain why for Rimbaud in his *Vowels* the letter A was black? Or why Beethoven thought that the key of B minor was black? No, enigma is only another word for black. We spend half our lives in curved shadows and in the sleep of dark, occlusive nights that are as "sloeblack, slow, black, crow black," as Dylan Thomas said of his own Welsh ("fishing-boat-bobbing") sea, and that are every bit as vast and profoundly mysterious.

Wet *is* black. On a gray day, in neutral light, with a faint drizzle, stones of almost any stripe quite vividly take on colors. As Adrian Stokes writes, the passing of water on stone gives a sense of organic formation and erosion, so that the stone seems "alive." Robert Frost in "The Black Cottage" notes, "A front with just a door between two windows/Fresh painted by the shower a velvet black." Cactus spines shine strangely red or gold in deserts during wet weather, just as creosote bushes become olive after rain. Most things darken when wet. And brighten when dark. And glisten when bright. Even swimmers. Harry Cohn of Columbia Pictures even said of his swimming star, Esther Williams, "Dry, she ain't much. Wet, she's a star." Darkness is also depth. The depth of black is determined by the penetration of light, which equals color when light is translated to pigment. A color with great tinting power allows in a lot of light. The stronger a tint is, the more transparent it may seem. The darker the wampum, the more valuable it was in trade. Native Americans sought *dark* clam shells from the English colonists who were compelled to use wampum in trading with them. Fr. Joseph François Lafitau, the French Jesuit, wrote in *Manners of the American Savages* in 1724 that in his time the usual strand of a wampum belt was eleven strands of 180 beads or about 1,980 beads. Three dark (or six white) beads were roughly the equivalent of an English penny. Black water in its stillness goes deeper than the ramparts of Dis. Clouds loom high above us, ominous, profoundly dark, yet shifting. There is a "black wind," the *beshabar,* a dry melancholy wind that blows northeasterly out of the Caucasus. "Even such winds as these have their own merit in proper time and place," declares Robert Louis Stevenson on the chiaroscuro wrought by wind, observing how "pleasant [it is] to see them [the clouds] brandish great masses of shadow."

Black is a maelstrom oddly inviting, winding about, ever beckoning us. It is a veiled temple, emptiness, the Balzacian abyss, "the mystery for which we are all greedy." Just as darkness is depth, corners are hidden and dark and inaccessible. Black is not only recessed but even in its most noble aspects never far from surreption and stealth. Is that not why silos are round? (Silage *spoils* in corners.) Black can be sullen as distant thunder, heavy as lead, here starkly blunt, there preternaturally atralumi-nous. It is also unlived-in, too authentic, embowered, conspirato-rial, rarely tender-hearted, cruelly cold, uninviting, casket-heavy, thick, explosive, mum and uncatalogably dead.

I think of Peggy Lee, singing the heartbreaking "Yesterday I Heard the Rain."

> Out of doorways
> black umbrellas
> come to pursue me
> Faceless people
> as they passed
> were looking through me
> No one knew me

Gene Lees, who wrote it, around 1962, told me it was a song about the loss of faith.

Black is the color without light, curtain dark, the portcullis-dropping color of loss, humility, grief and shame. Although to the human eye everything visible has a color, where color exists as an optical phenomenon, with a place already constructed for it in the human imagination, what can be said of the color black? *Is* black visible? Is it even a color? Or in some kind of grim, ruinous thunderclap and with a sort of infernal and ghastly force does it somehow smother color? Wholly destitute of color, is it the result of the absence of—or the total absorption of—light? It is pa-tently not included among Andrew Lang's color fairy books. It is, oddly, *not* the color of blindness. "I can still make out certain colors. I can still see blue and green," said Jorge Luis Borges, who added, ironically, that the one color he did not see in his blindness was black, the color of night. He said, "I, who was accustomed to sleeping in total darkness, was bothered for a long time at having to sleep in this world of mist, in the greenish or bluish mist, vaguely luminous, which is the world of the blind." Achromatopsy can involve partial or complete loss of color vision, where shades of gray are seen. (Robert Boyle spoke of this phenomenon as early as 1688.) To sufferers of such color deficiency, most foods appear disgusting—things like tomatoes appear black, for example. A patient of Dr. Oliver Sacks in 1987 became a victim of such dislocating misperception: "His wife's skin seemed to him to be rat-colored," Sacks observed, "and he could not bear to make love to her. His vision at night was so acute that he could read license plates for four blocks away. He became, in his words, 'a night person.' "

Many World War II pilots had the singular experience of actually *seeing* black, when, during "blackouts," pulling out of a dive—they could often hear but not see—blood quickly drained out of their heads and flowed into their abdomen and legs, whereupon immediately they "sticked" high to gain altitude and usually came fully alert. There are no commercial airplanes painted black. It is far too inkily deathful and crepuscular a hue. Most modern aircraft, in fact, have bright white fuselage tops largely to reflect sunlight and reduce rising cabin temperatures. Flight data recorders, introduced in 1965 and dubbed "black boxes" by the media, in spite of the fact that they are invariably orange, traditionally share that nickname with any electronic "box of tricks," as I learned when, teaching at MIT, I found twenty examples so named.

Black, unlike white, has comparatively far less of what Francis Crick in *The Astonishing Hypothesis* calls "pop-out." Crick speaks of the "spotlight" of visual attention regarding the matter of human perception. "Outside the spotlight, information is processed less, or differently or not at all." In relation to what the Hungarian psychologist Bela Julesz calls "preattentive processing," boundaried objects—and colors—are targets, as it were. According to Monet, Cézanne habitually kept a black hat and white handkerchief next to a model in order to ascertain, to fix, to examine the two poles between which to establish his "values." Although white can be considered a highly "salient" color, black with its remorseless absorption, assimilating all wavelengths, utterly engorging light, lacks such definition. Any radiation that strikes a "black hole," for example, is utterly absorbed, never to reappear. "A material that absorbs all light that falls on it is black, which is how this particular beast received its ominous name," write Robert Hazen and James Trefil in *Science Matters*. You could say that the color black is an "unattended" event, as it were, with no "fixation point." It detargets a visual place by its very nature, blots things out, becomes the ultimate camouflage. It is, as a distractor, the color of grimness and good-night. The high dark fog in San Diego is called *El velo de la luz,* the veil that hides the light. F.D.R. had the metal parts of his leg braces ("ten pounds of steel," he once pointed out) painted deep black at the ankles, so as to escape detection against his black socks and shoes. "Gobos" (or "flats," "niggers" or "flags") are those large black cloth shades used on Hollywood sets to block out unwanted light from the camera lens in order to avoid hala-tion and other undesirable effects. Black by definition scumbles objects.

Where is it half the time when we *can* discern it? Isn't rude, unforgiving black, impossibly covert like midnight and air-port macadam and prelapsarian ooze, merely a spreading brain-less giant without shape or contour? Contour, remember, almost always changes a color's tone. A square centimeter of blue, Ma-tisse argued, is not the same as a square meter of the same blue. Beyond that even, the extent of the area changes the tone, as well. And isn't black in its fat merciless gravitation almost by definition arealess? Without boundaries, at least without easily perceptible boundaries, black can be comfortless for that. If it doesn't threaten us, it can make us feel uneasy. Purple, which comes between blue and ultraviolet, resembles black in this. Al-though we accept that ultraviolet exists, there is little evidence of it in our daily lives. (The best evidence we have is sunburns and cataracts, neither of which are close to purple.) Black is bottom-less, autogyromotive and indirigible. Given Spinoza's observation that everything longs to endure in its being, doesn't black, more than any other struggling tinct, show an unpardoning tendency to be its own archetype, traveling, not like night, but with a kind of deep and unspellable horror reaching, stretching out, gathering, by way of everything from the monstrositous depth of children's formless nightmares to the gruesome hood-black anonymity of an executioner's reality, very like bony Death's harvesting hand?

I wonder, does black invoke what might be called "enemy-memory"? Or is black *itself* the enemy-memory? The witches on the back fence? The wreck into which we dive? Didn't Italo Calvino warn us, "The eye does not see things but images of things that mean other things"?

We tend to go wild in lunar light, in dark light, in the grip of the "night mysterious," as the song lyric goes. As Sky Masterson (Marlon Brando) tells Sarah Brown (Jean Simmons) in the film of the Broadway musical *Guys and Dolls,* "Sarah, I know the nighttime. I live in it. It does funny things to you." The question we pose of night, when we do not recoil from it, recalls for me certain lines from "Night Voices," a passionately personal poem which the young German pastor Dietrich Bonhoeffer wrote in 1943, two years before he was hanged by the Nazis in the Flossenburg concentration camp:

> I sink myself into the depths of the dark.
> You night, full of outrage and evil,
> Make yourself known to me!
> Why and for how long will you try our patience?
> A deep and long silence;
> Then I hear the night bend down to me:
> "I am not dark; only guilt is dark!"
> —*translated by Keith R. Crim*

As a color, black goes in more than several directions. It is the color of Saturn; the number 8—if for Pythagoras numbers have designs, why can't they have colors?—and symbolizes in China the North, yin, winter, water, as well as the tortoise among the Four Spiritually Endowed Animals. Ek Xib Chac, the western spirit of the Mayan rain-god, Chac, was black. In the Kabbala, black carries a value of understanding, while black in heraldry stands for prudence and wisdom. In the world of alchemy it is the color of fermentation. To ancient Egyptians, black symbolized rebirth and resurrection. Many Native American tribes who held the color black to be a powerful talisman wore it as war paint in battle and for feathers, because it made the warrior invulnerable. It is the fathomless color of everything from Nazi parachutes to Hernando's Hideaway, "where all you see are silhouettes," to the famous lunar eclipse on August 27, 413 B.C., which contributed to the terrible defeat of the Athenians (soothsayers, seeing the portent, advised delay) at the hands of the Spartans under Gylippus. What metaphor of need or hope or aspiration cannot be constructed of the ongoing paradox that black attracts the sun? The whole idea recapitulates the entire historical phenomenon of opposites: of the Beauty and the Beast, of Venus and Vulcan, of Plus and Minus, of Innocence and Guilt, of Death and Transfiguration. Noctiluca, "she who shines by night," wonderful paradox, is a classical synonym for Diana. Among some of the wilder, more extravagant and overingenious schemes presented over time to deal with the threat of dangerous, destructive glaciers, such as blowing them up, towing them, etc., someone once seriously suggested painting them solid black so that they would melt under the hot sun!

Although no two color blacks are alike—some would argue that one can almost always find a subtle and misleading gradualness of tone in whatever two examples are set side by side—as a basic color black seems, more often than not, invariable, solid, like no other, *la verità effetuale della cosa*, the nature of fact, true, although it has as many adjectives as it has hues—jet, inky, ebony, coal, swart, pitch, smudge, livid, sloe, raven, sombre, charcoal, sooty, sable and crow, among others. Things get smutched, darkened, scorched, besmirched in a thousand ways. (Common black pigments like ivory, bone, lamp, vine and drop black all basically consist of carbon obtained by burning various materials.) It is a color that reminds me in its many odd morphs of what photographer Diane Arbus chose to call freaks, "the quiet minorities," for its hues seem never the same, seem never alike, and in their enigmatic sombreness, like freaks, having passed their trials by fire—black is *the end*—are, as Arbus once said of her odd subjects, often ogled by people pleading for their own to be postponed. Isn't it strange that if you're "in the black," you are doing well, but if your "future looks black," things are bad? Its profundity is its mystery. The way of what the depth of black in going beyond deepness hides of, as well as defines in, the color reminds me of what Martin Heidegger once said of Carl Orff's musical language, *"Die Sprache der Sprache zur Sprache zu bringen,"* that it gives voice to the language of language. The color is an irrational and complicated achromatic, a tetrical, heat-eating, merciless, unforgiving and obdurate color, jayhawking you in a hundred ways, and in certain riddling guises it often reminds me of Frank Sinatra's "It Never Entered My Mind," a song Ol' Blue Eyes sings quite brilliantly but which, filled with sharps and flats and atonal glissandi, constantly strikes me, an amateur, mind you, as almost impossible to sing. There are many shades and faded grades in the parade of black, very like the turbid and half-turbid sounds found in Japanese writing and pronunciation.

It is not commonly compared to song, however. The spoken word sounds like a gunshot. *Blak!* As a pronounced word it has the sudden finality of a beheading. *Blak!* What a convinced declaration is made, for example, in Rouault's black line! Or Beckmann's! Or de Kooning's! Henri Rousseau did not want lines. He sought to make a line happen, as in nature, by arranging the delicate contrast between contingent colors. Art, it may be argued, like personality, like character, like human behavior, is fractal—its contours cannot be mapped. Who first conjured the color black, however, sharing with Robert Frost, who frequently wrote of the dark, the stormy "inner weather" within us, surely insisted fences made good neighbors.

What is of particular interest is that Frost, a poet often highly pessimistic and more than well acquainted with the night, also believed that blackness had to be faced. Remember in his poem "The Night Light" how he chides a woman who while she sleeps burns a lamp to drive back darkness, declaring, "Good gloom on her was thrown away"?

The origins of the word black (ME *blak*, OE *blāēc*, ON *blakkr*) go back to *flamma* (flame), and *flagrare* (L, to blaze up), words having to do with fire, flame, things that have been burned—compare *blush, bleak, blind, flare* and *flicker*—and is ultimately formed from the Indo-European *bhleg*, to burn with black soot or to burn black with soot. There are several Anglo-Saxon and Early English words for black or darkness: *piesternesse* (darkness), *blāēqimm* (jet) and *blakaz* (black). We find "blake" in *The Ancren Riwle*, or "Rule of Nuns," ca. 1210, and in *King Horn*, before A.D. 1210 ("He wipede bat blake of his swere"). A couplet from *The Story of Havelock the Dane*, an Anglo-Saxon tale, before A.D. 1300, goes as follows:

> In a poke, ful and blac,
> Sone he caste him on his bac

But do we in fact get our English word from sound symbolism or mispronunciation? Different meanings, amazingly enough, have derived from the very same original word by way of a sequence of semantic shifts and in the process ironically have moved in the opposite direction, as is evident in Old English in which *blāēc* is "black." But the word *blac*, with no other phonetic difference than that of a vowel, actually once denoted, according to Anglo-Saxon scholars W. W. Skeat, Rev. Richard Morris and T. Wedgwood, what we now think of as its opposite. The original meaning of *black* is "pale," "colorless," "blank" or "white." Is this not astonishing? The word *black* (Anglo-Saxon *blac, blāēc*), which is fundamentally the same as the old German *blach*—a word now only to be found in two or three compounds, e.g., *Blachfeld*, a level field—originally meant level, bare and by extension bare of color. According to William S. Walsh's *Handy-Book of Literary Curiosities*, the nasalized form of black is blank, a word which originally signified bare, and was used in the sense of white specifically and logically because white is (apparently) bare of color. In Anglo-Saxon we read, *"Se mona mid his blacan leōhte"*—the moon with her pale light. An old poet praises the beauty of *"blac hleor ides"*—the pale-cheeked girl or woman. *Blac* in *Beowulf* means "bright," "brilliant." In the great hall, Beowulf sees Grendel's mère for the first time by the bright firelight—*"fȳr-leōht zeseah, blācne leōman"* (l. 1516). The Old English infinitive *blāēcan* means not "to blacken" but rather "to bleach." Our words *bleak* and *bleach*—is this not passing strange?—are from the same root. In the north of England, the word *blake,* as applied to butter or cheese, means "yellow." So now you know the essential difference between black and white. *There is none!* Weirdly, in the etymological sense, black means white. Black *is* white!

Emily Fox Gordon

My Last Therapist

When I remember Dr. B's office I envision it from an aerial angle. I see myself slightly hunched at one end of the comfortable leather couch. I see him flung back in his specially designed orthopedic rocker, his corduroy-sheathed legs outstretched, his ankles crossed, his bald pate gleaming. I see the two of us looking out from our lamp-lit island into a parcel of shadowy office space, in the direction of the darkened alcove where Dr. B typed up his bills and displayed the photographs of his wife and children, which, squint and peer and crane my neck as I might, I could never quite make out.

Dr. B was a fit and pleasant-looking man in his early forties with a rather long and slightly horsey face, a little like Prince Charles's, or a Semitic version of John Updike's. He emanated sensitivity and good will and he had a fine speaking voice, an anchorman's baritone, which tended to lighten as he grew animated. When I first met him—nearly fifteen years ago—I was impressed by his handshake, a firm grasp, two hard pumps, and a quick release. By the time our acquaintance was five minutes old I had formed an opinion of him which I never entirely abandoned, though I did revise and expand it: ordinary!

Dr. B led me to his office, a small utilitarian space on the top floor of the local hospital. On the wall facing the patient's chair, he had displayed his diplomas and a poster-sized photograph of a sailboat in a storm, its deck half-swamped and drastically tilted. He observed me as I took inventory of his office and smiled. "Checking things out?" he asked. "Yes, indeed," I answered. "As well you should!" he said, emphatically. I recognized the language of consumerism, then a fairly new trend in therapy.

Dr. B declared himself available to work with me before the first session was over. His eagerness did not surprise me: I was a literary kind of person, wasn't I, and didn't he have a reputation as a psychiatrist with a special interest in literature and the arts? Surely I was brighter, I found myself thinking, than a lot of his patients, and more interesting. Reasonably stable, free of drug dependency, capable of humorous self-deprecation, even charm. And almost simultaneously I recoiled: was this what I had come to—finding gratification in the imagined prospect of becoming some shrink's prize patient?

I

Surely I was too much of a veteran for that. By the time I arrived in Dr. B's office I had been through five therapists, three before the age of seventeen. Two of these were almost comically inappropriate; between the ages of eleven and thirteen, I was the patient of two separate classically trained psychoanalysts.

The first was Dr. V, who was Viennese and practiced on the Upper East Side of Manhattan. Dr. V kept a tank of exotic fish in her waiting room. She had mismatched eyes, one small and weepy, the other hypertrophied and glaucous, like an eye behind a jeweler's loupe. Dr. V was followed by Dr. H, another middle-aged woman, but midwestern and more motherly. Like Dr. V, she put me on the couch and maintained a silence throughout the hour.

But she knitted me a sweater. The cables fell out of her needles fully articulated, like great ropes heaved length by length over the side of a ship. I appreciated the symbolism; the developing sweater was meant to suggest that something was being made here, that in spite of my nearly complete silence, progress of some kind was happening. At the end of my therapy with Dr. H—why it stopped, I had no idea: I could only guess it was because the sweater was finished—she presented it to me. It was very handsome and unbecoming and smelled ever after of Dr. H's Pall Malls.

I failed in these early therapies, or attempts at analysis, as I suppose they should properly be called. How could I have succeeded? And what could Drs. V and H have been expecting? Thrown into deep waters without instruction, I floated mute, Dr. V's great eye like an implacable sun above me. My silence was both anxious and voluptuous. I felt a gentle pressure to speak, but I also felt pillowed by the assurance that silence was all right—good, in fact. It established my bona fides as a sensitive person, because only a sensitive person would remain silent when given the opportunity to speak. The more silence, the more certainty that the surface tension of the silence would break; the more prolonged the silence, the more import it would be seen, once broken, to have had. The first would be last and the last would be first: I had internalized this, the fundamental psychoanalytic dialectic, before I turned thirteen. On the couch I felt like a passenger on a night train, lying in a closed compartment on a gently rocking bed, passive and inert, but hurtled forward by the process of travel.

The waiting rooms of Drs. V and H had the feeling, for me, of sanctified space. I understood Dr. V's aquarium as a metaphor for the unconscious mind: those glittering bits of protein flashing through it—how I wished I could pinch the tails of their analogs in my brain, draw them out wriggling and present them to her. And the framed reproduction of Rouault's little king which dominated Dr. H's waiting room seemed to me the focal point of a shrine.

I brought a free-floating ardor to my first encounters with psychotherapy, a kind of religious hunger which had gone unfed by my parents' agnosticism, their skepticism, their pragmatic liberalism. As I lay on the couch, my thoughts were runnels of dreamy speculation just below the translucent skin of consciousness, monitored, but not entirely registered. I never actually expressed these thoughts, not because I was secretive—nobody could have been more eager to reveal herself than I—but because I had childishly misunderstood the rules of free association. Somehow I had picked up the idea that only unconscious thoughts were to be spoken. An obvious contradiction, but I blurred this impossibility into a kind of Zen koan. Once I had solved it, I felt sure that enlightenment would follow.

My therapeutic education broke off while I went away to boarding school for two years. After I was thrown out, I returned to Washington, D.C., where my parents now lived, and began therapy with Dr. G, the first male. He was the most genuinely detached of all my therapists. When I remember him I bring to mind a cartoonist's doodle-drawing of a shrink—one quick unbroken line describing a domed, balding head, continuing with a substantial hooked nose and receding chin, and petering out after tracing the swell of a modest professional's paunch. He had a wry decency that was mostly, but not entirely, lost on me at the time. He seemed, emotionally, to be a smooth dry surface; no burrs to snag my creepers or wet spots to which I might adhere.

My therapy with Dr. G was the first in which I sat up and faced the therapist, the first in which I talked freely, and also the first in which I withheld or distorted the truth. I never mentioned how mortified I was, for example, to notice that the patient who walked out of his waiting room as I entered was a fat obnoxious girl from my school with alopecia and a steady rapid blink, and I never confided my fear that perhaps Dr. G had made the treatment of fat adolescent girls—I *was* fat, though not nearly as fat as she was—his specialty.

With Dr. G, I learned to "talk therapy." This was not a matter of using jargon—I'm proud to say I've never done that—but of recognizing which gambits and attitudes cause the therapist to signal his receptiveness. Even the most poker-faced practitioner will always reward an attentive patient with some small sign, a subtle alteration in the set of facial muscles, a dilation of the pupils. So with Dr. G I reached the "clever Hans" stage of my development as a patient.

And like the novice painter who has learned to use the entire canvas, I finally learned how to fill the hour; now I saw that anything I said could be depended on to color the silences which followed, giving them a plausible opacity behind which I could hide until I found another thing to say. Often what I said was about loneliness, or feeling as if I were enclosed in a glass box. These themes seemed to engage Dr. G, and they gave me a pleasant feeling too. I enjoyed the waiflike image I conjured up of myself, and the resultant gentle tide of self-pity which washed over me, raising the hair on my arms and leaving my eyes prickling with tears.

Throughout my three years as Dr. G's patient, I felt a guilty and unshakable conviction that I was completely sane and that I had health to squander. Of course, my notion that patients were expected to be crazy was a naive one, but I had swallowed whole the familiar ideology that connects madness to beauty of spirit. My knowledge of my strength and sanity was a secret I did my best to keep from Dr. G. I wanted him to see me as vulnerable and sensitive rather than robust. I loved the notion of myself as saucer-eyed and frail, and I was ashamed of the blunt and caustic person I knew I was. I hoped that if I applied myself, I might evolve toward becoming the fragile and purely lovable being I so wished to be. I was looking for transformation, not cure. I wasn't interested in being happier, but in growing more poignantly, becomingly, meaningfully unhappy.

Perhaps the reader wonders: why did my parents put me into these psychoanalytically oriented psychotherapies at such an early age? My mother would have explained that my chronic underachievement in school was the reason, and later she would have added my bad and wild behavior (mild by today's standards).

And what was wrong with me? A family systems therapist would have identified me as the family scapegoat, the child designated to "act out" the conflicts between my tense, driven father and my incipiently alcoholic mother, the vent through which the collective rage escaped; a Winnicottean would point to the consequences of early maternal inadequacy (my mother was bedridden with phlebitis for most of my first year); a practitioner with a neurological bent could find evidence of a learning disability.

All these hypotheses have explanatory power. I tend to favor the last one, at least on days when I feel inclined to believe that there *is* such a thing as a learning disability. But they were all equally irrelevant to the subjective reality of the adolescent I was. About her I can only say that if she was angry, she was also extremely passive, and mired in a deep helplessness, and that therapy became a means by which she became even more so.

My therapeutic education did me harm. It swallowed up years when I might have been learning, gathering competence and undergoing the toughening by degrees that engagement in the world makes possible. But worse than this was the effect of my therapies on my moral development: seedlings of virtues withered. An impulse that might have flowered, for example, into tact—the desire to gently investigate another's feelings—fell onto the stony ground of the therapist's neutrality and became manipulativeness, a tough perennial better suited to these desert conditions.

I acquired the habit of the analysand, the ruthless stripping-away of defenses. But in my case not much self had yet developed, and surely none of it was expendable. I was tearing away not a hardened carapace, but the developing layers of my own epidermis. By reducing myself to a larval, infantile state I was doing what I felt I was expected to do, and what would please the therapist.

I I

By the time I was sixteen I had given up any serious college ambitions. I spent the days sulking and smoking in the snack bar of a bowling alley with a group of fellow truants. At the age of eighteen, at loose ends and living with a boyfriend's mother in suburban Indianapolis, I scratched my wrists with a pair of nail scissors. The boyfriend's mother put me on a train the next day, and when I arrived in Washington my parents lost no time in taking me to Dr. G, who suggested that I spend some time in a therapeutic community—Austen Riggs, an open psychiatric hospital in the Berkshires, was his recommendation.

For years life had been retreating and the space it left filling up with therapy; at Riggs life *was* therapy. Here I was surrounded by young people, most of them no more apparently disturbed than I was. Our physical circumstances were comfortable; we lived in private rooms in a big high-ceilinged residence, ate good food, and were offered the usual diversions—volleyball and tennis, ceramics and woodworking. We were free to come and go.

From the first I felt something anomalous in our interactions with one another. It was as if we had been positioned at oblique angles to one another and had gotten stuck that way, unable to twist ourselves free so as to stand face to face. We had been planted in therapy, like rows of sunflowers. Our gazes were tilted upward, each toward the face of the therapist. Like acolytes at the feet of masters, we were taught to cultivate a contempt for the distractions which surrounded us. So we lived in communal loneliness and restless boredom. I can still "taste" these feelings; the sight of a jewel-green expanse of lawn or a hanging pot of pink and purple fuchsia can set it off in me as surely as an electrode probing brain tissue can evoke a hallucination.

I stayed for three years, years which I would otherwise have spent in college. I was assigned to an incompetent neophyte I'll call Dr. S (number four in the running count), a research psychologist. After the first year I became an outpatient and Dr. S, who was married and soon to become a father, began to show up at my door with bottles of wine and sheepish smiles. I got no help from the Riggs bureaucracy in my effort to extricate myself from this embroilment; firmly gripping my upper arm, the senior psychiatrists steered me out of their offices. One and all, they told me the same story: what I had mistaken to be Dr. S's feelings for me were merely projections of my own transference.

Here I felt for the first time the chill of an encounter with psychiatry in its systematic aspect.

Then Leslie Farber arrived at Riggs, coming in to serve as director of therapy for the new administration. He listened to my complaint about Dr. S, believed me, and—eventually—took me on as a patient.

Dr. Farber never found Riggs congenial, and he was suspicious of Stockbridge, which he regarded as a kind of Potemkin village. He left for New York after a little more than a year, taking me and two other patients with him. It is no exaggeration to say that Dr. Farber rescued us.

How difficult it is to abandon the ironic mode and speak enthusiastically! Although I list Dr. Farber as one in the succession of my shrinks, I do so apologetically, recognizing that this is a gross miscategorization—something like including Kafka in a roundup of Czech insurance underwriters. He was something other and larger than the rest of them, so much so that he eludes easy characterization. I write about him troubled by the well-founded fear that I will fail to do him justice.

He was a thinker and writer as well as a psychoanalyst, the author of three books of remarkable essays. His critique of psychoanalysis began in his understanding of human will, a category which he believed had been "smuggled into" psychoanalytic explanations of motive without acknowledgment, an element anatomized in literature, philosophy and theology, but neglected in psychoanalytic theory.

To understand people only in the reductive terms of the "medical model" was a drastic impoverishment of human possibility. Dr. Farber shared this belief with others associated with the humanistic or existential schools, but he never shared their woolly and inspirational leanings. He was tough-minded, pessimistic by temperament, and a man of deep emotional conservatism. He was a believer in God who protected his belief from any but the most serious inquiry.

Dr. Farber was in his late fifties when I met him. Though less ravaged, his small-chinned, delicate-boned Eastern European face was nearly as seamed and pouched, expressive and revelatory of character, as W. H. Auden's at the same age. He was a small man, plump and sedentary, but his walk had verve and his motions were graceful. I remember the elegant and efficient way he handled his keys as he opened his office door, one eye squeezed shut against the updraft of smoke from the cigarette in the corner of his mouth.

He exuded melancholy and humor. His gravitas, his distinction, were so immediately and overwhelmingly apparent that even in my deteriorated and boredom-numbed condition I recognized them. It was a revelation to me, this full, rich, pungent, complex humanity. It was as if another self continued to live inside the therapeutic self I had become, lying slack but fully jointed, waiting for some salutory yank to spring alive.

My sessions with Dr. Farber were entirely unlike my earlier experience of therapy. I had learned to think of my utterances as soap bubbles rotating in midair, to be examined by me with the help of the therapist. They were the matter of the enterprise. But with Dr. Farber, no such "work" was being undertaken. Instead, we talked. He talked—for example—about his childhood in Douglas, Arizona, and how growing up in the desert had affected his inner life. We talked about his marriages, my boyfriends, his children, my parents, his dismay at watching Riggs patients, most of them young and few really sick, loitering in a psychiatric limbo. We talked about movies and TV and the youth culture; we gossiped freely about the Riggs staff and patients. Dr. Farber expected me to hold up my end of these conversations, to keep him interested. Was I up to it? Mostly, but not always.

My reaction to my earliest view of Dr. Farber's world was something like the "wild surmise" of stout Cortez's men at their first sight of the Pacific. I knew quite suddenly not only that this world was *there* but also what that signified. This was my first apprehension of the realm of the moral, about which my parents had taught me very little, and therapy had taught me nothing.

The notion that another person might have a moral claim on me, or that I might have such a claim on another, was a novel one. So was the idea that a moral worldview had an intellectual dimension which required the careful working-out of distinctions, the most significant of which was the distinction between the moral and the aesthetic. This is the one I had, and still have, the greatest trouble understanding. Is there such a thing as a moral style? It has always troubled and confused me that Dr. Farber's influence on me had so much to do with traits that were really more aesthetic than moral—his worldly panache, his toughness.

With Dr. Farber I felt free to express the caustic and humorous judgments which I had been squelching for years. He enjoyed and encouraged my rude health. The world, which my therapeutic existence at Riggs had bleached of color and emptied of content, began to fill up again with the materials furnished in my sessions with Dr. Farber—with serious and light talk, with movies, books, music, with gossip and stories—with all the stuff of life.

I I I

My move from Austen Riggs to New York City was a jarring transition. I wanted life, unfiltered and unprocessed. Here it was, the real thing, lonely, grubby and full of jolts. I lost jobs, lived in chaos, and kept my money in a bureau drawer. My gums bled and my menstrual cycle went haywire. I cut my hair myself to save money, and the result made me look like the mental patient I had been pretending to be at Riggs. I got robbed, mugged, raped. At one point, the cockroach colony in my apartment grew so large that it produced an albino strain—translucent creatures whose internal workings were visible in certain lights.

I was living on my own, away from home or institution for the first time, and I simply did not do very well. I had envisioned an exhilarating life in some vaguely imagined bohemia. But there was no bohemia anymore, none that I could find. Instead there was poverty and disorder and a series of bizarre low-paying jobs which seem funny and picaresque only in retrospect.

Dr. Farber charged me an income-adjusted fee of $7.50 a

session. He and his wife went out of their way to help me get established in New York; they paid me handsomely to stay with their children while they went to Paris for a week, and during one of my homeless intervals Dr. Farber arranged for me to sleep on a cot in his brother's empty studio. They fed me, regularly. How warm and inviting the prospect of roast chicken at their table seemed, as I sat on the clanking, hissing subway train, fighting the temptation to get off at the Farbers' Upper West Side stop, how appealing when contrasted to my hotplate, my canned chili and saltines, my cockroaches. And indeed, it was wonderful to spend time in that bustling, musical, intellectually lively household, which eventually came to serve as a sort of salon for a certain group of New York intellectuals.

Other patients also visited the apartment and got to know the family—Dr. Farber never observed the psychiatric taboo against associating with patients, and for him therapy and friendship were inextricable. But I grew dependent on the Farber household, and as my dependency deepened I grew closer to Dr. Farber's wife and more distant from him. I often felt that he was getting sick of me, always there as I was, in his office and in his home, across the room and across the table, asleep on the couch so that he could not feel free to indulge his habit of wandering through the apartment late at night in darkness.

I knew that my contributions to our talks had grown stilted and falsely animated—willed, as Dr. Farber would have put it. I found that I suddenly had very little to say. The struggles of my daily life—getting to work on time under threat of being fired, making it to the laundromat, avoiding crime and trying to stay clean when the hot water in my building was more often off than on—all this had apparently drained my head of anything interesting. I arrived at Dr. Farber's comfortable Riverside Drive office, with its high views of the streaky Hudson, blinking in the strong light, feeling dirty and uncertain about how I smelled.

I had found it easier to hold up my end of talks with Dr. Farber at Riggs, where we had the shared world of the institution to complain and gossip about. In New York Dr. Farber offered me a sort of substitute by asking me questions about the culture of protest, the rallies and shutdowns then in progress a few blocks away at Columbia. But I was no authority on this subject; my life was far too proletarian to put me in the way of any student revolutionaries.

The fact is, I had very little to offer. My education had been so impoverished, so radically incomplete, that I had grown up to be a creature of hunches and blurts, and soon even these had dried up. My sketchy views had long since been outlined and exhausted, and all I had to give back to Dr. Farber were flimsily disguised recapitulations of his own.

George Eliot, in a reference to phrenology, the psychology of her day, once spoke of her oversized "Organ of Veneration." Apparently I had one too. I became a furtive taxonomist, dividing up the world into the Farberian and the non-Farberian. What was Farberian I would embrace; what was non-Farberian I would reject. But sometimes—frequently—I got it wrong. Once I told Dr. Farber that I wanted to explore orthodox Judaism. What I knew of his own tightly guarded belief and his interest in Martin Buber gave me confidence that this would please him. Dr. Farber looked at me with amused incredulity: you want to wear a wig? he said. You want to take a ritual bath every month? Seriously?

Daniel was another of Dr. Farber's patients in New York, an intellectually promising and sensitive young man with a Yeshiva background who, like me, had languished for several years at Riggs, his prognosis growing steadily worse, before Dr. Farber came along to rescue us.

I had found a job, my most respectable yet, as a glorified coffee fetcher and Xeroxer in the Academic Placement office at Columbia, where Daniel had resumed his interrupted education. I often ran into him on Broadway, at Chock Full o' Nuts and in the bookstores. We talked sometimes on the phone, and though we were not intimate, we maintained a concern for one another's fortunes in the city, a kind of sibling connection.

For a year or so Daniel stayed on the dean's list, but then something gave way in his life and he began to skip classes.

Eventually he dropped out. During one of our phone conversations, Daniel sheepishly confided to me that he had not yet told Dr. Farber about this. A year passed, and Daniel continued the deception. I mentioned this to Dr. Farber's wife, during one of our cozy late-night gossips after the children had been put to bed. She passed the information to Dr. Farber, who confronted Daniel during his next session. They agreed that their friendship had been ended by the lie, and parted ways.

The explosion, when it came, was directed at me. I noticed, as Dr. Farber ushered me quickly into his office—no leisurely small talk, no smiles—that he looked grim and haggard, as if he had not slept well. I began to feel anxious, and I searched my mind frantically. Had I forgotten to pay? Had my check bounced?

I knew that Daniel had been dismissed. In fact, I had come to Dr. Farber's office that morning glowing with *Schadenfreude* and braced by the prospect of a ready-made interesting discussion. I was even prepared to plead Daniel's case a little; I wanted to remind Dr. Farber about Daniel's history, the oppressively high expectations of his parents, the overshadowing intellectual success of his older brother.

So it was disturbing to me that Dr. Farber stared at the floor. His reaction to my introductory stammerings was a long silence. When he finally raised his head and engaged my eyes, his face was full of angry puzzlement. "How could you . . ." he began, then shook his head and fell silent. I was already weeping.

When he spoke again Dr. Farber's voice was low and hoarse, his speech discontinuous, as if he were vocalizing only random chopped-off segments of a tormented thought process. But I got the idea. I had colluded with a lie, and that had compromised my friendship with Dr. Farber, and my whisperings to his wife had in turn contaminated, if only briefly, even his marriage: "How could you come into my home and . . . solicit . . . my wife?"

I had meanwhile pitched myself out of my chair onto my knees. Panic and grief had transported me, busted up some internal logjam, and for the first time in months I spoke fluently to

Dr. Farber as I crouched on the carpet, sobbing, tears springing from my eyes.

Please forgive me, I said. I had forgotten. Or maybe I never learned. Never learned what? asked Dr. Farber. That things matter, I said. For the first time since I had entered his office Dr. Farber looked at me as if I were a fellow creature. "Yes, they do," he said, and I was so relieved at this turning that I burst into fresh sobs.

Dr. Farber granted me a kind of amnesty, but never, I think, real forgiveness. He waved me out of his office with an air of preoccupied disgust, but I could sense that in his exasperation his sense of humor had wanly reasserted itself. Before I left I won from him the assurance that I could return the next week.

I had gotten it wrong, unconsciously slipped back to the precepts of my early therapeutic education. I had reverted to understanding the relationship between Dr. Farber and Daniel, between Dr. Farber and me, as a game played for therapeutic chips, not as a reality in which human connection was at stake. And while I had never deceived Dr. Farber, I had been less than honest. I had been dealing with him strategically, trying to hold on to a friendship which had lost meaning months earlier, and I had allowed Daniel's deception to continue unchallenged because its feloniousness made my more subtle dishonesty feel like a misdemeanor.

The most painful irony in this painful situation was that eventually I came to envy the seriousness of Daniel's transgression. I suspected that Dr. Farber cared more about Daniel than me; his anger was like a father's toward a beloved errant son. And like an errant son, Daniel had been cut decisively free; he left New York and moved to Israel, joined the army and married there, returning to the States years later with his young family. His dismissal from Dr. Farber's office left him bereft, but it also served to jolt him out of a rut. He got to keep, I think, some of his legacy from Farber, while my lesser, weaker, more equivocal offense kept me tied to Dr. Farber for another year, during which I used mine up.

Or so I understood myself to be doing. But meanwhile I

had found a boyfriend and moved in with him. This boyfriend, who was later to become my husband, took a satirical view of my attachment to Dr. Farber. He often compared me to a character in one of R. Crumb's underground comic books, the goofy, loose-limbed Flakey Foont, always in pursuit of his guru, Mr. Natural, an irascible little visionary in flowing robes with a white beard and giant flapping bare feet. At the end of that year, my wedding a few months off, I ended things with Dr. Farber myself. I confessed to him that I had had little to say to him for years. I need to leave, I told him, because I'm in danger of becoming the acolyte who gets the master's message wrong. I knew how little Dr. Farber wished to serve as my guru, and I knew how particularly inappropriate my idealizing impulse toward him was. His tendency was deflationary: he nearly always preferred a modest exactitude to a rapturous generality.

I can see myself, I said, twenty years from now as a barfly, the regular who climbs onto her stool every afternoon at two and by four o'clock is mumbling to anyone who will listen to the incoherent tale of the wise man she once knew in her youth. Dr. Farber accepted my resignation with warmth. My confession was true, and he liked it because it was true, and because it had a self-immolating boldness calculated to appeal to him. I offered it not because it was true, but because it was the only way I knew to please him.

I V

When, twelve years after I exiled myself from Dr. Farber, I first walked into Dr. B's office, I was just emerging from the sea of early motherhood onto some indeterminate shore. I felt that my relation to the future had undergone a subtle change, one which signaled, I can see in retrospect, the onset of middle age. I found I lacked, and had been lacking for longer than I wanted to admit, the unshakable confidence in my own sanity and stability that I had once considered such an embarrassing encumbrance. I felt a vague sense of balked urgency. My husband and I were constantly fighting. I brought with me a tangle of confusion and sadness about Dr. Farber, who had recently died.

Dr. B passed one crucial test during the first session. He recognized Dr. Farber's name and knew a little about him. "Irreplaceable," he said, "life-saving," and I loved him for that. He went on to link Dr. Farber with my father, who had also died recently. "A lot of loss," he said, shaking his head deploringly. My reaction was mild disappointment and annoyance. I didn't like the idea of packaging Dr. Farber and my father together, but I let it pass.

Then, a few weeks later, Dr. B said something almost unforgivable; he interrupted one of my many anecdotes about Dr. Farber with what he called "a reality consideration." Dr. Farber, he said, had been well known in the profession as a sufferer from depression. Wasn't it possible, he suggested, that during my years as Dr. Farber's patient, I had tried to compensate him for his sadness, just as I had done with my unhappy mother?

How many things could be wrong with this? Could anything be right? First the "reality consideration": was it implied here that the profession had a corner on reality? And depression: Dr. Farber had his own views about depression. I suggested that Dr. B go to the library and look them up. What the profession took to be Dr. Farber's depression was actually despair.

But I was too angry to argue; instead I picked up the first wad of ad hominem that came to hand and flung it in Dr. B's direction. I looked up at the ship photograph. That put me in mind of an analogy; I compared Dr. Farber to an oceangoing liner with a great deep hull, and Dr. B to a surface-skimming sailfish. Two spots of bright pink appeared just below Dr. B's cheekbones, and I pointed them out to him, literally pointed with my finger, all the while registering in one corner of my mind the appalling rudeness of the gesture.

I was working myself into a rage, and I could see that he was calculating how best to backtrack and calm me down. He threw up his hands. OK, he said. You're quite right. I was out of line. I'm not perfect. Do you need me to be perfect?

No, I said. I need you to be smart. Dr. B absorbed that

without comment and we sat in silence for several minutes. I was registering my disgust at the hokeyness of the "I'm not perfect" line and the seductive pseudo-intimacy of "Do you need me . . . ?" I was also fuming at the realization that Dr. B had saved his remarks about Dr. Farber until he had me well roped in as a patient. He had waited until it seemed safe to introduce his revisionist agenda. He was getting off, no doubt, on the idea of rescuing me from my thralldom to a distinguished dead practitioner; this was the old supplanter's story so familiar to the profession.

Here I was, seated in the office of my sixth therapist. Hadn't I decided, with Farber's help and long ago—as far back as Austen Riggs—that what I needed was to recover *from* therapy? Why, then, was I even here? One thing I was *not* doing was undertaking a revision of my views of Dr. Farber. This was such a touchy subject that Dr. B, as far as I can remember, never raised it again. My dismay at my own ugly and fluent anger was apparently to be my punishment for my recidivist slide back into psychotherapy, for my bad faith.

It seems that my life has not been so much examined as conducted in therapy. I brought into my therapies not the problems of life but the problems of therapy. Even the glowingly subversive moral lessons of Dr. Farber came to me under the cloak of therapy.

In the early months with Dr. B I assumed a new persona. I became hostile and prickly. I sneered at the nautical decor in his new office, especially the coffee table, which was a sheet of glass affixed to an old lobster trap. I took out after his ties, particularly a forest-green one printed with a repeating pattern of tiny mud boots and the legend L. L. BEAN. It's not lost on me, by the way, that the sadistic and grandiose tendency of my behavior toward Dr. B was the mirror image of the masochistic self-abnegation I had shown with Dr. Farber.

I behaved unpleasantly because I was paying to behave any way I pleased, and also because this was my emotionally primitive way of staying loyal to Dr. Farber. I would never

have felt free to be so nasty if I had not been supremely confident of Dr. B's regard for me. It was, after all, overdetermined;
Dr. B told me that his positive feelings for me were highly useful to our work together, as were my negative ones for him. He
explained that he could not will affection for a patient, but if
he happened to feel it he made sure to cultivate it for the sake
of the therapy.

Dr. B kept his face in profile, his eyes lowered and shadowed, but he inclined his large listening ear toward me, and
somehow he used that appendage expressively; something about
its convoluted nakedness reassured and invited me. He also had
a particular gift—how he learned to do this I can't imagine—for
conveying, simply by sitting there, a warm satisfaction in the fact
of my existence. His body's attitude seemed to say, "You're quite
something, all right!"

Dr. B's physical expressiveness sometimes betrayed him;
his face colored easily, and I could often see a look of eager
anxiety spring into his eyes just as he was about to offer an
interpretation. I liked him better silent than talking, because
when he spoke he sometimes said the wrong thing, jarring me
out of my meditations. His unquestioning acceptance of the tenets of his profession often angered me, and so did the way he
turned my challenges back on me by engaging their emotive
content rather than their substance.

The only topic I was willing to talk about in more or less
conventional therapeutic terms was my marriage. Here Dr. B
acted like an advocate, pushing me to articulate my rancors and
to assert what he saw as fundamental rights. He threw into question all my efforts to accommodate my husband's needs—What
about *yours?* was his refrain. Of course I enjoyed being the innocent one, the hotly defended one, but I knew that if my husband
were the patient he would receive the same treatment—at least
he would if Dr. B had determined this to be in his therapeutic
interest. I was dismayed by Dr. B's lack of concern for the complex, nuanced picture of my marriage—indeed, of the whole
"life-world" that I was struggling to present. Often I felt as if I

had spent the better part of the hour constructing an elaborate imaginary house, trying always to balance a wing of self-justification with one of judicious self-criticism, only to watch Dr. B carelessly kick the thing over in his hunt for the hurt.

Dr. B's advocacy was gratifying, but it unnerved me deeply. To feel rancor was to feel self-pity, and I feared being caught up in its familiar dialectic. The more I struggled against it, the more touchingly valiant I appeared to myself, and the further I felt myself sucked back into a destructive self-cherishing. I learned to hate a certain look on Dr. B's face, a steady wide-eyed gaze qualified by a faint enigmatic smile. I'm waiting patiently, his face said, for you to come off it. To him, my resistance to self-pity was simply a form of denial. To me, resistance was necessary; if I yielded my efforts to construct, a self would collapse and I would find myself falling back into a kind of watery Boschian hell, a bog where I would rot slowly in a solution of my own tears.

Dr. B and I were talking past one another. When I asked whether my marriage was a good one or not, he understood me to be asking "Is it good for me?" I wanted to know the answer to that question, but I was really after something else, something which I can only phrase, awkwardly, as follows: is my marriage part of "the good"? It should hardly have surprised me that from him I got psychological answers to philosophical questions.

V

I think of Dr. B as a *tinted* man, an updated and affectively colorized version of the psychoanalytic "gray man." In his office I never endured the silences of Drs. V, H, and G. He was quick to move into relation with me, to offer me a kind of friendship. He was frank about the uses of this relationship: it would serve as a kind of mock-up. Our work together would consist not only of shuffling through my past, but also of examining our own relationship for patterns and tendencies applicable to my outside life. What about his own patterns, I asked. Wouldn't they complicate the matter? I could trust him, he assured me, not to let his own needs intrude, or if that was impossible, to inform me of their presence. This he did, sometimes rather oddly. When I was talking, for example, about having been raped when I lived in New York, he interrupted me and confessed that this story was making him very anxious, and that I should probably discount any reaction he offered.

Dr. B operated under an extraordinary constraint, which was to keep his own humanity out of our relationship unless it served a therapeutic purpose. If that was not possible, if some errant tendril worked loose and struggled past the therapeutic boundary, it was subject to examination and extirpation on the spot. But he was also quite free to stir up my feelings deliberately, to flirt, to manipulate, to do any and all of these things as long as they were justified by the realistic expectation that they would serve a therapeutic end.

For my part, I was also severely limited. I was free, of course, to express anything, but the rules of the game did not allow me, like Dr. B, to manipulate without disclosure. I was also obliged to live with the knowledge that what transpired in Dr. B's office, however powerful its emotional charge, was not real. Dr. B was fond of saying that what went on between us was *very* real, but of course the use of the intensifying "very" immediately threw up scare quotes around the "real."

Therapeutic gerrymandering had shaped the territory of our relationship strangely. Between us we had it all covered, but the shared portion was nearly nonexistent. Everything was possible between us—everything, that is, but mutuality. It's not exactly accurate to say that I longed for that crucial element—I was too wary of Dr. B to really miss it much.

What I did feel was an intensification of my growing disgust at myself for having returned to therapy like the proverbial dog to his vomit, and for staying in therapy in spite of that disgust. After all, I knew better! I knew that whatever its ends, therapy was a sad, manipulative parody of authentic relation. But I also knew that in the outside world, therapeutic notions had become so omnipresent and pervasive as to be inescapable.

❄   ❄   ❄

Why did I go back into therapy? I was very unhappy when I sought out Dr. B, but I don't believe that unhappiness was the proximate cause of my return. I think it was more a pervasive social loneliness that herded me back, a sense of panicky disconnection from a central social tradition—a feeling to which young mothers have become particularly susceptible.

I believe I returned to therapy not only because it had been my element for so much of my life, but because it was the place I had seen everybody *else* go. By the time I became Dr. B's patient, therapy had overflowed its professional vessels, flooded the culture, and seeped into the groundwater. However I resisted it, every one of my interactions—as wife, daughter, sister, friend, and especially as mother—was subject to mediation by my own therapeutic notions and those of others. I was like an ex-smoker trapped in an unventilated designated smoking area, inhaling so many secondhand fumes that continued abstaining seemed pointless. I returned to therapy because, in a sense, I was already *in* therapy, but I felt myself to be placed uncomfortably on its periphery rather than securely inside it. I went back into therapy because it had become the central institution, the hearth, of my society.

Once when I had been agonizing about my husband and the difficulty of keeping myself from being swamped by the intensity of his ambition, the vehemence of his anxiety, I ended my catalog of complaint by saying: but he's a good person. Dr. B leaned forward and whispered, in audible italics, *"You've never said anything different!"* At this I burst into tears of gratitude. I was touched that Dr. B had been keeping track and that he handed me back the raw data in such a generous spirit.

In retrospect it seems to me that this incident marked an end to the struggle between Dr. B and me, and the beginning of a real, if very minimal, friendship. Human nature is such, after all, that given time and proximity, mutuality will take root even in the least hospitable of environments.

More and more now—as the leaves turned red and yellow outside Dr. B's windows, as fast food restaurants and discount outlets sprang up on the outskirts of the small New England city where we all lived, as the snow flew and the years passed and my daughter grew and my husband wrote his books and my hair began to turn gray—I did the talking. I did the interpreting too, in my own terms. My hand was on the tiller and I was yawing wildly all over the lake in my maneuverable little Sailfish, and it was fun. It occurs to me now that perhaps one of my many motives to return to therapy was a desire to try my mettle against it, to seize control of therapy for my own purposes.

My talking was mostly narrative and descriptive; I went on at great length about faces, recounted events in intricate detail. When I spoke analytically or speculatively, I did so in general or philosophical, rather than psychological, terms. Sometimes Dr. B's eager-to-interpret look flashed momentarily across his face, but I could usually depend on him to quash the impulse. What I had begun to do, of course, in Dr. B's office, was to write aloud.

In the years since I left Dr. B's office I've begun to write in earnest, and writing has allowed me—as nothing else, even the wisdom of Dr. Farber, ever has or could—to escape the coils of therapy. I don't mean that writing has been therapeutic, though sometimes it has been. The kind of writing I do now is associative and self-exploratory—much like the process of therapy, except that the therapist is absent and I've given up all ambition to get well.

Let me give Dr. B his due. He was more than competent; he was really good at what he did, and got better as he went along. Eventually he became a kind of adept. He learned to vaporize at will like the Cheshire cat, leaving nothing behind but a glow of unconditional positive regard, allowing me a spacious arena in which to perform my dance of self. In resisting his impulse to lure me back into the charted territory of psychoanalytic explanation, he granted me my wish to be released into the wilds of narrative.

VI

Once, five or six years before I became Dr. B's patient, I left my husband and took a Greyhound bus to New York City. I moved in with an ex-roommate, found another job at Columbia, and made an appointment with Dr. Farber.

He had given up his office now, and was seeing patients at the apartment. When I arrived, late in the afternoon, he shook my hand cordially and led me through the living room, past the familiar row of big dusty windows overlooking West End Avenue, and into the kitchen, where he fixed us both old-fashioneds. I stood at the counter and watched the assembly process, the slicing of the orange and lemon, which he carefully dotted with drops of bitters and sprinkled with sugar, the "muddling" with the back of a spoon, and the pouring of a jigger and a half of good bourbon into each sturdy glass.

We retired to Dr. Farber's study with our drinks in hand. When I asked Dr. Farber for permission to smoke—he had suffered a mild stroke a few years earlier, and had given up his cigarettes—he encouraged me to do so, and to blow the smoke his way. When I told Dr. Farber of my decision to leave my marriage he nodded gravely and with evident approval—he was no fan of marital strife.

I had a sudden impression that in the five years since I'd last seen him, Dr. Farber had moved into old age. He looked wryer, more elfin, a little in need of a haircut. The essential strength and depth of his spirit was still present, but it seemed to me that he had begun to conserve and protect himself. The Sturm und Drang of my life was only one of many clamorings, I felt sure, from which he had now begun, gently but implacably, to turn away.

When I asked Dr. Farber if he would take me on as a patient once again he said no. We continued to talk for another half hour, reminiscing about Riggs and my New York days, and the tone of our talk was warm and relaxed. I returned to my husband and my life in New England a few days later. I believe, though I'm not entirely sure, that this was the last time I saw Dr. Farber. The news of his death reached me five years later, when I was on sabbatical with my husband in North Carolina and happened upon his obituary in the *New York Times*.

The last two years of my therapy with Dr. B were marked by a long wrangle about what he called "the termination process." We had not yet entered this phase, he cautioned, and so the end of therapy could not yet be envisioned. How far away in time was the beginning of the termination phase from the end of therapy? That varied, said Dr. B. How would we know that the process had begun? When the work of therapy had been completed.

But it seemed that under the terms of our therapeutic détente, the work of therapy could never begin, and so, of course, it could never end. I could go on writing aloud, basking in the warmth of Dr. B's unconditional positive regard forever, or until my insurance ran out.

Real life intervened in the form of my husband's second sabbatical leave. Dr. B and I both accepted this as a stalemate-breaker, and the termination process was compressed into a few summer months just before my family's yearlong removal to Princeton. During these last sessions Dr. B often interrupted my monologues to introduce the theme of attachment and loss, but the stream of my thought continued to ripple along as it always had, picking up no traces of this effluent.

So it was a surprise to me when at the end of our last session, just as I was about to stand up, Dr. B, who since our initial handshake seven years earlier had never once touched me, rose from his orthopedic rocker and stood before me. In what took me a moment to realize was a clumsy, mistimed attempt at a hug, he grasped my head in his hands and pressed it against his stomach, hard enough so that I could hear the gurgle of his digestion and feel his belt buckle bite into my cheek.

Never have I felt such a congestion of sensations; only in retrospect can I separate and order my reactions—first bewilderment, then a panicky vicarious embarrassment, then a flash of sexual arousal quickly extinguished by my realization that Dr. B's embrace was an awkward eruption of affection and not a pass, then a suffusion of amusement and tenderness. I got to my feet and returned Dr. B's hug, planted a kiss on his cheek, and left the office.

The Lens of Art

Susan Sontag

Pelléas et Mélisande

All art, it has been said, aspires to the condition of music. And all arts made with music—but, more than any other, opera—aspire to the experience of ecstasy.

Originally, opera's ecstasies were provided by the singers. Stories—well-known intrigues from classical mythology, ancient history, and Renaissance epic—were dignified pretexts. The music, often glorious, was a platform. Whatever the pleasures afforded by the other elements (music, dance, poetry, scenography), opera was above all a vehicle for a unique reach of the human voice. This was something much more potent than "beautiful singing." What was released by the dramatic and musical occasion of opera was a substance experienced as sublime, virtually transhuman (in part because it was often transgendered), and so erotically affecting as to constitute a species of ravishment. (Think of the swoons and delirium that Farinelli and the other legendary castrati of the eighteenth and early nineteenth centuries provoked in their publics, among men and women both—echoed, in diminuendo, by the adulation offered the great bel canto singers of our own century.) The model register was soaring, feminine; the gender line was arbitrary (men sang women's parts) and opera aroused emotions, excesses of reaction identified as feminine.

A more civically responsible idea of the ecstasies delivered by opera emerged when the devoted audience expanded from its aristocratic core to a much larger public, and attendance at "opera houses" became a ritual of urban bourgeois life. Opera experienced as preeminently a vehicle for the voice declined in favor of opera as the most inspiring, irresistible form of drama. Singing was a heroic rather than an uncanny enterprise, which furthered the "progressive" idea that the work of the voice and of music were at parity. It is about this time that opera began to reflect the nationalist projects of the European nineteenth century. The enthusiasm produced in opera houses fed on something the audience brought to the occasion: tribal self-congratulation. Being construed as an achievement of a national culture resulted, inevitably, in a certain normalization of opera ecstasies: sexual roles were locked into place; stories chosen (historical or folkloric) were constructed around the contrasts of feminine and masculine traits, vocal and characterological. The model responses of audiences became less outrageously feminine: invigoration, inspiration, exaltation.

It was precisely the composer with the largest ambition for opera, Richard Wagner, who brought this second idea of what opera can be—the apotheosis of a collective spirit—to its greatest, most solemn conclusion, who also ushered in the third, or modern, idea of what opera can be: an isolating, ecstatic commotion of feeling aroused not by the sublime feats of a human voice but by exhausting, relentlessly ecstatic music. The voice rides the music; the music, rather than an independent ideal of vocal virtuosity, makes ever more difficult (initially felt to be impossible) demands on the voice. Music, Wagner's music, depicts the very condition of being flooded by feeling that the uncanny voice once provoked in audiences. The consequence was to weaken the authority of sharply contrasting feminine and masculine styles of emotional reaction—both on the opera stage (for all the masculinist pretensions of Wagnerian ideology) and in the opera public. But how could reinstating the goal of providing an immoderate, ravishing experience not entail a re-feminizing (in terms of the cultural stereotypes) of the most acute pleasure taken in opera?

For Wagner, who created the idea of opera as overwhelming experience—and whose supreme dramatic subject is the progression of consciousness through ecstasy into oblivion—certain strictures about the story still held. Wagner could not have accepted as satisfying any drama left unresolved by an epiphany of acceptance, of understanding. Since Wagner, however, the stories that operas tell are more likely to end with collective dismay, with the defeat of understanding.

To be sure, some of the greatest operas (*L'Incoronazione di Poppea, Così Fan Tutte, Fidelio, Don Carlo, Moses und Aron*) carry real arguments, real debate. But more commonly favored in opera are stories which are, in effect, tragedies of cognition. This is particularly true of what we could properly call modern opera, the transition to which is made by Wagner's last opera, *Parsifal,* whose protagonist enters the story as a child, a holy innocent, a fool. Subsequently, Parsifal does attain enlightenment—offstage. In later versions of this story the naïf remains in a state of unknowing. The central figure of modern opera is often someone in a state of deficient consciousness, of pathological innocence.

Pelléas et Mélisande is one of the masterpieces in this evolution. Upon one of the most traditional opera stories, that of a young man whose love for a woman his own age or younger is thwarted because she is promised or already married to an older relative (*Tristan und Isolde, Don Carlo, Eugene Onegin,* inter alia), is grafted the modern story about not understanding, not knowing, being balked by a mystery; or creating a mystery, by being afflicted by an unexplained injury or suffering.

Dubussy's opera (following the Maeterlinck play, used, almost in its entirety, as the libretto) has its special inflections. We are in the world without clear borders and fixed dimensions of Symbolist enigma: where appearances are known by their shadows or reflections, where debility and inexplicable affliction are equated with voluptuousness, and the emblematic object of desire is a languid childlike woman with art nouveau long hair.

In this kingdom of stretched, fairytale dualities—ancient and juvenile, ill and well, dark and light, wet and dry—is set a neo-Wagnerian tale of yearning and thwarting, of incurable vulnerability. Maeterlinck's drama can be read as an idealization of depression. It can also be seen as a representation, a literalizing, of once widely accepted ideas about physical illness—which attributed many illnesses, tautologically, to an illness-producing atmosphere ("miasma"). The story is set in precisely such a damp, sun-deprived environment, replete with water sources and subterranean spaces. Debussy began at the play's second scene, with Mélisande at a forest spring: "une petite fille qui pleure au bord de l'eau." (It was surely not for lack of thematic aptness that he cut the first scene of Maeterlinck's play: a chorus of castle servants calling for water.) The omnipresence of water, which generally signifies purity—or emotional volatility—here signifies a generalized unhealthiness.

Most characters are ill (Pelléas' father, Pelléas' friend Marcellus) or wounded (in the course of the story, Golaud) or infirm (the grandfather, Arkel) or physically weak (Golaud's little son, Yniold, who sings of his inability to lift a stone.) Mélisande, of course, is the epitome of fragility—and dies of a wound that, the doctor says, would not kill a bird. (In Maeterlinck's play, the doctor adds, "Elle est née sans raison . . . pour mourir; et elle meurt sans raison . . .") Every reference to Mélisande emphasizes her smallness (her hands are always her "petites mains"), her untouchability (her first words are "Ne me touchez pas! Ne me touchez pas!"). Her benign discoverer, Golaud, who appears to her like a giant—and, possibly, a rapist—wins Mélisande by promising not to touch her, and by avowing his own vulnerability ("Je suis perdu aussi"). But when he brings Mélisande back to his family and begins to treat his child-bride as a woman, he becomes, despite himself, a brute.

Thus the love of Pelléas and Mélisande cannot be consummated not because the young woman is married to an older relative of the young man, the usual story, but because she is too fragile, sexually immature. Any adult sexuality would constitute an aggression against the heroine. Golaud is the story's one normally mature male character—in contrast to the ancient grandfather, whose request to kiss Mélisande is ostentatiously chaste, and to Golaud's young half-brother, still a boy, who, when he wishes to embrace and be embraced by Mélisande, wraps himself in the part of her body that is not solid, not flesh: her hair. Mélisande seems endowed with a body only for others to marvel at its delicacy. It is startling to realize (I have never seen it depicted in any production of the opera) that Mélisande would be nine months pregnant when she and Pelléas finally do confess their love to each other, only immediately to be torn apart by the jealous Golaud. But her altered, swollen body is unmentionable, perhaps unstageable, and, in a certain sense, unthinkable. It is as if Mélisande herself cannot realize she is pregnant (and therefore a woman), for the same reason that, at the story's close, she cannot take in that she now has a daughter and is about to die.

Eventually the lovers do embrace, body to body, but this moment of shared immolation-in-feeling is cut short, to be followed by amnesia (Mélisande) and excruciating mental confusion (Golaud). Mélisande doesn't remember that Pelléas has been slain by Golaud, isn't aware that she has just given birth ("Je ne sais pas ce que je dis . . . Je ne sais pas ce que je sais . . . Je ne dis plus ce que je veux . . ."), and is genuinely incapable of giving the frantically bereaved Golaud the relief of knowing that, however much he regrets what he has done, he was not wrong in suspecting that Mélisande and Pelléas were in love.

The well-intentioned Golaud has turned into one of opera's remorseful, inadvertent murderers, who kills an innocent woman whom he truly loves. For in this story in which not just a protagonist but everyone feels inadequate, helpless, baffled by what she or he is feeling, Golaud is the only character physically capable of violence. Mental deficiency or frustrated understanding (combined with feelings of helplessness) is, indeed, a recipe for violence. Like *Wozzeck* and *Lulu*, like *Bluebeard's Castle*, *Pelléas et Mélisande* is a story of blind cruelty—with the difference that the cruelties perpetrated are not transactions between adult men and women but of adults against children. Mélisande is a lost child, whom Golaud rescues and pledges to protect but cannot help destroying; in the anguish of jealousy he also manhandles his little son. But all this does not make the ogre any less a victim—like Wozzeck, like Peter Grimes, Golaud is innocently guilty—and therefore a proper object of the audience's pity.

Pity for the innocent lovers; pity for Yniold and the infant Mélisande has left; and pity for Golaud—*Pelléas et Mélisande* completes the process begun long ago whereby opera exalts the feelings regarded as feminine. No work that is now part of opera's standard repertory is so devoid of the triumphalist accents by which opera, traditionally, gives such pleasure. A robust art (compared to, say, chamber music), opera has specialized in broad—broadly contrasting, broadly legible—emotions. The emotional stream of Debussy's masterpiece is deliberately narrower: he wagers on a more harrowing, more finely calibrated intensity. But the great modern tragedies of deficient consciousness propose their own voluptuous standards as they rise to an ecstasy of lament. Debussy's portrayal of lacrimae rerum is unlike any other in opera: it must be the saddest opera ever composed. (The only rival of *Pelléas et Mélisande* in this respect is *Wozzeck*, which also ends on the excruciating presence of a just-orphaned child.) As the heartbroken Arkel sings: "Mais la tristesse, Golaud . . . mais la tristesse de toute que l'on voit!"

Martha Nussbaum

Victims and Agents

The principal characters in ancient Greek tragedy are often depicted as victims of circumstances beyond their control. They ask
for compassion and help by pointing out that they are victims,
that they did not bring disaster (enslavement, rape, hunger,
death of loved ones) upon themselves. Consider one central case,
Sophocles' *Philoctetes,* produced in 409 B.C. at a time when Athens, involved in a costly war, had good reason to ponder the toll
taken on human beings by disasters not of their own making.

Philoctetes was a good man and a good soldier. On his way
to Troy to fight with the Greeks in the Trojan War, he had a
terrible accident. He stepped by mistake into a sacred shrine,
and his foot was bitten by the serpent who guarded the shrine. It
began to ooze with a foul-smelling pus, and his cries of agony
disrupted the religious observances of the troops. The com-
manders therefore abandoned him on a deserted island, with no
resources but his bow and arrows. Ten years later, having learned
that they cannot win the war without him, they return, determined to trick him into rejoining them. Sick, lonely, hungry,
exhausted from hunting his own food, Philoctetes still longs for
friendship and activity. He greets his visitors with joy, delighted

that he can interact with others after his long solitude. And he asks them to have compassion for him, seeing the troubles that life has brought him, troubles from which no human is safe:

> . . . Have compassion for me.
> Look how men live, always precariously
> balanced between good and bad fortune.
> If you are out of trouble, watch for danger.
> And when you live well, then think the hardest
> About life, lest ruin take you unawares.

Compassion proves crucial to the subsequent plot. The younger of the two leaders, Neoptolemus, witnesses an attack of Philoctetes' terrible pain. At this point, he is seized by what he calls "a fearful compassion," a compassion that strikes terror into him because it makes him see that the plan to snare Philoctetes into helping the Greek war effort by deceit is morally wrong. Reflecting, he recognizes that they ought not to use this man merely as a means of political ends. Seeing Philoctetes in his pain, he sees him as human and therefore worthy of respect. Sympathy for weakness and respect for human agency are allies, because once Neoptolemus understands the magnitude of Philoctetes' suffering, he can no longer regard him as simply a thing to be manipulated, or an animal to be pushed around. He cries out in pain himself, with a sharp cry of *moral* pain (guilt at his deception) that mimics Philoctetes' inarticulate cry of bodily pain. From then on he refuses to lie to him, insisting that Philoctetes must be treated as someone entitled to decide without being manipulated.

In our society today, we often hear that we have a stark and binary choice between regarding people as agents and regarding them as victims. We hear this contrast in debates about social welfare programs: it is said that to give people various forms of social support is to treat them as mere victims of life's ills, rather than to respect them as agents, capable of working to better their lot.

We hear the same contrast in recent feminist debates, where we are told that respecting women as agents is incompatible with a strong concern to protect them from rape, sexual harassment, and other forms of unequal treatment. To protect women is to presume that they can't fight on their own against this ill treatment: this, in turn, is to undermine their dignity by treating them as mere victims. For Katie Roiphe, for example, "the image that emerges from feminist preoccupations with rape and sexual harassment is that of women as victims."[1] an image that reinforces an antiquated perception of women as frail and helpless. Betty Friedan, similarly, criticizes the rape-crisis movement: "Obsession with rape, even offering Band-Aids to its victims, is a kind of wallowing in that victim state, that impotent rage, that sterile polarization."[2] Naomi Wolf decries a "victim feminism" that "[c]harges women to identify with powerlessness."[3]

We hear the same contrast, again, in debates about criminal sentencing, where we are urged to think that any sympathy shown to a criminal defendant on account of a deprived social background or other misfortunes such as child sexual abuse is, once more, a denial of the defendant's human dignity. Supreme Court Justice Clarence Thomas, for example, went so far as to say, in a 1994 speech, that when black and poor people are shown sympathy for their background when they commit crimes, they are being treated like children, "or even worse, treated like animals without a soul."[4]

Interestingly, we do not take this attitude in all areas. Even if we believe that people are capable of much resourcefulness under adversity, we still hold that law should protect them against many of life's ills. We all know that writers and artists are capable of extraordinary resourcefulness and cunning when their

---

[1] Katie Roiphe. *The Morning After: Sex, Fear, and Feminism* (Boston: Little, Brown, 1993), p. 6.
[2] Betty Friedan. *The Second Stage* (New York: Summit Books, 1981), p. 362.
[3] Naomi Wolf, *Fire With Fire: The New Female Power and How to Use It* (New York: Fawcett, 1993), p. 136.
[4] "Justice Thomas blames 'rights revolution' for increase in black crime." *Chicago Tribune*, 17 May 1994.

freedom of speech is suppressed by a brutal regime: and yet we do not hold that we are undermining their dignity, or turning them into soulless victims, when we defend strong legal protections for the freedoms of speech and press, protections that make it unnecessary for them to struggle against tyranny in order to publish their work. Some people have held this: the philosopher Friedrich Nietzsche wrote that liberties of speech and press undermine "the will to assume responsibility for oneself," making people "small, cowardly, and hedonistic." Calling John Stuart Mill a "flathead," he pronounced that "[t]he highest type of free men should be sought where the highest resistance is constantly overcome: five steps from tyranny, close to the threshold of the danger of servitude."[5] But we do not accept Nietzsche's view about liberty. Legal guarantees, we think, do not erode agency: they create a framework within which people can develop and exercise agency.

Again, we do not believe that strong law enforcement in the area of personal property turns property-holders into victims without dignity. Laws protect citizens from theft and fraud: these laws are backed up by state power, in the form of a police force supported by tax money. Nonetheless, we usually do not hear arguments that such uses of public money turn property owners into victims. Even though we are of course aware that people are sometimes capable of fighting to defend their homes and their possessions from theft, we think it's a lot better for law and the police to get involved, so people don't have to spend all their time fending off attack, and can get on with their other business. Often, Americans support even stronger protections of personal property, without thinking that in that way they are turning property owners into helpless victims. Those who support a repeal of the capital gains tax do not hold that this handout from the government would turn investors into victims without honor. Even though they are aware that investors are quite capable of doing

---

[5]Friedrich Nietzsche, "Skirmishes of an Untimely One," from *Twilight of the Idols*. in *The Viking Portable Nietzsche,* ed. and trans. Walter Kaufmann (New York: Viking Penguin, 1959), §38.

pretty well even with current tax levels, they do not regard this legal change as producing passivity or turning people into soulless animals. If, then, we hear political actors saying such things about women, and poor people, and racial minorities, we should first of all ask why they are being singled out: what is there about the situation of being poor, or female, or black that turns help into condescension, compassion into insult?

The *Philoctetes,* I believe, helps us to understand this issue better. Greek tragedy is preoccupied with the portrayal of human beings as victims. As Aristotle says, its governing emotions, the emotions that hold the audience to the plot, are compassion and fear. Compassion, as he tells us, requires three thoughts: that the suffering we see is significant, has "size": that the suffering person did not deserve to suffer to this extent; and that we too share certain general human possibilities with the suffering person—so we too, or people we know and care about, may suffer similar catastrophes. The occasions for compassion that he mentions are the common bases of tragic plots: illness, old age, hunger, disability, solitude, loss of one's friends, loss of one's children, loss of one's citizenship or money or well-being. Sometimes people face such disasters because of their own wickedness: but, as Aristotle says, tragedy focuses on cases where this is not so, where a pretty good person gets hit very hard by life. Our compassion itself acknowledges that Philoctetes doesn't deserve to suffer as he does; and our fear acknowledges that something similar might happen to us, or someone dear to us.

So, that means, we are seeing Philoctetes as a victim. And so, commonly, we see a host of other tragic characters: women who get raped in wartime, little children who are sold into slavery, men who lose their families or see their loved ones being raped, and so on. When we see them as victims, we are seeing something true about them and about life: we see that people can be harmed on a large scale, in ways that even the best efforts cannot prevent. As the *Philoctetes* suggests, this gives people of good will strong incentives for doing something about such disasters, and bringing relief to the afflicted.

And further, the *Philoctetes* suggests that the victim shows us something about our own lives: we see that we are not any different from the people whose fate we are watching, that we too are vulnerable to misfortune, and that we therefore have reason to fear a similar reversal. But if we are ourselves vulnerable, we had better think about what we would wish if we were to find ourselves in a situation of tragic reversal. If people think themselves exempt from misfortune, they can easily harden themselves to the cry of the afflicted. But if they truly see their own vulnerability, they will move close in thought to the victims they see, and this very movement will lead them to want structures that provide support for people against life's ungovernable disasters. Rousseau puts it this way:

> Human beings are by nature neither kings nor nobles nor courtiers nor rich. All are born naked and poor, all are subject to the misfortunes of life, to difficulties, ills, needs, pains of all sorts. Finally, all are condemned to death. . . . Each may be tomorrow what the one whom he helps is today. . . . Do not, therefore, accustom your pupil to regard the sufferings of the unfortunate and the labors of the poor from the height of his glory. . . . Make him understand well that the fate of these unhappy people can be his, that all their ills are there in the ground beneath his feet. . . . Show him all the vicissitudes of fortune.[6]

Rousseau thought that to focus on the pain of others, through stories that arouse emotion, was a good way of reminding people of the truth of their own condition and of giving them incentives to make the lot of the victim less bad than it would otherwise be.

But isn't this treating people as passive rather than active? Is this victim role compatible with being seen as an agent? En-

---

[6]Jean Jacques Rousseau. *Emile*, trans. Allan Bloom (New York: Basic Books, 1979), pp. 222, 224. I have altered Bloom's translation in several places, in particular substituting "human being" for "man."

tirely compatible, as we see from Philoctetes' story. We see him as a victim, in the sense that we see his loneliness, his poverty, his illness as things that he did not bring upon himself. But we also are led by the play to see him as capable of activity of many kinds. We hear him reason, we see his commitments to friendship and justice. Seeing that he can't be active in some parts of his life is fully compatible with observing that in other ways he remains very active. Seeing this, we are led to admire the dignity with which he confronts these ills, and to notice the yearning for full activity that he displays even in the most acute misery.

It is precisely this combination of dignified agency with disaster out of which the tragic response is made. If we just saw the hero as a worm or an ant, a pathetic low creature grovelling in the mud, we would not have the intense concern we do have with the forces that have inflicted suffering on him. Sophocles takes great pains to show Philoctetes' suffering as fully human: even when he screams out in unbearable pain, his cry is metrical—a human cry of pain. What inspires our compassion (and also our self-interested fear) is in fact this combination of human dignity with disaster. It is because we respect his humanity that we come to hate the forces that bear down upon him, and to think that something ought to be done about them. It is precisely because Philoctetes is shown to be capable of a human use of his faculties that Neoptolemus eventually shrinks from treating him like an animal or a thing. Tragedy shows us that disasters do strike at the heart of human action: they don't just cause superficial discomfort, they impede mobility, planning, citizenship, ultimately life itself. On the other hand, when we see that such a disaster strikes a human being, it is then that we feel the sense of tragic compassion: for we don't want humanity to be wasted, or even callously pushed around.

Let me now return to the three contemporary issues, and see how tragedy helps us think about them. We should begin by observing that all Americans in countless ways receive financial assistance from government, and are highly dependent on that assistance. State money and state power support laws without which most of us would not know how to live: laws protecting public order, personal safety, private property, the ability to make a binding contract, freedoms of assembly, worship, speech, and press. Of course people could learn to live without the expenditure of public money protecting those rights, but as a society we have decided that we think human agency is worthy of a basic concern that involves protecting these rights as prerequisites of meaningful human action.

Take the case of poverty and welfare reform. There are of course many complex empirical questions in this area, and this is why every society must experiment with programs and policies to understand their effects. It's not evident that direct relief is the best way to promote flourishing lives, and we should explore other alternatives. But there is one thing we should not say. We should not say that financial assistance for basic food, child welfare, and other prerequisites of meaningful human life is a way of dehumanizing people or turning them into passive victims. Human beings can struggle against all sorts of obstacles; frequently they succeed. But middle-class parents typically reveal in their own lives the belief that young children should not be hungry or neglected, that they should have the basic necessities of life provided to them so that they can develop their agency richly and fully. It is strange that we so often speak differently about the poor, suggesting that cutting off basic social support is a way of encouraging agency in poor mothers and children and improving their character, rather than a way of stifling agency, or stunting it before it gets a chance to develop. If we do respect agency and its dignity, we owe it a chance to develop and flourish.

The late Justice William Brennan made precisely this connection between dignity and luck in one of his most memorable opinions—in *Goldberg v. Kelly* (1970), a case that established that welfare rights could not be abridged without a hearing:

From its founding the Nation's basic commitment has been to foster the dignity and well-being of all persons within its borders. We have come to recognize that forces not within the control of the poor contribute to

their poverty. . . . Welfare, by meeting the basic demands of subsistence, can help bring within the reach of
the poor the same opportunities that are available to
others to participate meaningfully in the life of the community. . . . Public assistance, then, is not mere charity,
but a means to "promote the general Welfare, and secure the Blessings of Liberty to ourselves and our Pos-
terity."

It is certainly legitimate, and even desirable, for states to experiment with different welfare strategies. But something more sinister is currently in the air, a backing away from the "basic
commitment" to dignity and well-being that Brennan finds, plausibly, at the heart of our traditions.

Think now of women who demand more adequate enforcement of laws against rape and sexual harassment. They are asking
the state to do something about this problem. Are they therefore
asking to be treated as people who have no ability to stand up for
their rights? Of course not. Women do manage to struggle
against sexual harassment. Most working women of my generation have done so—sometimes with relatively little damage to
their careers, sometimes with great damage. But should women
be required to wage this struggle? Or do we think that a woman's
dignity demands that she not have to fight this struggle all the
time, that part of the respect we owe to a woman as an agent is
to let her get on with her work in an atmosphere free from such
intimidation and pressure? It seems plausible that women will be
more productive in the economy and in their homes with these
pressures minimized.

Finally, let us consider Justice Thomas's observations about
criminal defendants. This is the most difficult of the cases we
have before us: it requires us to depart from the comfortable
framework of ancient tragedy. Sophocles shows us good people
whose suffering was not their own fault. Even in tragedy, however, we now notice, the distinction between innocent and
blameworthy conduct is not always terribly clear. Aristotle insisted that the hero should not be shown as falling through wick-

edness, or deep-seated defect of character. He preferred plots where the bad consequence came about through a chain that involved a mistake of some type made by the leading character, sometimes innocent, but sometimes at least partly blameworthy. His general attitude to such errors was that we should be forgiving of people who go wrong, seeing the difficulty of judging well in circumstances of great complexity. So we may begin our response to Justice Thomas by pointing out that even basically good people go wrong, and that a forgiving attitude may be appropriate to the general frailty and weakness of human judgment. In judging a person's blameworthy errors in a forgiving spirit, we record that we ourselves are not perfect in judgment, even when we have the best intentions.

But what if the person who is asking for our sympathy is a criminal who has done bad things from a genuinely bad character? Justice Thomas says that it is insulting to a black defendant to treat him as not responsible for his criminal acts on account of a bad social background. To deny responsibility is to treat the criminal as no more than a "soulless animal." And this claim seems plausible if we were to say that people who grow up in the inner city will all, as a group, be treated as not guilty by reason of insanity, that would indeed be to negate their human potential.

But this is not the way the issue typically comes up in the law. The law typically uses a conventional standard of sanity when assessing guilt or innocence, and introduces the deprived background in a separate phase of the trial, the sentencing phase, in order to plead for some leniency. And in fact, there is a long tradition in the law that this sympathetic assessment of the defendant's life story in the penalty phase, far from treating people like animals, is an essential part of treating them as fully human. An opinion written by Justice Potter Stewart in a 1976 capital sentencing case, *Woodson v. North Carolina,* held that a process lacking this opportunity to hear the life story

> excludes from consideration . . . the possibility of compassionate or mitigating factors stemming from the diverse frailties of humankind. It treats all persons con-

victed of a designated offense not as uniquely individual
human beings, but as members of a faceless, undifferen-
tiated mass. . . .

So Stewart is claiming more or less the opposite of what Thomas
claimed: he says that when we *do not* take the opportunity to
show compassion to a defendant's background, we treat that person as not fully human. What does he mean? The law's two-stage
process asks us to assess guilt or innocence by looking to the
state of mind with which the person did the act: if the person is
not insane, he is responsible. But it says, as well, that people are
not always fully in control of the factors that form their state of
mind. And here we get back to tragedy. The standard tragic
hero, like Philoctetes, grows to adulthood, becomes a good person, and then gets clobbered by life. But people get clobbered by
life, sometimes, before they become good and grow to adulthood. The sentencing process recognizes that we may at times
encounter a criminal who meets the conditions of basic responsibility, but whose moral development was subject to unusual
hardships, and who therefore deserves to be seen as a kind of
victim of life, one who did not get the support that life should
have provided. When we recognize the "diverse frailties of humankind" and the way in which these are brought out by social
circumstances, we recognize that few human beings are so firm
that they can resist temptations to wrong, even under the prolonged effect of extremely bad circumstances. Sometimes they
will make the type of error that is compatible with a basically
good character. But sometimes damage has set in earlier, and the
character itself is deformed by what it has encountered. Even
this type of criminal defendant can be regarded as not a breed
apart, intrinsically evil, but a human being like us, with diverse
frailties and weaknesses, who has encountered circumstances—
whether personal or social—that bring out those weaknesses in
the worst possible way. And this, of course, creates incentives,
once again, to think hard about those circumstances, so that we
do not put people under pressures that many normal agents cannot stand.

✿   ✿   ✿

In November 1996, I was mugged while walking from my office to a meeting on the other side of the Midway at 5 o'clock in the evening. My assailant was a short, timid, young black man, only about 5'2", wearing a thick parka and a blue wool hat. He said he had a gun, although I wasn't sure this was true: he seemed very inexperienced and tentative in his actions. After a certain amount of negotiation, I managed to get away losing only the cash in my wallet. But I spent some hours the next day in the police station, looking at hundreds of mug shots and talking to Officer Queenola Smith about the crime. I didn't find my suspect, and Officer Smith was not surprised. Given the recent cutbacks in welfare support and the high unemployment, she said, so many people have no money for their families, no warm clothes, and not enough food as winter approaches and the holidays draw close. So there are many new offenders.

Officer Smith was a very zealous officer; she boasted to me of the dangerous felons she had apprehended, the high-stakes chases she had conducted with aplomb. But she also had a sense of tragedy. And she saw these criminals not as a breed apart, but as members of her own community and her own race, who deserved a chance to exercise basic human agency, and therefore deserved the basic support to make that possible. Most who lose that support are like Philoctetes, good people hammered by circumstances, and it is—or at least it should be—easy to sympathize with them. But some get pushed harder and earlier, and don't resist the temptation to commit a crime. She did not deny that the mugger was responsible for his act. But she thought it was a humanly comprehensible act, an act many of us would have committed had we faced similar pressures. She saw my assailant as both victim and agent: someone trying to get a job, to support a family, someone hit hard by all kinds of circumstances, from the welfare cuts to unemployment to the harshness of the Chicago winter. She said in effect, see how hard it is to be good, with adversities like these. Now Queenola Smith didn't think we should stop arresting these criminals—as I say, she was proud of her work. But, she argued, we should think hard about our own responsibility in creating a situation in which some people so unequally face poverty and closed doors, and also, therefore, the temptation to do wrong. That's what it would mean to take their human agency seriously, and not to treat them as animals who could not help being bad.

A few days later the president of the university phoned me and said, "I heard about this terrible thing that happened." And I felt that we were talking about the wrong event—for the loss of $40 by a professor was a trivial thing, compared to the tragedy that was going on all around us in our community. Who is the victim, and who the agent?

As a society we are in grave danger of losing our sense of tragedy. I am arguing that if we lose this sense of tragic compassion for people who unequally suffer the misfortunes of life— including both those who remain good and those who turn to the bad—we are in danger of losing our own humanity. We are in danger of forgetting something central about ourselves—that we don't become agents automatically; that our own relatively comfortable lives typically need, but also get, much support from government and from the material world; that we too would suffer terribly, and perhaps even become worse, were that support to be withdrawn. By thinking like the audience at an ancient tragedy, we may possibly move closer to building a community that does indeed "foster the dignity and well-being of all persons within its borders." "Thus from our weakness," Rousseau observed, "our fragile happiness is born."

Aging and Fate

Jenny Diski

At Fifty

I'm nine years old, in bed, in the dark. The detail in the room is perfectly clear. I am lying on my back. I have a greeny-gold quilted eiderdown covering me. I have just calculated that I will be 50 years old in 1997. "Fifty" and "1997" don't mean a thing to me, aside from being an answer to an arithmetic question I set myself. I try it differently. "I will be 50 in 1997." 1997 doesn't matter. "I will be 50." The statement is absurd. I am nine. "I will be ten" makes sense. "I will be 13" has a dreamlike maturity about it. "I will be 50" is simply a paraphrase for another sense-less statement I make to myself at night: "I will be dead one day." "One day I won't be." I have a great determination to feel the sentence as a reality. But it always escapes me. "I will be dead" comes with a picture of a dead body on a bed. But it's mine, a nine-year-old body. When I make it old, it becomes someone else. I can't imagine myself dead. I can't imagine my-self dying. Either the effort or the failure to do so makes me feel panicky.

Being 50 is not being dead, but it is being old, inconceiv-ably old, for me, that is. I know other people are old, other people are 50, and I will be 50 if I don't die beforehand. But the best I can do is to imagine someone who is not me, though not someone I know, being 50. She looks like an old lady; the way old ladies currently look. She looks like someone else. I can't connect me thinking about her with the fact that I will be her in 41 years' time. She has lived through and known 41 years to which I have no access. I can't believe I will become her, though I know, factually, that I must. I can't dress myself in her clothes and her flesh and know what it feels like being her. This is immensely frustrating. I do the next best thing. I send a message out into the future, etch into my brain cells a memo to the other person, who will be me grown to be 50, to remember this moment, this very moment, this actual second when I am nine, in bed, in the dark, trying to imagine being 50.

I was 50 in the summer of 1997 and for the past year I have been recalling the nine-year-old who tried to imagine me. I mean, I have been recalling her trying to imagine me, at that moment, in bed, in the dark, some 41 years ago. I have finally received the memo. It is easier for me to acknowledge her than the other way round, for all that I have learned about the unreliability of memory, because I have lived the missing 41 years she could know nothing about. There is a track back. The vividness of her making a note to remember the moment when she is 50 is startling. But it's not a simple, direct link. I have the moment, but the person I connect with is someone whose future I know. I do not know the nine-year-old as she was then, at all; the one who had not yet experienced the life I led between her and me. I can't imagine her as a reality, in her striving to understand what kind of 50-year-old woman she would be, because she doesn't exist anymore except as a pinpoint in time. She now has an indelible relation to me back through time, that I could not have for her aiming forward. There is a sense of vertigo, something quite dizzying about having arrived at the unimaginable point she reached out towards, at recalling her message and being in a position—but not able—to answer it: here I am, it's like this.

It is not just the nine-year-old's illusive reality that prevents me from responding, it is also my own present inability, aged 50, to imagine what it is like to be 50. I've heard a lot about it, read plenty, seen numbers of 50-year-olds, both depicted and in real life, but that seems to be no help at all. This isn't surprising. The 50 that I seek to understand is the same 50 I wondered about as a child, it has nothing much to do with having lived for 50 years or more. It is, as Richard Shweder and the other anthropologists insist in the coyly named collection of ethnographical essays *Welcome to Middle Age!*, a "cultural fiction."[*] Faced with the label, I find it hard not to wonder what use such a designation could be. Presumably everything cultural is a fiction by definition, and come to that everything natural is fiction too since it is named as such and viewed always by acculturated eyes. "Fictional," Shweder explains, does not mean "unreal"; he uses the term, he says, in an (oh dear) "affirmative Post-Modern sense." Things that are fictions are "fabricated, manufactured, invented or designed, but they are not necessarily false."

It's funny how, when social theory is teased out for the unspecialised reader, it splats to earth like a water bomb. The term "cultural fiction" is manufactured, but it's not necessarily false, it just returns us to the knowledge we started with. The designation of middle age as a cultural fiction is necessary, however, to make this book of essays more than a Disney travelogue of just so stories. "Middle age" we learn is simply the story we tell ourselves in this part of the world at this time about a stage in life that has an alternative narrative in other places. That is the premise. "There are alternative ways of representing the temporal dimension of life without relying on the idea of middle age. For example, in some cultural worlds described in this book, the stages of life (including mature adulthood) are represented in terms of a social history of role transitions within the context of a residential kinship group." The last phrase, far from radically resetting notions of middle age, seems to describe our current Western point of view quite as well as it describes any alternative cultural formulation of the middle years of life. But there is a real sense of crusade from Shweder and other contributors to

---

[*]*Welcome to Middle Age! (And Other Cultural Fictions)*, edited by Richard Shweder (Chicago, 302 pp., 14 July, 0 226 75607 6).

enlighten us, and show how we could have other, better ways of designating mature adulthood. Those better views ("better fictions," if we are using Shweder's terminology) are, of course, to be found in faraway places with strange-sounding names.

A definition of the current Western discourse on middle age is offered by Margaret Morganroth Gullette, who opens the debate with an evangelically strong social-constructionist approach in which she calls for "critical age studies," which start with the assumption that "little in midlife ageing is bodily and that nothing considered 'bodily' is unaffected by culture." It's radical stuff, demanding a new negative category "middle-ageism," born of power, hierarchy and resistance; familiar to readers of Foucault everywhere. Middle age in our culture is a decline narrative that begins at adolescence and peaks in the forties and fifties as midlife crisis. Since it is taken to be a cultural category, there appears to be no way out of this discourse; the "ideology of 'decline' raining over us" includes those who claim to experience no such thing: "there may be some people for whom life-course optimism or pessimism is a solid and relatively unshakeable given, so that they infallibly pick out only those elements of the available discourses that support their chosen worldview." The counter-discourse is dependent on the prevailing discourse. There's no wriggling out of it, Gullette informs us. Those who refuse the narratives of "crisis-and-fall or crisis-and-cure" are "also, but unwittingly, taking a stance toward midlife decline ideology: they are supporting it."

For most of my life, I've felt quite cheery about aging. It always seemed to me to be better to be older, and on the whole my experience has borne this suspicion out. I have, with each decade, better liked the way my life was; there has been increasing real autonomy, less anxiety, more confidence, greater physical pleasure, fewer physical pressures. This, of course, is all predicated on good luck and relative affluence. I don't feel clever about it, only remarkably fortunate. Even so, I have to report, among other signs, a certain loss of muscle tone, an alarming decline in the ability to recall names and the reason I have just walked into the living room, and the arithmetical certainty that I am nearer to inescapable death than I have ever been before. As a woman on a plane bound for sun and sea said to her friend to explain her anxiety about wearing bikinis, "My gravity's going." Of course, we might rejoice in the new sensuality of soft, pliable flesh, and be grateful for the opportunity to let go of names that no longer concern us. We could look on short-term absentmind-edness as a newfound advantage: the excitement and infinite pos-sibilities of arriving in a room without a clue why you are there are surely more interesting than just going to the cupboard to get a new roll of lavatory paper. Certainly, there are culturally im-posed feelings about the bodily changes of aging, and let's sup-pose it's possible consciously to alter our attitudes to them. But, for those lacking a conventional religious faith, how are we to celebrate the increasing proximity of death, which includes the loss of all these new advantages we've discovered? When we feel concern about aging, we are not just kowtowing to received opin-ion, we are also gripped by panic at the remorselessness of time. Things are not going to get better, there is a definite direction to the physical changes those in middle age experience, from soft-ening flesh and forgetfulness to arthritic immobility and oblivion. We might be lucky and stay relatively fit and mentally alert until the end, but the end is getting closer faster, and the end is foreordained. What exactly is there to look forward to? How do these other cultures avoid the glummest of conclusions?

The answer in almost all the essays is that they replace a decline narrative with one about life stages. In this view, middle age is a time of authority, less work and higher social standing. What is common to the alternative view is a strong sense of hierarchy. In Samoa, Kenya and rural India, middle life is a time when maximum political power, social status and family respon-sibility (though I'm not sure this follows) are achieved. Those at this stage are functioning at the center of life and therefore are not much given to introspection. In Samoa, the physical move-ment and hard graft of the young are replaced with passive au-thority. Birthdays are insignificant, what matters is where you have got to in the life plan. "In age my parents are only fifty-five and forty-five, but I call them 'old' because I am in a stage of being responsible for taking care of them," one informant explains. In Hindu families in rural India, people live in three- or four-generation families. Parents cease sexual activity when their firstborn son brings home a wife. The youngest daughter-in-law is entirely subservient to the mother-in-law, who rules and runs the house. A twenty-three-year-old daughter-in-law cooks and cleans for a household of twelve and, after washing the feet of her parents-in-law, drinks the water.

We are warned by the authors of this essay, Usha Menon and Richard Shweder, not to make cultural assumptions about this, nor to take a dim Western feminist view of the life of young women. What we see as an appalling daily grind has moral meanings of service to the family. They report relative contentment in their informants: well-being scores an average of 8 on a scale from 0 to 16. Mothers-in-law, of course, report high levels of well-being. But time passes not just for the daughters-in-law who will progress to higher and lighter duties. Mothers-in-law become grandmothers who are marginalized, lonely and feeble. A sense of community may have avoided midlife crisis, and a belief in the hereafter apparently prevented a premature despair at a blank end, but it seems to be replaced by a miserable youth and old age. We are told it is inappropriate to judge these lifestyles negatively, but at the very least my culturally conditioned eyes look without envy on the culturally conditioned contentment described in these pages. These other ways reject the individualism, the narcissism of Western attitudes to the life course. Instead, they embed it in social relations hedged with rigid rules about appropriate aging and duty. This may be a more comfortable way to live, it may even be more virtuous, but we've lost it, for better or worse, and the tales of middle age in other places are not alternative ways of being that we can slip on like a kimono; they are no more than interesting ethnographical data.

So we're stuck with where we are. A notional 50 that is related to but not coterminous with our experience of ourselves. A cultural fiction, but in our present culture, lacking firm rules. In all probability everyone is startled by the fact of their having aged and has to align inner confusion with social perceptions, but in our society the signs are unclear. Beyond the notion of "50" that I had as a child, that I have now, there are no guidelines. How is one supposed to be 50? There used to be a dress code, as clear as Greeks swathed in black, or white-haired old ladies in shawls who were "mothers" in old movies. The nearest thing we have now is people who have stuck to whatever style was fashionable when they were young: the middle-aged in miniskirts, too-black eye makeup and the wrong kind of jeans. "Turn your collar down," I'm warned by my young. "You look Sixties." There are specialist shops. Invisible for most of my life, there is a shop in Kentish Town which, even now, I think of as always closed. When should I begin getting my clothes from here? Inspired by the fieldwork of *Welcome to Middle Age!*, I took a trip to Burston's Jackets and Gowns. It has a permanent window display of shapeless pleated skirts, floral frocks, cardigans and fully fashioned jackets in 100 percent polyester and crimplene and nylon. I toured the double-fronted windows. Middle age isn't expensive. Even the "Model Coat" was just £52, while 'Latest' dresses could be had for as little as £12. I hovered at the door. Inside, clothes were neatly racked and under polythene wraps. Two women I could easily identify as middle-aged were sitting chatting to some children who called one of them Granny. It was my intention to go in and try on some of these clothes, to see if I would be transformed into somebody appropriately "50," but I couldn't get through the door. What if it worked, what if "50" and me converged as I put on the clothes? And what if it didn't work? By which I mean, what if wearing the clothes made no difference to the image I thought I was seeing in the mirror, because the image I have of myself is entirely subjective? I remember sitting opposite a man at dinner, who was wearing a wig so obvious that it was hard to drag your eyes away from it. What, I wondered, did he see when he looked into his mirror before he left the house? Not what I and the others around the table were seeing, surely? Which thought led inexorably to the question of what I saw when I looked in the mirror before leaving the house, and what the other people around the table, included the wigged gent, were seeing when they looked at me.

Ditto the music I listen to. The books I read. The opinions I hold. My sex life. The variables are too great, the truths are too relative for a simple, satisfactory definition of middle age. Here I am, I might say to the nine-year-old, I have turned 50 and it is like . . . well, it's rather like not knowing what 50 is like when you are nine, but with the added certainty now that time is passing and will pass with increasing speed. And time, as I suspected all those years ago, is strictly limited. Time, of course, is another cultural fiction, but from one end of the planet to the other, for each individual, it comes to an end. And no, I am no better at imagining my own death than I was at nine. A memo then, for myself at the moment of death.

Floyd Skloot

Kismet

My brother Philip was buried on the morning of my fiftieth birthday. Earlier that week, he had decided to stop dialysis treatments, so his death was not really a surprise.

But it was a shock. My sister-in-law called just after dawn and I snatched up the phone, turning on my knees, naked, to lean over the bed as though in prayer. Elaine said hello, then issued a sound I did not at first recognize. The phone in our bedroom is an ancient, staticky cordless with a replacement universal antenna that falls off whenever I pick up the unit, so I assumed that the sound was just her voice breaking up over the thousand miles between us.

But my wife Beverly knew at once what she heard coming through the unit and the bones of my skull. She bounded out of bed, ran into the next room, picked up the phone in there and began comforting Elaine before I could let the truth seep in.

We had last seen Philip two months earlier. During that visit, for the first time, he had begun to speak about dying. On Friday night, he interrupted a dinner-table discussion of the virtues of root vegetables to say he thought he had about six months left. Provided he continued receiving dialysis four times a week.

I'm okay with this. I've had a good life. He gestured toward Elaine and his left hand landed on top of his buttered bread, which made him chuckle, then shrug, then eat the chocolate chip cookie he had been hiding in his right hand.

Near the end, when he weighed 264 pounds, my brother was a vestige of his former self. He sat quietly in his recliner or wheelchair, listening, a mellow smile on his face, gray hair flattened in back and spread like a fan above his ears. When he spoke his voice was deeper and slower than it had ever been, tamped down. What he had to say was offered in counterpoint, as comment on what he heard rather than as part of the main melody.

Philip was 57. In his apartment, he liked to strip right down to basics, white boxer shorts and v-neck tee shirt, or maybe a pair of loose sweatpants while the air conditioning blasted. Without the black wraparound shades, he kept his sightless eyes closed. Without the false teeth, he kept his mouth shut but loved to work his gums sideways across each other. His skin, stippled with odd growths, bore the soft ocher shade of renal failure and stung whenever he was touched. There was a hump at the base of his neck. He could barely walk, soles numbed, muscles atrophied, balance in shambles. He needed help to stand and could not get himself up off the toilet or take a shower by himself. He had trouble breathing and when he slept, slumped in the recliner, his face erupted in tics.

He looked exactly like our grandmother Kate in the months before she died in 1965. She was then 79.

In his heyday my brother weighed 375 pounds but moved with uncanny grace, as though the planet held him in place with a different kind of force than the rest of us. He was a successful gambler, a savvy player of games, an unlikely ladies' man. He knew odds; he counted cards. Over the years, he sold pressure-sensitive papers or envelopes or shoes or metals, always expanding his territory, on-the-go. When he could no longer walk well or see well enough to drive, he sold computer hardware by phone, what he disdainfully called Inside Sales. He was the kind of guy you instinctively trust, a sell-sand-to-the-Saudis type, and his word was good. He was the joke a minute sort, the life of the party, suavely smiling, cigarette cupped in his palm, wise to the ways of the world. Even blind, he would give his wife directions when they drove together through the streets of San Francisco, saying "turn left here," or "bear right at that Texaco station." He knew what he knew. He loved the spotlight, the lead, and he was never very interested in blending into the background.

For casual wear, my brother favored brightly colored shirts and contrasting golf slacks. He claimed visual space, flaunting his size, proclaiming that he had nothing to hide. I have a photograph of Philip posed beside his tall, slender wife before a fancy evening out; he is wearing a red sports jacket with fuschia accents, a fuschia tie and red shoes to go with the white shirt and red-and-white checked slacks. As always, the thick black hair is carefully pompadoured.

To eat with him was to witness pleasure carried to the level of torture. Restaurant owners and chefs fawned over him, the maître d'hotel and maître de cuisine lavishing attention on his vast table of friends, waitresses bringing free desserts and aperitifs. He tipped everyone twice. I remember eating a five-course dinner with him one Saturday night at an Italian restaurant in New York's East Village, Mario's, then stopping for donuts on the short drive to his home in New Jersey, then watching him eat a sandwich before going to bed. My sleep that night was one endless nightmare. Early next morning, there was a full table of traditional Jewish Sunday brunch foods, bagels and nova with cream cheese, smoked sable and sturgeon, whitefish chubs, lox wings, ruggelach.

Afterwards, we drove to the batting range and swatted line drives in the blistering August heat. I weighed less than half of what he weighed, but felt rotund as Babe Ruth and was not sure I could manage a swing without my arms thumping my belly.

Our grandfather Philip, my brother's namesake, was born in the old country in the fall of 1880. The old country was Russia or Poland or Lithuania, depending on the year in question, though in the late nineteenth century it was part of the Russian empire designated as The Pale of Settlement by Tsar Alexander III, the only place where Jews were legally authorized to settle. Skluts came from Volozhin, between Minsk and Vilnius, in what was known as White Russia and is now part of Belarus.

It was and remains a small town. But its renowned Jewish Academy or Yeshiva was known throughout the Jewish world, a place that was led by such great rabbis as Rav Chaim or Rav Joseph Baer Soloveichik and that attracted talmudic scholars. The Hebrew poet Hayyim Nahman Bialik and essayist/fiction writer Micah Joseph Berdichevsky studied there.

As Paul Johnson notes in his book *A History of the Jews,* "In the last half-century of imperial Russia, the official Jewish regulations formed an enormous monument to human cruelty." It was a preview for Nazi policy. To be a Jew in Volozhin was to be constantly at risk from Poles, Cossacks, Catholics, Tsarist loyalists, Nazis, and to survive required both vigilance and resilience.

Beset by violence, transformed by invasion the way a cell is transformed by a virus, Volozhin's destiny was to be always under attack. Like a human body perpetually challenged by pathogens, the community's collective defense mechanisms became rewired, organized to be continually on alert. We became a people focused on self-defense, locked into patterns of resistance, guarded even when there was no threat.

Prayer, communal solidarity, the development of niche skills, bribery, conversion—these were typical external forms of coping. In *A Promised Land,* Mary Antin's classic 1912 memoir of east European Jewish life and immigration, a sense of resignation underlies Jewish creativity in the face of continued calamity: "But what can one do? the people said, with a shrug of the shoulders that expresses the helplessness of the Pale. What can one do? One must live."

At constant risk, people either adapted or perished. Current theories about evolutionary biology suggest that there would have been internal forms of coping as well, biological adaptations to prolonged stress that mirrored the external adaptations, ultimately weakening the body as they preserved it, overburdening the immune system. In time, a pattern of neurologically mediated behavior evolved that closed off responses irrelevant to self-protection. In a sense, my brother and I came from people whose biological adaptation to stress had a self-destructive component. Programmed to biologically circle the wagons, our immunological responses were maladaptive—we ate ourselves up with worry. This was the secret baggage brought to America from the old country, and whether or not the theory is correct, the metaphorical implications are compelling.

After increasingly anti-semitic restrictions imposed by Alexander III, and an escalation of pogroms, four Sklut brothers left Volozhin in 1892. Two settled in South Africa, where the family name became Sloot; two, name Eliahu and Samuel, came to New York, where they were processed at Ellis Island as Skloot.

Grandfather Philip, a scholarly former student prepared to enroll at the Volozhin Yeshiva, a reader of books and nascent arguer of interpretive points, went to work in an undershirt factory. Shortly afterwards, his father—our great-grandfather Eliahu—died of a heart attack. Eliahu was in his mid-fifties when he died. He never got to see his younger son save enough money to own his own grocery store, or marry an emigree from Bialystok named Kate Tatarsky and open his own live Kosher poultry market.

Like Eliahu's, grandfather Philip's life was short and his end sudden. A diabetic, he died of a heart attack in his eldest daughter's arms in 1939. He was 59. And like the two generations before him, our own father's life, also etched with diabetes, ended by heart attack. He was 53.

It is easy to look at this pattern and conclude that our destiny is to die young of heart disease and the complications of diabetes. It is fate, Kismet. The three generations of fathers we know about all did so. Whether due to evolutionary biology's maladaptive changes or to long-standing genetic tendencies, we are genetic patsies and there is not much we can do.

In essence, this was my brother's view. He ate wildly, almost contemptuously, in the face of his inheritance. He smoked to the same rhythm, often four packs of cigarettes a day. Aggressively sedentary, he was an accomplished napper, a spectator and kibitzer of fine style and volume. He was resigned to the inevitability of early death and chose to live high while he lived. In a sense, he converted; he joined the enemy.

My own view was the exact opposite. I dieted fanatically, buying ever more sensitive bathroom scales and kitchen scales, measuring and apportioning nearly everything I took in, keeping elaborate diaries of my running with details added of sleep and weight and estimated calories burned. Never smoked, logged nearly 2,500 miles of running a year, ate all the miracle foods from oat bran to salmon to Egg Beaters omelettes, and took all the supplements. I worried and wrote poems about dying young, and had a will drawn up before I had anything of value to leave behind. I also thought I was managing stress, having developed all those outlets for it, but of course was so intense about this that it made my brother laugh. Then, in 1988, my health collapsed utterly. During a long airplane flight, I was exposed to a virus that targeted my brain, scarring it with lesions that remain today, and my already-compromised immune system misread all the signs, going into permanent overdrive. I remain, nine years later, totally disabled, neurologically impaired and confined, for the most part, to home.

There was something romantic about the assumption of being marked for an early end. Like Mickey Mantle, our hero when we were growing up, or like settlers beyond The Pale who hear Cossacks in every shift of the wind, my brother and I felt shadowed by mortality. Philip, adopting the Mantle method, went for broke, living it up in the terms that made most sense to him; I became something of a genetic ascetic, denying nearly everything that my brother emphasized. He was a hellion and I was a good boy. We were, as ever, quite a team.

But the truth of the matter is that genetic tendencies toward diabetes, heart disease, and obesity, however evolved, are not necessarily death sentences. The geneticist Steve Jones writes, in *The Language of Genes,* that "a harmful gene can sometimes become obvious only when the environment

changes." Both Philip and I have a genetic predisposition to diabetes, but it is not a genetic sentence to the disease unless we
create the right environment for the harmful gene to flourish.

According to *The Merck Manual*, 80 to 90 percent of the
people with type II diabetes mellitus, the common adult-onset,
non-insulin-dependent form of the disease which my brother
developed, are obese. In these cases, the body still produces
insulin—the hormone responsible for absorption of glucose into
cells for energy production—but insufficient amounts to meet
the body's needs, especially when the body is overweight. Not
only is it possible to prevent, or at least to delay the onset of
diabetes, but the disease can be controlled through careful management of diet, exercise, and the use of drugs. My brother did
none of these things, either before or after diabetes began to
change his life.

I remember visiting Philip in Fremont, California, in 1984.
He took me on a sightseeing tour of the area, driving up into the
hills of Alameda County and the Sunoi Regional Wilderness,
weaving all over the road in his struggle with fading eyesight.
After dinner at his favorite restaurant, which included a double
order of zabaglione—a beaten egg yolk, sugar and liqueur con-
coction—for dessert, he insisted on driving home. Suddenly, he
pulled onto the shoulder of the highway, sighed, and just made it
over to the passenger seat before falling into a sleep that approached coma.

In 1991, Philip flew up to visit me in Portland, Oregon. He
was the last to emerge from the plane and I was glad he could
not see my reaction. He was gray-haired and his teeth, which had
steadily begun to spread into gaps, were now a gleaming row of
ill-fitting chompers that distorted his mouth. His eyeglasses were
thick and sturdy as mugs, with a special insert in the right lens
for magnification. Only his right eye had vision, but he obviously
could not see well enough to walk with confidence and held his
arms poised in front of his chest like a wrestler. He was hungry
after the flight and wanted to stop for a sweet roll before we left
the airport.

The last meal we ate together in a restaurant, in early

spring of 1997, culminated in Philip's ordering baked Alaska. He had not liked his appetizer of raw clams, nor his shrimp cocktail, and had not been able to finish his salmon. Wheelchair tucked under the table's edge, he signalled for the waitress all throughout the meal, wanting dessert before our entrees had arrived, lost in time, and unaware that we had been seated for just twenty minutes. He could not get enough water, though he was not supposed to drink much in the days between dialysis. He was edgy, unable to listen to conversation, and his usual smile was gone. I knew that we were seeing the end of Philip's journey, when even a fine meal could no longer please him. Only when his dessert arrived did he settle down, and when it was done he smiled in turn at each of us.

One Monday evening in the fall of 1958, my brother announced that he wanted to audition for a local theater production of "Kismet" on Thursday. "What else am I going to do?" he asked. He figured he would play Hajj the poet-beggar and get to sing "Fate!" in his rich baritone. *What fate, what fate is mine?* Hajj had easy songs to put over on an audience, Philip thought, songs that took acting talent rather than operatic pipes. It would be a cinch. Or maybe he would play the Caliph, lighten up the voice a little so he could be the beau and croon the great lovesongs like "Stranger in Paradise."

We had moved from Brooklyn to Long Island the year before, following his high school graduation, and Philip knew no one in the town where we lived. Stranded, he said, just like Hajj. So it would be method acting. Being in the play might be a good way to make friends, to meet girls. Especially girls, since he was spending all his free time now driving to and from Brooklyn for dates and was too tired to get up for work in the mornings.

At nineteen, he was finished with his half-hearted attempt at college, where playing intramural football had gradually become his major. Employed in the Manhattan garment district, he was learning the children's dress business from our mother's Uncle Sam, who owned Youngland. He wanted to sell, but had to begin by sweeping floors. He hated it. He would drive into the city from our new Long Island home every morning at 7:00, leaving a half-hour after our father, who worked only a few blocks from Youngland. They would arrive back home in their separate cars at nearly the same time, ravenous for dinner, but would never commute together, for reasons they seemed to agree upon without ever having to talk about them. After dinner, there was nothing for him to do but sit around the house and bicker with our parents or play endless games of Careers with me. He hated that too.

I was eleven and my job for Wednesday afternoon was to prepare Philip's audition song for him. He was not supposed to sing anything from "Kismet" and had chosen Tennessee Ernie Ford's hit from three years earlier, "Sixteen Tons." I had to listen to the record and write down the lyrics. And they had better be perfect, even if I had to listen to it a thousand and one times. *Some people say a man is made out of mud. A poor man's made out of muscle and blood.*

"What's this?" he asked on Wednesday night, when I handed him the page of lyrics. Certain lines had a heavy X in the margin.

"Snaps. You have to snap your fingers there when you sing."

He shook his head. "I'll do the snapless version. You never see an Arab snap his fingers when he sings."

"Kismet," which opened on Broadway in December of 1953, has an unusual pedigree. Basing a musical's book on an existing novel or play was a Broadway tradition—the Gershwins did it with "Porgy and Bess," Rodgers and Hammerstein did it with "Carousel" and "South Pacific." The script of "Kismet" is based upon a popular WWI-era play by Edward Knoblock, set in Baghdad, that used the grandeur of the Arabian Nights as background for romance between a beggar's daughter and noble caliph despite the machinations of the Wazir. But unlike the great musicals of the period, the score of "Kismet" was completely unoriginal. Its music actually came from mid-nineteenth century Russia, composed there by a chemist and professor of medicine named Alexander Borodin. Its lyrics, however, were written nearly a century later by two Americans, Robert Wright and George Forrest, who made a theatrical career out of putting words to the melodies of dead composers. They had already turned Edvard Grieg's music into "The Song of Norway," Sergei Rachmaninoff's into "Arya" and Victor Herbert's into "Gypsy Lady," so their formula was well-tested. For "Kismet," they applied lyrics to Borodin's *Polovtsian Dances* for "Stranger in Paradise," "He's in Love" and "Not Since Ninevah." They used a love duet from the opera *Prince Igor* for "The Olive Tree" and another melody from earlier in that opera to create "Rhymes Have I." The Notturno of Borodin's String Quartet No. 2 in D major was used for "And This Is My Beloved" and a theme from elsewhere in the Quartet gave them "Was I Wazir." Symphony No. 1 yielded "Gesticulate," Symphony No. 2 produced "Fate," and *In the Steppes of Central Asia* turned into "Sands of Time." Listening to a recording of Borodin is like listening to Wright and Forrest's Overture. At a Portland Chamber Orchestra performance of the D Major Quartet, I drew angry stares for singing along with the Notturno.

Clearly, "Kismet" is a classic of adaptation. Taking the genetic code of Borodin's music, grafting it onto an ancient Middle Eastern fable and writing fresh lyrics, Wright and Forrest did something wholly new with what they were given. They created an alternative destiny, a new life out of Borodin's material, giving it quintessentially American features. Fittingly, the winner of Broadway's Tony Award in 1953 for excellence in musical composition was Alexander Borodin, who had died in 1887.

Philip's audition for "Kismet" was a success in the sense that he got a part in the production. But he was cast as the Wazir and had only one song to sing. He would be going to rehearsals every night for two months in order to sing one song! I knew he would hate that and thought it was my fault.

But I was wrong. He reveled in the cruelty of the character, the wicked Minister of State who dismembered suspects arm by arm and ear by ear and joint by joint, who sealed an embezzling tax collector in a pot of glue and hung seven hundred men "by their fuzz" in a prison pen. *Was I Wazir? I was!* Philip played the

Wazir as a Cossack, modeling the role on those stories we had grown up with, tales of vicious torturers who preyed on Jews. I read him his cues in our living room and saw how hard he worked. Eyes bulging and fists clenched like our mother's when she was angry, voice going flat like our father's when he was about to erupt, he used everything he knew. In performance, he was riveting; with his sinister and musical laugh, his relish in delivering the song, even in his death by drowning, he stole the show. *I hacked and hatcheted and cleft until no one but me is left!*

"Kismet" has an underlying motif of sensory confusion, of difficulty in figuring out how to read the signs. "Fate," Hajj sings, "can be the trap in your path." It can "weave the evil and good in one design." *Is it good? Is it ill? Am I blessed, am I cursed? Is it honey on my tongue or brine? What fate what fate is mine?*

I cannot listen to the soundtrack without chills. It speaks to something so deep within me, a mix of fraternal memories and fears and pride that seem never to have released their hold. I also hear in the exotic music and backstory a theme that has dominated our lives: the mysteries of fate, of kismet, as played out in the blood. My brother and I share a legacy of bad genes and confusion over what to do about them.

I have never forgotten a childhood dream about my brother. It probably occurred in 1954, when I was six, since I woke up in the room we shared in our Brooklyn apartment. I got out of bed and went across the room to his, carefully leaning over his body to determine whether he was still there and still alive.

The dream was set in that room, which was four stories above the building's enclosed courtyard and looked down a brick alcove onto the space where we played stickball. My brother, glasses off, dressed in an undershirt and pajama pants, was clinging to the window ledge. He was calling to me. I tried to get out of bed, but the covers were too heavy. Just as he lost his grip, I managed to squirm free and run to the window. But the air was thick, like the ocean at Long Beach where we went on hot spring afternoons, and I could not move fast enough. He began to drift away, floating like a feather rather than plummeting to the court-yard. His right hand still reached for me; his eyes were fixed on mine. He was silent, all his hopes grappled to my outstretched arms that could do nothing for him.

Beverly and I began visiting Philip regularly in 1995. Every three months, we would fly to San Jose on a Thursday afternoon and stay until early Monday morning. It was the end game. We all knew that, but since he never spoke about being terminally ill, we only discussed such matters out of his hearing.

At first, he would be sitting in his wheelchair at the gate to greet us, duded up in shades and windbreaker, head tilted back to hear what Elaine whispered as she bent over the chair's back with her hands on the grips. He loved to hug Beverly, this tall and willowy blonde sister-in-law of his that he had never actually seen but clearly approved of. We would head for the baggage claim together, me with my cane and Philip being pushed in his chair, and he would lay out the weekend's plans for where we ate each night.

A rhythm developed through the next two years. Thursday evening we would dine at a vegetarian restaurant in San Jose, in honor of Beverly's preferences, and Philip would joke about his passion for bok choy. I had never known him to compromise when it came to food, but he was elegant in his consideration now. On Friday we would drive him to dialysis in the morning, dropping him off at 9:00 and returning at 1:00. Then we would bring him home, keep him company as he ate a sandwich and napped until the cooking programs came on television at 4:00. We prepared dinner on Fridays, since Elaine worked all day. Saturdays were for rest and then dinner at fancy restaurants in San Francisco; Sundays were for dinner with their two grown children.

Gradually, time fell apart. Philip was no longer able to meet us at the gate, waiting instead in the car while we got our baggage. We began eating in restaurants closer to their apart-ment on Thursdays and then, by mid-1997, went straight home and ordered take-out dinners. Friday, his stays at the dialysis center got shorter, until at last he was there for less than an hour, gradually diminishing his treatments and growing ever sicker as the toxins normally removed by dialysis built up. After being hooked to the machine through an indwelling catheter directly above his heart, Philip would doze for a few minutes. Awake, he could not remember how long ago he had arrived, but believed that he had to get home immediately. Neither the attendants nor the nurses nor the doctors nor I could convince him that he had only been there a half hour. He slept for six hours afterwards instead of three and could not eat the dinners we prepared. On Saturdays, he could not venture out for the trips to Monterrey or to San Francisco, as before, and on Sundays he could barely stay awake during the family visits. He talked less and less.

Then over dinner the last Friday we saw him, Philip spoke about being okay with death, about having a good life, and stuck his hand in the butter. He was surrounded by pill bottles and the apparatus for injecting himself in the abdomen with insulin. He was surrounded by cookies. He was surrounded by family and love. He was surrounded.

One morning in September of 1997, about two months after my brother died, I was sitting on the living room couch listening to music. It was just after breakfast. Across the room was the collage of photographs I had assembled on the weekend he died. One showed my brother, aged eight, holding me in his arms shortly after I was born. He is dressed in an undershirt and striped pajama pants, sitting on the edge of his bed, and has unwrapped me like a gift. My discarded blankets lie next to him. Not quite smiling, hunched there in a room crowded by the crib crammed against the wall behind him, Philip looks confused but resigned. *Am I blessed? Am I cursed?* In a second photograph, I stand between him and our cousin Phyllis, both squatting before a parking lot fence through which the rear ends of late-1940s Oldsmobiles and Chevrolets can be seen. Philip is displaying a white wind-up toy dog to the camera, obviously something just given to me, and Phyllis holds a plastic dog bone. They are both smiling and I have the same resigned, confused look on my two-year-old's face that Philip had in the earlier photo. The final image was taken a half year ago, after our last restaurant meal with Philip. He is at the head of the table, his wife beside him with her hand clasped in his, and a single red tulip juts from its vase, tilted toward them as though drawn to their warmth. I am next to Elaine, looking across the table at my wife. We are all smiling. We seem almost giddy with being together. There is nothing held back and there are no questions in the air. His expression says *I've had a good life.*

As the sun rose just high enough above the oaks to shine into our windows, the Notturno from Alexander Borodin's D Major Quartet began. Its exquisite, tender theme—the movement essentially has only one theme, repeated and varied among the strings for eight minutes—was announced by the cello and floated across the air. For the first time since my brother died, I began to cry and could not stop until the music ended.

My brother had been dying for so long that I had time to prepare myself. As his physical presence dwindled, memories of him loomed everywhere. The transition to holding on to him as pure memory was relatively simple. But somewhere along the way, I had skipped a step, held my grief in and instead built a shrine to my brother's dogged destiny.

Now I see it all tinged with regret, even anger, because his death was unnecessary. Through the years of excess, he could be provoked to fury by any suggestion that he temper his behavior; at the end, he acknowledged his mistakes and worried about the fate of his son, whose habits are a direct copy of Philip's. The riddle of "Kismet" remained unsolved for my brother. The honey on his tongue was in fact brine and what he construed as good was ill. He sought to embrace in life the very things that would kill him. That, rather than the more mundane genetic inheritance or the facts of renal failure, is the real end of the story.

Marilynn Robinson is the author of the novel *Housekeeping* and of *Mother Country*, an examination of Great Britain's role in the radioactive pollution of the world's environment. She teaches at the University of Iowa Writers' Conference.

Margaret Talbot is a contributing writer for the *New York Times Magazine* and a Senior Fellow at the New America Foundation. She lives in Washington, D.C.

Richard Rorty is University Professor of Humanities at the University of Virginia. He is the author of *Philosophy and the Mirror of Nature; Contingency, Irony and Solidarity*; and *The Consequences of Pragmatism*.

George Packer is the author of *The Village of Waiting*, a memoir about Africa, and two novels, *The Half Man* and *Central Square*. His work has appeared in *Harper's*, *Dissent*, the *New York Times*, and *Doubletake*. His next book, *Blood of the Liberals*, from which the essay in this volume was adapted, will be published in 2000.

Andre Dubus was the author of nine works of fiction. He received the PEN/Malamud Award, the Rey Award for Excellence in short fiction, the Jean Stein Award from the American Academy of Arts and Letters, the *Boston Globe*'s first annual Lawrence L. Winship Award, and fellowships from both the Guggenheim and MacArthur foundations. He died in February 1999.

Thomas Beller is the author of *Seduction Theory*, a collection of stories. He has worked as a staff writer at *The New Yorker* and is currently a contributing editor at *Elle* and *The Cambodia Daily*. His essays have appeared in *The Literacy Insomniac*, the *New York Times Magazine*, and the *New York Observer*. He was editor of *Personals: Dreams and Nightmares from the Lives of Twenty Young Writers*, and co-founded and edits the literary journal *Open City*. His first novel, *The Sleep-Over Artist*, is forthcoming in the spring of 2000.

Jonathan Rosen is the cultural editor of *The Forward* and a creator of the newspaper's Arts and Letters section. His essays have appeared in the *New York Times Magazine*, the *New York Times Book Review*, and *Vanity Fair*, among other publications.

Kathleen Norris is the author of *Dakota: A Spiritual Geography*, *Amazing Grace*, and *The Cloister Walk*.

Siri Hustvedt is the author of the novels *Blindfold* and *The Enchantment of Lily Dahl*, and the essay collection *Yonder*. She lives with her husband, the novelist Paul Auster, in Brooklyn, New York.

Wayne Koestenbaum is the author of *The Queen's Throat*, *Jackie Under My Skin*, and most recently the poetry collection *The Milk of Inquiry*.

Vijay Seshadri is the author of *Wild Kingdom* (Graywolf Press), a book of poems. His work has appeared in many periodicals, including *The Nation, The New Yorker, Antaeus*, and *Three-penny Review*, and in several anthologies. He has received grants from the New York Foundation for the Arts and the N.E.A., and has been awarded the *Paris Review*'s Bernard F. Conners Long Poem Prize. He is on the editorial staff of *The New Yorker* and teaches at Sarah Lawrence College. About "My Pirate Boyhood," he writes, "I was inspired to write the piece by my now six-year-old son, whose newborn enthusiasm for baseball brought me back in touch with my own childhood love for the game— one of the many things I'm grateful to him for."

Gerald Early is the author of *Tuxedo Junction*, a collection of essays on American culture; *The Culture of Bruising: Essays on Prizefighting*, winner of the National Book Critics Circle Award; *Lure and Loathing*; and *One Nation Under a Groove*. He has edited *My Soul's High Song: The Collected Writings of Countee Cullen, Voice of the Harlem Renaissance, Speech and Power*, and an anthology of African American essays. He is the recipient of a

Whiting Award and a General Electric Foundation Award and lives in St. Louis, Missouri.

George Orwell, author of some of the most famous and influential novels, essays, and nonfiction works of the twentieth century, died in 1950.

Derek Walcott received the Nobel Prize for Literature in 1992 for his poetry.

Gordon Grice is a contributing editor at *Oklahoma Today*. His work has appeared in *Harper's, Granta*, and other magazines and has been anthologized in *Best American Essays*, among other places. He teaches film, humanities, and English at Seward Community College in Liberal, Kansas. He lives in Oklahoma with his wife and children.

Anne Fadiman is the editor of *The American Scholar*, and the author of *The Spirit Catches You and You Fall Down*, which won a National Book Critic's Circle Award for nonfiction, and the essay collection *Ex Libris*.

Bliss Broyard is the author of the forthcoming short story collection *My Father Dancing*. Her stories have appeared in *The Best American Short Stories 1998, Ploughshares, Open City, Grand Street, Five Points*, and *The Pushcart Anthology*. She lives in Brooklyn, New York.

M. G. Stephens is a poet, playwright, and essayist. He is the author of the novel *The Brooklyn Book of the Dead*, and the essay collection *Green Dreams*.

Marcus Laffey is the pen name of a New York City police officer who writes for *The New Yorker*. *Blue Blood*, a family memoir of the NYPD, will be published in 2000. He lives in the Bronx, New York.

Miroslav Holub was the author of a number of poetry collections, and of the recent collection of literary-medical essays *Shedding Life: Disease, Politics, and Other Human Conditions*. He died in 1999.

Edward Hoagland is the author of more than sixty books, most recently *Balancing Acts, In the Country of the Blind*, and *Tigers and Ice*. He is the guest editor of *The Best American Essays 1999*, forthcoming in October 1999. He has taught at ten colleges, including Bennington, Brown, Columbia, Beloit, the City College of New York, the University of Iowa, and the University of California at Davis. About one third of his titles are fiction, but for the last thirty years he has specialized in personal essays.

Erin McGraw is the author of two collections of short stories, *Lies of the Saints* (Chronicle Books, 1996) and *Bodies at Sea* (University of Illinois Press, 1989). Her essays have appeared in *The Gettysburg Review*, the *Cleveland Plain Dealer*, and elsewhere. She teaches at the University of Cincinnati.

Alexander Theroux has taught at Harvard, MIT, Yale, and the University of Virginia. He is the author of two books of essays, a collection of poems, as well as several books of fables. He lives in Barnstable, Massachusetts.

Emily Fox Gordon's essays have been reprinted in all three issues of the anchor essay annual. Her memoir *Mockingbird Years*, forthcoming from Basic Books, is based partly on "Mockingbird Years," which appeared in the inaugural issue, and partly on "My Last Therapist," which appears here.

Susan Sontag has written and edited more than twenty works of fiction and nonfiction. She is the author of *On Photography*, winner of the National Book Critics' Circle Award for Criticism, and the novel *The Volcano Lover*, among other works.

Martha Nussbaum is Ernst Freund Distinguished Professor of Law and Ethics at the University of Chicago, with appointments in the Philosophy Department, the Law School, the Divinity School, and the College; she is an associate member of the Classics Department and an Affiliate of the Committee on Southern Asian Studies. Her most recent books are *Cultivating Humanity: A Classical Defense of Reform in Liberal Education* (1997) and *Sex and Social Justice* (1999).

Jenny Diski lives in London. She has published seven novels, a volume of short stories, a collection of essays, and a memoir.

Floyd Skloot is the author of three novels, two collections of poetry, and a book of essays about the illness experience. His essays have appeared in *The American Scholar, Southwest Review, The Gettysburg Review, Boulevard, Antioch Review, Threepenny Review, Witness, Commonweal,* and elsewhere, and have been reprinted in *The Best American Essays 1993, Survival Stories,* and other anthologies. Born in Brooklyn, New York, in 1947, he now lives in rural western Oregon, in a small round house that his wife built herself in the middle of twenty hilly acres of woods. "Kismet" is part of a new collection entitled *In the Shadow of Memory*, nearing completion, which concerns the experience of living with brain damage and with the reconstruction of shattered memory.

ACKNOWLEDGMENTS

Grateful acknowledgment is made for permission to reprint copyrighted material as follows:

"Family" by Marilynn Robinson from *The Death of Adam* by Marilynn Robinson. Copyright © 1998 Marilynn Robinson. Reprinted by permission of Houghton Mifflin.

"The Perfectionist" by Margaret Talbot. Copyright © 1998 Margaret Talbot. First published in *The New Republic*.

"The Eclipse of the Reformist Left" by Richard Rorty from *Achieving Our Country*. Copyright © 1998 the President and Fellows of Harvard College. Reprinted by permission of Harvard University, Cambridge, Mass.

"Sisyphus in the Basement" by George Packer. Copyright © 1998 George Packer. First published in *Harpers*.

"Digging" by Andre Dubus from *Meditations from a Movable Chair*. Copyright © 1998 Andre Dubus. First published in *Epoch*. Reprinted by permission of Alfred A. Knopf.

"Portrait of the Bagel as a Young Man" by Thomas Beller from *Personals*. Copyright © 1998 Thomas Beller. Reprinted by permission of Mary Evans, Inc.

"The Talmud and the Internet" by Jonathan Rosen. Copyright © 1998 Jonathan Rosen. First published in *The American Scholar*.

"Annunciation" by Kathleen Norris. Copyright © 1998 Kathleen Norris. First published in *Image*. Reprinted by permission of Riverhead.

"A Plea for Eros" by Siri Hustvedt. Copyright © 1998 Siri Hustvedt. First published in *Yonder*.

"Masochism" by Wayne Koestenbaum. Copyright © 1998 Wayne Koestenbaum. First published in *Venue*.

"My Pirate Boyhood" by Vijay Seshadri. Copyright © 1998 Vijay Seshadri. First published in *Threepenny Review*.

"Ali, the Wonder Boy" by Gerald Early from *The Muhammad Ali Reader*. Copyright © 1998 Gerald Early. First published in *The New York Review of Books*. Reprinted by permission of Ecco Press.